WEAVING HISTORIES

A British Academy Monograph

British Academy Monographs showcase work arising from:

British Academy Postdoctoral Fellowships
British Academy Newton International Fellowships

WEAVING HISTORIES

The Transformation of the Handloom Industry in South India, 1800–1960

Karuna Dietrich Wielenga

Published for THE BRITISH ACADEMY
by OXFORD UNIVERSITY PRESS

Oxford University Press, Great Clarendon Street, Oxford OX2 6DP

First edition published in 2020

British Library Cataloguing in Publication Data
Data available

Library of Congress Cataloging in Publication Data
Data available

Typeset by Mach 3 Solutions Ltd

Printed in Great Britain by TJ Books Ltd, Padstow, Cornwall

ISBN: 978-0-19-726673-1

Contents

Figures

Abbreviations

EEIC (EIC)	English East India Company
G. O.	Government Order
HCPP	House of Commons Parliamentary Papers
ICCC	Indian Central Cotton Committee
ILC	Industries, Labour and Co-operation (department)
IOR	India Office Records
MDR	Madura District Records
PBR	Proceedings of the Board of Revenue
RMHK	Real Madras Handkerchiefs
TDR	Tinnevelly District Records
TNSA	Tamil Nadu State Archives
V&A	Victoria and Albert Museum

Maps

Plates

Colour plates (swatches) between pages 78 and 79

Colour plates (paintings and photos) between pages 142 and 143

Acknowledgements

My fascination with crafts goes back to my childhood, when I observed the clanking of handlooms first-hand while growing up in Madurai. My interest in history was kindled by my parents Bastiaan Wielenga and Gabriele Dietrich, though I came to it late, after taking a degree in chemistry. My teachers in Delhi University—Sumit Sarkar, Shahid Amin, Dilip Menon and Chitra Joshi—along with Uma Chakravarty and V. Geetha transmitted their passion for the discipline to me. Prabhu Mohapatra was a generous and accommodating supervisor, giving me the flexibility to juggle research with childcare, allowing me to develop my own ideas, and contributing critical insights when I got stuck.

Douglas Haynes was incredibly helpful, always willing to comment on drafts or write a reference. Ravi Ahuja has given me sustained encouragement and sound criticism throughout the course of my career. In Oxford, where I began reworking the manuscript, Matthew McCartney and Barbara Harriss-White were an unfailing source of ideas (and humour). Barbara encouraged me to present my work to different audiences, sharpened my ideas about the informal sector and provided reams of readings.

Professor Maxine Berg went through the manuscript with a fine-tooth comb and suggested many improvements. Dorothy Ko and Prachi Deshpande generously took time off from busy schedules to give detailed comments. The British Academy's anonymous reviewer made some helpful suggestions towards the end.

I would also like to thank Judith Heyer for stimulating discussions in Oxford and Chennai. Neeladri Bhattacharya in Delhi and Padmini Swaminathan gave useful advice on enlarging my thesis. In Tamil Nadu, Tho. Parmasivan, Sivasubramanian, Sundar Kali and Dhananjayan shared their knowledge and insights freely with me.

The staff, faculty and fellows at the School of Interdisciplinary Area Studies in Oxford, especially Stephen Minay, Victoria Hudson, Miriam Driesen, George Kunnath and Kate Sullivan, were warm and helpful, as was

Nikita Sud of the Oxford Department of International Development. They made my time in Oxford even more rewarding than it would otherwise have been. My students and colleagues in Azim Premji University, especially Venu, Meghna, Varuni, Tarangini, Toy, Rajendran, Sunandan, Vasvi and Priya have been incredibly welcoming and supportive.

A big thank you to fellow historians for conversation, advice, tips on sources, discussions and much else—to Shahana Bhattacharya, Vidhya Raveendranath, Bhavani Raman, Aditya Menon, Ponni Arasu, Aparna Balachandar, Senthil Babu, Prasannan Parthasarathi, Aditya Sarkar, Rana Behal, Dhiraj Knight, Shabnam Tejani, Eleanor Newbegin and many others. Some of them have become close friends over the years.

Shahana was an unfailing source of support during my doctoral dissertation—thanks to her, I always had a home in Delhi. Our journeys as doctoral candidates also overlapped; her practical advice and support were invaluable during the last stages of my dissertation. I also owe a debt of gratitude to Vivek Oak for his work on the maps and graphs (and many stimulating discussions on the future of handlooms in India). The work of Malkha and the Decentralised Cotton and Yarn Trust in Hyderabad encouraged me to deepen my exploration of the links between cotton cultivation, spinning and weaving. Uzramma, in particular, has been an inspiration: her insights and engagement fed into this book in many ways. Arvind, Sarita, Annapurna, Mohan Rao, Durgalakshmi and other activists working with weavers were source, not just of ideas, but hope.

My time as an observer in a handloom factory in Madurai helped me to understand the rhythms of work and the life experiences of ordinary weavers. Chinnu Ayya, Dravida Selvi, Mariappan, Valli, Sekar and others welcomed me into their work lives, taught me how to weave, and shared skills, tea, food and stories. Union organisers such as Comrade Murugan, P. M. Kumar, Mayandi Bharathi, Iswaran, K. K. Pillai and Gandhi shared their memories with me. A special thank you to Meena Krishnaswamy, who agreed to speak to me about her experiences as an organiser.

This book would have been impossible without the holdings of the Tamilnadu State Archives and help of its staff (especially Mr Neelavannan and Mr Suresh) and the ever helpful and well-informed librarians, curators and assistants at the British Library, the Victoria and Albert Museum (especially Rosemary Crill), the School of Oriental and African Studies, and the Bodleian Library in Oxford. I also consulted books and papers in the Madras Institute of Development Studies and the offices of the Communist Party of India in Chennai; the Centre for Social Analysis in Madurai; the National Archives and the Nehru Memorial Museum and

Library in Delhi; and the United Theological Seminary in Bangalore. I owe a debt of gratitude to the staff of all these institutions.

The British Academy handled my manuscript expertly on its long journey to publication. A big thank you to all the people there, particularly Portia Taylor, who answered all my queries patiently; and to Elizabeth Stone of Bourchier who oversaw the last stages of its publication. Professor Hamish Scott facilitated the book by smoothing out practical problems during my time as Newton International Fellow at Oxford. The V&A gave permission to reproduce images of some Company paintings. The Harris Museum and Art Gallery at Preston generously allowed me to use images of swatches from the Forbes Watson collection without payment. Thanks to Uzramma and Pankaj Sekhsaria for generously allowing me to use their photos; and to the director of Kalakshetra Foundation for giving me permission to photograph one of the looms in their craft centre. The Charles Wallace Trust, the Indian Council for Historical Research and the Newton International Fellowship provided indispensable funding for archival work, travel and research at different stages of my career.

This book rests upon the warmhearted support of friends in many cities. Iona and Alfy (along with Carenza and Kabir) were a dependable rock in Oxford, likewise Usha and Murali in Delhi. A big thank you to all of them: to Tara, Bonojit, Vidhya, Mythri, Ravi, Indira, Kamla and others in Delhi; Madhu, Shalini, Aravind, Bhavani, Frank, Karen, Nity, Chandrika, Karuna and Ally in Chennai; Adlin, Jeyaharan and Rajendran in Madurai; Sabine and Yolanda in Berlin; Judith, George, Pablo and Patricia in Oxford; Murad and Leena in London; Premi, Rosie, Hugo and other friends from the Tamil Nadu Theological Seminary in different parts of the world; and, finally, to Jayashree, Amit, Kailash and Rehmat in Badwani and Sakad. Thanks also to Binayak, Ilina and Nalini who taught me a great deal by example.

Thambu (Prasad) and Ojas helped in all kinds of ways, from booking tickets to typing and sharing care of Appa. My mother was always encouraging and supportive. My father-in-law Kamlkishore Kela opened his house and garden in Nagpur to us over many summers. Rienk, Angelique, Margriet, Bert, Paul and the rest of the tribe in Holland were warm, funny and welcoming. Thanks also to Prema, who has been a reliable and loving presence in our household: we could not have managed without her. Ammlakka, Deviakka and Surya helped with childcare during our time in Madurai.

This book would have been impossible without Shashank and his support. Both of us have a shared passion for history and a longstanding commitment to each other's work. I have lost count of the number of times he ploughed through my manuscript and discussed its ideas. He also edited it painstakingly and patiently—his skill in adjusting my text has made it clearer and much more readable. Our children Mahil and Lyra kept my feet (and eyes) planted firmly on the ground.

Some of the ideas in this book were tested in conferences organised by the Association of Indian Labour Historians in Delhi. I have presented other bits at seminars in London, Göttingen, Oxford and other places. I thank all the scholars who discussed them in all these fora. Early versions of Chapters 1 and 6 appeared in the *Indian Economic and Social History Review* and the *International Review of Social History* respectively. Chapter 5 appeared in a slightly different form as a paper in *Towards a New History of Work* edited by Sabyasachi Bhattacharya. Needless to say, any errors and omissions that remain are mine alone.

I miss my father's presence as the book makes its way into the world. I am certain it would have made him very happy. To him, and to his influence in my life, I dedicate this book.

Map 1: South India showing the districts of the Madras Presidency, 1920

Source: Based on *Cotton Map of India*, 1917. All maps created by Vivek Oak.

Map 2: The Madras Presidency with places mentioned in the text

Note: All locations marked on this map are approximate. Stars represent cities that carry the same name as the district

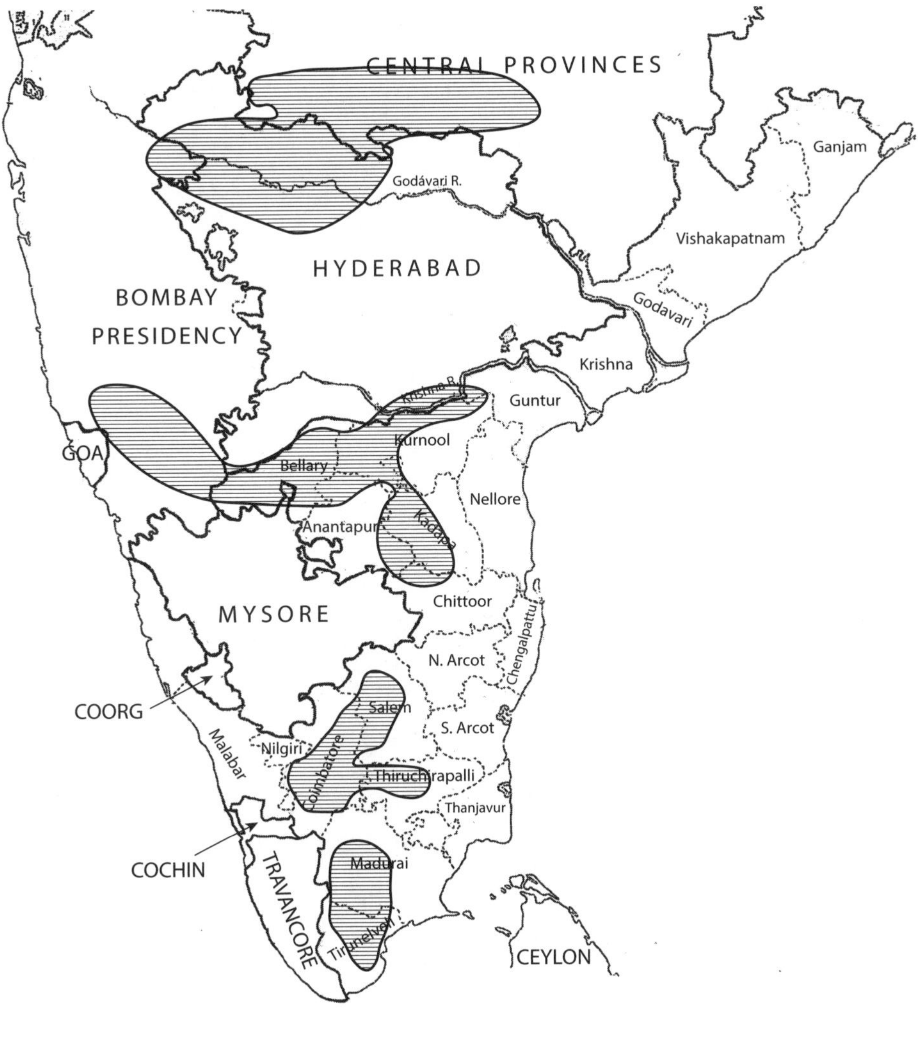

Map 3: The cotton-growing regions of the Indian peninsula

Source: Based on the map in Forbes Watson, *On the Growth of Cotton in India: Its Present State and Future Prospects, with Special Reference to Supplies to Britain* (London, 1859), IOR/V/27/631/1, India Office Records, British Library, London.

Map 4: Cotton varieties cultivated in the Madras Presidency, 1948

Source: Based on Cotton Map of Madras, in *Memoirs of the Department of Agriculture, Madras* (Madras, Government Press, 1954), p. 483. The numbers represent acres in thousands.

Introduction

The word 'handlooms' conjures up contradictory images—of skilled weavers making exquisite cloth on the one hand, and an industry mired in crisis, with low-paid workers condemned to a precarious living on the other.[1] As a craft, it is one of the oldest known to humankind, with deep roots in different parts of the world. Handlooms were one of the most important industries of the pre-modern age. With the coming of the industrial revolution, the craft weaver gradually disappeared from Western Europe. But, in other parts of the world, the handloom industry proved more durable. In India, it continues to be a significant source of employment, despite a gradual decline spanning several decades.[2] South India remains an important hub of production, with a substantial proportion of handloom cloth being exported. A small minority of weavers are organised into cooperatives; the remainder work from home and in small workshops, forming part of the informal sector of the economy.

Handlooms also play a prominent part in historical debates about the impacts of colonialism and divergent trajectories of economic development. Contemporary debates about sustainable development—fuelled by jobless growth, increasing inequality and an impending ecological crisis—stress their relevance.

The survival of handloom weaving as a commercially viable sector into the twenty-first century highlights its resilience. It also casts doubt upon conventional theories of industrialisation based on the inevitability

[1] See, for example, https://www.thehindu.com/society/Life-on-the-loom/article16729565.ece; https://www.vogue.in/content/jamdani-saree-history-origin-technique-indian-handloom (accessed 19 April 2020).

[2] The number of looms in India fell from 3,778,583 in 1987–8 to 3,486,308 in 1995–6 to 2,377,331 in 2009, a decline of 37 per cent in 21 years. In Tamil Nadu and Andhra Pradesh, they fell from 648,260 in 1987–8 to 615,274 in 1995–6 to 279,223 in 2009, a decline of 57 per cent. *Joint Census of Handlooms and Powerlooms, 1995–96: Handloom Sector* (Delhi, NCAER, 2004), p. 35; *Handloom Census of India, 2009–10* (Delhi, NCAER, 2010), p. 99.

of mechanisation. But this resilience is accompanied by a chronic vulnerability. Uncertain employment and low wages are a fact of life for weavers caught up in a global capitalist economy. The fact that handloom weaving remains largely home-based, with family labour at its core, gives a misleading impression of continuity with the past. In fact, from the mid-nineteenth century, the structures of handloom production in South India were transformed and reorganised. This book tells the story of that transformation and examines its implications.

2

Early scholarship on cloth production focused largely on trade, stressing the importance of Indian cloth in the expanding world market of the sixteenth and seventeenth centuries.[3] More recent studies examine the global reach of Indian textiles in terms of production, exchange, consumption and diffusion. The emergence and subsequent development of the European textile industry was made possible by artisanal skills and knowledge obtained from regions outside Europe, especially India, Persia and China.[4] Textiles also dominate historical debates about economic trends and economic development. For the period between the sixteenth to the eighteenth centuries, these are about the degree of commercialisation attained by the Indian economy.[5] For the nineteenth century, the focus shifts to deindustrialisation. Handlooms also play an integral part in

[3] K. N. Chaudhuri, *The Trading World of Asia and the English East India Company 1660–1760* (Cambridge, Cambridge University Press, 1978); Tapan Raychaudhuri, *Jan Company in Coromandel 1605–1690: a Study in the Interrelations of European Commerce and Traditional Economies* (The Hague, Martinus Nijhoff, 1962); Sinnapah Arasaratnam, *Merchants, Companies and Commerce on the Coromandel Coast 1650–1740* (Delhi, Oxford University Press, 1986).

[4] Giorgio Riello, *Cotton: the Fabric that Made the Modern World* (Cambridge, Cambridge University Press, 2013). See also Giorgio Riello and Tirthankar Roy (eds), *How India Clothed the World: the World of South Asian Textiles, 1500–1850* (Leiden, Brill, 2009) and Giorgio Riello and Prasannan Parthasarathi (eds), *The Spinning World: a Global History of Cotton Textiles, 1200–1850* (Delhi, Primus Books, 2012).

[5] Sanjay Subrahmanyam, *The Political Economy of Commerce in Southern India, 1500–1650* (Cambridge, Cambridge University Press, 2004); David Washbrook, 'The Textile Industry and the Economy of South India, 1500–1800', in Giorgio Riello and Tirthankar Roy (eds), *How India Clothed the World: the World of South Asian Textiles, 1500–1850* (Leiden, Brill, 2009), pp. 173–99; Frank Perlin, 'Proto-Industrialisation and Pre-Colonial South Asia', *Past and Present*, 98 (February 1983), 30–95.

studies exploring the role of small-scale industry in economic growth and development during the twentieth century.[6]

Studies dealing with the seventeenth and eighteenth centuries examine the *process* of cloth production: its links with agriculture; the relationship of weavers to merchants; their living conditions, social organisation, forms of collective action, and so on.[7] By contrast, scholarship on the nineteenth century ignores the components, internal structures and participants of the handloom industry almost entirely. Instead, it is placed at the centre of the debate on deindustrialisation conducted largely through macro-economic statistics. Astonishingly, there exists no detailed book-length study of the industry for this period.[8] This book aims, among other things, to remedy the omission.

One group of scholars argues that colonialism was responsible for large-scale deindustrialisation in South Asia; others contest this claim. Both groups use loom counts, census figures and statistics of trade to make their cases.[9] More recent studies have shown that any unitary picture, whether

[6] Tirthankar Roy, *Traditional Industry in the Economy of Colonial India* (Cambridge, Cambridge University Press, 1999); Douglas E. Haynes, *Small Town Capitalism in Western India: Artisans, Merchants and the Making of the Informal Economy, 1870–1960* (Cambridge, Cambridge University Press, 2012).

[7] Broadly speaking, all these studies agree that the position of weavers vis-à-vis merchants was relatively strong. Joseph J. Brennig, 'Textile Producers and Production in Late Seventeenth Century Coromandel', *The Indian Economic and Social History Review*, 23(4) (1986), 334–55; Prasannan Parthasarathi, *The Transition to a Colonial Economy: Weavers, Merchants and Kings in South India, 1720–1800* (Cambridge, Cambridge University Press, 2001); P. Swarnalatha, *The World of the Weaver in Northern Coromandel, c. 1750–c. 1850* (New Delhi, Orient Longman, 2005); Sinnapah Arasaratnam, 'Weavers, Merchants and Company: the Handloom Industry in Southeastern India, 1750–1790', *The Indian Economic and Social History Review*, 17(3) (1980), 257–81; K. N. Chaudhuri, 'The Structure of the Indian Textile Industry in the Seventeenth and Eighteenth Centuries', in Tirthankar Roy (ed.), *Cloth and Commerce in Colonial India* (Delhi, Sage Publications, 1996); Ian Wendt, 'The Social Fabric: Textile Industry and Community in Early Modern South India', PhD thesis (University of Wisconsin – Madison, 2005); Hameeda Hossain, *The Company Weavers of Bengal: the East India Company and the Organization of Textile Production in Bengal, 1750–1813* (Delhi, Oxford University Press, 1988).

[8] Konrad Specker's monograph is a notable exception; however, it is only available in German. Konrad Specker, *Weber in Wettbewerb: Das Schicksal des suidindischen Textilhandwerks im 19.Jahrhundert* (Wiesbaden, Steiner, 1984). Haynes' detailed and insightful monograph on western India, *Small Town Capitalism*, which I draw upon throughout this book, deals primarily with twentieth-century developments.

[9] Scholars arguing for decline include Amiya Kumar Bagchi, 'Deindustrialization in India in the Nineteenth Century: some Theoretical Implications', *Journal of Development Studies*, 12(2) (1976), 135–64; Michael J. Twomey, 'Employment in Nineteenth-Century Indian Textiles', *Explorations in Economic History*, 20(1) (1983), 37–57; J. Krishnamurty, 'De-industrialization in Gangetic Bihar during the Nineteenth Century: another Look at the Evidence', *The Indian Economic and Social History Review*, 22(4) (1985), 399–416. Articles and books arguing against

of decline or progress, cannot be sustained: the trend varied by region, period and sector.[10] However, the debate remains rooted in statistics and oriented towards generalised, industry-wide developments. The output and productivity of the handloom industry as a whole are placed at the centre of narratives of both decline and expansion.

According to Tirthankar Roy (the most influential of the revisionist historians), the handloom industry was restructured in response to market forces during the nineteenth century: the effect of this restructuring was to eliminate redundant elements and organise the remainder more efficiently.[11] This process is presented as natural and organic; the only human actors discussed in any detail are the 'weaver-capitalists' who emerged from this transformation. His argument can be criticised on two grounds. In the first place, it incorporates some hidden assumptions about the teleology of industrialisation (based on mechanisation) in the Indian context. Secondly, its contention that capitalist reorganisation led to sustained growth and greater stability is open to question.

Teleological assumptions about the emergence of industrial capitalism have been questioned by many scholars. Nowadays, most historians would agree that there was no 'standardised' path to the development of mass production through the factory system. The precise manner in which different regions industrialised (or failed to industrialise) was determined by a range of factors, including state policy, technological choices and class conflict.[12] As for stability and growth, Douglas Haynes shows that

---

deindustrialisation include Morris D. Morris, 'Towards a Reinterpretation of Nineteenth-Century Indian Economic History', *The Indian Economic and Social History Review*, 5(1) (1968), 1–15; Tirthankar Roy, 'De-industrialization: an Alternative View', *Economic and Political Weekly* 35(17) (2000), 1442–7. Thorner and Vicziany question the sources on which the deindustrialisation thesis is based. Daniel Thorner, 'De-industrialization in India, 1881–1931', in Daniel Thorner and Alice Thorner (eds), *Land and Labour in India* (Bombay, Asia Publishing House, 1965), pp. 70–81; M. Vicziany, 'The De-industrialization of India in the Nineteenth Century: a Methodological Critique of Amiya Kumar Bagchi', *The Indian Economic and Social History Review*, 16(2) (1979), 105–46. An overview of these debates can be found in Colin Simmons, '"Deindustrialization", Industrialization and the Indian Economy, *c.* 1850–1947', *Modern Asian Studies*, 19(3) (1985), 593–622.

[10] Konrad Specker, 'Madras Handlooms in the Nineteenth Century', *The Indian Economic and Social History Review*, 26(2), 131–66; Sumit Guha, 'The Handloom Industry of Central India: 1825–1950', *The Indian Economic and Social History Review*, 26(3) (1989), 297–318; Peter Harnetty, 'Deindustrialization Revisited: the Handloom Weavers of the Central Provinces of India, *c.* 1800–1947', *Modern Asian Studies*, 25(3) (1991), 455–510.

[11] See Tirthankar Roy, *Artisans and Industrialisation: Indian Weaving in the Twentieth Century* (Delhi, Oxford University Press, 1993), pp. 1–25.

[12] See Tessie P. Liu, 'Introduction', in *The Weaver's Knot: the Contradictions of Class Struggle and Family Solidarity in Western France, 1750–1914* (Ithaca, NY, Cornell University Press, 1994),

the actual picture was much more complex. Everyone involved in weaving did not prosper. There were failed entrepreneurs, and weavers working for wages were confronted with chronic insecurity and became more, not less, dependent on their masters.[13] Even if the story of growth and expansion is accepted for some sectors of the handloom industry, significant questions remain. Who were the people excluded or forced to drop out of weaving? What happened to those who failed to become successful entrepreneurs? What were the living conditions of the vast majority of weavers?

The corpus of revisionist historiography, and Roy's work in particular, played a key role in putting small-scale industries at the centre of Indian economic history. Before this, it was focused largely upon the factory sector: small, craft-based industries received short shrift. This bias reflected the assumption that large-scale mechanisation was the only rational and desirable direction of economic development. By contrast, Roy pointed to the vibrancy of artisanal industries and their economic significance. However, as Haynes points out, there remains a teleology in his narrative too, albeit of a different kind. Roy sees artisanal industries as moving towards a model of small capitalist firms (regarded as being more efficient and productive). In the case of handlooms, this progression leads 'organically' to small-scale powerlooms. Haynes casts doubt upon this assumption by showing that twentieth-century structures of cloth production in western India were in fact remarkably diverse.[14]

The gradual evolution of artisanal industries—central, as Roy shows, to India's modern economic history—needs more nuanced and detailed treatment than has hitherto been the case. This can only be done through regional studies and Haynes' monograph on western India shows the way. He situates the process of change in interactions between various actors: traders, consumers, weavers and weaver-capitalists, faced with the 'external forces' of global capitalism and the state. Drawing upon oral interviews and archival sources, he shows how social forces—including consumer choices, the availability of new technologies and raw materials, the flexibility and enterprise of weaver-capitalists, and caste and kinship networks—shaped the character of the industry and its production relations. In this analysis,

pp. 1–21, for a discussion of this stream of history writing. Also, Charles Sabel and Jonathan Zeitlin, 'Historical Alternatives to Mass Production: Politics, Markets and Technology in Nineteenth-Century Industrialization', *Past and Present*, 108 (1985), 133–76; Michael J. Piore and Charles Sabel, *The Second Industrial Divide: Possibilities for Prosperity* (New York, Basic Books, 1984).

[13] Haynes, *Small Town Capitalism*.

[14] Haynes, *Small Town Capitalism*, pp. 1–22.

global capitalism and state policy are explicitly subordinated to politics at the point of production.

This book is also a regional study—it complements Haynes' monograph and derives inspiration from it. However, there are some significant differences in our theoretical approach that will be outlined in the last section of this chapter.

3

Early narratives of industrial capitalism paid little attention to artisanal or small-scale industries on the assumption that they were destined to disappear. In recent years, scholars have begun questioning this assumption, turning their attention to patterns of production and work outside large factories.[15] In Britain, the persistence of craft-based, small-scale production outside factories well into the nineteenth century has been pointed out.[16] Nineteenth-century economic development in France, marked by small-scale and specialised production, was once designated as a failure, but this judgement is being questioned now. Instead, it is seen as a viable alternative to factory-based mass production.[17] The theory of proto-industrialisation recast dispersed, rural, craft-based industries as essential precursors to industrialisation in many European regions.[18]

We now possess a critical mass of historical scholarship challenging the idea of a single, linear, pre-determined path of industrial development. In actual fact, there were a range of diverse industrial transformations in different parts of the world.[19] Many explanations have been offered for this divergence. Earlier narratives (liberal as well as Marxist) stressed the

[15] For an overview of debates on small-scale and craft-based production in industrialisation and economic development, see Maxine Berg, 'Skills, Craft and Histories of Industrialisation in Europe and Asia', *Transactions of the Royal Historical Society*, 24 (December 2014), 127–48.
[16] Maxine Berg, *The Age of Manufactures: Industry, Innovation and Work in Britain, 1700–1820* (London, Fontana Press, 1985).
[17] Patrick O'Brien and Caglar Keyder, *Economic Growth in Britain and France, 1780–1940: Two Paths to the Twentieth Century* (London, Allen and Unwin, 1978); Jeff Horn, *The Path not Taken: French Industrialisation in the Age of Revolution, 1750–1830* (Cambridge, MA, MIT Press, 2006). Piore and Sabel, in *The Second Industrial Divide*, use the term 'flexible specialisation' to describe an alternative path to mass production.
[18] Not all regions with a flourishing 'proto-industry' industrialised. Peter Kriedte, Hans Medick and Jürgen Schlumbohm, *Industrialization before Industrialization: Rural Industry in the Genesis of Capitalism* (Cambridge, Cambridge University Press, 1981).
[19] Jeff Horn, Leonard N. Rosenband and Merritt Roe Smith (eds), *Reconceptualizing the Industrial Revolution* (Cambridge, MA, MIT Press, 2010).

inherent logic of industrialisation driven by technology. By contrast, the new scholarship explores a range of factors including the social and cultural determinants of consumption, the role of the state, the creation and spread of 'useful knowledge', wage rates, work culture, and so on.[20] It also places special emphasis on the centrality of *political* choices in determining the direction of change. Patrick O'Brien, Charles Sabel and Jonathan Zeitlin stress state action; Jeff Horn and Tessie P. Liu examine pressures from below (politics at the point of production).[21] For South Asia, Rajnarayan Chandavarkar was among the first to raise important questions about technology-driven teleological assumptions of industrialisation.[22]

Many of these studies were inspired by contemporary problems in periods of economic instability. The work of Sabel and Zeitlin has its roots in the economic crisis of the seventies and the search for alternatives to mass production. In recent years, there has been renewed emphasis on the small and local (expressed in the phrase 'small is beautiful').[23] The search for alternatives recurs throughout the history of modern industrialisation: it is driven by its inherent inequality, periodic crises of mass underemployment and unemployment and a deepening ecological crisis.

The critique of capitalism and the search for alternative visions of economic development has a long tradition in India. Its most important theorist was Gandhi. His economic vision revolved around the idea of local self-sufficiency: the city and the village were depicted as oppositional entities, representing different models of development. Spinning and weaving were central to this vision.[24] Despite being pushed to the margins

[20] Horn, Rosenband and Roe Smith, *Reconceptualizing the Industrial Revolution*. The literature on the causes of the industrial revolution is too large to discuss here.

[21] See the papers by Patrick O'Brien and Jeff Horn in Horn, Rosenband and Roe Smith, *Reconceptualizing the Industrial Revolution*, pp. 21–46; Sabel and Zeitlin, 'Historical Alternatives'; Liu, *The Weaver's Knot*.

[22] Rajnarayan Chandavarkar, *The Origins of Industrial Capitalism in India: Business Strategies and the Working Classes in Bombay 1900–1940* (Cambridge, Cambridge University Press, 1994); Rajnarayan Chandavarkar, 'Industrialisation in India before 1947: Conventional Approaches and Alternative Perspectives', *Modern Asian Studies*, 19(3) (1985), 623–68.

[23] E. F. Schumacher, *Small is Beautiful: a Study of Economics as if People Mattered* (London, Blond and Briggs, 1973).

[24] Rahul Ramagundam, *Gandhi's Khadi: a History of Contention and Conciliation* (Delhi, Orient Longman, 2008); Kazuya Ishii, 'The Socioeconomic Thoughts of Mahatma Gandhi as an Origin of Alternate Development', *Review of Social Economy*, 59(3) (2001), 297–312. Gandhian economic ideas are (imperfectly) explored through the autobiography of an important collaborator and fellow traveller in Venu Madhav Govindu and Deepak Malghan, *The Web of Freedom: J. C. Kumarappa and Gandhi's Struggle for Economic Justice* (Delhi, Oxford University Press, 2016).

by policy-makers in post-independence India, Gandhi's ideas retained a symbolic value.[25] They also influenced state policy towards small-scale industry, sometimes in unintended ways.[26] Social movements against displacement and non-government organisations (NGOs) working with artisans and farmers to revive traditional skills still draw upon them. They continue to inspire experiments to recast and revive weaving (by using hand-spun or machine-spun yarn produced by decentralised methods).

A hallmark of the search for alternatives is the uncritical celebration of smallness as a virtue in itself. As Haynes points out, Gandhi remained blind to the fundamental transformation of traditional crafts during his own lifetime.[27] One might add that his followers showed little interest in addressing social inequalities in the village economy (the structural inequality of caste or the unequal distribution of resources). Critics of mass production, as Liu points out, usually equate small-scale production with greater dynamism, equity and so on, ignoring sweating and exploitation in workshops. In actual fact, the forms assumed by labour-intensive production systems depend upon a range of factors, including state policy and struggles at the point of production. Liu's study of conflicts between handloom weavers and merchants in one French region shows how decentralised weaving persisted until the end of the nineteenth century alongside new industries employing women from weaving households as sweated labour.[28]

4

This book rests on the premise that there was nothing predetermined about the evolution of the handloom industry in South India—or indeed the Indian economy as a whole—from the early nineteenth century. It draws upon the work of scholars like Haynes and Liu who place human agency and politics at the centre of economic change. I argue that the modern contours of the handloom industry emerged out of a complex process of conflict, compromise and adaptation at many different levels and sites. It involved different social groups or actors embedded in distinctive social, economic and political hierarchies. These intersectional forces are examined

[25] The place of crafts in the idea of India as a nation are discussed in Abigail McGowan, *Crafting the Nation in Colonial India* (New York, Palgrave Macmillan, 2009).

[26] Nasir Tyabji, *The Small Industries Policy in India* (Calcutta, Oxford University Press, 1989), pp. 112–48.

[27] Haynes, *Small Town Capitalism*, p. 2.

[28] Liu, *The Weaver's Knot*.

primarily from the perspective of *labour* or the people whose work went into making cloth.[29]

As late as the 1960s, the Indian economy remained predominantly agricultural, with a very small organised or formal sector. The bulk of manufacturing and processing was done by decentralised, small-scale units in the informal sector: the handloom industry formed a key part of this system. The evolution of a very large informal sector is one of the key characteristics of the Indian economy. This study seeks to provide a historical explanation for its emergence.

Both Haynes and Liu emphasise politics at the point of production. Other factors—the emergence of textile mills, the forces of global capitalism, state policy—are viewed as external, providing context and helping to shape choices made by those involved in the production process. By contrast, I argue that these factors were not 'given' and cannot usefully be regarded as external: instead, they should be viewed as conflicts at *different levels* of the system.

Not all battles were fought at the point of production. Supposedly external forces exerted a decisive influence on the handloom industry: one example is the abrupt severance of the link between spinning and weaving during the late nineteenth century. The shift from hand- to machine-spun yarn played a key role in the disappearance of many coarse cloth weavers and instigated the reorganisation of production systems. Pariar weavers were forced out of weaving before struggles at the point of production could commence.[30] Instead of viewing mechanisation as an external force acting on them, it makes more sense to see it a socio-political conflict in a very different arena. Its impacts were variable; unlike Pariars, specialist weaving castes with social capital were able to adapt to the new systems of production. Contemporary activists working with weavers in South India have highlighted the link between spinning and weaving, and sought to revive it by finding alternative sources of yarn supply.[31]

[29] As labour history has widened to encompass overlooked and invisible forms of work (such as women in the domestic sphere), it has also moved away from teleological narratives of proletarianisation and class consciousness. For an overview of recent trends in Indian labour history writing, see Chitra Joshi, 'Histories of Indian Labour: Predicaments and Possibilities', *History Compass*, 6(2) (2008), 439–54.

[30] The Pariar were a so-called untouchable caste. The term Pariah (used in colonial records) has derogatory connotations; many scholars prefer to replace it with the term Dalit, encompassing all 'untouchable' castes. In this book, different groups of weavers are described by caste affiliation, using the Tamil honorific modifier 'ar' (which is also the plural form) as a sign of respect: the Pariar, Kaikolar, Saliar and so on.

[31] Notably in Uzramma Bilgrami's analytic work as well as her practical interventions. See Meena Menon and Uzramma Bilgrami, *A Frayed History: the Journey of Cotton in India* (New Delhi, Oxford University Press, 2017).

Ranking causative drivers of change, even in rough order, is an inherently difficult task—instead, this study seeks to trace critical *conjunctures*, when social, economic and political forces came together to reshape the lives of weavers in fundamental ways. This approach is especially fruitful in interpreting state policies. The colonial state loomed large in the writings of most nationalist historians; conversely, it has been downplayed in revisionist historiography. Chandavarkar advocated an intermediate approach based on the interplay between social structures and the state.[32] My analysis of state action (and inaction) rests upon a close examination of departmental struggles, larger battles over policy within and outside government, and political contests between interest groups seeking to establish their dominance. In turn, state policy affected social groups in different ways, depending upon their position in the production system. Labour legislation came to exert a strong influence on the organisation of the handloom industry after the Second World War. Here, I seek to uncover the range and complexity of forces affecting the lives of various participants in the world of weaving.

Regional studies play an important role in clarifying larger narratives of economic change. This book is a study of the handloom industry in South India, roughly coterminous with the borders of the Madras Presidency and Mysore state. Most studies focus on the Coromandel coast, where cloth was produced primarily for export. This book takes the opposite tack: here, I focus on cloth production for domestic consumption, especially in inland regions, and map the diversity of producers, markets, intermediaries and consumers in the early nineteenth century.

During this period, a substantial proportion of cloth was made by part-time weavers from so-called untouchable castes. Makers of fine and specialised cloth lived mostly in larger villages and towns, but the production of coarse cloth was decentralised and dispersed all over the countryside. Production systems varied. Some weavers made cloth with yarn supplied by customers; others bought yarn and sold their cloth in local markets; some worked for merchants who provided them with cash advances. The first part of the book also maps the work of non-specialist, part-time groups: plebeian weavers such as the Pariar and the Mala as well as spinners, mostly women. A gendered division of labour organised around the household lay at the heart of cloth production.

[32] Chandavarkar, 'Industrialisation in India'.

The rest of the book examines the subsequent process of change. My aim is to move from macro-economic narratives to the lived experience of social groups. In addressing the deindustrialisation debate, I seek to differentiate the process of change by mapping its human costs and identifying social groups forced out of weaving and those who managed to adapt. The focus throughout is on structures of production and their impact on different *kinds* of weavers. I compare the trajectory of Pariars—coarse cloth weavers belonging to a so-called untouchable caste—with that of specialised weavers from the upwardly mobile Pattunoolkarar or Saurashtra caste to uncover the effects of caste and social status in determining divergent outcomes.

By the 1950s, the handloom industry had been transformed. Spinning was mechanised, the practice of making cloth with yarn supplied by the customer had disappeared and the weaver's control over the production process had been significantly eroded. There was some variation in production systems, which ranged from home-based weavers working on their own looms to small workshops, factories and cooperatives. Their common factor was centralisation: this was achieved through tight control of consumer markets and yarn by intermediaries. The master-weaver had become a key figure in the landscape of handloom production.

This process did not entail a wholesale shift to large-scale handloom factories or even powerlooms. Instead, the handloom industry dissolved into what was to become the informal economy along with industries like beedi making, leather processing, tile making and so on. The informal economy is characterised by small units; identities based on caste, gender and religion are used to recruit and control workers. The absence of state regulation with regard to capital accumulation, labour markets and capital-labour relationships is viewed as its defining characteristic.[33] It is marked by the absence of any form of legal protection for workers.

Sociologists and economists take the existence of the informal sector for granted. Most historians view it as a residue or holdover from those parts of the traditional economy that failed to modernise.[34] A few scholars situate it within a historical process, examining the role of the state in its evolution.[35]

[33] There is much disagreement over definitions of the informal sector (and whether it can be defined at all). For a summary, see Elisabetta Basile and Barbara Harriss-White, 'Introduction', *International Review of Sociology*, 20(3) (2010), 457–71.

[34] Peter Robb, 'Introduction' and Michael Anderson, 'Work Construed: Ideological Origins of Labour Law in British India to 1918', in Peter Robb (ed.), *Dalit Movements and the Meanings of Labour in India* (Delhi, Oxford University Press, 1993), pp. 44–7, 118–19.

[35] Haynes, *Small Town Capitalism*; Prabhu Mohapatra, 'Regulated Informality: Legal Construction of Labour Relations in Colonial India, 1800–1926', in Jan Lucassen and

My study seeks to throw light on this long-term process, by using the handloom industry as a case study.

Chapter 1 sets the scene by recovering and describing the physical and human geography of cloth production in South India. Chapter 2 outlines the process of change during the nineteenth century, paying close attention to different groups of weavers. Chapter 3 examines the links between cotton cultivation, spinning and weaving, and shows how these were ruptured and reconfigured. Chapter 4 looks more closely at the production structures of weaving. Chapters 5, 6 and 7 deal with social and political factors, showing how caste networks, collective mobilisation and state policies came together to shape the handloom industry from the mid-nineteenth century. I end with some reflections on the implications of this study for our understanding of the economic trajectory of India after 1947.

A final note on the period of this study. It begins in the early nineteenth century, when the English East India Company (EIC) had consolidated its rule, and just before the effects of the industrial revolution affected cloth production in South Asia. It ends not in 1947, but in 1960. 1947 is a somewhat artificial dividing line, for the demise of the colonial state did not lead to overnight change in the economic realm. It is more rewarding to view the period between 1935 and 1960 as a single unit, when many political battles broke out to shape the contours of the Indian state, its economy and society. The process of devolving power begins with the Government of India Act of 1935. By 1960, the dust had settled and many conflicts over policy had been resolved, for the time being at least. In this unstable equilibrium, it is possible to discern the contours of future developments.

Sabyasachi Bhattacharya (eds), *Workers in the Informal Sector: Studies in Labour History, 1800–2000* (Delhi, Macmillan, 2004), pp. 65–95; Karuna Dietrich Wielenga, 'The Emergence of the Informal Sector: Labour Legislation and Politics in South India, 1940–1960', *Modern Asian Studies* (2019), 1–36.

1

The Geography of Weaving

South India in the Early Nineteenth Century

Indian textiles are usually associated with fine muslins, woven silks and cloths printed with vivid, decorative motifs. These were made for elite consumption and export to many parts of the world from at least the sixteenth century onwards.[1] Archival sources for the export trade are abundant and varied, but very little is known about ordinary cloth woven for local consumption. This chapter seeks to reconstruct the human and spatial geography of textile production in nineteenth-century South India, not for export but for *domestic* use. This involves mapping the varieties of cloth produced, and identifying their consumers and producers. In order to do this, I draw upon a range of source materials largely ignored by historians.

I begin by reconstructing the actual clothing of different social groups during this period, using textual descriptions and visual representations. While doing this, I pay close attention to the cloth itself: the material (whether cotton or silk), its texture (whether coarse or fine), its colour (whether bleached or unbleached, plain or coloured), the decorative element (whether patterned on the loom or printed) and so on.[2] The nature of cloth provides important clues to its makers.

The next stage is to track down these makers, unearthing their geographical and social position. Finally, I examine the interrelated flows of cotton, yarn and cloth, systems of cloth production, and networks of exchange and trade. The aim of this exercise is to uncover the basic structures of textile production in the early nineteenth century. The picture

[1] For an overview, see Riello, *Cotton*, pp. 17–36. Also, Riello and Roy, *How India Clothed the World*.

[2] My focus is on cotton and cotton textiles, for the vast majority of weavers made cloth from cotton. During the nineteenth century, the production of silk textiles fell; I refer to silk mainly in the context of specialist weavers who wove in silk or some combination of silk and cotton.

is partial and tentative, but serves as a baseline for the transformation of the handloom industry during the rest of the century.

Reconstructing clothing in early nineteenth-century South India

One reason for the scholarly neglect of cloth production for domestic markets is the nature of the sources: these are largely records of various European companies involved in the export trade. Since equivalent records for domestic trade are very sparse, I have adopted a different approach. This involves the use of visual sources—primarily Company paintings and specimens from textile collections—combined with statistical data on looms and cloth production whenever it is available.[3]

Cloth production in South India was marked by pronounced regional variations. Styles of wearing or draping cloth also varied—clothing might change from one locality to another and between different social groups. Some varieties were produced for restricted or specialised markets: large quantities of mundus or veshtis (cloths for men) and tortas or towels for the Travancore market were made in the districts of Tinnevelly (Tirunelveli) and Madurai; they were even called Travancore cloths.[4] The weavers of Kodali Karuppur, a village near Kumbakonam, made fine cotton cloth for the Maratha nobles of Thanjavur.[5]

The sources: an appraisal

For information on clothing, I draw upon contemporary observations in personal narratives, travelogues and official records. Another source material is visual in nature; for the late eighteenth and early nineteenth century, I use Company paintings depicting various castes and occupations.[6] These were

[3] Giorgio Riello uses material and visual evidence in conjunction with concepts from material culture in his work. Here, I use material and visual evidence to reconstruct production systems, putting questions of consumption and culture to one side.

[4] Tinnevelly District Records (TDR) vol. 3600, 22 October 1805, p. 82, Tamil Nadu State Archives (TNSA); Proceedings of the Board of Revenue (PBR) vol. 1937, 7 November 1844, no. 48–9, pp. 14949–55, TNSA; India Office Records (IOR) H/misc/791, 1834, London.

[5] W. S. Hadaway, *Cotton Painting and Printing in the Madras Presidency* (Madras, Government Press, 1917), p. 9.

[6] Most Company paintings were made in the late eighteenth and early nineteenth centuries; my examples are from the collections of the Victoria and Albert Museum (V&A), London.

commissioned by Europeans and painted by Indian artists in the local style or modified versions of it (by incorporating some elements of perspective). The painters probably came from specific caste groups: in Thanjavur, they were called Moochys. Other sets were painted in Trichinopoly (Thiruchirapalli) and Madras.[7] For a slightly later period, I draw on textile collections: the largest was made by Forbes Watson, who collected, classified and described different varieties of cloth woven in the Madras Presidency in two large albums of 18 volumes each.[8] Before examining these sources, a few things must be said in order to place them in context.

Watson's collection does not provide *quantitative* information—it tells us nothing about how much of what kind of cloth was actually produced. He notes that white, unbleached cloth (or coarse white cloth with minimal decoration) formed the commonest article of clothing. But among his samples, this is obviously not found in proportion to the quantities produced.[9] His primary interest was in design, represented by clothes of intricate pattern and colour. His albums contain many colourful samples made and worn by the Lubbays of Tamil Nadu, a relatively small community.[10] The usefulness of Watson's work lies elsewhere—his collection maps the sheer *variety* of textiles in South India and provides information about the dimensions of each sample, its price and the exact locale of production.

While interpreting Company paintings both the social context and their actual purposes must be kept in mind. In the words of Captain Charles Gold who commissioned some of them:

> on the suggestions of Europeans, some of the artists had been induced to draw series of the most ordinary casts or tribes, each picture representing a man and his wife, with the signs or marks of distinction on their foreheads, and not in their common but holiday clothes.[11]

Many paintings are clearly of this description: the men and women appear to be dressed in their best clothes, wearing their 'caste marks' and posing with implements of work or trade in their hands. Many women wear ornaments

[7] Modern equivalents of nineteenth-century place names are given in brackets wherever possible and used subsequently; otherwise, they are left as written in the sources.

[8] These can be found in the V&A. The second series is also available in the IOR. Forbes Watson, *The Textile Manufactures and the Costumes of the People of India* (London, India Office, 1866).

[9] Watson, *The Textile Manufactures*, pp. 21, 83.

[10] Watson, *The Textile Manufactures*, pp. 27–9.

[11] Mildred Archer, *Company Paintings: Indian Paintings of the British Period* (London, Victoria and Albert Museum, Indian Art Series, 1993), p. 17.

and jewellery.[12] Here, it should be borne in mind that what people choose to wear is often governed by the social context and the audience.[13] However, there are also paintings that depict men and women in working postures and what appear to be their working or everyday clothes. It is likely that the artists who painted them used their own knowledge to create composite types. A close examination of both kinds of paintings offers valuable clues. It becomes clear, for example, that a very large proportion of clothes worn by men and women during the nineteenth century were unstitched, that is they came off the loom ready to wear.[14] This was particularly true for South India.[15] The sari, the dhoti and the turban are obvious examples.

Men's clothing: dhotis, angavastrams, rumals and turbans

Most men wore a cloth around the lower part of their bodies—the dhoti, mundu or veshti—paired with a similar piece thrown across the shoulders. This was called the dupatta or angavastram.[16] The two parts might be woven as a single piece joined by a narrow band of warp threads, where they could be separated. The upper cloth often served as a sheet at night. It was also common practice to cut up piece goods of suitable breadth into dhotis and upper cloths.[17] Where winters were cold, the cumblee or woollen blanket doubled up as a body cloth.[18]

Young boys wore a shorter version of the dhoti.[19] Most men wore turbans albeit in different styles. Rumals, shorter in length and square in shape, were also used to cover the head.[20] The poorest castes usually wore only the dhoti or a very short loincloth called langotee: quite often they were

[12] These paintings formed part of the colonial project of labelling and classifying 'Indian' subjects. For this aspect of their history, see Emma Tarlo, *Clothing Matters: Dress and Identity in India* (Chicago, University of Chicago Press, 1996), pp. 2–6.

[13] See Tarlo, *Clothing Matters*, p. 14; Arjun Appadurai, 'Introduction', in Arjun Appadurai (ed.), *The Social Life of Things: Commodities in Cultural Perspective* (Cambridge, Cambridge University Press, 1986), pp. 3–56.

[14] Watson, *The Textile Manufactures*, p. 4.

[15] The spread of stitched clothing is usually traced to Mughal influence. Some scholars believe that it was extant before the Mughal period, but, if so, its actual use in South India was limited. See Vijaya Ramaswamy, *Textiles and Weavers in Medieval South India* (Delhi, Oxford University Press, 1985), p. 17; and Tarlo, *Clothing Matters*, p. 28.

[16] Watson, *The Textile Manufactures*, p. 21.

[17] Watson, *The Textile Manufactures*, pp. 21–2.

[18] Hamilton F. Buchanan, *A Journey from Madras through the Countries of Mysore, Canara and Malabar*, vol. 1 (London, British Library Historical Print Editions, 1807), p. 40.

[19] Buchanan, *A Journey from Madras*, vol. 1, pp. 207, 208.

[20] Watson, *The Textile Manufactures*, p. 20.

prohibited from wearing turbans or upper cloths, for these were regarded as badges of respectability and social status.[21]

Cloths of this kind were usually unbleached or white. Hoole, describing a Christian congregation in Madras, writes that the

> men were neatly attired in white cotton cloths ... [They] wear turbans. The rest of their dress consists of two cloths, one disposed about the loins, forming something like a pair of loose trousers; the other gracefully thrown across the shoulders.[22]

A missionary in Cudappah (Kadapa) district describes a congregation assembled for the Christmas celebration:

> [M]en, women and children [are] dressed in their best and gayest clothing, mostly snow white garments but relieved continually by contrast with the brightest of colours—a scarlet jacket or turban etc.; many of the women wear flowers in their hair and the children have garlands of marigold and chrysanthemum.[23]

This mode of dress seems to have continued until the late nineteenth century, when changes began to set in.[24]

These accounts are confirmed by Company paintings in which the vast majority of men wear white dhotis of varying lengths with little or no embellishment. In a collection from 1770 showing 36 castes and occupations, 26 out of 37 men wear white.[25] In two collections dating from 1790 and 1805, 63 and 72 per cent of men respectively are clothed partly or wholly in white.[26] Most working clothes were plain and unbleached. In an 1840 set depicting artisanal occupations, men and women are shown in working postures; all the men are wearing white dhotis, tucked tightly between their legs, and almost all the turbans are white. While working, the upper cloth was abandoned, probably for comfort (see, for example,

[21] For attempts to adopt turbans and upper garments by social groups forbidden from wearing them, see Tarlo, *Clothing Matters*, p. 7.

[22] Elijah Hoole, *Madras, Mysore and the South of India: or a Personal Narrative of a Mission to those Countries, 1820–1828*, 2nd edn (London, Longman, Brown, Green and Longmans, 1844), pp. 39–40.

[23] The Budwail Mission, Cuddapah, Society for the Propagation of the Gospel to Foreign Parts, Quarterly paper no. 136, May 1866, Rhodes House Library, Oxford.

[24] For an examination of changing fashions in the late nineteenth and early twentieth centuries, see Tarlo, *Clothing Matters*; and some of the contributions in Douglas E. Haynes, Abigail McGowan, Tirthankar Roy and Haruka Yanagisawa (eds), *Towards a History of Consumption* (Delhi, Oxford University Press, 2010).

[25] A set of thirty-six paintings, Museum Number AL. 9128, V&A, London.

[26] A set of sixteen paintings, Museum Numbers 0923, 0924, 0925 and 0926; and a set of thirty-six paintings, Museum Number AL. 9254, V&A, London.

Plate 1).[27] In comparison, Company paintings from the north show a larger proportion of men wearing an upper cloth or some form of stitched clothing: seasonal variations in temperature are much greater in the north than the south.[28] Much the same observations can be made about paintings depicting agricultural work.

By contrast, paintings of religious and marriage processions usually show men dressed in dhotis and upper cloths with ornamented, coloured borders and bright turbans.[29] Men in 'holiday' clothes are dressed in much the same way. Watson observed that Indian weavers were economical with decoration—it was never in excess but served to highlight the beauty of the cloth when worn the right way. One side of turbans and dhotis might be decorated with coloured bands using silk or gold thread; borders running along the long edges were made with coloured cotton (or silk or gold) thread.[30] Even coarse cloth was decorated with red, brown or blue borders that assumed a prominent position when it was worn: Burghers, a farming caste in the Coimbatore region, wore coarse cloth with blue and red borders (Plate 1).[31] Togataru weavers living in the region around Bangalore made coarse white cloth with red borders, the staple dress of the poor.[32]

Coloured clothing was popular with some social groups. The Lubbay, a group of Muslim traders and weavers, wove coloured cloths in checks or stripes to be tied around the waist (Plates 4 and 5). In Company paintings, they are shown wearing this garment loose and not tucked between the legs (Plate 22).[33] In the twentieth century, it came to be called the lungi and passed into common use, largely for wearing at home, in private rather than public spaces. From the 1930s on, lungis were exported to countries where Tamil migrants had settled.[34] More usually, coloured clothing was worn on festive occasions and those of religious significance: a painting shows

[27] A set of sixteen paintings, Museum Number IS 97-1989 to IS 104-1989 and IS 1-1990 to IS 8-1990, V&A, London.

[28] See Company Paintings Series with Museum Number 4656, Benares, 1870; Series with Museum Number 4675, Benares 1870, V&A, London.

[29] For example, IS 39:28-1987; IS 39:27-1987, V&A, London.

[30] Watson, *The Textile Manufactures*, pp. 5, 14.

[31] Watson, *The Textile Manufactures*, p. 23; Sample no. 80, Forbes Watson Textile Collection, First Series, V&A, London.

[32] Buchanan, *A Journey from Madras*, vol. 1, p. 217.

[33] Company Paintings Series, Museum Numbers 0927:3/(IS), 0923:2/(IS), AL.9128:12, V&A, London.

[34] D. M. Amalsad, 'The Development of the Madras Handkerchief and Lungi or Kily Industry in the Madras Presidency', Department of Industries Bulletin no. 22 (Madras, Madras Government, 1926).

a man on a pilgrimage clad in an ochre dhoti.[35] According to Buchanan, sanyasis or Brahmins in temples and monasteries usually wore yellow or red dhotis.[36] In Company paintings, religious mendicants are clad in yellow or ochre robes. Muslim mendicants also wore coloured garments (Plate 22).[37] Not unsurprisingly, the most striking clothes in terms of colour and design were worn by members of prosperous and powerful groups (like the money lender in Plate 23). Foreign travellers in India were struck by the costly attire of rulers and local elites.[38] By the early nineteenth century some of them had declined in wealth and power and the use of expensive textiles fell proportionately.

Not all men wore the same kind of clothes. Some wealthy individuals, especially members of the bureaucracy and the army, are dressed in tunics or kurtas in Company paintings. By the early nineteenth century many cultural influences were at work upon clothing. Nayaka chieftains, Muslim rulers, the Marathas and the British brought new forms and fashions to South India. Stitched clothing became more common. Strikingly, all the local terms used by Watson to describe tunics are derived from Urdu and other North Indian dialects: this would indicate that they arrived with migrants from the north.[39]

In Company paintings, men of the ruling classes and those belonging to immigrant groups (Muslim nobles, Marathas and Sikhs) wear long robes or kurtas with trousers or dhotis. Some are white, but most are coloured and patterned; others are heavily embellished with gold. According to Hoole, 'native men, in the service of Europeans, generally wear also a close jacket, of muslin or calico, with sleeves down to the wrist'.[40] Company paintings show dubashes, shroffs, cooks, soldiers, barbers and tailors in stitched upper garments (Plate 21). Cooks and soldiers are clad in trousers of varying lengths. This influence also extended to designs and patterns. South India does not appear to have had any indigenous tie and dye tradition: this was popularised by Pattunoolkarar weavers who migrated into the Tamil

[35] Company Paintings Series, Museum Number AL.9128:9, AL.8940J, AL.9254:29, AL.9254:36, V&A, London. For the significance of colours, see C. A. Bayly, 'The Origins of Swadeshi (Home Industry): Cloth and Indian Society, 1700–1930', in Arjun Appadurai (ed.), *The Social Life of Things: Commodities in Cultural Perspective* (Cambridge, Cambridge University Press, 1986), pp. 290–2.

[36] Buchanan, *A Journey from Madras*, vol. 1, p. 21.

[37] Company Paintings Series, Museum Number 0923:2(IS), AL.9254:29, AL.9254:14, AL.9254:15, AL.9254:28, AL.9254:36, V&A, London.

[38] Ramaswamy, *Textiles and Weavers*, pp. 67–8; Bayly, 'The Origins of Swadeshi', pp. 298–302.

[39] Watson, *The Textile Manufactures*, p. 56.

[40] Hoole, *Madras, Mysore and the South of India*, pp. 39–40.

country during the reign of the Nayakas (1529–1736) (Plate 12). Maratha nobles in Thanjavur (a Maratha kingdom from 1674 to 1855) were said to be especially fond of tie and dye textiles.[41]

The turban was universally worn during the nineteenth century, though the custom has almost died out in present-day South India. Turbans were usually of fine texture, for they had to be wound many times around the head; they came in varying sizes and were worn in myriad styles (Plate 13). The length of a turban was usually between 15 and 25 yards (but some could be as long as 60); it was about 9 to 12 inches wide.[42] Shorter turbans or rumals (literally handkerchiefs) were widely used, white being the most common colour (Plate 15).[43] The cheapest turbans usually had red borders along the long sides. Coloured turbans were usually of red or yellow. Printed turbans were also worn. The most expensive method of ornamentation involved the use of gold threads in borders and ends. Other kinds of head dress included stitched caps made from dyed cotton cloth, worn by some Brahmins.[44] Soldiers wore caps too. Coloured scarves and shawls, made of silk and embellished with gold, were also worn.

Women's clothing

Most women wore saris, called by various names in different regions and languages.[45] In a Christian congregation in Madras, the women were clad in

> red or blue cloths, of the same material [cotton], or of silk, one piece of about nine yards in length being disposed (without the aid of pins or sewing) into a modest covering of the whole person; one end being drawn over the head, to serve as a veil when they assemble in a public congregation. ... Some of the hindoo women wear under the cloth a ravvikei, or body-dress, usually of fancy silk, fitting close to the person, and only long enough to cover the bosom; it has short sleeves, reaching half way to the elbow. Many of them have gold or silver bracelets and anklets of large size on their arms and ankles, and an abundance of rings and jewellery about their noses and ears, fingers and toes; they wear no shoes and no head dress.[46]

[41] Veronica Murphy and Rosemary Crill, *Tie-dyed Textiles of India: Tradition and Trade* (London, Victoria and Albert Museum in association with Mapin Publishing, 1991), p. 105.
[42] Watson, *The Textile Manufactures*, pp. 13–14.
[43] Watson, *The Textile Manufactures*, p. 14.
[44] Watson, *The Textile Manufactures*, p. 54; Company Paintings, Museum Number AL. 9128:13, V&A, London.
[45] Watson, *The Textile Manufactures*, p. 40.
[46] Hoole, *Madras, Mysore and the South of India*, pp. 39–40.

According to Buchanan, women around Mysore wore the 'shiray', which they 'wrap around their haunches and then throw over their heads and shoulders'. A slightly shorter version of this was the 'kirigay' for girls. In addition, there was the 'cuppisa', a 'little jacket which the women at this place wear'. The cloth was woven in long pieces, and one piece could be used to make as many as twelve jackets.[47]

Saris came in different dimensions. There were many ways of draping the garment. Some women wore ravikkais or bodices under the sari, but this practice was relatively uncommon. Most saris were coloured, although white saris with coloured borders and ends were also made. White clothing predominated in some regions: Company paintings from the Malabar coast show men and women, Brahmins and plebeian castes, toddy tappers and fisher-people, in white clothes of various styles.[48] As late as the twentieth century, white saris with coloured borders were commonly worn in Visakhapatnam district.[49] Togataru weavers around Bangalore wove a white cloth with a red border for men and women.[50] Mothasaudys (coarse saris) produced in the Ceded Districts were also white.[51] Plates 6, 7 and 8 show examples of coarse white cloths with simple borders.

Poor women are usually shown wearing white clothes—often only a waist cloth, with the upper body left bare. In three sets of Company paintings dating from 1770, 1790 and 1805, showing grass-cutters, basket makers, mud-wall builders, rat-catchers, toddy tappers, tank builders, firewood sellers, jugglers and beggars (a catalogue of the poorest and most menial occupations), the women are depicted in plain white clothes without even a border. Often the cloth reaches only to the knee (Plates 3 and 4). Some of them carry babies in slings made of white cloth partly covering their bodies. In paintings showing potters, carpenters, weavers, bricklayers, blacksmiths, butchers, bracelet or necklace sellers, washermen, and shoemakers—artisanal groups, somewhat higher up the social scale—women wear white saris with red or blue borders, or coloured ones (Plates 1 and 2). In the 1770 collection (consisting of 36 paintings), 17 out of 32 women are shown in white.[52] One wears a fine muslin dress, but about half are clad in simple

[47] Buchanan, *A Journey from Madras*, vol. 1, pp. 207, 208.
[48] Company Paintings, Museum Number IS.251-1951 to IS.265-1951, V&A, London.
[49] W. Francis, *Vizagapatam District Gazetteer* (New Delhi, Asian Educational Services, Reprint, 1992), p. 69.
[50] Buchanan, *A Journey from Madras*, vol. 1, p. 217.
[51] PBR vol. 382, 21 June 1804, p. 5075, TNSA.
[52] Series with Museum no. AL.9128, V&A, London.

white clothing. In the 1790 set, 25 per cent of the women are in white saris; in the 1805 series, this percentage rises to 32.[53]

In general, it would appear that most women wore coloured saris, especially in the regions corresponding to modern Tamil Nadu and the southern districts of Karnataka and Andhra Pradesh. Joseph Mullens, a missionary, noted that 'the women are fond of coloured dresses, which they wear rather short; and often leave the head uncovered out-of-doors: a thing never done in Upper India'.[54] Buchanan wrote that women in the Mysore country generally wore coloured saris.[55] Poor women used white saris with borders of indigo blue or madder red. Dyeing in red was easier and cheaper than dyeing in blue.[56] Dyed saris might be plain, with the whole garment in one colour but for a border and end dyed in a contrasting shade. Nearly all saris had borders and some kind of design at the shorter end draped across the shoulder or over the head, or tucked into the waist.[57]

Saris were patterned in many ways, by using threads of different colours to make checks or stripes (Plates 9, 10 and 11). The borders might be woven with threads of a different colour, sometimes of silk or interwoven with gold thread (called zari). Tie and dye was another method of making patterns albeit restricted to a few centres: Madurai was famous for its tie and dye saris in dark red (Plate 12).[58] Block printing was a specialty of other centres.[59] The sari was ubiquitous, but women from some social groups preferred to wear other clothes. Lambadi women favoured a petticoat with a kind of blouse or ravikkai. So-called dancing girls are often shown in skirts or petticoats with a ravikkai and davani (upper covering cloth).[60]

Thus, a large proportion of everyday clothing in nineteenth-century South India was coarse and white (with coloured borders and ends). But cloth was also woven for other purposes. Textiles were used for decoration

[53] Series with Museum no. 0923, 0924, 0925, 0926 and AL.9254, V&A, London.

[54] Joseph Mullens, *Missions in South India: Visited and Described* (London, W. H. Dalton, 1854), p. 64.

[55] Buchanan, *A Journey from Madras*, vol. 1, p. 135.

[56] Buchanan, *A Journey from Madras*, vol. 1, pp. 209–15, 224–5.

[57] Watson, *The Textile Manufactures*, pp. 39–40. Some idea of the sheer variety of saris can be obtained from the Forbes Watson Textile Collection.

[58] J. H. Nelson, *The Madura Country: a Manual* (Madras, The Asylum Press, 1868), p. 874; Tie and dye samples from Madurai in the Forbes Watson Textile Collection, Series I, no. 33, 36, 37.

[59] Benjamin Heyne, *Tracts Historical and Statistical, on India; with Journals of Several Tours through Various Parts of the Peninsula: also an Account of Sumatra, in a Series of Letters* (London, Robert Baldwin; and Black, Parry and Co., 1814), p. 326.

[60] Watson, *The Textile Manufactures*, pp. 57–8; Company Paintings, Museum Number: AL.545, V&A, London.

and ornamentation in the homes and palaces of dominant social groups.[61] These included jamakalams or carpets in many colours and designs.[62] The nobles and rulers of Thanjavur favoured carpets made of silk. Cotton tapes were used for stringing cots.[63]

Ordinary cloth also had plenty of other uses: this was true of a thick, plain cloth called khadi. Khadi was used as a tent cloth, either plain or printed, and some varieties were used to make sails. It was also employed 'for packing goods, and as a covering for the dead, for which last purpose a large quantity is employed both by Hindoos and Mahomedans'.[64] The thicker varieties, sometimes called Dungarees, were used for tents and sails (Plate 14). Watson took particular note of the 'strength, lightness, and other good qualities of the cotton sailcloth manufactured in India'.[65]

Quality and quantity

We have seen that most clothing was made of coarse but durable varieties of cloth: plain white garments with some decoration formed the everyday wear of the poor and middling classes. But we need to know more about their gross value in terms of output and their actual contribution to cloth production. According to Watson,

> common unbleached fabrics, under names varying in different localities, constitute a large proportion of the clothing of the poor. … In Western and Southern India they are known under the more general term of khadi, which includes a great variety in quality of material.[66]

Watson also noted that 'the quantity of cotton annually consumed in India in the manufacture of sail and tent cloth is very large'.[67] This, as we have seen, was strong, unbleached cloth sold under the umbrella term of khadi or parkalla.

A discussion between the Board of Revenue and the collectors of various districts in 1837–8 over the suggested abolition of duties on cheap cloth offers another entry point. The collector of Coimbatore estimated that if

[61] For a description of this use in the Vijayanagara court, see Ramaswamy, *Textiles and Weavers*, p. 68.
[62] Watson, *The Textile Manufactures*, p. 142.
[63] Watson, *The Textile Manufactures*, p. 95.
[64] Watson, *The Textile Manufactures*, p. 83.
[65] Watson, *The Textile Manufactures*, p. 85.
[66] Watson, *The Textile Manufactures*, p. 83.
[67] Watson, *The Textile Manufactures*, p. 85.

cloths worth less than 2 rupees were exempted from paying duty on inland transit, collections would fall by 70 per cent, for

> the piece goods priced at one rupee and four annas, and one rupee form the chief articles upon which the customs [are] levied, being of a description adopted for the trade to the western coast and Bombay, and being in great demand in various markets supplied from thence. ... The cloths in ordinary use by coolies and daily labourers whose wages do not exceed three or four rupees monthly are chiefly those bearing a value below one rupee.[68]

In Nellore, it was estimated that the loss would amount to roughly one fourth of the total sayer revenue (derived from all kinds of trade and not just the trade in cloth). The collector added that

> cloths of the value above mentioned (1½ rupees) are not exclusively worn by the poorer classes. Though persons in good circumstances and those generally in the public employ will not use such cloths when they appear in public, it is notorious [*sic*] that they are used by them in their houses.[69]

In two taluks of Thiruchirapalli, 75 per cent of the cloth consumed was of the coarsest quality, as Table 1.1 shows.[70]

A rough estimate of the relative proportions of coarse and fine cloth can be obtained by examining figures for different categories of looms. In an 1804 report on cloth production in the Ceded Districts, Thomas Munro, a colonial official who went on to become Governor of the Madras Presidency, wrote that 'by far the greatest proportion of the looms are employed in the fabrication of the coarser and low priced cloths'.[71] The lowest monthly production of a loom was estimated to be 8 rupees and the highest 60 rupees. Munro calculated the average to be only 10.5 rupees: clearly, looms producing cheap cloth (or working part-time) far outnumbered those producing expensive cloth.

[68] PBR vol. 1583, no. 34, 16 November 1837, pp. 14917–18, TNSA.

[69] PBR vol. 1554, no. 18, 10 April 1837, pp. 1848–50, TNSA. The author of the Salem Manual noted that 'the wealthier classes dress in public more richly, as may be warranted by their means, though in their houses their attire is very scanty'. H. Le Fanue, *A Manual of the Salem District in the Presidency of Madras* (Madras, Government Press, 1883), p. 141.

[70] PBR vol. 1690, no. 26, 6 January 1840, p. 327, TNSA. A taluk is an administrative unit or sub-division of a district. Before the metric system was introduced, the Indian rupee had 16 annas, with each anna divided into 12 pice. Amounts were written as rupees-annas-pice.

[71] PBR vol. 382, 21 June 1804, p. 5075, TNSA.

As many as 16,298 out of 19,626 looms in the Ceded Districts (83 per cent) produced white cloth. However, some of this may have been dyed later on and the figure also includes fine varieties of muslin. The largest number of looms—40 per cent—made khadi.[72] If looms weaving mothasaudys are added, the percentage rises to 48. In terms of value, white cloth, coarse and fine, accounted for 72 per cent of cloth production. Khadi comprised 40 per cent of this figure and 29 per cent by value of *all* cloth. Together khadi and mothasaudys made up 36 per cent by value of all cloth produced. Since its price was low, the figures indicate a much larger quantitative contribution to total output (see Table 1.2).[73]

In 1846, 78 per cent of looms in Thanjavur wove cloth estimated to be less than one pagoda in value; 21 per cent wove cloth valued at between one to five pagodas; and less than 1 per cent wove cloth valued at between five and ten pagodas. Only one village, Vijayamandapum, had weavers making cloth worth more than ten pagodas. This was alienated to the Raja of Thanjavur and paid no loom tax to the Madras government.[74] In 1844, there were only two silk looms and 1,215 fine cloth looms, but as many as 9,725 coarse cloth looms in South Arcot.[75] In 1842, the collector of Tirunelveli reported that only 15 per cent of looms in his district wove cloth valued at above 5 rupees; 34 per cent wove cloth valued at between 2.5 to 5 rupees; but as many as 50 per cent wove cloth valued at *less* than 2.5 rupees.[76]

It seems clear that a very large proportion of cloth made in South India was of coarse quality, usually unbleached or white. Coloured cloths of varying fineness were woven, especially for women, and the emphasis on ordinary cloth should not obscure very fine and intricately decorated textiles produced by skilled weavers. Nevertheless coarse, unbleached cloth

[72] In the sources, 'kaudie', 'kadi' and 'khadi', refer to coarse, strong, mostly unbleached varieties of cloth. Here, I use a single spelling (khadi) for all of them. Much later, Gandhi was to apply the word khadi to cloth woven from handspun yarn, but the khadi of the nineteenth century (discussed here) is emphatically not the same as the Gandhian khadi.

[73] For more details, see the tables in D. W. Karuna, 'Weaving Histories: the Handloom Industry in South India: Aspects of Production, Work and Identities, *c.* 1800–1960', PhD thesis (University of Delhi, 2014), pp. 319–25.

[74] PBR vol. 1967, no. 65, 22 May 1845, p. 6303, TNSA. One English Pagoda was worth 3.50 rupees. Pagodas were minted by the French and Danish as well: their value was less than the English pagoda. My source does not specify which pagoda (whether English, French or Danish). Joseph Blunt, *The Shipmaster's Assistant and Commercial Digest: Containing Information Useful to Merchants, Owners and Masters of Ships* (New York: E. and G. W. Blunt, 1837), p. 372.

[75] PBR vol. 1980, no. 46, 4 September 1845, p. 10844, TNSA.

[76] PBR vol. 1820, no. 31, 29 September 1842, p. 11066, TNSA.

dominated total output in terms of the number of looms and weavers, and, above all, quantity.

The rest of this chapter will examine the spatial geography of cloth production and the diversity of its structures. Before this, it may be useful to take note of some debates on the nature of textile production in early modern India, for their implications extend to the economy as a whole. One group of historians holds that cloth production was commercialised and market oriented; according to another group, it formed a part of self-sufficient village economies with a small exchange component.

It has been argued that, unlike other societies where peasants wove cloth in their spare time, the handloom industry in South India was significantly more commercial and specialised, dominated by full-time weavers from specialist castes.[77] According to Sanjay Subrahmanyam and Prasannan Parthasarathi, the bulk of cloth was produced by these groups. Subrahmanyam describes settlements comprising weavers, merchants and other groups involved in textile production; he argues that its rhythm cut across the temporal rhythm of the agricultural cycle.[78] Social groups engaged in agricultural tasks could not weave part-time; although some cloth was produced by part-time weavers, often from 'untouchable' castes, this was insignificant in terms of quantity and quality.[79]

Historians who hold that cloth production was dominated by full-time weavers regard the merchant as an organic intermediary; he provided weavers with advances to buy yarn and sold the finished cloth.[80] His presence is held to denote an advanced stage of commercialisation: there are discussions on whether a putting-out system had evolved during this period and its possible contours.[81] These feed into wider debates about the nature of the

[77] Wendt refers to 'specialised spaces where many weavers as well as commercial groups lived and focused their livelihoods on textile production and commerce'. Wendt, 'The Social Fabric', p. 180.

[78] Parthasarathi, *The Transition to a Colonial Economy*, pp. 10–11. For a similar argument see Sanjay Subrahmanyam, 'Rural Industry and Commercial Agriculture in Late Seventeenth-Century South-Eastern India', *Past and Present*, 126 (February 1990), 76–114 at 92–7, and *The Political Economy of Commerce*, pp. 28–30, 71–7.

[79] Parthasarathi, *The Transition to a Colonial Economy*, p. 11; Subrahmanyam, *The Political Economy of Commerce*, p. 29.

[80] Parthasarathi, *The Transition to a Colonial Economy*, p. 14; Wendt, 'The Social Fabric', p. 248.

[81] Brennig, 'Textile Producers and Production', 351–2. The putting-out system in eighteenth-century Europe involved merchants (or their agents) supplying manufacturers and craftsmen who worked from home with raw materials to make goods and paying them wages for their labour. In this system, the manufacturer exerted little control over the product. See the entry for 'Domestic industry', in Joel Mokyr (ed.), *The Oxford Encyclopedia of Economic History*

pre-colonial economy, the extent of monetisation and commercialisation, and whether India was capable of moving towards some form of capitalist development in the absence of colonialism.[82]

Historians of the nationalist school viewed cloth production as forming part of a largely self-sufficient village economy—in their view, it was colonialism that disrupted these structures and led to deindustrialisation. Interestingly, revisionist historians challenging the deindustrialisation thesis hold roughly similar views on the *nature* of cloth production. According to Tirthankar Roy, most cloth production during the pre-colonial period was for 'subsistence' under 'various types of non-market and barter distribution arrangements such as "jajmani"' and for 'local, rural periodic and other spot markets'. He holds that the Indian economy was very imperfectly commercialised: wide-ranging commercialisation took place much later, during the late nineteenth century.[83] Essentially Roy is arguing against generalisations based on a small sector of the weaving industry, namely the export trade.[84] The point is a valid one, but he fails to provide convincing arguments in support of his own view.

The evidence from South India indicates that the actual structures of cloth production were much more diverse than these arguments would suggest. There were many kinds of weavers: some worked part-time and others full-time. Some belonged to specialist castes while others were scattered through the countryside. Some formed a part of long-distance trade networks while others supplied local demand. Cloth production was marked by a diversity of makers, markets and methods of production and sale.

(Oxford, Oxford University Press, 2005), https://www.oxfordreference.com/view/10.1093/acref/9780195105070.001.0001/acref-9780195105070 (accessed 26 May 2020).

82 C. A. Bayly and Sanjay Subrahmanyam, 'Portfolio Capitalists and the Political Economy of Early Modern India', *The Indian Economic and Social History Review*, 25(4) (1988), 401–24; Perlin, 'Proto-industrialization'; David Washbrook, 'India in the Early Modern World Economy: Modes of Production, Reproduction and Exchange', *Journal of Global History*, 2(1) (2007), 87–111.

83 Roy, 'De-industrialization', 1445; Roy, *Traditional Industry*, pp. 31, 63.

84 Roy estimates the proportion of exports (principally textiles) to national income at the end of the eighteenth century to be between 1 and 2 per cent. Tirthankar Roy, *The Economic History of India, 1857–1947* (New Delhi, Oxford University Press, 2000), p. 36.

The physical and human geography of textile production

Cotton, yarn and the cloth trade

Cotton grew well in some places—this was true of the black cotton soils of the Deccan and the region around Coimbatore and Tirunelveli. However, weavers were scattered all over the peninsula and cloth was made almost everywhere. Cotton and yarn were transportable commodities forming part of a range of commercial networks. Ian Wendt and Parthasarathi provide a good deal of information about cotton cultivation in the eighteenth century.[85] Very little was grown in the Coromandel districts of Ganjam, Visakhapatnam and Godavari. Some cotton could be found in the Krishna and Guntur districts, but the bulk of it came from the inland districts of Cuddapah (Kadapa), Bellary and Kurnool. Cotton was also an important crop in the Maratha territories and Hyderabad state. In the far south, the main centres of cultivation were the inland districts of Coimbatore, Salem, Madurai and Tirunelveli.[86] Map 3 shows the regions where cotton was cultivated.

Black soil districts in the interior of the Deccan grew the bulk of cotton and exported it in large quantities. A limited quantity was grown in other regions for local use. In Guntur and Malabar, cotton was planted in conjunction with paddy.[87] Small amounts of cotton were grown in Nellore and Mysore.[88] Almost all of it was made into cloth by local weavers; Buchanan notes that around Narasinghapura in South Mysore, cotton was sold at weekly markets and 'wrought up into coarse cloths for country use by the casts [*sic*] called Whalliaru, Devangars and Tricoluru Dasas who reside in the neighbourhood'.[89] In the Tumkur region, farmers were unable

[85] Wendt, 'The Social Fabric', pp. 29–47; Parthasarathi, *The Transition to a Colonial Economy*, pp. 50–3.

[86] Parthasarathi, *The Transition to a Colonial Economy*, pp. 67–71; Wendt, 'The Social Fabric', pp. 29–47.

[87] House of Commons Parliamentary Papers, *A Return of 'Papers in the Possession of the East India Company, Showing what Measures have been Taken since 1836 to Promote the Cultivation of Cotton in India'*, 21 May 1847 (hereafter Cotton Report of 1847, HCPP), p. 61.

[88] House of Commons Parliamentary Papers, *Report from the Select Committee on the Growth of Cotton in India; together with Minutes of Evidence*, 17 July 1848 (hereafter Select Committee Report, HCPP) p. 386; Buchanan, *A Journey from Madras*, vol. 1, pp. 378, 411.

[89] Hamilton F. Buchanan, *A Journey from Madras through the Countries of Mysore, Canara and Malabar*, vol. 2 (London, T. Cadell and W. Davies, 1807), p. 158.

to give any precise estimate of their cotton because it was 'spun by the women as [soon as] gathered'.[90]

Large quantities of cotton and thread were exported from inland districts. A good deal of cloth was also made there for local use as well as export. Northern Coromandel was supplied by the region around Nagpur and the black cotton soils in the Krishna-Tungabadhra doab (the land lying between the two rivers). Central Coromandel (comprising the districts of Nellore, Madras and the two Arcots) obtained cotton from Kadapa and Bellary. These districts also supplied cotton to Mysore. Southern Coromandel was supplied from Coimbatore, Tirunelveli and Madurai.[91] Cotton from Coimbatore was also exported to Malabar and Mysore; cotton from Tirunelveli found its way to Travancore. Much of this transport trade was in the hands of Banjaras and merchants.[92]

The Bellary-Adoni region produced white and red yarn along with many varieties of coarse and fine cotton cloth sold in Mysore.[93] The Ceded Districts grew indigo and exported blue cloth.[94] Thread from Coimbatore was exported to Malabar; yarn from Tirunelveli and Madurai went to Travancore and Ceylon along with finished cloths.[95] Thread and cloth were exported from the Baramahal region (in Salem) to Mysore; some fine varieties of cloth also went to Thanjavur. Chintzes (printed and painted cloths) were imported into Baramahal from the Coromandel coast.[96]

This trading web included local networks as well as routes criss-crossing the peninsula. Both converged at weekly markets which served as meeting points for traders from different places. A description of the weekly market of Gubi in Mysore illustrates their importance.

> At Gubi is one of the greatest weekly fairs in the country .... The country, for ten or twelve cosses round, produces for sale coarse cotton cloth both white and coloured, blankets, sackcloth, betel-nut ... coconuts, jagory, tamarinds, capsicum, wheat, rice, ragy and other grains, lac, steel and iron. Beside the sale of these articles and of those imported for the consumption

[90] Buchanan, *A Journey from Madras*, vol. 1, pp. 378–9.
[91] For the routes traversed by cotton, see Wendt, 'The Social Fabric', pp. 115–23.
[92] Wendt, 'The Social Fabric', pp. 115–23.
[93] Buchanan, *A Journey from Madras*, vol. 1, pp. 218, 302, 416.
[94] Buchanan, *A Journey from Madras*, vol. 1, p. 302.
[95] IOR H/misc/791, 1834, London.
[96] English East India Company, *The Baramahal Records*, Section VII: Imposts (Madras, Government Press, 1920), pp. 4–9, 64–5 and *The Baramahal Records*, Section IV: Products (Madras, Government Press, 1912), p. 110.

> of the neighbourhood, this is also an intermediate mart for the goods passing through the peninsula.[97]

Coarse cloths made in the neighbourhood of Gubi sold at 2 to 6 fanams a piece: approximately one hundred pieces were sold at each fair.[98] Merchants from Coorg, Canara and Malayala came to Gubi to sell spices; traders from Bangalore, Colar (Kolar), Salem and Krishnagiri sold fine cloth and bought betel nut and spices. Merchants from Gubi travelled to Wallajapet near Arcot to buy cloth from the Carnatic and goods imported by sea at Madras to sell in the weekly market.[99]

Raw cotton and hanks of white and red thread from Dharwar and Hubli were sold at the weekly market of Sira. The region grew a small quantity of cotton, made into coarse cloth by local weavers. The dyeing was done by the Niligaru who made blue cloth and Marathas who used red dye extracted from the Cossumba flower. Coarse and fine cloths from the Maratha country and Hyderabad state sold at higher prices, for the colours were better fixed.[100]

Cotton, yarn and cloth formed an integral part of local and long-distance trade networks. Buchanan remarked that 'at all these markets business is carried on by sale; no barter is customary, except among a few poor people, who exchange grain for the produce of the kitchen garden'. Farmers 'carry their produce, and sell it, partly to consumers by retail; and partly by wholesale to traders. In the early part of the day they endeavour to sell their goods by retail, and do not deal with the traders unless they be distressed for money'.[101] Much the same could be said of weavers—most transactions, even when subsistence oriented, involved cash.[102]

The geography of weaving

Up until now, most accounts of weavers and their settlements are derived from the Coromandel coast. Wendt describes villages occupied by weavers and other groups involved in textile production, called weaving villages in

[97] Buchanan, *A Journey from Madras,* vol. 2, pp. 31–3.

[98] Fanam was a currency used in the Madras Presidency until 1815. It was a small silver coin divided into 80 copper *cash.* The gold pagoda was worth 42 fanams and the Indian rupee 12 fanams.

[99] Buchanan, *A Journey from Madras,* vol. 2, pp. 31–3.

[100] Buchanan, *A Journey from Madras,* vol. 1, pp. 416–18.

[101] Buchanan, *A Journey from Madras,* vol. 1, p. 125.

[102] See Chapters 2 and 3.

contemporary records.[103] Many had little or no connection with agriculture; others combined cloth production with cultivation. Netramangalam near Nagapattinam had 30 merchants, 48 weavers and 47 cultivators. Padapah, a weaving village near Madras, was inhabited by weavers, merchants and washers, with just a few households practising other occupations.[104] Wendt argues that 'these rural spaces … were essentially geared toward market production activities, which must radically revise our equation of the rural with the agrarian'.[105]

Settlements like Padapah reinforce the view of weaving as a specialised, full-time occupation tied to market forces. There is no doubt that weaving was commercialised along the coast and in some centres of the hinterland, but the inland districts present a more complex picture. There were some villages and towns where large numbers of weavers lived, but most of them were scattered across the countryside, a few to each village. These weavers made cloth principally for local consumption. This dispersed distribution was a hallmark of districts where cotton was grown.

Some groups specialised in weaving specific varieties of cloth. Centres of textile production might grow or decline for different reasons—migration, famine, shifts in demand or political change—but an underlying pattern persisted. The coarsest and strongest kinds of cloth were made all over the countryside, especially in cotton-producing regions. By contrast, the production of fine varieties, and coloured saris in particular, was a more specialised affair associated with specific weaving centres and groups of weavers.

A good deal of evidence for this dual system can be found in the sources. There is direct evidence in the form of observations or descriptions, but a large mass of indirect evidence also exists. This can be extracted by examining the geographical distribution of looms, the tax paid on them and the value of cloth produced by weavers.

The Coimbatore-Salem region

The town of Coimbatore had many weavers, chiefly Jadars, Pattunoolkarars and Coiculurs (Kaikolars). In the surrounding villages lived Bestas, Canara

[103] Wendt, 'The Social Fabric', p. 223; Brennig, 'Textile Producers and Production', 338–40; Subrahmanyam, *The Political Economy of Commerce*, pp. 71–7.
[104] Wendt, 'The Social Fabric', p. 234.
[105] Wendt, 'The Social Fabric', p. 230.

(Kannada) Devangars and Pariars.[106] The Pattunoolkarar and Jadar specialised in making fine cloth.[107] The Kaikolar and Pariar wove coarse cloth—khadi and 'shirays' (saris) with red or blue borders.[108] The samples collected by Forbes Watson include a coarse, white cloth with red and blue borders sold to cultivators (Plates 1 and 8).[109]

In 1824, the collector of Coimbatore reported that

> there are very few large towns, the population is scattered over a large extent of country and in the numerous petty hamlets. In each of these hamlets, two or three looms are to be found, the person who has no loom will get his thread manufactured into cloth at the loom of his neighbour.[110]

A large proportion of these weavers were Pariars.[111] The town of Salem contained a small settlement of Pattunoolkarar (or Saurashtra) weavers. They could also be found, albeit in smaller numbers, in the villages of Paramapatti and Namakkal.[112] The Jadar and Pattunoolkarar of Salem specialised in making fine cloths for export to Mysore and Thanjavur.[113] Salay (or Saliar) and Seniyar weavers also lived in Salem and Rasipur.[114] The Saliar and Jadar made roughly similar kinds of cloth while the Seniyar specialised in women's clothing.[115]

There were many weavers' settlements producing cloth for export in the Salem region; merchants collected these piece goods for sale. Ammapettai near Bhavani was a village of forty households comprising merchants and weavers.[116] The village of Doddarapalayam had fifty Jadar households.[117] Komarapalayam, Puttur (Puthur), Mohanur, Velur and Satimangalam were weaving settlements inhabited by Jadars, Kaikolars and

[106] Buchanan, *A Journey from Madras*, vol. 2, pp. 261–2; PBR vol. 1325, no. 47, 24 May 1832, p. 5011, TNSA; PBR vol. 1942, no. 49, 25 November 1844, p. 16125, TNSA.

[107] Buchanan, *A Journey from Madras*, vol. 2, pp. 261–2.

[108] Buchanan, *A Journey from Madras*, vol. 2, pp. 261–2.

[109] Watson, *The Textile Manufactures*, p. 23.

[110] PBR vol. 984, no. 42, 17 May 1824, pp. 4439–40, TNSA.

[111] Buchanan, *A Journey from Madras*, vol. 2, p. 261; PBR vol. 1942, no. 49, 25 November 1844, p. 16125, TNSA. The Pariar were the prototypical 'untouchable' caste of the Tamil country; their name will crop up repeatedly in connection with the weaving of coarse cloth.

[112] *The Baramahal Records*, Section VII: Imposts, p. 71.

[113] Dhotis with red borders, several kinds of saris, striped cloths (white and blue, or red and yellow) made with a mixture of silk and cotton for drawers and petticoats. Some of them also made carpets or jamakalams. *Baramahal Records*, Section VII: Imposts, p. 65. Watson had some very fine dhotis made in Salem for his collection.

[114] *The Baramahal Records*, Section VII: Imposts, p. 70.

[115] *The Baramahal Records*, Section VII: Imposts, pp. 64–5.

[116] Buchanan, *A Journey from Madras*, vol. 2, p. 199.

[117] Buchanan, *A Journey from Madras*, vol. 2, p. 242.

some Pattunoolkarars.[118] By contrast, the Koliar were scattered all over the region: they produced coarse cloths called Mota khadis and parkallas.[119] Chembadavars, said to be inland fisherfolk, also wove coarse cloth. Another group called the Manniwar (possibly a sub-division of the Pariar) lived in the northern part of the Baramahals, making fine turbans and body cloths.[120]

The Mysore region

The Mysore region grew very little cotton. Weavers in Bangalore made fine silk and cotton cloth and some coarse cloth was exported to Malabar, but Mysore was a net importer of cloth. The finest cloth was woven by Puttuegar and Cuttery weavers.[121] The Shayanagaru and Devangar specialised in coloured saris.[122] Like the Saliar, the Shayanagaru also wove white muslins; each pattern had three degrees of fineness. The Togataru made coarse, white cotton cloth with red borders.[123] The Whalliaru, also called Deds, are described as the equivalent of Pariars: they lived 'scattered in … villages', making coarse parkallas.[124]

Waluru, Colar (Kolar) and Sirijapura (Sarjapur) are described as weavers' settlements. Many Devangar, Padmasalay, Shayanagaru, Togataru and Kaikolar weavers lived in Lacor near Waluru: they sold cloth at weekly markets to merchants from Bangalore, Kolar and Krishnagiri.[125] Kolar had once been an important weaving centre: its Devangar and Shayanagaru weavers made muslins, turbans and cotton cloth with silk borders. These piece goods were bought by merchants from Gubi (Gubbi) and Seringapatam (Srirangapattanam). 'Much coarse cloth was made by the Whalliaru' in villages around Kolar.[126] The Devangar, Saliar and Togataru weavers of Sarjapur also made coarse cloth; they claimed that once upon a

[118] *The Baramahal Records*, Section IV: Products, pp. 138–9. The weaving settlements of the Salem region resemble those described by Wendt for the Coromandel coast. Buchanan, *A Journey from Madras*, vol. 2, p. 239. See PBR vol. 1312, no. 78, 2 January 1832, p. 238, TNSA for weaving castes in Salem district.

[119] *The Baramahal Records*, Section IV: Products, pp. 64–5, 70, 115.

[120] *The Baramahal Records*, Section IV: Products, p. 27. Strikingly, they are the only group of 'untouchable' weavers reported to make fine varieties of cloth.

[121] Buchanan, *A Journey from Madras*, vol. 1, pp. 210–13.

[122] Buchanan, *A Journey from Madras*, vol. 1, p. 213.

[123] Buchanan, *A Journey from Madras*, vol. 1, p. 218.

[124] Buchanan, *A Journey from Madras*, vol. 1, pp. 218, 313.

[125] Buchanan, *A Journey from Madras*, vol. 1, p. 272.

[126] Buchanan, *A Journey from Madras*, vol. 1, pp. 277, 302.

time they used to weave fine cloth too.[127] The town of Silagutta had a small settlement of Padmasalays making coarse cotton cloth with red borders, but the bulk of coarse cloth was made by the Whalliaru.[128]

In the town of Sira, Billi Muggas wove a coarse muslin called Shilla. The Devangar made two kinds of coarse cloth: one resembled the khadi woven by the Whalliaru; another, with red borders, resembled that made by the Togataru.[129] Gubi with its large weekly market contained no weavers, but 'the country, for ten or twelve cosses around, produces ... coarse cotton cloth both white and coloured' made by Devangar, Togataru and Whalliaru weavers.[130] In Priyapattana at the border of the Coorg region, cloth was imported from Mysore, but a small quantity of coarse cloth was woven by the Torearu.[131] In some places, Buchanan reported 'no commerce; nor any manufactures, except the coarse cloth which the Whalliaru weave'.[132]

The Madurai-Dindigul region

The city of Madurai, with its large settlement of Pattunoolkarars, was an important weaving centre. They made fine, white dhotis with patterned borders in gold thread (zari), cloth with silk borders, white and red turbans, and fine saris.[133] Another group of Pattunoolkarars lived in Paramakudi, a large village east of Madurai on the banks of the Vaigai.[134] But the district also had many weavers belonging to other castes. There were many Pariar weavers, who produced much of the cloth used for ordinary wear.[135]

In Dindigul, fine cloth weavers were concentrated in the town and larger villages, but there were looms in almost every village weaving cloth of the coarser kind. It was reported that the town had

> 20 kinds of looms, consisting of about 93 in number, for the manufacture of different sorts of cloth, both fine and coarse, comprising long cloths, muslin, handkerchiefs, turbans, doopetahs, shomens, vaties and various kinds of women's cloth. Besides the above, there are 146 looms in the villages

[127] Buchanan, *A Journey from Madras*, vol. 1, p. 271.
[128] Buchanan, *A Journey from Madras*, vol. 1, p. 327.
[129] Buchanan, *A Journey from Madras*, vol. 1, p. 418.
[130] Buchanan, *A Journey from Madras*, vol. 2, pp. 34, 36.
[131] Buchanan, *A Journey from Madras*, vol. 2, p. 116.
[132] Buchanan, *A Journey from Madras*, vol. 2, p. 151.
[133] Forbes Watson Textile Collection, vol. 2, Man's Garments, Sample no. 41.
[134] Rev. James Kearns, *Report of the Puthiamputhur Mission*, SPG E2, Missionaries Reports, June 1856, Archives of the Society for the Propagation of the Gospel in Foreign Parts, Rhodes House Library, Oxford, p. 451.
[135] PBR vol. 1325, 21 May 1832, no. 44, p. 4901 onwards, TNSA.

> dependent to [*sic*] the cusbah talook, where coarse cloths are manufactured by parayars, which serve the purposes of the inhabitants in the country.[136]

The Ceded Districts

The Ceded Districts grew cotton: much of this (40 per cent, according to Munro) was consumed locally.[137] The remainder, along with substantial quantities of thread and cloth, was exported to the Coromandel coast and Mysore. The sub-divisions of Goorankondah (Gurram Konda), Pooley-Wandrah (Pulivendula), Chittawail (Chitvel) and Dummalmudgoo (Jummalamadugu) produced coarse to middling varieties of cloth. The main staples were khadis of low counts and coarse saris. Some 68 per cent of looms in Pulivendula and 67 per cent in Chitvel made khadis and mothasaudys, mostly with yarn provided by their customers.[138] The collector of Kadapa reported that 'the practice of supplying the material and getting cloths made for home use obtains to a great extent in this district'.[139]

By contrast, the sub-divisions of Bellary, Compli (Kampli), Harpanhally (Harpanahalli), Goottee (Gooty) and Koilhonttah (Koilkuntla) contained fewer looms but produced finer textiles. A total of 44 looms spread over Kampli (which had 19 of them), Gooty, Yadhi (Yadiki), Chennumply (Chennampalle), Tarputree (Tadipatri) and Adhoni (Adoni) made silk cloth. Bellary produced middling to fine textiles: 41 per cent of its looms made red and blue saris. Kamalapuram was a centre for fine dupattas and saris.[140] In the late nineteenth century, Uppalur in Kamalapuram developed into an important silk-producing centre.[141]

In Gooty, 38 per cent of looms wove khadi; the remainder made different varieties of fine cloths, up to 32 punjams in some cases.[142] It also contained six silk looms and was a centre for saris (36 per cent of looms made red and blue saris). Coarse chintzes (printed and painted) were made around the town.[143] Part of the cotton-producing black soil tract, the sub-division had the usual combination of fine cloth production in a

[136] Madura District Records (MDR), vol. 1258, 1816, TNSA.
[137] PBR vol. 382, no. 18, 21 June 1804, p. 5078, TNSA.
[138] PBR vol. 382, no. 18, 21 June 1804, p. 5075, TNSA.
[139] PBR vol. 1494, no. 16, 7 March 1836, p. 4088, TNSA.
[140] PBR vol. 382, no. 18, 21 June 1804, p. 5075, TNSA.
[141] C. F. Brackenbury, *Cuddapah District Gazetteer* (Madras, Government Press, 1915), p. 110.
[142] Punjams refer to the number of warp threads in a cloth; the finer the cloth, the greater the number of warp threads (and hence punjams). PBR vol. 382, no. 18, 21 June 1804, p. 5075, TNSA.
[143] Heyne, *Tracts Historical and Statistical*, p. 326.

few weaving centres while coarser varieties were made in the countryside. Red saris were produced in Pulivendula, Gooty, Roydoorg (Rayadurgam), Bellary and Naguldinnah; blue saris were woven in Gooty, Chennampalle, Rayadurgam, Darmavar (Dharmavaram), Kamalapuram, Naguldinnah, Bellary, Kampli and Koodligah.[144]

Munro provides a good deal of information on looms and kinds of cloth, but has little to say about the weavers themselves. For this, we must look elsewhere. One of the largest groups of weavers in this region were Malas: like the Whalliaru and the Pariar, they were an 'untouchable' caste, and, like them, made strong, coarse cloth used by poor folk. Many Malas lived in the districts of Kadapa, Kurnool and Bellary, where their primary occupation is described as weaving. According to a missionary, 'the Malas are not mere coolies; the majority of them weave with the handloom, and their wives spin thread; some are cultivators, others field labourers'.[145] As late as 1896–7, an official estimated that one third of the weavers in the Deccan districts were Malas making coarse cloth 'worn by the Malas themselves and by the cultivating classes'.[146] The Kapu—a caste of farmers and landowners—paid Mala women to spin their cotton into yarn and Mala weavers for turning yarn into cloth.[147] Padma Sales (or the Saliar) and Pattu Sales (another group among the Saliar), the Togataru and Devangar were some of the weaving castes in Kadapa; the Togataru and Saliar made silk and fine cotton cloths.[148] A large number of Muslim carpet-makers also worked in towns like Adoni and Kurnool.[149]

Chingelput (Chengalpattu) and North Arcot

Most looms in Chengalpattu were located in the taluks of Conjeevaram (Kanchipuram) and Manemungalum (Manimangalam); the sub-divisions of Nayer and Teruporoor (Tiruporur) had fewer than hundred looms

[144] Also Chennampalle, Tadipatri, Tarnurrie, Dharmavaram, Nauguldinnah. For details, see the tables in D. W. Karuna, 'Weaving Histories' (2014), pp. 319–25.

[145] C. F. Pascoe, *Two Hundred Years of the S.P.G.: an Historical Account of the Society for the Propagation of the Gospel in Foreign Parts 1701–1900* (London, SPG, 1901), p. 566b.

[146] *Report of the Famine in the Madras Presidency During 1896 and 1897* (Madras, Government Press, 1898), Appendix I, p. 356.

[147] Edgar Thurston, *Castes and Tribes of Southern India*, vol. 4 (Madras, Government Press, 1909), p. 351.

[148] Brackenbury, *Cuddapah District Gazetteer*, pp. 110, 115, 206–7, 216.

[149] *Report of the Famine*, Appendix I, p. 356.

each.[150] Loom tax figures indicate that Kanchipuram town and Arnee (Arani) were centres for fine cloth.[151] This is corroborated by evidence from other sources.[152] This data combined with statistics of cloth duties reveals that dispersed looms produced cheaper cloth: indeed, weavers in some parts of the district made nothing else. The collector of Chengalpattu opined that if cloth worth less than 2 rupees was to be exempted from duties, several chowkis or collection centres could well be abolished.[153]

The geographical distribution of cloth production in the Madras Presidency falls into a distinct pattern. Towns and larger villages acted as centres of fine cloth production, but a very large proportion of cloth for ordinary use was made by weavers scattered throughout the countryside. Some castes specialised in weaving certain varieties of cloth: coloured or patterned cloth and fine varieties of cotton and silk were made by the Pattunoolkarar, Pattu and Padma Saliar, Devangar, and some Muslim weavers. Coarse cloth was the preserve of the Kaikolar, Togataru, some Devangar, and, above all, the Pariar and other 'untouchable' castes: Malas, Koliars, Manniwars and the Whalliaru, many of whom worked part-time.

Part-time and full-time weavers

The evidence shows that part-time weaving in South India was nowhere near as unusual as historians have assumed. A large proportion of coarse cloth was made by part-time, non-specialist weavers who practised two or more trades. Apart from weaving, they also worked as cultivators, fishermen, labourers or petty traders: this phenomenon is very marked in cotton-producing regions. The bulk of part-time weavers belonged to the so-called untouchable castes traditionally associated with agricultural labour. Their numbers were far from negligible, especially in the case of the Pariar.

Let us look, first of all, at the occupational strategies adopted by part-time weavers. The Chembadavar (or Cheniwar) of the Baramahal

[150] PBR vol. 1324, no. 18, 14 May 1832, p. 4746, TNSA.

[151] PBR vol. 1906, no. 30, 29 February 1844, p. 3823, TNSA. Loom tax rates might vary widely within a district for no discernible reason, but a higher rate usually indicates fine cloth production.

[152] Watson, *The Textile Manufactures*, pp. 76–80; Madras Exhibition of Raw Products, Arts and Manufactures of Southern India, 1855: *Reports by the Juries* (Madras, Government Press, 1856), p. 93; Heyne, *Tracts Historical and Statistical*, pp. 19–21.

[153] PBR vol. 1583, no. 23, 23 November 1837, p. 15071, TNSA.

region worked as inland fisher folk.[154] The Toreas, also known as Bestas, are described as farmers, ferry-men, armed messengers, burners of lime, fishermen and porters.[155] Some castes associated with cultivation—the Agamudiyar, Velamavamloo, Balijavanloo, Agamadiah, Pullee, Gollavar and Iendravar—are also described as weavers, albeit in smaller numbers.[156] The Coravur, a caste of nomadic, petty traders, also wove cloth. Some part-time weavers belonged to the Polavur, Sevyar and Andie castes about whom little is known.[157]

Many members of specialist weaving castes also owned land. The Pattunoolkarar were renowned for making fine varieties of cloth. Yet, at the beginning of the nineteenth century, 550 out of 2,200 Pattunoolkarars in Baramahal are listed as cultivators, not weavers.[158] In 1824, the collector of Nellore reported that many weavers in his jurisdiction owned farmland.[159] According to Buchanan, some Kaikolars around Coimbatore rented land, which was worked for them by others (presumably labourers or sharecroppers).[160] In 1844, most weaving households in Coimbatore were said to obtain their livelihood from money earned from agriculture or trade in addition to weaving.[161] Of the Jadar, the collector wrote that 'many of these persons, if not all, employ half their time in weaving and the other portion in cultivation'.[162] Weavers in some villages of Thiruchirapalli paid a tax to the local temple: in return, they were allotted plots to cultivate.[163] A few Janmavar (or Devangar) weavers in

[154] *Baramahal Records*, Section VII: Imposts, pp. 18 and 27.

[155] Buchanan, *A Journey from Madras*, vol. 2, pp. 116, 152.

[156] PBR vol. 1906, no. 30, 29 February 1844, pp. 3825–6, TNSA, gives a list of castes making cloth in Chengalpattu district.

[157] PBR vol. 1942, no. 49, 25 November 1844, pp. 16133–5, TNSA. Details of castes involved in weaving can be found in PBR vol. 1325, no. 47, 24 May 1832, p. 5011, TNSA; PBR vol. 1942, no. 49, 25 November 1844, p. 16125, TNSA; PBR vol. 1334, no. 22, 13 August 1832, pp. 7768–9, TNSA; PBR vol. 1641, no. 42, 24 December 1838, p. 17250, TNSA; PBR vol. 1937, no. 80, 7 November 1844, p. 14954, TNSA; PBR vol. 1312, no. 78, 2 January 1832, p. 238, TNSA.

[158] English East India Company, *The Baramahal Records*, Section III: Inhabitants (Madras, Government Press, 1907), p. v. Many of them owned land in the early twentieth century. Albert James Saunders, *The Saurashtra Community in Madura, South India* (unpublished manuscript available in the library of the American College, Madurai, n.d.), p. 26.

[159] PBR vol. 987, no. 27, 5 July 1824, p. 5732, TNSA.

[160] Buchanan, *A Journey from Madras*, vol. 2, p. 265.

[161] PBR vol. 1942, no. 49, 25 November 1844, p. 16125, TNSA.

[162] PBR vol. 1942, no. 49, 25 November 1844, p. 16131, TNSA.

[163] PBR vol. 1554, no. 9, 10 April 1837, pp. 3971–3, TNSA.

South Arcot owned large holdings.[164] Some heads of weaving castes also acted as renters of revenue.[165]

A small proportion of specialist weavers turned their hands to trade. Poor castes, on the other hand, did not have the luxury of choosing—the evidence indicates that they adopted a variety of occupations.[166] This was especially true of the so-called untouchable castes, the most despised and oppressed of all: Malas, Pariars, Koliars, Manniwars and the Whalliaru living in different regions occupied roughly the same position in the caste hierarchy. All of them wove large quantities of coarse and durable cloth.

'Untouchable' castes and part-time weaving

We have seen that Pariar weavers generally worked part-time but this does not imply that their output was negligible. It should be remembered that part-time weaving might be pursued for eight months of the year given the intrinsic character of the agrarian economy in regions of dryland cultivation. Thus, Mala weavers in Kadapa spent eight months of the year making cloth, turning to agricultural work for the other months.[167] The Whalliaru of Mysore would 'hire themselves out as day-labourers to farmers, or other persons who will give them employment'.[168] In the Ceded Districts,

> many of the looms belong to Barbers-Chucklers and Dhers who only weave occasionally and many of the weavers themselves have not always employment in their own profession and are engaged several months in the year as field labourers.[169]

Part-time weavers made enough cloth to pay the loom tax. In Bellary

> looms are kept not only by the distinct classes of weavers, namely, Pudmasalawar, Davangumwar, Togatewar, Hatakar, Heracooroovany and Chickcooroovany, but also by some other castes such as Lublaree/Cubbaree, Momeens, Barbers and *Parias* who assume the profession and all these are invariably taxed more or less with moturpha.[170]

164 Arasaratnam, 'Weavers, Merchants and Company', 263–4.
165 Wendt, 'The Social Fabric', p. 233.
166 Washbrook argues that occupational diversity was common in 'the subsistence-via-exchange economy' of early modern India. Washbrook, 'India in the Early Modern World Economy', 96–7.
167 Thurston, *Castes and Tribes*, vol. 4, p. 350.
168 Buchanan, *A Journey from Madras*, vol. 1, p. 218.
169 PBR vol. 382, no. 18, 21 June 1804, p. 5075, TNSA.
170 PBR vol. 1925, no. 42, 8 August 1844, p. 10276, TNSA.

The Koliar, another 'untouchable' caste, occupy a somewhat anomalous position in that weaving was said to be their primary occupation in the districts of Salem, Madurai and Tirunelveli, even though they also did agricultural work.[171] Some Koliars were totis or village servants working part-time as weavers; an observer noted that they 'do not constantly apply to their trade as weavers but as they have time to spare from their ordinary occupation or ability to purchase the raw materials'.[172]

In Dindigul, the Dhan, an 'untouchable' caste, were

> taxed in proportion to the time they work at their looms and the produce of the time since in the months of cultivation they leave their craft to attend on that particular business.[173]

We have already noted that Nellore, Guntur and Kadapa contained large numbers of Mala weavers. In some districts, 'untouchable' weavers might own one third to half the total number of looms.[174] Cumulatively, they produced a very large quantity of cloth.

Conclusion

A wide range of clothing was made for the domestic market in early nineteenth-century South India. Some of it was fine, but all of the clothing worn by the poor—and even the everyday wear of the middling classes—consisted of coarse, strong and durable cloth, mostly white or unbleached. Between half to two thirds of all looms in the Madras Presidency made coarse cloth. The main categories were khadis and mothasaudys or coarse saris. Khadis were used for making clothes as well as tents, sails, shrouds and so on.

The spatial distribution of weavers in inland districts differed significantly from the Coromandel coast. The production of coarse cloth was dispersed and decentralised: its makers lived in villages scattered through the countryside. Many worked part-time, combining weaving with some other occupation. 'Untouchable' castes wove a great deal of coarse cloth, especially khadis. Some of them—notably the Malas of Kadapa and the Koliar in Salem, Madurai and Tirunelveli—were almost indistinguishable from full-time weavers.

[171] *The Baramahal Records*, Section VII: Imposts, p. 115.

[172] *The Baramahal Records*, Section VII: Imposts, p. 115.

[173] PBR vol. 383, 25 June 1804, p. 5285, TNSA.

[174] Chapter 2 will discuss these estimates.

By contrast, fine or patterned cloths were made by full-time weavers from specialist weaving castes living in towns and large villages. The categories are porous—the Manniwar in Baramahal made fine cloth while many specialist weaving castes also made coarse cloth. But until the mid-nineteenth century, the broad pattern held—coarse cloth was usually made by plebeian, often part-time weavers and fine or patterned varieties by specialist weaving castes. Much of this coarse cloth was sold in local markets and some was exported to other regions. Trade networks ranged from the local to the regional to the supra-regional—they overlapped in weekly markets, where weavers, spinners and merchants came together to buy and sell.

This picture occupies a middle ground between two opposing positions. The evidence shows that a large part of cloth production in South India was subsistence oriented and geared to local markets. In that sense, it supports Tirthankar Roy's warning against extrapolating from the export trade. However, it would be a mistake to see it as being primitive or non-commercial. For one thing, it incorporated a great many cash transactions even if the amounts involved were small. Munro avers that the sale of yarn was an important source of cash for farmers in cotton-producing regions.[175] Wendt uncovers the scale of incomes derived from cotton: every stage from cultivation and processing, to spinning and weaving involved cash payments.[176]

Most transactions in weekly markets were also in cash. This brings to mind David Washbrook's argument that subsistence and markets were not necessarily inimical—a close interface exists between markets and the subsistence economy.[177] The second component of the domestic market was the long-distance trade. Here, the level of commercialisation was obviously higher; although it is not possible to compare its scale to the local trade, it was by no means insignificant.

The actual structures of cloth production were marked by considerable diversity and complexity. The social status of its makers varied—from specialist weaving castes, whose members invested in land and went into trade, to 'untouchable' castes at the very bottom of the social structure. Cloth production was oriented towards local *and* distant markets; transactions took place in cash, but also in kind. The remainder of the book will examine the process of change in the decades that followed.

[175] *The Baramahal Records*, Section VII: Imposts, p. 28.
[176] Wendt, 'The Social Fabric', pp. 155–6.
[177] Washbrook, 'India in the Early Modern World Economy', pp. 95, 99. Frank Perlin argues that the use of money had reached very small, local exchanges by the early modern period. Frank Perlin, 'Growth of Money Economy and Some Questions of Transition in Late Pre-Colonial India', *Journal of Peasant Studies*, 11(3) (1984), 96–107.

2

Statistics, Looms and People

The Changing Contours of the Handloom Industry

The handloom industry lies at the heart of the deindustrialisation debate. This is largely concerned with the number of looms and the number of people employed in weaving and its preparatory processes: the figures are used to make broad generalisations about the trajectory of the handloom industry and the economy as a whole. An older view argued for a sharp decline in the number of weavers and non-agricultural workers during the nineteenth century.[1] More recent scholarship holds that there was no significant fall; on the contrary, the output of some sectors increased during this period.[2] Much of the debate about the extent of growth or decline, its period, and causal factors rests upon statistical data.[3]

Revisionist scholarship has uncovered considerable regional diversity in the actual effects of colonialism on the handloom industry; regional studies present a more nuanced picture of developments.[4] Some of its leading representatives have argued that the decline of certain sectors of the handloom industry was balanced by growth or gain in terms of new kinds and forms of cloth production.[5] According to Tirthankar Roy,

[1] See Bagchi, 'Deindustrialization in India'; Twomey, 'Employment in Nineteenth-Century Indian Textiles'; Krishnamurty, 'De-industrialization in Gangetic Bihar'.

[2] The key figures are Morris D. Morris and Tirthankar Roy. See Roy, 'De-industrialization'. Thorner and Vicziany have questioned the sources on which the deindustrialisation thesis is based. Thorner, 'De-industrialization'; Vicziany, 'The De-industrialisation of India'.

[3] David Clingingsmith and Jeffrey G. Williamson, 'Deindustrialization in 18th and 19th Century India: Mughal Decline, Climate Shocks and British Industrial Ascent', *Explorations in Economic History*, 45(3) (2008), 209–34.

[4] See Specker, 'Madras Handlooms'; Guha, 'The Handloom Industry of Central India'; Harnetty, 'Deindustrialization Revisited'.

[5] Most proponents of deindustrialisation lay stress on the fact that colonialism failed to develop or foster modern industry in South Asia; a third stream deriving from Gandhi criticises industrialisation as unsuitable, indeed harmful, in the Indian context.

the 'decline was milder if measured as net rather than gross decline and measured as income rather than employment'.[6] In general, he holds that the decline in employment was balanced by increases in productivity, output, profits and wages (although they did not rise uniformly): thus, lost earnings from hand spinning were offset by a fall in yarn prices that benefited the weaver.

Much of the controversy centres around the exact period of decline and whether a revival did in fact occur. Roy argues that any fall in cloth production is only tenable for the early part of the nineteenth century. The period after 1870 was one of growth, when the industry expanded, and productivity and wages rose (albeit unevenly). In any case, Roy holds that decline was restricted to certain sectors: hand spinning became obsolete; the 'backward' segments of handloom production declined while 'progressive' segments expanded.[7]

It is quite true that different parts of the handloom industry were affected very differently: revisionist scholars are right to stress that these varied effects should be examined closely. Its survival against so many odds should be acknowledged, indeed celebrated. But the survival of the industry—or the achievements of artisans who became industrialists—tells us nothing about the human costs of the transition. Statistics, valuable though they are, do not help us recover the lived experience of real people navigating a period of considerable upheaval. In this chapter I take a closer look at the process of change in the handloom industry of South India during the nineteenth century, using descriptive reports to foreground and interrogate the statistical data.

Counting the looms: 1800–50

It should be stated at the outset that counting looms is not a reliable method of estimating employment in the handloom industry. The numbers do not reveal patterns of use or productivity; they do not tell us how many people actually worked each loom or for how long. Looms were simple wooden machines installed in houses. They might vanish from a region if their owners migrated; for the rest, they remained *in situ*, whether they were used or not. But in the absence of any other source to shed light on employment or output, we must make do with them.

[6] Roy, 'De-industrialization'; Roy, *Artisans and Industrialization.*

[7] Roy, *Artisans and Industrialization*, pp. 5–8.

Appendix Table 2.1 shows the number of looms in various districts of the Madras Presidency from 1821–2 to 1843–4 and Table 2.2 shows the increase/decrease in numbers over time.[8] Looms were counted for the purpose of levying the loom tax: this formed part of a set of taxes called the moturpha.[9] This data is not very reliable, especially for the early years. The loom tax, like all moturpha taxes, was variable and arbitrary. Some villages, and sometimes entire districts, were exempted from it—it was not levied throughout the district of Madurai from early on in the century.[10] Weavers in Thiruchirapalli town were exempt from the loom tax.[11] Some individuals in a village might obtain exemption: head weavers and even Pariar weavers who performed specified village duties in addition to weaving often had their looms exempted.[12] In the same way, head weavers responsible for collecting the loom tax on behalf of the government did not have to pay tax on one or two of their own looms.[13] Where the tax was paid to a temple or zamindar instead of the government, the looms in question were not recorded or counted.[14] Some looms were exempted by 'custom', without specifying a reason.[15]

Until the end of the eighteenth century, local rulers tried to encourage weavers to settle in their territories by offering exemption from the loom tax—the aim was to increase revenues from cloth manufacture and trade. As a consequence, the EIC was also forced to adopt this practice. In many districts of the Madras Presidency, weavers working for it were exempted from the loom tax.[16] As a result, the number of looms recorded in reports during the late

[8] Specker draws up a table similar to Table 2.1, but rounds the figures. I have kept the original numbers. Discrepancies between his figures and mine are marked in the table.

[9] The moturpha tax was ostensibly levied on manufacturing occupations. But its application (and rates) varied widely between (and even within) districts. Traders and houses were taxed in some districts but not in others; certain castes were taxed only in some districts. See Appendix 2 for a note on the loom tax and moturpha taxes in general.

[10] PBR vol. 854, no. 61, 29 May 1820, p. 3790, TNSA; PBR vol. 1325, no. 44, 21 May 1832, p. 4901, TNSA.

[11] PBR vol. 1359, no. 40, 15 April 1833, pp. 3690–5, TNSA.

[12] In the district of Nellore, 350 to 450 weavers were exempted from the loom tax between 1821 and 1830 on the grounds that some of them were also cultivators and village servants. PBR vol. 1334, no. 22, 13 August 1832, p. 7769, TNSA. Exemptions of this kind were also common in Thiruchirapalli and Kadapa. PBR vol. 1359, no. 40, 15 April 1833, p. 3695, TNSA; PBR vol. 1325, no. 46, 24 May 1832, p. 5005, TNSA.

[13] PBR vol. 1359, no. 22, 11 April 1833, pp. 3506–7, TNSA.

[14] For examples from Salem, Masulipatnam, South Arcot and Tirunelveli, see PBR vol. 1333, nos 1–2, 2 August 1832, p. 7492, TNSA; PBR vol. 1376, no. 38, 22 August 1833, p. 10031, TNSA; PBR vol. 1359, no. 22, 11 April 1833, pp. 3506–7, TNSA.

[15] PBR vol. 985, no. 45, 31 May 1824, p. 4829, TNSA; PBR vol. 1359, no. 40, 15 April 1833, pp. 3690–5, TNSA.

[16] Swarnalatha, *The World of the Weaver*, pp. 149–51.

eighteenth and early nineteenth century is much lower than the actual number in operation. During the course of the nineteenth century, and especially after the EIC had ceased investing in cloth production for export, the state began investigating the moturpha tax with a view to increasing its revenues. Many looms that had hitherto been exempt came under the ambit of the loom tax. Thus, loom figures for the twenties are lower than they should be and their putative increase from the thirties on is overstated, for some proportion of the 'new' looms existed already; they just had not been counted until then. This anomaly is freely acknowledged in the reports.

In 1830–1, the number of looms in Nellore increased sharply—this was because the sub-collector had 'made a minute inquiry into the moturpha tax generally in this division and the result was a considerable increase in the loom tax'.[17] Another rise of 1,086 looms between 1840–1 and 1843–4 was attributed to the moturpha of three taluks being brought under the circar (government) account. In Kadapa, the rise between 1834–5 and 1843–4 was attributed 'partly to certain looms having been occasionally brought to account on a more careful scrutiny which had previously escaped observation'.[18] In 1826–7, there was a very large increase in the number of looms in Rajamundhry after the EIC stopped buying cloth and the loom tax was imposed on the weavers who used to work for it.[19] These examples can be multiplied; the notes accompanying Table 2.1 give the reason for sudden jumps whenever the relevant information is available.

To sum up: the statistical data is subject to three caveats. We have already seen that loom figures for the early years were underestimations.[20] In addition, they do not reflect actual production or the length of the time each loom was actually worked. The collector of Nellore pointed out that 'the loom is taxed whether worked or not. The loom, which is full from the beginning to the end of the season pays the same as that which has been once worked to make a cloth for some of the family of the owner'.[21] Finally, there is a margin of uncertainty in that numbers in different reports sometimes vary.[22]

[17] PBR vol. 1931, no. 47, 23 September 1844, p. 12541, TNSA.
[18] PBR vol. 1931, no. 48, 23 September 1844, p. 12548, TNSA.
[19] PBR vol. 1335, no. 17, 20 August 1832, p. 8187, TNSA.
[20] This is true for population statistics as well; it has been shown that population figures for the early nineteenth century are underestimations and that their accuracy improves over time. Dharma Kumar, *Land and Caste in South India* (Delhi, Manohar, 1992), p. 103; Sumit Guha, *Health and Population in South Asia: from Earliest Times to the Present* (Delhi, Permanent Black, 2001), pp. 50–1.
[21] PBR vol. 1931, no. 47, 23 September 1844, p. 12522, TNSA.
[22] See the figures for Rajamundhry and Nellore in Table 2.1.

It is only after making these corrections that loom figures can be used as indicators. Let us return to Rajamundhry, where they rose by 66.5 per cent between 1825–6 and 1826–7. A regular settlement of moturpha taxes was not made until 1824 and the steep rise of 1826–7 can be traced to the withdrawal of the EIC from the cloth trade: the weavers who worked for it, hitherto exempt from the loom tax, were now included in the list.[23] Another notional increase occurred in 1836–7, when 1,500 looms in the Pettapore zamindary were transferred to the government account. After correcting for these distortions, there were probably over 12,000 looms in the district at the beginning of our period (1824–5) or 80 per cent more than recorded. Even this may be a conservative estimate, for, according to another report, the EIC employed approximately 15,000 looms until the 1820s in Rajamundhry. If we add weavers supplying other merchants and the local market to this figure, the probable number of looms in 1824–5 would be even higher.[24]

Underestimations of this kind can be corrected in the case of some (but not all) districts. Therefore, the remainder of the chapter interprets statistical data in conjunction with descriptive accounts in order to obtain a more reliable picture. My findings are broadly as follows: a real decline in cloth production appears to have occurred in the northern Coromandel districts that provided the bulk of the company's investments and exports. Other districts show little change or a modest increase in output.[25] Four districts show a substantial increase in the number of looms and this data is corroborated by descriptive accounts: these are the inland cotton-growing tracts of Kadapa, Bellary, Madurai and Tirunelveli.[26]

The number of looms in the coastal districts declined steeply between 1830–1 and 1834–5. In common with other artisans and poor peasants, weavers suffered disproportionately in famines: there were several of them during the first half of the nineteenth century, but the effects of the famine of 1833–5 were especially marked.[27] It occurred not long after the

[23] PBR vol. 1379, no. 35, 19 September 1833, p. 11225, TNSA; PBR vol. 1953, no. 26, 27 January 1845, p. 1147, TNSA.

[24] PBR vol. 1953, no. 26, 27 January 1845, p. 1147, TNSA.

[25] Chengalpattu appears to be an exception in that it shows an *increase* of 38 per cent. However, data for this region is very sparse; there was continuous resistance to the loom tax and it had to be imposed gradually over a long period of time. It is quite likely that the initial loom counts do not reflect the actual number in operation.

[26] However, Coimbatore—another cotton-producing inland district—shows a decline in the number of looms. Its collector gave three reasons for this: a fall in cloth exports to Bombay (from where they were trans-shipped to Arabia), several bad seasons and competition from imported textiles. PBR vol. 1942, no. 49, 25 November 1844, pp. 16128–9, TNSA.

[27] Specker, 'Madras Handlooms', 138.

withdrawal of the EIC from the cloth trade and the closing down of its factories in the 1820s. In 1833, the collector of Rajamundhry reported a deficit in the collection of the loom tax: a large number of weavers were left without work because of the EIC's withdrawal; many of the poorest died of hunger and cholera.[28] There was considerable migration from the districts of Godavari, Rajamundhry and Visakhapatnam during this period: many of those who went to work as indentured labourers were erstwhile weavers and washermen thrown out of work.[29] High rates of death and out-migration were also reported from Nellore and Guntur.[30]

The increase in looms in the inland districts of Kadapa, Bellary, Madurai and Tirunelveli was partly the result of more systematic counting. In Bellary, numbers rose when the practice of excluding 'infant' or balike looms was abandoned.[31] In Kadapa, part of the rise was attributed to 'careful scrutiny' and to 'the increase and separation of families'. Weavers also arrived from adjoining districts where the trade had suffered.[32] But there was also a real increase. The collector of Bellary noted that imports of cloth into the district fell from a tariff value of 130,884 rupees to 72,506 rupees, a decline of 44.6 per cent. Home consumption, including exports to other British provinces (accounting for most of the cloth trade), increased from a tariff value of 1,241,009 rupees to 1,751,767 rupees, a rise of 41.2 per cent. Cloth exports to other states increased from a tariff value of 299,736 rupees to 445,323 rupees, a rise of 48.6 per cent.[33]

The first half of the nineteenth century: a closer view

The collectors of the coastal districts at the heart of the export trade were unanimous in declaring that the value and quality of cloth production had fallen. Weavers producing for the export market suffered the most, along with those making fine varieties of cloth. Masulipatnam had once been a centre for painted goods or chintz for export: these exports fell steeply

[28] PBR vol. 1379, no. 35, 1 September 1833, pp. 11225–6, TNSA.
[29] Kumar, *Land and Caste*, pp. 130–1, 139.
[30] PBR vol. 1062, no. 35, 1 May 1826, p. 4079, TNSA; PBR vol. 1379, no. 43, 23 September 1833, pp. 11471–2, TNSA.
[31] PBR vol. 1925, no. 42, 8 August 1844, p. 10277, TNSA.
[32] PBR vol. 1925, no. 42, 8 August 1844, p. 10277, TNSA; also PBR vol. 1931, no. 48, 23 September 1844, p. 12548, TNSA.
[33] PBR vol. 1925, no. 42, 8 August 1844, p. 10281, TNSA.

from 1,050,000 rupees in 1819–20 to just 2,750 rupees in 1843–4.[34] Much of this trade had been with Persia; it vanished under competition from British chintz.[35] A steep fall in cloth production was reported from Nellore, where much of the cloth printed in Masulipatnam was woven.[36] Exports of madapollams and punjams fell from 11,925 bales to 541 bales. By 1855, these varieties were no longer being made.[37]

In 1826, the collector of Nellore reported that weavers in his district were 'daily diminishing in wealth and number'. He estimated that the number of looms had declined by approximately 2,000 in a single year as 'many weavers have died, many have left the district and many who remain are very poor'. The reasons ranged from the loss of eastern markets to competition from British goods to the withdrawal of the EIC from the cloth trade.[38] Between 1836–7 and 1842–3, inland duties collected on cloth fell by 14,398 rupees as production of fine cloth slumped. A comparison of duties charged on different varieties of cloth in 1817–18 and 1842–3 is revealing: of 27 varieties sold in 1817–18, 17 were no longer being made by 1842–3. The manufacture of coarse cloth had gone up while the production of the 'finer description of goods' had been 'almost entirely discontinued'.[39]

In Pundlapully and Jaundrapett, hamlets of Chirala in Nellore district, red and black handkerchiefs were made against orders from mercantile houses in Madras: their inhabitants were reported to be 'much depressed' as this trade had 'greatly fallen off' and they were not used to making any other kind of cloth. Exports from Visakhapatnam district declined steeply.[40] Rajamundhry had once been a centre of production for fine punjams and muslins for the EIC. With its withdrawal, the average export of piece goods fell from 6,000 corges valued at 974,000 rupees to 2,000 corges valued at 107,000 rupees.[41] The weavers of Palicole in Mogultoor estate, who used to make punjams, turned to cloth of inferior quality and price. Some migrated to Mauritius; others enlisted as sepoys. In general, reported the collector,

[34] PBR vol. 1955, no. 21, 10 February 1845, p. 1853, TNSA.

[35] PBR vol. 1061, no. 26, 24 April 1826, p. 3828, TNSA; PBR vol. 1955, no. 21, 10 February 1845, p. 1853, TNSA.

[36] PBR vol. 1931, no. 47, 23 September 1844, p. 12519, TNSA.

[37] *Reports by the Juries*, p. 92.

[38] PBR vol. 1062, no. 35, 1 May 1826, pp. 4078–9, TNSA.

[39] PBR vol. 1931, no. 47, 23 September 1844, pp. 12516–17, TNSA.

[40] Specker, 'Madras Handlooms', 140; PBR vol. 1982, no. 73, 22 September 1845, p. 11628, TNSA.

[41] A corge was a unit used to calculate quantities of cloth, especially piece goods. Twenty pieces of cloth made one corge. PBR vol. 1982, no. 73, 22 September 1845, p. 11627, TNSA. For details, see Table 2.3.

> the profits of the craft are now very considerably less (on the finer cloth) than they used to be, so that in the present day a much smaller value of cloth is made by a much greater number of workmen, and the profit upon each piece of cloth is a great deal less than was formerly the case.[42]

Weavers in other districts to the south, where production was oriented towards export, suffered much the same fate.[43]

Production for the domestic market

Weavers dependent upon export markets and those producing fine cloth for the domestic market were hit hard during this period. However, those making coarse cloth for local consumption fared better. Almost every report makes a distinction between weavers making cloth for local consumption and for export. The collector of Nellore reported that, in contrast to weavers in the south of the district producing for export, those in the north had not suffered too much, for they made 'coarser kind of cloths for home consumption, in use amongst the cultivating class of the district'.[44] A report from one sub-division had this to say:

> With the exception of those resident in certain villages in the Chendalore talook the weavers in this division are employed generally in the manufacture of coarse cloth and the common cloth in ordinary use among the less opulent inhabitants of the country and have never been in the habit of manufacturing much cloth for exportation beyond the limits of the district. The weavers therefore have not suffered to any material extent from the introduction of the finer cloth of English manufacture which is not used by the class above referred to.[45]

However, they were affected by the depression in agricultural profits that reduced their customers' purchasing power.

In Thiruchirapalli, weavers making cloth for local consumption were largely unaffected: 'their present compared with their former condition admits of no cause of complaint'.[46] The collector of Guntur, singling out weavers serving local markets, reported that the number of looms appeared to be on the increase and that the profits of the trade were either the same

42 PBR vol. 1953, no. 26, 27 January 1845, p. 1147, TNSA.

43 PBR vol. 1925, no. 19, 5 August 1844, p. 10199, TNSA; PBR vol. 1929, no. 29, 5 September 1844, p. 11761, TNSA; PBR vol. 1925, no. 43, 8 August 1844, pp. 10296–9, TNSA.

44 PBR vol. 1931, no. 47, 23 September 1844, pp. 12522–3, TNSA.

45 PBR vol. 1931, no. 47, 23 September 1844, pp. 12538, TNSA.

46 PBR vol. 1062, no. 41, 8 May 1826, pp. 4298–9, TNSA; PBR vol. 1925, no. 43, 8 August 1844, p. 10296, TNSA.

or improving.[47] In Rajamundhry, the collector noted that 'the making up of coarse piece goods is carried on with great activity in this district'.[48] Reports from Masulipatnam and South Arcot include similar observations.[49] The inland districts of Kadapa and Bellary exported little cloth before this period: the rise in the number of looms strengthens the view that weaving for the domestic market remained strong. Within this market, it was coarse cloth production that dominated.

Almost all official reports from the mid-1840s report a fall in cloth production in terms of value.[50] The period from 1825 to 1853 was marked by declining prices and a general depression, especially in agriculture.[51] Both grain and cloth prices fell in varying degrees. This was because of falling input costs (the price of raw cotton also decreased), but competition from imports also played a role in some districts.[52] Konrad Specker calculates that the prices of textiles in the Madras Presidency fell by an average of 30–40 per cent during this period.[53] This translated into a generalised fall in production (in terms of value) even in regions where more looms were installed. In Kadapa, cloth production fell by 333,122 rupees, for fewer looms were now fitted for weaving the finer kinds of cloth:

> the merchants and weavers without exception declare that fine cloths of all descriptions being imported from Europe and other parts of India at a lower price than they could produce them for, they have been generally obliged to employ themselves in the manufacture of the coarser kinds of cloth.[54]

Specker shows that cloth imports from Britain during this period consisted of middling to fine varieties. It was only in the later part of the century that coarse cloth began to be imported in large quantities.[55]

[47] PBR vol. 1929, no. 29, 5 September 1844, p. 11761, TNSA.
[48] PBR vol. 1064, no. 35, 5 June 1826, p. 4990, TNSA.
[49] PBR vol. 1061, no. 26, 24 April 1826, p. 3828, TNSA; PBR vol. 1925, no. 19, 5 August 1844, p. 10199, TNSA.
[50] In Thanjavur, a rise in the total number of looms was accompanied by a fall in looms making higher-priced cloth (valued at five pagodas or more). PBR vol. 1942, no. 66, 28 November 1844, p. 16367, TNSA. There are similar reports from Rajamundhry and Nellore. PBR vol. 1953, no. 26, 27 January 1845, p. 1147 onwards, TNSA; PBR vol. 1931, no. 47, 23 September 1844, p. 12517, TNSA.
[51] Dharma Kumar and Meghnad Desai (eds), *The Cambridge Economic History of India*, vol. 2, *c.*1757–*c.*1970 (Cambridge, Cambridge University Press, 1983), p. 361.
[52] The impact of this competition was felt much more acutely in the later part of the nineteenth century. See Figure 2.1 for a graph depicting cloth imports into the Madras Presidency.
[53] Specker, 'Madras Handlooms', 154.
[54] PBR vol.1931, no. 48, 23 September 1844, p. 12548, TNSA.
[55] Specker, 'Madras Handlooms', 144.

Impact on incomes

Descriptive accounts of the period report falling incomes based on discussions with merchants and weavers, not upon comparison with statistical data from earlier periods (which did not exist). Nevertheless these calculations and impressions are worth looking at.

Weavers forced to make coarse instead of fine cloth saw a fall in income. Apart from this, many collectors reported that earnings from weaving had been badly affected as a result of competition from English imports and a decline in the purchasing power of farmers and peasants.[56] In Rajamundhry, the collector opined that incomes had fallen by approximately a third.[57] The collector of Bellary calculated that between 1815–16 and 1843–4, weavers of fine cloth saw a fall of 75 per cent in their earnings and those weaving coarse cloth of 62 per cent. The price of a piece of cloth fell by 35 per cent on average during this period. However, the decline is less steep once food prices are factored in: 'this cannot be altogether considered as loss when we compare the present low price they pay for grain and every kind of food'.[58]

Reports from other districts agree that falling cloth prices were offset to some degree by the decline in grain and cotton prices.[59] But this had a dual effect on weavers: they could buy grain (and thread) more cheaply than before, but the agricultural depression affected the *demand* for cloth in rural communities by reducing the purchasing power of farming households. It is estimated that grain prices fell by 40 to 50 per cent during this period; but in some regions cloth prices fell even more steeply (as much as 75 per cent in Bellary).[60] It is likely that the agricultural depression of the 1820s and '30s was magnified by the withdrawal of the EIC from the cloth trade, even though many officials believed that real incomes (especially for weavers making coarse cloth) were holding steady.[61]

[56] PBR vol. 1932, nos. 32–3, 7 October 1844, pp. 12998–9, TNSA; PBR vol. 1925, no. 19, 5 August 1844, p. 10199, TNSA.
[57] PBR vol. 1953, no. 26, 27 January 1845, p. 1147, TNSA.
[58] PBR vol. 1925, no. 42, 8 August 1844, p. 10284, TNSA.
[59] PBR vol 1929, no. 29, 5 September 1844, p. 11761, TNSA.
[60] For the estimated decline in grain prices, see Kumar and Desai, *The Cambridge Economic History of India*, vol. 2, p. 361.
[61] PBR vol. 1925, no. 43, 8 August 1844, p. 10298 (Trichinopoly), TNSA.

Some conclusions

Broadly speaking, Specker accepts the contention of the Madras Board of Revenue in 1845 that 'apart from a few exceptions, both the number of looms in operation and the number of weavers, underwent an increase over the preceding 25 years'.[62] He also contends that there was a pronounced tilt towards coarser varieties of cloth and a geographical shift of production southwards.[63] These conclusions are based on an ostensible decline in the number of looms in northern Coromandel during this period and a corresponding increase in loom figures for some of the southern districts.

My evidence shows that the actual picture was much more complex. A pronounced drift towards coarse cloth production is not in dispute, but Specker's argument about a southward shift appears less convincing; loom numbers rose significantly in the Deccan districts of Kadapa and Bellary. I would argue the primary distinction was sectoral rather than geographical. The steepest decline occurred in the coastal districts where production was geared towards export. By contrast, inland districts, where production was oriented to domestic markets, fared much better (with the exception of Coimbatore). Cotton grew there, transport costs were low, and yarn could be obtained both abundantly and cheaply.

Broadly speaking, weavers making cloth for domestic markets fared better than those locked into the export trade. At the same time, the domestic demand for fine cloth also fell. There appear to be two reasons for this: a decline in the fortunes of local elites and competition from British manufacturers.[64] Piece goods imported into India during this period were of middling to good quality, in demand among the 'better classes of people'.[65] Coarse country-made cloths remained the preferred choice of poor to middling folk.[66]

[62] Specker, 'Madras Handlooms', 133.

[63] Specker, 'Madras Handlooms', 145.

[64] In Rajamundhry, the collector noted that few of the fine varieties once bought in large quantities by zamindars and their retainers were made any longer. According to the collector of Coimbatore, the prosperous classes and those in public service were buying more imported cloth. PBR vol. 1942, no. 49, 25 November 1844, p. 16128, TNSA; PBR vol. 1953, no. 26, 27 January 1845, p. 1147, TNSA.

[65] PBR vol. 1942, no. 49, 25 November 1844, pp. 16128–9, TNSA.

[66] PBR vol. 1942, no. 49, 25 November 1844, pp. 16128–9, TNSA.

Counting the looms: 1850–1918

Data on looms for the second half of the nineteenth century is scarce. The moturpha tax was abolished in 1861. In 1871, the Board of Revenue conducted an enquiry into the state of the handloom industry from 1856–7 to 1869–70. Data collected from different districts indicated an increase in the number of looms by 40 per cent, but the Board rejected some figures as unreliable and incomplete (with data for the earlier period missing for whole districts): a rise of 20–25 per cent was considered more realistic.[67] Yet another estimate in 1889 calculated that the number of looms had risen by 7 per cent in the intervening period. If these estimates are correct, the number of looms increased from anywhere between 27–32 per cent in approximately 35 years.

By the mid-1840s, the crisis caused by the withdrawal of the EIC and a series of famines had begun to pass: officials noted that the handloom industry was showing signs of revival.[68] The withdrawal of transit duties on goods transported within British territory was another source of relief.[69] The evidence shows that cloth production for the domestic market was not affected until later. According to Sumit Guha, the population of South India (Mysore plus the Madras Presidency) doubled between 1800 and 1881.[70] Dharma Kumar estimates that the population of the Madras Presidency grew by 63 per cent between 1823 and 1851, and by 44.5 per cent between 1861 and 1891.[71] The most generous estimate of loom increase during a comparable period—between 1856–7 and 1889—is 32 per cent. Thus, despite an absolute increase in numbers, employment in weaving lagged behind population growth during the second half of the nineteenth century.

It is likely that the number of looms rose gradually after the 1840s as agricultural production expanded, lifting domestic demand. A large proportion of this demand was met by textile imports from Britain and the

[67] Board of Revenue Proceedings, 28 June 1871, TNSA. See Table 2.4.

[68] PBR vol. 1974, no. 31, 14 July 1845, p. 8627, TNSA; PBR vol. 1953, no. 26, 27 January 1845, p. 1147, TNSA.

[69] Borpujari examines the crippling effect of transit duties on trade and manufacture. Separate duties had to be paid on raw cotton, spun yarn, dyed yarn, finished cloth and so on. The cumulative duties on domestic products were much higher than those on imported goods, especially yarn and cloth. Jitendra G. Borpujari, 'The Impact of the Transit Duty System in British India', *The Indian Economic and Social History Review*, 10(3) (1973), 218–41. The withdrawal of these duties in 1842 in the Madras Presidency represented a significant relief; many collectors noted the benefit to weavers.

[70] Guha, *Health and Population*, p. 58.

[71] Kumar, *Land and Caste*, pp. 120–1.

nascent Indian mill industry; handlooms provided the rest. But the rise in loom numbers between 1856–7 and 1889 was followed by a steep decline at the end of the century. The loom figures for 1844 and 1901 are almost identical even though the population of the Madras Presidency increased by 73 per cent between 1851 and 1901.[72]

When did this decline commence? Cotton exports took off during the American Civil War, leaving less cotton for domestic consumption; this affected hand spinners in several parts of the country. Afterwards, these exports, despite declining, remained on average substantially higher than their pre-war levels. At the same time, the continued buoyancy of the agricultural economy probably fuelled demand for cloth. It is possible that the decline began in the late 1870s or early 1880s, even though the number of looms remained unaffected (being counted even when not in use).

The peak of 1889 is perplexing, especially in the light of contemporary accounts.[73] If the figure is accurate, all the gains between the 1840s and the 1880s were wiped out in a single decade, bringing the number of looms back to the level of 1844. This seems unlikely—it is more probable that the decline was gradual, setting in some time before this. However, there is other evidence for a sudden dip in numbers during the last decade of the nineteenth century. Village studies conducted in different parts of the Madras Presidency in 1917 show a sharp fall in the number of weavers making coarse cloth.[74]

This decline should be interpreted against a background of continuous increases in cloth imports and the rapid expansion of the domestic mill industry—both were magnified by the railway network that ferried machine-made cloth deep into the interior. The data on cloth imports shows a steady rise, with substantial jumps during the 1860s and again in the 1880s.[75] The number of mills in India increased from 47 in 1876–7 to 114 in 1889–90,

[72] Kumar, *Land and Caste*, pp. 120–1.

[73] Havell saw clear signs of decline in many places, especially for plain and coarse varieties of cloth. Noting that accurate statistics were difficult to come by, he made detailed inquiries in a town in Visakhapatnam district: these revealed that the output of ordinary cloth had fallen by 23 per cent in four or five years. In Havell's view, the town was representative of many places in the Presidency. E. B. Havell, *Reports Submitted by Mr. E. B. Havell During the Years 1885–1888 on the Arts and Industries of Certain Districts of the Madras Presidency* (Madras, Government Press, 1909), p. 28.

[74] In one village in Krishna district, the number of weavers fell from 69 in 1891 to 3 in 1911; in Mayavaram (Thanjavur) from 44 in 1891 to zero in 1911; in Polur (North Arcot), from 255 in 1891 to 80 in 1911 (census figures). All of them used to make coarse cloth. The only place where weaving still flourished was the region around Kanchipuram (North Arcot). Gilbert Slater (ed.), *Economic Studies*, vol. 1: *Some South Indian Villages* (London, Oxford University Press, 1918), pp. 90, 115, 208, 224.

[75] See Figure 2.1.

and the number of looms in mills rose from 9,139 to 22,078.[76] By 1900 there were 193 mills with 40,124 looms, an almost four-fold increase in a little over two decades.[77]

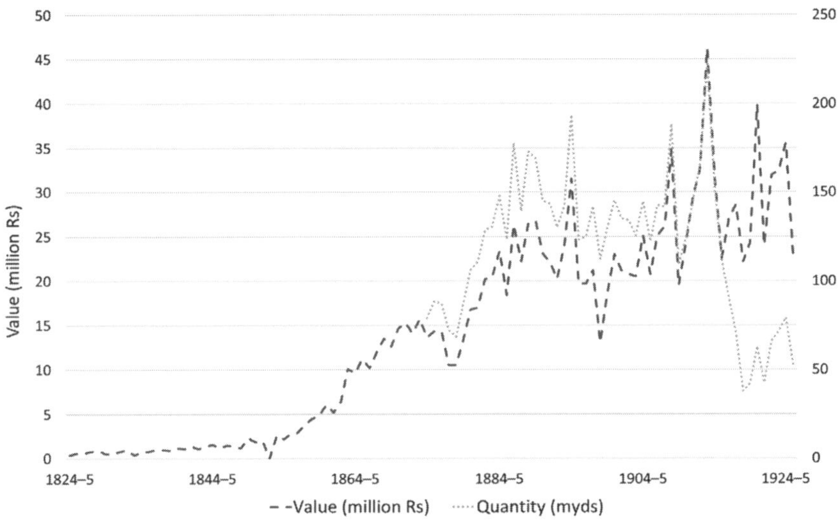

Figure 2.1: Quantity and value of cloth imports by sea into the Madras Presidency

Sources: Specker, *Weber in Wettbewerb*, p. 253; *Annual Volumes of the Sea-borne Trade and Navigation of the Madras Presidency and of its Chief Port and Each of the Subordinate Ports for the Year from 1874–75 to 1924–25* (Madras, Government Press).

The late nineteenth century: a closer view

A noticeable shift towards mill cloth becomes visible from this time. Havell provided first-hand reports on the struggles of makers of coarse cloth during the 1880s. According to him, 'the European goods have their great advantage in point of cheapness and consequently the native manufacturer who supplies the wants of the low caste and poorer classes has suffered most'. He distinguished between two kinds of clothes for men:

[76] Great Britain, India Office, *Statement of the Trade of British India with British Possessions and Foreign Countries for the Five Years 1883–84 to 1887–88* (London, HMSO, 1889), p. 10.
[77] K. S. Venkatraman, *The Handloom Industry in South India*, Supplementary to the Madras University Journal (Madras, Diocesan Press, 1936), p. 18.

> first, a plain white cloth with a narrow border of coloured cotton, and sometimes with a broader band woven across each end, which are worn by the low caste poor; and, secondly, superior cloths of fine texture in which the borders are broader and of silk and generally embroidered with a simple pattern, and the bands at each end either of silk or of silver lace ... The first of these has been almost entirely superseded for general wear by English long cloth, which is cheaper than the native cloth by about one half.[78]

The weaver who wove 'the common white cloths of imported twist selling for 2 or 3 rupees each' had to compete not only with the ordinary English and American long-cloth that could be cut to the required length,

> a piece of which, equal in length to a native cloth, can be purchased for less than half the price, but also with machine-made cloths precisely similar to their own production as regards size, pattern and quality of cotton, and selling for three-fourths the price.[79]

By 1892, weavers in the city of Madurai had taken to wearing mill cloth.[80] By 1917, so had 75 per cent of the inhabitants in a village in Krishna district.[81] According to an observer in Kumbakonam, 80 per cent of men living in towns now wore clothes made of mill cloth.[82]

The manufacture of coarse cloth did not disappear overnight, especially in cotton-growing regions. In the mid-1880s, coarse strong cloth made from hand-spun yarn was still woven in Coimbatore, Kadapa and the cotton-growing districts south of the Krishna river, albeit in smaller quantities.[83] It was regarded as more durable; besides, handwoven cloth was still preferred for ceremonial occasions.[84] By this time, weavers were making a shift that was to become much more pronounced in the twentieth century—towards cloth varieties that could not be easily replicated by mills. The output of some varieties of fine cloth fell: painted and printed cloths in Walajanagar, silk carpets in Thanjavur and cotton carpets in some centres.[85] But, on the whole, handloom varieties facing little competition from mills did much better: there was a boom in the chequered lungis woven principally for a Muslim clientèle in Chirala, Ventapalem and Peddana.[86]

[78] Havell, *Reports Submitted*, pp. 4–5

[79] Havell, *Reports Submitted*, p. 29.

[80] S. Srinivasa Raghavaiyangar, *Memorandum on the Progress of the Madras Presidency during the Last Forty Years of British Administration* (Madras, Government Press, 1892), p. 137.

[81] Slater, *Some South Indian Villages*, p. 115.

[82] Raghavaiyangar, *Memorandum*, p. 126.

[83] Havell, *Reports Submitted*, pp. 19, 50.

[84] Havell, *Reports Submitted*, pp. 4–5.

[85] Havell, *Reports Submitted*, pp. 6, 7, 29.

[86] Havell, *Reports Submitted*, p. 19.

Weavers making saris were also insulated from competition. Coarser saris had to compete with cheap printed goods from England and France, but a substantial quantity of coarse cloths patterned on the loom continued to be made, especially for overseas markets. Centres for fine saris (Thanjavur, Kuttalam, Koranad, Madurai, Gudiyattam, Rajam and Chirala) did reasonably well.[87] This sector benefited from the relative cheapness of imported machine yarn. Silk weaving was largely unaffected for much the same reason. Havell reported an increase in the weaving of pure silk and of cotton mixed with silk (usually in borders).[88] New varieties of cloth were developed to make garments like the ravikkei (a blouse), not in wide use before this period.[89]

Wherever possible, weavers sought to avoid competition with mills. In South Arcot, where the common fabrics woven were 'coarse cotton dupattis, white cloths for men and coloured cloths for women',

> the makers of the usual men's and women's cloths constantly complain that competition of foreign machine-made goods is ruining their market, but the weavers of *kambayam* fabric appear to be in a more flourishing condition, and in several villages ... the weaving castes are relinquishing the making of ordinary kinds of stuffs to take up the manufacture of these fabrics.[90]

But not everyone could make this transition and many weavers of plain cloth had to abandon their occupation: the decline in loom numbers around the turn of the century should probably be attributed to this.

The disappearance of the Pariar weaver

Our hypothesis that the production of coarse cloth fell substantially during the last decade of the nineteenth century is corroborated by the gradual disappearance of Pariar or 'untouchable' weavers. It is impossible to calculate the exact number of looms worked by them before this period, but a reliable picture of the extent of their decline can be put together from the sources. In 1796, the Baramahal region had substantial numbers of 'untouchable' Koliar and Manniwar weavers. The Koliar were concentrated in the southern division, where they comprised between 10 and 18 per cent of all weavers; in the central and northern divisions lived the Manniwar

[87] Havell, *Reports Submitted*, pp. 5, 19.

[88] Havell, *Reports Submitted*, Enclosure 1, p. 41.

[89] Havell, *Reports Submitted*, Enclosure 1, p. 41.

[90] W. Francis, *South Arcot District Gazetteer* (Madras, Government Press, 1906), pp. 156–7. Kambayam was another name for the lungi or kaili, a cloth with a chequered pattern.

(10 and 38 per cent respectively). Together, they comprised roughly 18 per cent of all weavers in the Baramahals. The proportion of specialist weaving castes in these three divisions was as follows: 36 per cent for Kaikolars, 23 per cent for Jadars and 8.5 per cent for Pattunoolkarars.[91] Manniwars formed the largest group of weavers in the northern division.

In Madurai district, Pariars comprised as much as 48 per cent of all weavers; by contrast, the Pattunoolkarar were 20 per cent, the Kaikolar 7 per cent, and the Shaider 16 per cent.[92] The town of Dindigul had 93 looms producing both fine and coarse cloth—presumably most of these were owned by specialist weaving castes. Pariar weavers in surrounding villages worked 146 looms making coarse cloth, 'which served the purposes of the inhabitants in the country'.[93]

Pariars comprised 15.5 per cent of all weavers in Coimbatore district.[94] In Thiruchirapalli, the District Manual estimated that 'dress is provided by weavers and Pariahs in nearly equal numbers, almost to the exclusion of other castes'.[95] In Tirunelveli district, Pariars made up 20 per cent of all weavers.[96] In Guntur district, the number of looms worked by the Saliar (a specialist weaving caste) were roughly equal to those worked by the Mala (an 'untouchable' Telugu caste) and some others.[97] In Nellore, Pariar looms comprised between 38 and 42 per cent of the total—they were the single largest group of weavers in the district. Next came the Saliar, comprising approximately a third of all weavers.[98] Many Pariar weavers lived in Masulipatnam although no numbers are extant.[99]

The districts of Kadapa, Kurnool and Bellary were inhabited by many Mala weavers. The Mala of Nundial (Kurnool) were said to be 'more industrious and more self-reliant; and besides following the *ordinary* occupation of weaving the common cloth of the country, many of them

[91] Figures based on tabulations in *The Baramahal Records*, Section VII: Imposts, pp. 18, 19, 27, 65. See Tables 2.5 and 2.6.

[92] PBR vol. 1325, no. 44, 21 May 1832, p. 4901 onwards, TNSA. The figures are estimates; the weavers of Madurai were resisting enumeration, for they feared that the loom tax (from which they had been exempt) would be imposed on them. But the very large number of Pariar weavers is significant. See Table 2.7.

[93] MDR, vol. 1258, 1816, TNSA.

[94] PBR vol. 1325, no. 47, 24 May 1832, p. 5011, TNSA. See Tables 2.8 and 2.9.

[95] Lewis Moore, *A Manual of the Trichinopoly District in the Presidency of Madras* (Madras, Government Press, 1878), p. 105.

[96] PBR vol. 1937, no. 80, 7 November 1844, p. 14594, TNSA. See Table 2.10.

[97] PBR vol. 1929, no. 29, 5 September 1844, p. 11761, TNSA.

[98] PBR vol. 1334, no. 22, 13 August 1832, pp. 7768–9, TNSA; PBR vol. 1641, no. 42, 24 December 1838, pp. 17296–9, TNSA. See Tables 2.11 and 2.12.

[99] Swarnalatha, *The World of the Weaver*, p. 31.

[are] engaged in agricultural work, having fields of their own which they till with their own cattle'.[100] As late as 1896, one official estimated that one third of the weavers of the Deccan districts (Kadapa, Bellary, Kurnool) were Malas, who made the coarse cloth 'worn by the Malas themselves and by the cultivating classes'.[101]

Thus, 'untouchable' groups comprised as much as half the total number of weavers in some regions of dryland cultivation. They find little or no mention *as weavers* in coastal districts like Visakhapatnam and Godavari.[102] But, if not as weavers, Pariars were omnipresent in these districts as specialist spinners: the finest thread was made by them.[103] Extrapolating from all these figures, it is likely that 'untouchable' weavers formed between 20 and 30 per cent of *all* weavers in the Madras Presidency during the first half of the nineteenth century. Most of them worked part-time, but in some regions of the dry interior they made cloth for eight months of the year.[104] Measured by value, their output was smaller than that of fine-cloth weavers; by quantity it constituted a very large proportion of the total output of cloth.

Reports from the 1920s reveal a significant decline in their numbers. They had all but disappeared from the southern or Tamil districts, but for some Koliars in Thanjavur and Thiruchirapalli.[105] They could still be found in the cotton producing districts of the Deccan, albeit no more than a 'sprinkling' in most places; Guntur was the only district where they retained a substantial presence.[106] K. S. Venkatraman, writing in 1936, refers to them in some

[100] Edwin Lewis, *History of the Telugu Missions of the London Missionary Society in the Ceded Districts* (Madras, Addison and Company, 1879), p. 12. Emphasis mine.

[101] *Report of the Famine*, Appendix I, Report by the Special Deputy Collector in Charge of Weavers Relief Operations in the Deccan Districts, p. 356.

[102] Swarnalatha, *The World of the Weaver*, p. 31. This may have prompted Brennig to argue that 'there is no evidence of low or outcaste weavers'. Brennig, 'Textile Producers and Production', 346.

[103] Wendt, 'The Social Fabric', pp. 135–7.

[104] Edgar Thurston, *Castes and Tribes of Southern India*, vol. VII (Madras, Government Press, 1909), p. 350. There were slack and busy seasons for full-time weavers as well: the monsoon was a slack season and festival times were busy. Parthasarathi, *The Transition to a Colonial Economy*, pp. 18–19.

[105] D. Narayana Rao, *Preliminary Report on the Survey of Cottage Industries in the Districts of Madura, Ramnad, Trichinopoly and Tinnevelly* (Madras, Government Press, 1928), pp. 17–18; D. Narayana Rao, *Preliminary Report on the Survey of Cottage Industries in the Tanjore and South Arcot Districts* (Madras, Government Press, 1929), pp. 11–12.

[106] D. Narayana Rao, *Preliminary Report on the Survey of Cottage Industries in the District of Guntur* (Madras, Government Press, 1929), p. 7; D. Narayana Rao, *Preliminary Report on the Survey of Cottage Industries in the Anantapur District* (Madras, Government Press, 1928), p. 2; D. Narayana Rao, *Preliminary Report on the Survey of Cottage Industries in the East Godavari District* (Madras, Government Press, 1929), p. 3; D. Narayana Rao, *Preliminary Report on the Survey of Cottage Industries in the Cuddapah District* (Madras, Government Press, 1927), p. 7; D. Narayana Rao, *Preliminary Report on the Survey of Cottage Industries in the Chittoor District*

districts.[107] Later reports barely mention them at all; the few that remained were considered new entrants to the industry. The decline in the production of coarse cloth runs parallel to the disappearance of 'untouchable' weavers. This, in turn, implies a fall of roughly 20–30 per cent in loom numbers.

Coarse cloth was also made by other castes like the Kaikolar and Togataru. Unlike 'untouchable' weavers, they did not abandon weaving en masse; instead, many of them shifted to making new varieties of cloth. Around 1800, the Kaikolar (and Pariar) of the Baramahal region were known as coarse cloth weavers.[108] A century later, in 1906, Kaikolar weavers in Salem (Baramahal) were weaving coarse piece goods called dupattis as well as special 'solid bordered' veshtis (also made by Pattunoolkarars) and patterned saris.[109] This transition can be traced in other districts as well.[110]

The twentieth century: numbers

We have already seen that the number of looms in the Madras Presidency barely changes between 1844 and 1901. From the 1820s to the 1840s, total output remained stagnant or fell especially in the coastal districts. There was a period of recovery from the 1840s to the 1880s when the number of looms rose significantly. Fine cloth production suffered and there was no recovery in exports; however, weaving of coarse cloth for domestic consumption did well. From the 1880s, another decline sets in. The output of coarse cloth falls and a very large number of weavers, especially from so-called untouchable castes, are pushed out of the industry.

The turn of the twentieth century marks the lowest point of this decline. From roughly the end of the First World War, an upturn sets in.[111] Between 1901 and 1941, the number of looms in the Madras Presidency approximately doubles. On the face of it, the handloom industry had succeeded in making a handsome recovery. The subcontinental picture is

(Madras, Government Press, 1929), pp. 2, 7; D. Narayana Rao, *Preliminary Report on the Survey of Cottage Industries in the Nellore District* (Madras, Government Press, 1929), p. 15.

107 Venkatraman, *The Handloom Industry*, pp. 180, 273.

108 *The Baramahal Records*, Section VII: Imposts, pp. 18, 19, 27, 65.

109 F. J. Richards, *Madras District Gazetteers: Salem*, vol. 1, part I (Madras, Government Press, 1918), pp. 265–6.

110 In Chengalpattu, Kaikolars who used to weave coarse cloth to sell in local markets shifted to making kailis for merchants. Some took up silk weaving. *Preliminary Report on the Survey of Cottage Industries in the Chingelput District*, pp. 2, 8; *Preliminary Report on the Survey of Cottage Industries in the North Arcot District*, p. 4; Venkatraman, *The Handloom Industry in South India*, p. 182.

111 See Table 2.4.

more mixed; some scholars, including Tirthankar Roy, argue that its decline was decisively arrested from the turn of the century, after which handlooms managed to sustain their share of the cloth production vis-à-vis mills. Over India as a whole, the number of looms actually fell, but *output* remained steady at about 25 per cent of total cloth consumption.

Cloth produced by textile mills equalled handloom output in 1910–11 for the country as a whole,[112] and overtook it during the First World War. From the 1920s, the two curves diverge more and more: mill production increased by 706 per cent between 1901–2 and 1936–7, but handloom production rose by only 53 per cent. During this period, cloth imports declined from 62.7 to 14.4 per cent and the share of cloth made by Indian mills rose from 11.9 to 61.5 per cent.[113] The first half of the twentieth century saw a rapid increase both in population and per capita consumption of cloth. Most of this increase was supplied by the mill sector (imported cloth in the beginning and later domestic mills). Handlooms comprised only 25 per cent of all cloth produced between 1901–2 and 1936–7. Measured in terms of yarn consumption and output of cloth, the industry grew—but the number of people employed in it fell.[114]

Cloth production by mills may have caught up with handlooms in other parts of the country before the First World War, but handlooms retained their dominant role in Madras for somewhat longer. Textile mills were set up much later in the Madras Presidency than elsewhere; for a long time, they made only yarn. Until the First World War, only two out of 11 mills in the Presidency were making cloth. As late as 1939, the Director of Industries estimated that the handloom industry of Madras was more than four times as large as mills in output and value, and many times more in terms of employment generated.[115] In 1940, the Madras Presidency was the largest producer of handloom cloth in the country.

The recovery and subsequent expansion of the handloom industry is not in doubt. However, loom numbers should be examined contextually, in conjunction with other data (such as yarn consumption) and descriptive

[112] *Report of the Fact Finding Committee (Handlooms and Mills)* (Bombay, Ministry of Commerce, 1942), p. 10. Roy argues that the calculation of yarn used for making handloom cloth by the Fact Finding Committee is an underestimation, chiefly because it does not reflect the consumption of non-cotton (synthetic) yarn. According to him, 30 per cent of cloth produced in the 1930s was by handlooms—but even this modified figure reveals that the lion's share of the market had been cornered by mills. Tirthankar Roy, 'Size and Structure of Handloom Weaving in the Mid-thirties', *The Indian Economic and Social History Review*, 25(1) (1988), 1–24.

[113] *Fact Finding Committee*, p. 157.

[114] Roy, 'De-industrialization', 1444.

[115] Development Department, G.O. no. 2058, 21 August 1939, TNSA.

accounts, in order to obtain an accurate picture of working conditions. The number of looms may have doubled but the yarn actually consumed by weavers increased by only 64 per cent between 1901 and 1940. This discrepancy is magnified by the fact that new technologies were raising output during this period: looms fitted with fly-shuttles consumed much more yarn.[116]

The most plausible reason is that many of these looms were wholly or partly idle. There is considerable evidence to support this: a textile expert investigating a crisis in Coimbatore in the mid-1930s reported that the number of looms had increased partly because the weaving population had increased. However, there was not enough work to keep them running at capacity:

> Weavers have been equipped with labour saving appliances and are now capable of producing an increased quantity of cloth on handlooms, but are compelled, owing to unfair mill competition, to keep their looms idle for a greater part of the year and thus restrict their output.[117]

According to the Fact Finding Committee of 1941–2, 13 per cent of looms in the Madras Presidency lay wholly idle.[118]

Between 1941 and 1948, the number of looms in Madras doubled again—once again, actual growth was less than this figure alone would indicate. Demand for cloth increased during the Second World War even as the introduction of yarn control and rationing artificially inflated loom numbers. Introduced in 1943 after widespread protests, these controls were applied on a per loom basis: each loom got a defined quantity of yarn. Master weavers and yarn dealers overstated the number of looms owned by them in order to obtain more yarn. New looms were installed and registered for much the same purpose—to obtain raw material for existing looms.[119] Large-scale unemployment and underemployment set in once the wartime stimulus had ended. In 1961, a study by the International Labour Organisation noted that the practice of registering false or idle looms still

[116] Fly-shuttles increased output by 200 per cent depending upon the kind of cloth—the largest gain was in coarse and plain cloths. International Labour Organization (ILO), *Handloom Weaving Industry in India with Special Reference to Madras State* (New Delhi, ILO India Branch, 1960), p. 37. Venkatraman estimated that the fly-shuttle doubled productivity when thread of coarse counts was used, and increased it by 50 per cent and 25 per cent for medium to fine counts respectively. Venkatraman, *The Handloom Industry*, p. 153.

[117] Development Department, G.O. no. 806, 3 April 1937, TNSA.

[118] *Fact Finding Committee*, p. 29.

[119] *Report of the Textile Enquiry Committee, September 1954* (Delhi, Government of India Press, 1954), p. 229.

continued, long after rationing had been abandoned: this was because state aid to the handloom sector was distributed on a per loom basis.[120]

There is little doubt that the handloom industry saw a revival from the 1920s despite competition from imports and the growth of mills. This recovery can be attributed to a number of factors. The most important was technology; the introduction of the fly-shuttle, dobby and jacquard improved productivity and aided the weaving of complicated patterns. By 1935, half of all looms had been equipped with fly-shuttles; by 1940, 81 per cent of looms in the Madras Presidency were fly-shuttle looms.[121] This revolution was accompanied by a shift towards fine and patterned cloth. Exports revived, especially the export of kailis or lungis to Southeast Asia and other places, and that of Madras handkerchiefs to Africa via Britain.

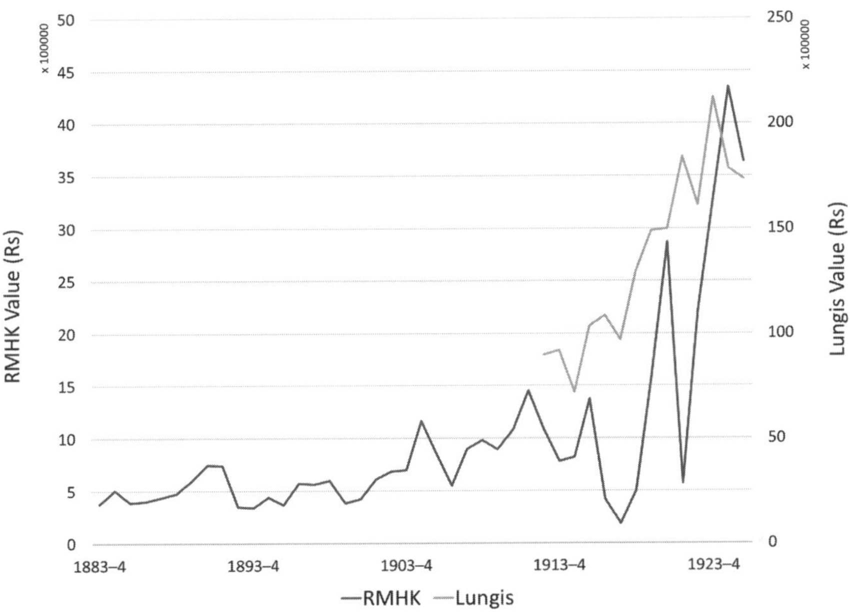

Figure 2.2: Value of exports of handkerchiefs and lungis from the Madras Presidency

Sources: Specker, *Weber in Wettbewerb*, p. 253; *Annual Volume of the Sea-borne Trade*; Amalsad, 'Development of the Madras Handkerchief'.

[120] ILO, *Handloom Weaving Industry in India*, p. 36.
[121] Venkatraman, *The Handloom Industry*, p. 276; *Fact Finding Committee*, p. 32.

The annual average of the export trade in Madras handkerchiefs between 1891 and 1900 was valued at 486,188 rupees. This rose to 820,565 rupees (1,442,993 yards) in 1914 and 3,298,372 rupees (2,642,107 yards) in 1923–4, with large fluctuations in the interim.[122] The lungi faced little competition from powerlooms, for a wide range of patterns in warp and weft of short lengths could be produced more economically by handlooms. Favoured by Muslims, they began to be exported to Penang, Singapore, Burma and the Malay states. Exports increased from 7,204,189 rupees in 1914–15 to 21,244,522 rupees in 1923–4.[123] By the end of the decade, about 25 per cent of looms in the Madras Presidency were making lungis and handkerchiefs for export.[124] Some saris were also exported to countries where Indians had migrated as guest-workers (though exact figures are not available). Export markets (combined with long-distance domestic trade) played a critical role in the expansion of the handloom industry.

The twentieth century: a closer view

The replacement of coarse cloth by mill cloth gained pace during this period; weavers sought new products and markets in the face of increasing competition from mills. Older markets were reshaped by changing habits and fashions; Emma Tarlo shows that men's clothing changed much faster than women's clothing.[125] Although it remained predominantly white, stitched garments came into common use. The angavastram was replaced by shirts and vests; shorts and trousers gained increasing acceptance. Mill cloth was cheaper and better fitted for making stitched clothes. However, women continued to wear the sari, and here handlooms had the upper hand for some time to come.

There was a noticeable shift towards fine varieties (including silk and synthetic cloth). Yanagisawa shows that the production of fine, coloured piece goods (using silk and gold thread) and coloured cloth made of artificial silk yarn (worn by the poor on special occasions) increased during this period. Some coarse cloth, especially coloured and patterned varieties, continued to be made, but much of it was for export to overseas markets.[126] Ranga notes

[122] See Figure 2.2.
[123] See Figure 2.2.
[124] Venkatraman, *The Handloom Industry*, p. 57; D. Narayana Rao, *Survey of Cottage Industries in the Madras Presidency* (Madras, Government Press, 1929), p. 75.
[125] Tarlo, *Clothing Matters*, pp. 46–7.
[126] Haruka Yanagisawa, 'The Handloom Industry and its Market Structure: the Case of the

the shift towards fine varieties, especially in silk. Weavers were also making special kinds of cloth (like pieces with solid or 'pettu' borders) difficult to reproduce on powerlooms.[127] After the 1920s, many silk weavers locked into competition with Japanese powerlooms shifted to artificial silk.[128]

A sample survey of handlooms in 1960 showed that 34 per cent of looms made super-fine cloth; 29 per cent made fine cloth; 24 per cent made cloth of medium quality; but only 13 per cent wove coarse cloth. The production of fine and super-fine cloth rose from 40.4 per cent in 1940 to 62.5 per cent in 1960.[129] This shift lies behind the argument that markets for mill and handloom cloth were segmented, with little competition between them: mills produced plain cloth (or patterns incorporating minor changes in the weft) used for stitched clothes, while handlooms produced garments that could be worn off the loom—saris, dhotis and turbans—with borders and coloured patterns woven into the body of the cloth.[130]

It should be pointed out that this segmentation begins only from the second half of the nineteenth century, when mill cloth arrived in Indian markets: before this all cloth was woven by hand and the bulk, as we have seen, was coarse and plain. During the twentieth century, weavers were forced to look for new markets as mills kept imitating their products. Diversification was essential for survival—but this is scarcely consistent with Roy's belief that handlooms did not face significant competition from mills because of market differentiation.[131] The Fact Finding Committee of 1941 compiled a list of cloth varieties made by mills and handlooms (with comparative prices), showing substantial competition.[132] From 1925, mills even began making saris, hitherto a preserve of handlooms.[133] The Committee noted that if weavers were to restrict themselves to cloth that mills could not make, only a fraction of them would be employed.[134] It is

---

Madras Presidency in the First Half of the Twentieth Century', *The Indian Economic and Social History Review*, 30(1) (1993), 1–27, at 14–18.

[127] N. G. Ranga, *The Economics of Handlooms: Being a Study of the Social and Economic Conditions of Handloom Weavers of South India*, Andhra Economic Series no. 3 (Bombay, Taraporewala and Sons, 1930), pp. 42, 51–2, 55–6, 75, 77, 80, 105, 120–1.

[128] Ranga, *The Economics of Handlooms*, pp. 106–7; *Census of India 1961*, vol. 11-A, Handlooms in Madras State (Delhi, Government Press, 1964), pp. 108, 163–8.

[129] *Census of India 1961*, p. 62. See Table 2.13.

[130] Roy, *Artisans and Industrialization*, pp. 105, 109–11.

[131] Roy, 'De-industrialization', 1445.

[132] *Fact Finding Committee*, pp. 322–9

[133] *Fact Finding Committee*, p. 12.

[134] *Fact Finding Committee*, p. 209.

clear that innovation was accompanied by a good deal of self-exploitation in order to keep afloat.

New forms of instability

Increases in yarn consumption and output have been taken as proof of the handloom industry's capacity to reorganise itself by adopting new technologies and shedding redundant labour.[135] But these figures do not reveal significant costs of readjustment for the mass of weavers. A close scrutiny of the evidence reveals that the twentieth century was marked by chronic instability and regular downturns.

During the First World War, imports of cloth fell steeply. This should have benefited weavers, but domestic mills promptly stepped up cloth production to take advantage of this opportunity. Yarn available to the handloom industry declined as mills began using more of it to make cloth themselves. Over the country as whole, handloom output fell by more than half, from 1,088 million yards in 1914–15 to 506 million yards in 1919–20, while the proportion of yarn consumed by mills increased.[136] It is from this period that many mills in the Madras Presidency began making cloth; new composite (spinning and weaving) mills were also set up. Weavers across the country bore the brunt of rising yarn prices and periodic shortages.[137] In Madurai, the dyeing industry ground to a halt once the import of chemical dyes from Germany ceased; many weavers were 'forced to do cooly work or starve'.[138] In Coimbatore, the scarcity of imported yarn and gold thread led to unemployment and wage reductions.[139]

Another crisis set in during the 1930s. The expansion of spinning mills meant there was more yarn for handlooms, but the cascading effects of the Great Depression produced a sharp contraction in demand.[140] Exports dropped sharply and even domestic demand was affected. The annual average export of piece goods from the Madras Presidency for the

[135] Roy, 'De-industrialization', 1445.
[136] *Fact Finding Committee*, p. 10.
[137] See Harnetty, 'De-industrialisation Revisited', p. 486. Douglas E. Haynes, 'Artisan Cloth-Producers and the Emergence of Powerloom Manufacture in Western India, 1920–1950', *Past and Present*, 172(1) (2001), 170–98, at 175.
[138] Saunders, *The Saurashtra Community in Madura*, p. 104.
[139] Indian Industrial Commission, Minutes of Evidence, 1916–17, vol. 3, Madras and Bangalore (Calcutta, Government Press, 1918), p. 445.
[140] C. J. Baker, *An Indian Rural Economy 1880–1955: the Tamilnad Countryside* (Delhi, Oxford University Press, 1984), pp. 351–4.

quinquennium 1921–2 to 1925–6 had been 27,468,000 yards and from 1926–7 to 1930–1, 24,752,000 yards; from 1931–2 to 1935–6 this fell to 14,841,000 yards.[141] Many weavers making cloth for export were thrown out of work. Centres like Madurai and Coimbatore, catering to the North Indian market, also suffered large-scale unemployment. Meanwhile, yarn prices began to rise as protective duties were applied. In 1936, large-scale unemployment among weavers was reported from Coimbatore: only 200 out of 1,200 looms were said to be in operation. They were 'driven to seek employment in textile mills, some have taken to hawking vegetables and fruits. Many of the people that could no longer earn their livelihood have left the town in search of work'.[142]

During the Second World War, weavers stood to benefit from rising cloth prices, for wages rose in tandem with demand. But this potential gain was offset by a steep increase in yarn prices and severe shortages. Mills, yarn merchants, cloth merchants and master weavers made very large profits, but most weavers enjoyed steady employment and good wages only for brief periods. Those who could obtain yarn prospered, but for those who could not, it was a time of unemployment and hunger. These developments will be discussed in more detail in later chapters.

After the war came the crisis of 1951–3, one of the worst of the twentieth century. Weavers were reduced to penury: centres for food distribution called *kanji thotti* (literally tanks or tubs of rice gruel in Tamil) had to be opened across the province.[143] With the end of the war, demand fell; markets like Ceylon and Burma (absorbing 73 per cent of pre-war exports of lungis and saris) vanished as import restrictions on cloth were imposed. Mill cloth, hitherto reserved for war supplies, was released on the market and mill production increased.[144] Faced with this glut, thousands of looms fell idle. There is no data on the number of weavers affected, but sample surveys conducted by the Textile Enquiry Committee show very high levels of distress: 66.2 per cent of looms in Chokkampatti (Tirunelveli) were reported to be idle, as were 50 per cent in Puthamputhur and 38 per cent in Melapalayam.[145]

[141] Baker, *An Indian Rural Economy*, p. 394.
[142] Development Department, G.O. no. 806, 3 April 1937, TNSA.
[143] Interview with P. M. Kumar, Madurai, 27 January 2009.
[144] *Census of India 1961*, p. 28.
[145] *Textile Enquiry Committee*, pp. 217, 228, 237.

Conclusion

Combining descriptive or qualitative evidence with statistics and estimates yields a substantially new picture of the handloom industry in South India during the nineteenth and twentieth centuries. Broadly speaking, weavers making cloth for export and fine cloth for the domestic market suffered disproportionately during the first half of the nineteenth century, from the 1820s to the 1840s. From the 1840s to the 1880s, there was a revival, dominated by coarse cloth weaving. From the 1880s, another decline set in—this time it was weavers making coarse cloth who were the worst affected. Weavers from so-called untouchable castes gradually abandoned weaving. This represented a very significant loss of numbers, for they comprised between 20 to 30 per cent of all weavers and supplied a substantial proportion of ordinary cloth.

Peter Harnetty's study of the handloom industry in the Central Provinces traces a broadly similar arc. He shows that it was chiefly fine cloth weavers who suffered during the first half of the nineteenth century, as the traditional aristocracy declined and fashions changed. Later on, and especially after the coming of the railways, the market was flooded with cheap imported cloth: this affected coarse cloth weavers the most but the earnings of fine cloth weavers also suffered. By the turn of the century, 'lower caste' weavers had either moved to other occupations, or spent much less time in making cloth. By 1931 most of them had stopped weaving altogether. 'Upper caste' weavers like Koshtis and Momins shifted to finer varieties.[146]

After the First World War, the handloom industry recovered by dint of adapting to new technologies, making new varieties of cloth and conquering new export markets: this allowed it to hold its own in the face of growing competition from mills. Tirthankar Roy presents these changes in wholly positive terms; in his view, they introduced greater productivity, stability of employment and enhanced wages (for some weavers at least). My evidence shows that the actual picture was much more complex.

We have seen that the apparent segmentation of markets between handlooms and mills emerged during this period. At the beginning of the nineteenth century, the handloom industry in South India supplied the entirety of domestic demand: the bulk of the cloth produced by it was plain and coarse. By the end of the century, it had largely ceased to

[146] Harnetty, 'De-industrialization Revisited', 496–8.

make coarse cloth. Some scholars have argued that mills provided poor consumers with greater choice, but it should not be forgotten that many of these consumers had originally been *producers* of cloth. A very large number of poor and especially 'untouchable' households were pushed out of the handloom industry during the late nineteenth century (both as weavers and spinners).

Other groups of weavers managed to adapt to new structures of production at the cost of increased instability and uncertainty. The revival and expansion of the handloom industry did not usher in a period of unfettered growth and prosperity—instead, it was marked by bouts of instability, with a major downturn punctuating almost every decade. A small minority of weavers became successful capitalists, but the vast majority had to live through periods of unemployment and falling wages. All these developments will be explored in the rest of the book—but before that, we will examine the actual web of processes and people that went into making a piece of cloth.

3

From Cotton to Cloth

The Linking Threads

Cloth making starts with the cultivation of cotton. In the nineteenth century, the transformation of cotton into cloth involved a number of stages, incorporating different technologies and skills. These interlinked processes formed a chain or, more accurately, a web of interlinked chains, for each process might be carried out in a number of ways. These chains were nourished by the labour of many people—men and women; cultivators, labourers and artisans; weavers, spinners, dyers and merchants—embedded in complex social and economic relationships. Much of this labour remains hidden and undervalued, for it was subsumed into the working rhythms of households who combined it with other kinds of work. This is especially true in the case of women workers.

Many of these processes have received scholarly attention.[1] Ian Wendt examines traditional methods of cultivating, cleaning, transporting, spinning and weaving cotton in some detail; he shows that a wide range of people, many of them women and many working part-time, contributed their labour and time to different stages of cloth making. Their earnings formed a crucial contribution to the income of poor households.[2] However, scholars have paid little attention to the complex linkages *between* different stages of

[1] Particularly for the seventeenth and eighteenth centuries. See Swarnalatha, *The World of the Weaver*, pp. 46–72; Wendt, *The Social Fabric*, pp. 25–225; Parthasarathi, *The Transition to a Colonial Economy*, pp. 9–77.

[2] The strength of Wendt's work resides in the quantity of data collated and analysed: the complex networks of labour and skill that went into cloth making, the earnings derived from various stages of processing and so on. His work is seminal in shifting focus from the weaver and drawing attention to the people who performed other kinds of work. However, the picture he draws is largely static, with little analysis of change; it fails to address the growing power of the EIC during the course of the eighteenth century, its withdrawal from the cloth trade during the nineteenth century, and the impact of industrialisation and mechanisation on handlooms.

cloth making and the knock-on effects of disruption to one stage upon the others. On the other hand, activists working with weavers see changes in production systems as playing a key role in shaping the handloom industry of today.[3]

During the nineteenth century, the stages of cloth production—and methods associated with them—were transformed utterly, with their links being broken and reforged in new configurations. All this had far-reaching consequences for different groups of workers. This chapter will examine the major stages of cloth making—cotton cultivation, cleaning and spinning—and the process of rupture, reconfiguration and reconsolidation for each of them during the course of the century.

Cotton: cultivation and marketing

The cotton plant

Cotton is one of the world's most botanically diverse crops, thanks largely to human selection. Seeds were selected over generations for certain qualities such as colour, strength and fineness of fibre, early maturity, resistance to drought, frost, pests, and so on. It has been cultivated in India since the time of the Indus Valley civilisation.[4] The oldest variety of cotton grown in the subcontinent is *Gossypium arboreum*. Nineteenth-century records mention many indigenous cotton varieties: from later botanical studies, we know that most of them descend from *G. arboreum;* by the 1920s, botanists had identified six varieties cultivated in different regions. Another species was *Gossypium herbacium*, largely confined to the western part of the subcontinent. This was originally domesticated in Africa and introduced into India through trade exchanges between the west coast and North Africa and West Asia.[5]

[3] Menon and Bilgrami, *A Frayed History*, pp. 1–80; C. Shambu Prasad, 'Suicide Deaths and Quality of Indian Cotton: Perspectives from History of Technology and Khadi Movement', *Economic and Political Weekly*, 34(5) (1999), PE-12–PE-20.

[4] Botanists now believe that cotton was domesticated independently in Asia, Africa and America. The four domesticated species of cotton are *G. arboreum* (Asia), *G. herbaceum* (Africa), *G. hirsuttum* and *G. barbadense* (the Americas). There are approximately 50 identified species of cotton. Jonathan F. Wendel and Corrine E. Grover, 'Taxonomy and Evolution of the Cotton Genus Gossypium', in D. D. Fang and R. G. Percy (eds), *Cotton*, 2nd edn, Agronomy Monograph vol. 57 (Madison, WI, American Society of Agronomy, 2015), pp. 25–44.

[5] B. L. Sethi and K. Dharmarajulu, *Indian Cotton: Its Past, Present and Future* (Bombay, ICCC, 1957), pp. 4–5.

Indigenous varieties of cotton, selected for specific attributes of fineness, strength or colour, were used to make cloth of that particular attribute or combination of attributes. Special methods of processing and treatment might be applied to a fine variety of short-staple cotton to convert it into yarn used for weaving fine cloth. Another variety known for the strength of its fibre might be used to make coarse, strong cloth. In central India, a variety called Nurma was grown in a few villages along the Narmada; it was dirty yellow in colour with the fibre clinging strongly to the seed. It was exported to Chanderi, where yarn made from it was used to weave ultra-fine cloths called mamoodies. Coarse cloths were woven from a different variety, more widely cultivated; Nurma was considered unsuitable for this.[6] The 'red cotton' grown in the Krishna district was used only by weavers in the neighbouring district of Rajamundhry.[7] The brownish cotton grown in Guntur district was 'much esteemed by the punjum weavers about Samulcotah'.[8]

The botanical history of the cotton plant, the range of its indigenous varieties and their specific attributes played an important part in cloth making. This will become evident while discussing changes in cotton cultivation and processing during the course of the nineteenth century. Once yarn production moved to mills, the range of attributes considered desirable contracted sharply: the question of staple (long rather than short) became all important. The long-term result was much greater homogeneity in cultivated varieties.

Methods of cultivation

The diversity of cotton varieties was matched by local and regional differences in methods of growing it. As a crop, cotton was both capital and labour intensive; it depleted the soil and could not be grown without rotation. In the early nineteenth century, the usual custom was to intercrop it with grain or plant it in a small part of the landholding, with other crops occupying the remainder. Field rotation allowed the soil to replenish itself. Mixed cropping also acted as a form of insurance. If the rains were scanty

6 Cotton Report of 1847, HCPP, pp. 118–20.

7 House of Commons Parliamentary Papers, *East India (cotton), Further Return: Copy of Correspondence between the Secretary of State for India, and the Governor General or Other Persons in India, on the Subject of Cotton Cultivation in India, and the Prospects of Supplies of that Article to this Country during the year 1863* (hereafter Cotton Report of 1863, HCPP), p. 264.

8 Heyne, *Tracts Historical and Statistical*, p. 239.

and the grain crop failed, cotton would do relatively well; if the rains were heavy or fell at the wrong time (when the cotton was ready to pick, for example), the farmer could be reasonably sure of getting a good harvest of grain. Different crops required variable amounts of rain and ripened at different times, so mixed cropping reduced the risks of failure and ensured some return in all but the worst seasons.[9]

Cultivators were willing to take the risks associated with growing cotton, for they needed the cash obtained from selling it. This went into paying the land tax. Some part of the cotton might be spun into thread; this could be used to make clothing for the household or sold on the market. Cleaned cotton was also used for stuffing quilts and cotton thread for making wicks. The actual amount grown depended upon the cultivator's means. Prosperous or middling farmers grew more cotton, poor farmers and small landholders planted less. The whole household was involved in growing and harvesting the crop: children helped to pick cotton (and often to clean and spin it). The collector of Coimbatore described cotton cultivation as being 'peculiarly a family undertaking'.[10] The labour of women was integral to it: men ploughed the land but women did much of the sowing, weeding and harvesting.

Cotton-growing techniques ranged from slash-and-burn cultivation to more intensive methods involving many ploughings and the use of special tools like drills.[11] They varied by social group, soil quality and cotton variety. A prosperous farming household with many ploughs and fieldworkers would sow cotton over a large part of its holding, manure it well, and plough and weed it more often. Methods of cultivation also varied by region. In general, the Deccan was more advanced: farmers used drills for sowing and had better implements for weeding.[12] By contrast, broadcast sowing was widespread below the ghats in the Tamil country. Systematic manuring was practised only in some regions, by farmers who could afford to do so.[13]

[9] Select Committee Report, HCPP, p. 26; *The Baramahal Records*, Section IV: Products, pp. 106–7. For a discussion of cotton cultivation, also see Wendt, 'The Social Fabric', pp. 25–37; and Parthasarathi, *The Transition to a Colonial Economy*, pp. 43–77.

[10] Cotton Report of 1847, HCPP, p. 410.

[11] Parthasarathi classifies cotton cultivation as being either extensive or intensive. According to him, the intensive method was more expensive, but yielded greater returns. The actual method adopted depended upon the means of the cultivator. Parthasarathi, *The Transition to a Colonial Economy*, pp. 62–6. See Wendt, 'The Social Fabric', pp. 25–37, for a similar argument.

[12] Select Committee Report, HCPP, p. 37.

[13] For a more detailed description of cotton cultivation, see D.W. Karuna, 'Weaving Histories' (2014), pp. 100–4.

Cleaning of cotton

Cotton was cleaned in two stages. In the first, the seed was separated; this was followed by the removal of dust and other particles adhering to the fibre. The most widespread technique of separation involved the use of the churkha. This was a 'small mill, consisting of two horizontal cylinders moved by a perpetual screw, and turned by the hand; while a semi-cylindrical cavity behind forces back the cotton to the person who feeds the mill'.[14] A foot roller could also be used to separate the seed. A woman sat on a three-legged stool and rolled an iron rod, thicker in the middle than at the ends, over cotton spread on a granite slab with her feet. The seeds, pushed forward, fell in front of the stone while the cotton was pushed backwards under the stool. This technique was widespread in the Maratha country.[15] When extremely fine yarn had to be spun, the separation of the lint from the seed was done with a small iron rolling-pin; by this very laborious process, only fine fibres were collected.[16]

After this, the lint was cleaned, and its fibres separated and aligned using a bow. This was beaten with a mallet, causing the string (made of leather) to vibrate: this fluffed up the cotton and aligned its fibres. 'The bowstring separates the fibres far and wide, the cotton flies up into the air, and any impurity or dirt, heavier than cotton, fall apart to the ground.'[17] This was normally done just before spinning. In the Deccan, craftsmen called Dudekalas specialised in bowing cotton, but in many regions it was spinners who took over this stage of cleaning. Cotton could also be cleaned by spreading it on a cot and beating it with a stick: the dirt fell through the meshes of the cot on the ground below.[18] When fine yarn had to be spun, a finer string was used in place of the coarse leather thong of the bow. After this, the fibres were carded or disentangled by hand with the upper jawbone of a freshwater shark called 'walagu'.[19]

[14] Hamilton F. Buchanan, *A Journey from Madras through the Countries of Mysore, Canara and Malabar*, vol. 3 (London, T. Cadell and W. Davis, 1807), p. 317. See Plate 24.

[15] English East India Company, *Reports and Documents Connected with the Proceedings in Regard to the Culture and Manufacture of Cotton-wool, Raw Silk and Indigo in India* (London, 1836; hereafter EIC, *Report on Cotton-wool*), pp. 294–5.

[16] Havell, *Reports Submitted*, p. 25.

[17] EIC, *Report on Cotton-wool*, p. 294. See Plate 24.

[18] James Talboys Wheeler, *Madras versus America: Handbook to the Cotton Cultivation in the Madras Presidency* (New York, Virtue and Yorston, 1866), p. 20.

[19] Havell, *Reports Submitted*, p. 25. This process is still followed by workers who prepare and spin yarn for the famous Ponduru cloth of Andhra Pradesh. See http://www.sarisafari.com/tour/ponduru.html (accessed 19 April 2020).

Organisation of cleaning

Cotton cleaning formed part of the usual work of farming households. The seed comprised almost three fourth the weight of raw cotton; for this reason, it made little sense to transport unprocessed cotton to any great distance.[20] In addition, its high oil content made the seed a valuable source of cattle fodder. Thus, farmers preferred to clean as much of their cotton as possible. Some of it was used to spin thread for household use; the rest was sold. Much of the cleaning was done by members of the household, mostly women, although there is some evidence of male workers being hired when de-seeding had to be done in bulk. It was customary for women to bring a churkha with them when they got married. It was quite common for old women, unable to do heavy work, to clean cotton along with children.[21]

Cotton sold locally with the seed might be cleaned by spinners. Cleaning was seen as part of the normal work of spinning and most of it was done by women.[22] In rare cases, raw cotton with the seed was transported long distances for cleaning. This was reportedly the case with cotton used to make fine Chanderi cloths: the process of cleaning and spinning its yarn required a high degree of skill.[23]

Not all cotton was processed by farmers and spinners. Merchants also hired workers to clean cotton, especially in large cotton markets. In the bazaar of Kosee near Agra, where cotton was exported to Calcutta, 400 to 500 churkha workers could be seen along the roadside.[24] There are similar descriptions from the Deccan as well.[25] These workers owned their own churkhas and were paid a piece-rate for a fixed quantity of cotton cleaned.[26] An American planter in Tirunelveli reported that there were men whose only job was to run churkha houses where cotton was cleaned.[27] There

[20] EIC, *Report on Cotton-wool*, p. 199; Cotton Report of 1847, HCPP, p. 395.

[21] Select Committee Report, HCPP, p. 253; Cotton Report of 1847, pp. 53, 63, 419; Cotton Report of 1863, HCPP, p. 264.

[22] Buchanan, *A Journey from Madras*, vol. 2, p. 221.

[23] Cotton Report of 1847, HCPP, pp. 120, 201–2.

[24] Cotton Report of 1847, HCPP, p. 118.

[25] Select Committee Report, HCPP, p. 38, Buchanan, *A Journey from Madras*, vol. 3, p. 317.

[26] EIC, *Report on Cotton-wool*; Amalendu Jha, 'Raw Cotton of Western India: 1750–1850', *The Indian Economic and Social History Review*, 9(1) (1972), 1–41, at 16–17.

[27] House of Commons Parliamentary Papers, East India (cotton), *Return to an Order of the Honourable House of Commons, Dated 24 August 1857 for a Selection of Papers Showing, the Measures Taken since 1847 to Promote the Cultivation of Cotton in India* (hereafter, Cotton Report of 1857, HCPP), pp. 198, 203. This may have been a nineteenth-century development in Tirunelveli; it was only from the beginning of the century that large quantities of cotton began to be exported from the region to China.

is some evidence to show that cotton processing by merchants increased during the nineteenth century thanks to a growing export market.

Household processing fetched a gain reflected in the higher price of cleaned cotton: the notional wages of the women doing this work were subsumed in the household's income. By contrast, workers hired to clean cotton had to be paid a wage. Wendt, after comparing a range of figures, concludes that a moderate monthly wage for a woman cleaning cotton full-time was around 0.44 to 0.66 pagodas on average.[28] Most women did not do this work full-time and their earnings were seasonal; yet, along with earnings from spinning, they formed a substantial part of the household income. The cleaning and spinning of cotton was usually done in the dry season when there was little or no agricultural work, making it doubly useful as a source of supplementary income.

Cleaned cotton reached the weaver in a variety of ways. The shortest and most direct was when a farmer had cotton cleaned and spun in his own household, with the yarn being given to a weaver to make cloth. Other routes were longer; sometimes cotton might pass through many hands before reaching the weaver. Complex circuits involving farmers, merchants, spinners and weavers have already been described, but two points made by Wendt are worth reiterating. Cotton merchants were distinct from cloth merchants, for the sale of these two commodities was largely separated. And even where cotton travelled long distances, it was usually sold in small quantities to spinners.[29]

Spinning in the early nineteenth century

The most widely used method of spinning cotton involved the spinning wheel (Plate 25). In Coimbatore, a kind of distaff was also reported to be in use, 'a bobbin which they turn on the knee'. Even children could spin.[30] In and around Bangalore, where cotton was imported

> at the weekly markets, the cotton wool is bought up in small quantities by the poor women of all casts [*sic*], except the Brahmans; for these never spin, nor do their husband ever plough the soil. The women of all other casts spin, and at weekly markets sell to the weavers the thread that is not wanted for family use.[31]

[28] Wendt, 'The Social Fabric', pp. 98–105.
[29] Wendt, 'The Social Fabric', pp. 108–14. For the Banjara trade in cotton during the seventeenth century, see Brennig, 'Textile Producers and Production', 335–8.
[30] Select Committee Report, HCPP, p. 195.
[31] Buchanan, A *Journey from Madras,* vol. 1, p. 218. There are similar descriptions from other places. Buchanan, *A Journey from Madras*, vol. 3, p. 317. For another example, see *The Baramahal Records,* Section IV: Products, p. 59.

Spinning was an important part of household work; women picked it up whenever they had a 'free' minute. Even women from communities not primarily associated with agriculture spun yarn. This was true of the Koravas who were involved in long-distance trade, carrying grain, salt, cotton and other commodities on pack-cattle; they were a mobile group, travelling with their families. Amongst the Shanars (Nadars) of the Tirunelveli region, the men were 'almost all "climbers" of the palmyra ... [and] the women are generally employed in spinning thread for the coarse cloth of the country'.[32] Labourers hired to pick cotton were often paid in kind; it is likely that this cotton was cleaned and spun for sale in markets.[33]

Weaving was marked by diverse supply chains. In some regions, farmers took yarn spun in the household to a weaver in order to make cloth. Other weavers bought yarn from spinners: by offering advances they could obtain an assured supply of yarn and keep track of its quality and price. The weavers of Tiruchengode in the Baramahals got yarn more cheaply than their counterparts in Mallasamudram, who could not advance money to spinners.[34] The full-time weaver required a good deal of yarn of uniform thickness, and not all of this could be provided by a single spinner. Fine cloth weavers had to be particularly watchful while buying yarn: the weavers of Chanderi selected yarn of uniform fineness from different spinners.[35]

There is abundant evidence of spinners acting as buyers of cotton and sellers of yarn. Around Bangalore, women bought cotton in small quantities to spin and sell at weekly markets: this is specifically described as being 'the thread that is not wanted for family use'.[36] In the Baramahal region, several hundred weavers bought thread at these markets. Attempts to prevent the sale of yarn by farmers and spinners in the local market in order to divert supply to weavers working for the EIC led to protests.[37] Yarn markets are described as follows: 'Pariahs, poor wives and spinners ... spin [cotton] into yarn and bring it to the market for sale; there it is taken up by the weavers in various quantities, as each desires or has need.'[38] Joseph Brennig shows

[32] Journal of Bishop Spencer quoted in Pascoe, *Two Hundred Years*, p. 536. Also, Caldwell's memoirs, USPG X Series, no. 1085, Archives of the Society for the Propagation of the Gospel in Foreign Parts, Rhodes House Library, Oxford.
[33] *The Baramahal Records*, Section IV: Products, p. 34; Cotton Report of 1857, HCPP, p. 161.
[34] *The Baramahal Records*, Section VII: Imposts, pp. 17, 23.
[35] Cotton Report of 1847, HCPP, pp. 134–6.
[36] Buchanan, *A Journey from Madras*, vol. 1, p. 218.
[37] *The Baramahal Records*, Section VII: Imposts, pp. 28–9.
[38] Quoted in Wendt, 'The Social Fabric', p. 177.

that merchants were not involved in providing yarn to weavers but only contracted with them for cloth, for which cash had to be advanced.[39]

It has been suggested that some merchants operated a kind of putting-out system, employing women to spin thread, perhaps for export.[40] This cannot be ruled out, but it was rare in comparison with the direct sale and purchase of yarn. Elijah Hoole describes this scene in a village near Pondicherry (Puducherry):

> I walked into [a man's] house and found several women employed in spinning a coarse description of cotton, and another winding the yarn off the cop into hank. He told me that they received raw cotton from their employer, a native manufacturer, and returned it in hank, their delivering the whole being ascertained by weight.[41]

It is not clear whether the 'manufacturer' was a weaver or a merchant. But Wendt's contention that merchants do not appear to have been involved to any great extent in the production and sale of yarn seems to hold true. This process was largely restricted to spinners and weavers, whether mediated through the marketplace or relationships of credit.[42]

Women in most households spun thread, but certain regions and communities were renowned for their skill in making specialised thread. Chief among them were the Pariar. Weavers' settlements along the coast often contained hamlets of Pariar spinners. They were regarded as the most skilled of all; very fine yarn was usually made by them.[43] In Chanderi in central India, cotton was cleaned and made into thread by the 'Ballaees (outcastes) whose males make the finest of the thread employed in Indian fabrics'.[44] Similarly, in the region around Nagpur in Central India the finest thread was spun by the Dhers, the social equivalent of Pariars.[45]

Some yarn was transported long distances, mostly from districts where cotton was grown to weaving centres without a source of supply of equivalent quality closer by. For example, cotton thread travelled from Coimbatore to Palghat.[46] Silk and gold thread, along with the best quality

[39] Brennig, 'Textile Producers and Production', p. 351.
[40] Parthasarathi, *The Transition to a Colonial Economy*, p. 60.
[41] Hoole, *Madras, Mysore and the South of India*, pp. 247–8.
[42] Wendt, 'The Social Fabric', p. 141.
[43] Buchanan, *A Journey from Madras*, vol. 2, p. 263. There are references to skilled Pariar spinners in Wendt, 'The Social Fabric', pp. 141, 169.
[44] Cotton Report of 1847, p. 203.
[45] HCPP, East India (Cotton), *A Copy of the Report of Mr. H. Rivett-Carnac, Cotton Commissioner for the Centrap Provinces and Berars, on the Operations of his Department for the Year 1867*, pp. 58–9.
[46] PBR vol. 369, no. 43, 23 January 1804, p. 980, TNSA.

Plate 1

A man's garment (dhoti or veshti) in cotton, apparently unbleached. Worn by an agricultural group called 'burghers'. The cloth is of coarse quality with the ends (shorter sides) woven with strips of red and blue. Obtained from Coimbatore. The length is 5 yards and 9 inches; width, 1 yard; weight, 3 lbs. and 1 oz. Price not stated. No. 80, Forbes Watson collection.

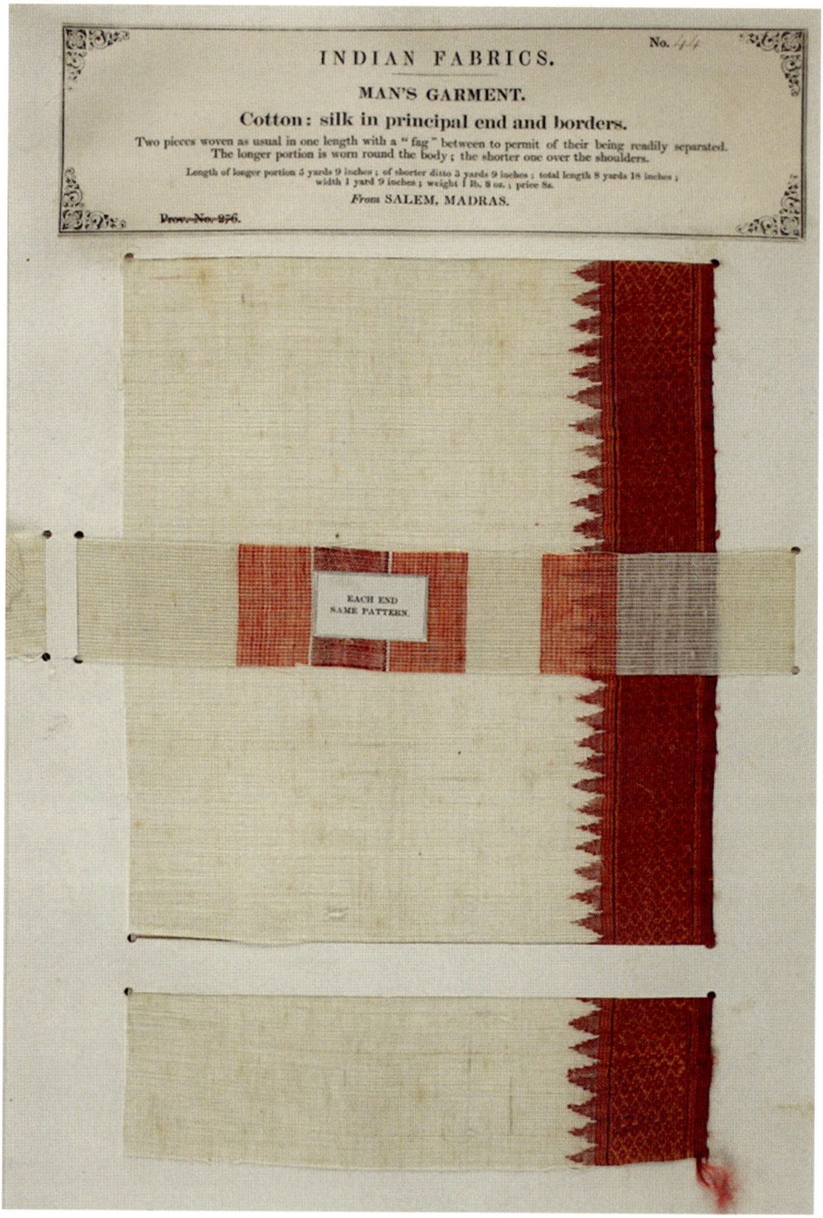

Plate 2

A man's garment in cotton consisting of two pieces of cloth woven with a fag in between, allowing them to be separated easily. One piece to be used as a lower garment (dhoti/veshti), the other to be thrown around the shoulders (angavastram). The cloth is moderately fine, with silk used in the red border (longer side), which is woven in the 'gopuram' (temple tower) pattern. Obtained from Salem, a weaving centre famous for men's cloths. The length is 8 yards and 18 inches; width, 1 yard and 9 inches; weight, 1 lb. and 8 oz. Price: 8 shillings. No. 44, Forbes Watson collection.

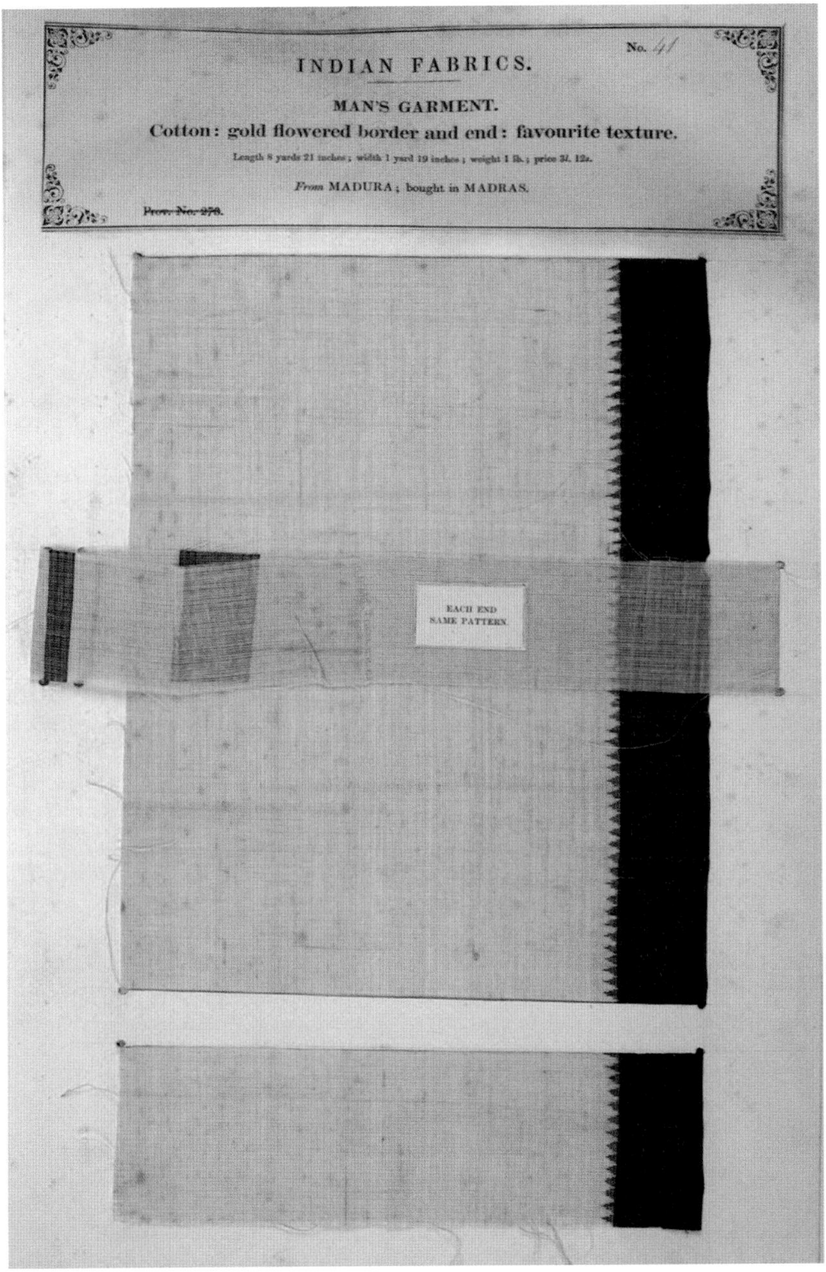

Plate 3

A man's garment (dhoti/veshti) in cotton. Of fine texture, with a finely woven red and black border in the 'rudraksh' (a seed used to make prayer beads) and 'gopuram' patterns. Embellished with zari (gold wire). Obtained from Madurai, a town well-known for fine textiles. The length is 8 yards and 21 inches; width, 1 yard and 19 inches; weight, 1 lb. Price: 3 pounds and 12 shillings. No. 41, Forbes Watson collection.

Plate 4

A man's garment (lungi) in cotton worn by the Lubbay (a Muslim group). These were also exported, especially to south-east Asia. This piece was made in Pulicat, near Madras. The length is 3 yards and 18 inches; width, 1 yard and 2 inches; weight 1 lb., 1 oz. Price: 3 shillings. No. 65, Forbes Watson collection.

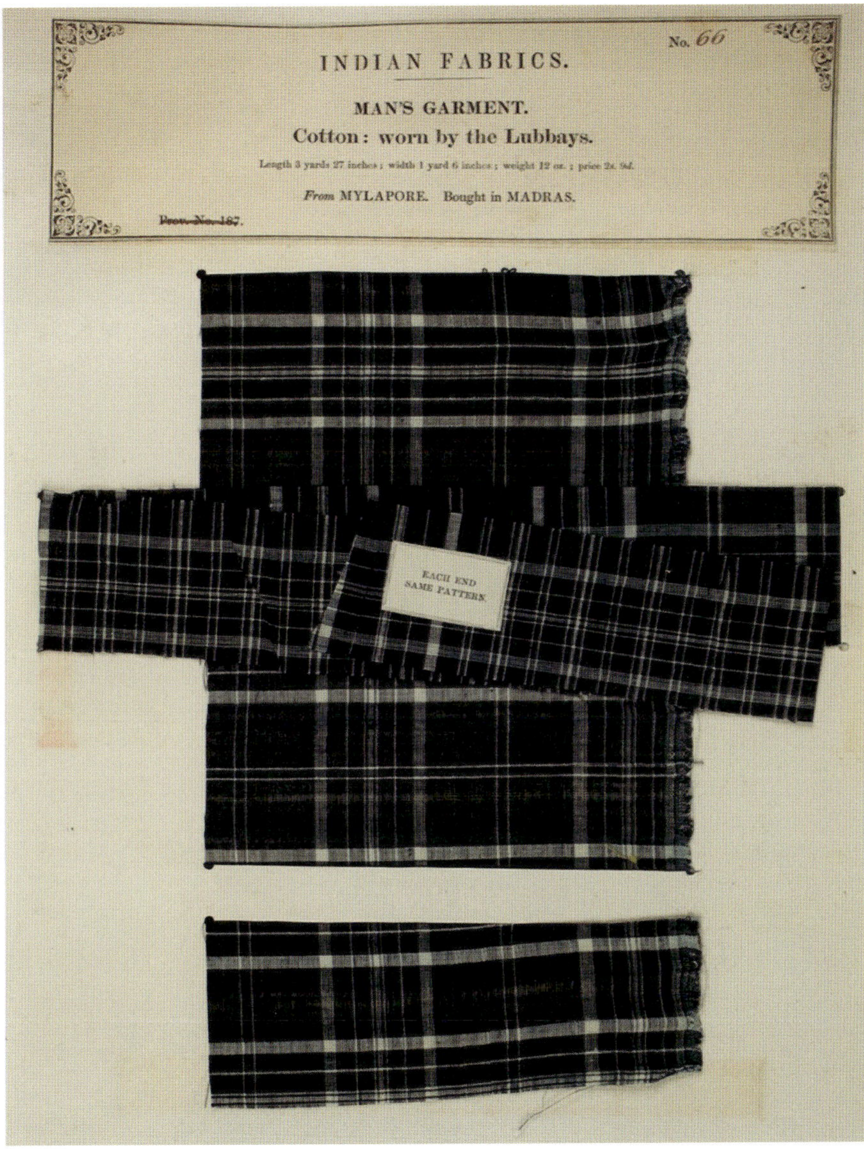

Plate 5

A man's garment (lungi) in cotton worn by the Lubbay (a Muslim group). These were also exported, especially to south-east Asia. This piece was made in Mylapore, Madras. The length is 3 yards and 27 inches; width, 1 yard and 6 inches; weight, 12 oz. Price: 2 shillings and 2 pence. No. 66, Forbes Watson collection.

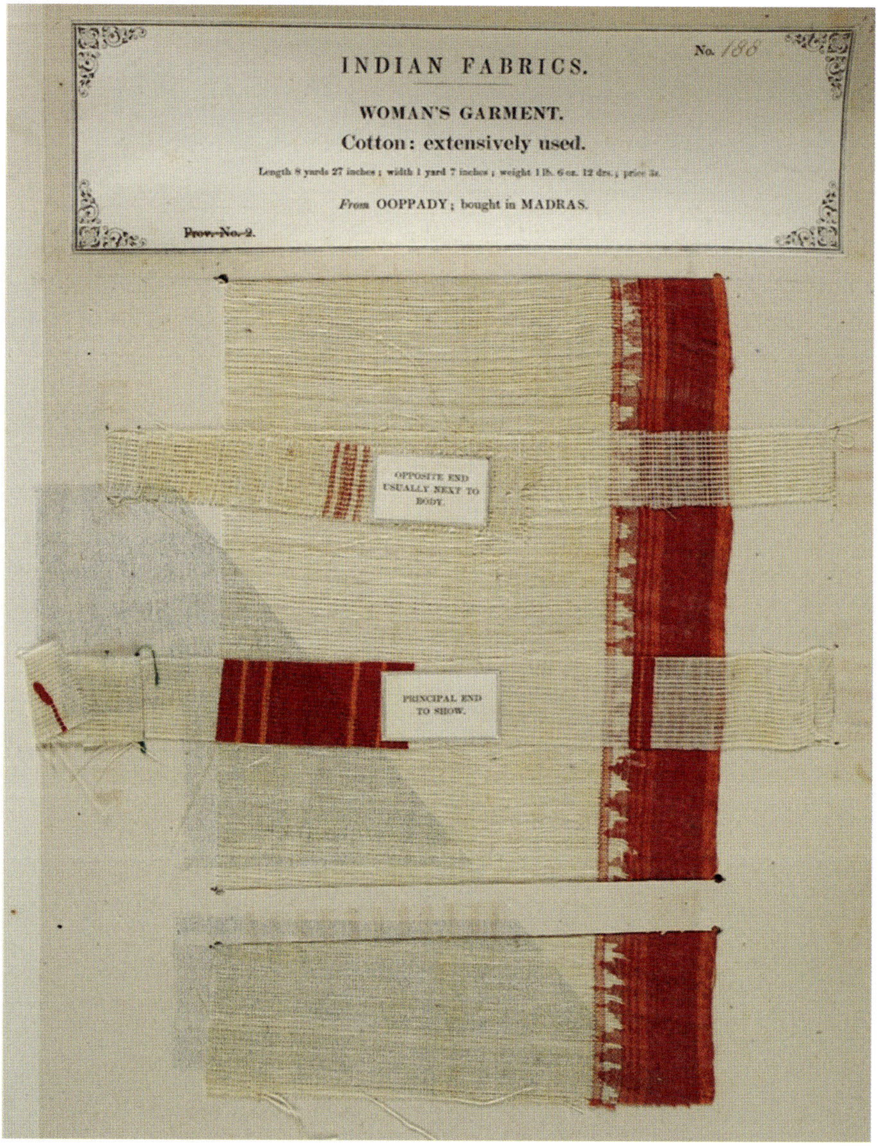

Plate 6

A woman's garment (sari) in cotton. Fairly coarse. Its body is plain with an orange and red border. Produced in large numbers and extensively worn. Made in Ooppada. The length is 8 yards and 27 inches; width, 1 yard and 7 inches; weight, 1 lb. and 6 oz. Price: 3 shillings. No. 188, Forbes Watson collection.

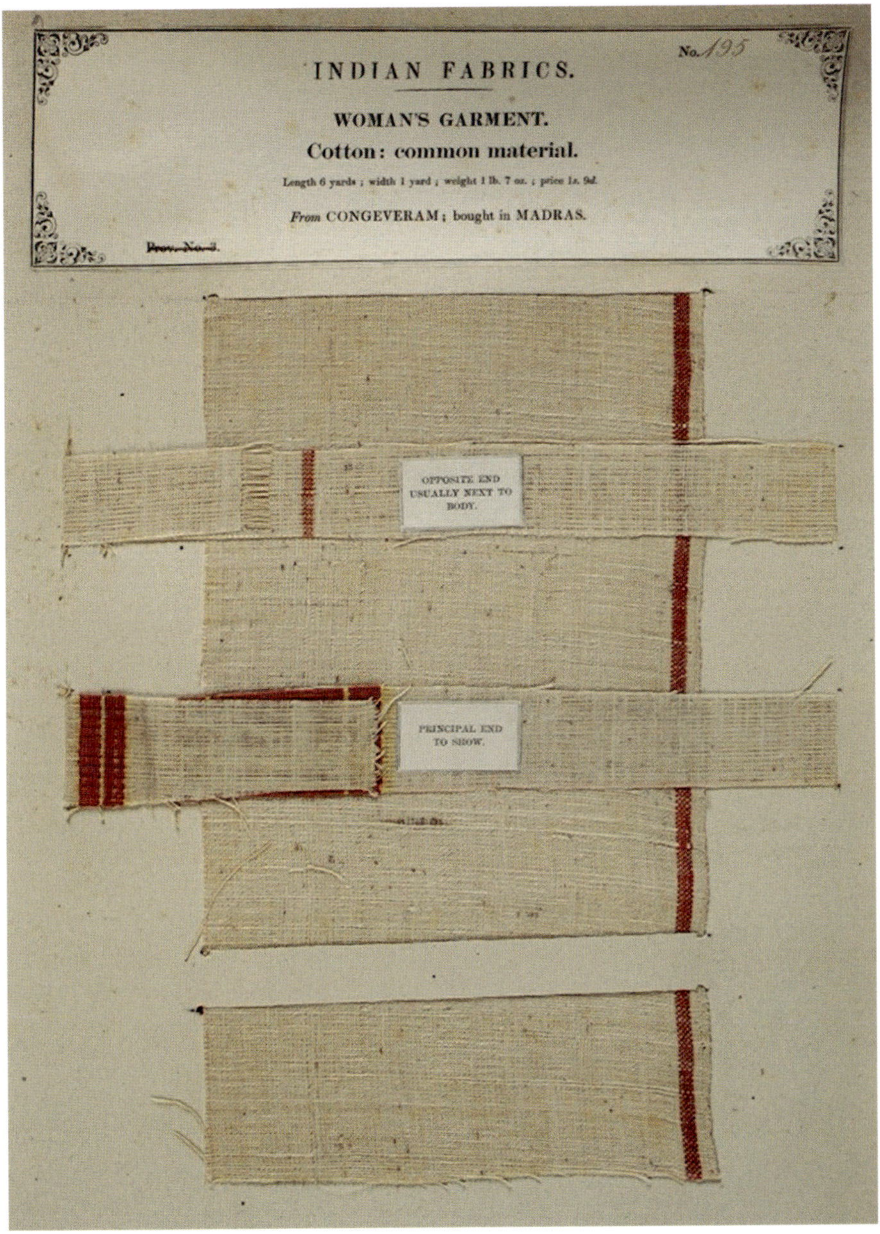

Plate 7

A woman's garment (sari) in cotton. Described as being of 'common material'. Plain and coarse in texture, with a thin red border. Made in Kanchipuram. The length is 6 yards; width, 1 yard; weight, 1 lb. and 7 oz. Price: 1 shilling and 9 pence. No. 195, Forbes Watson collection.

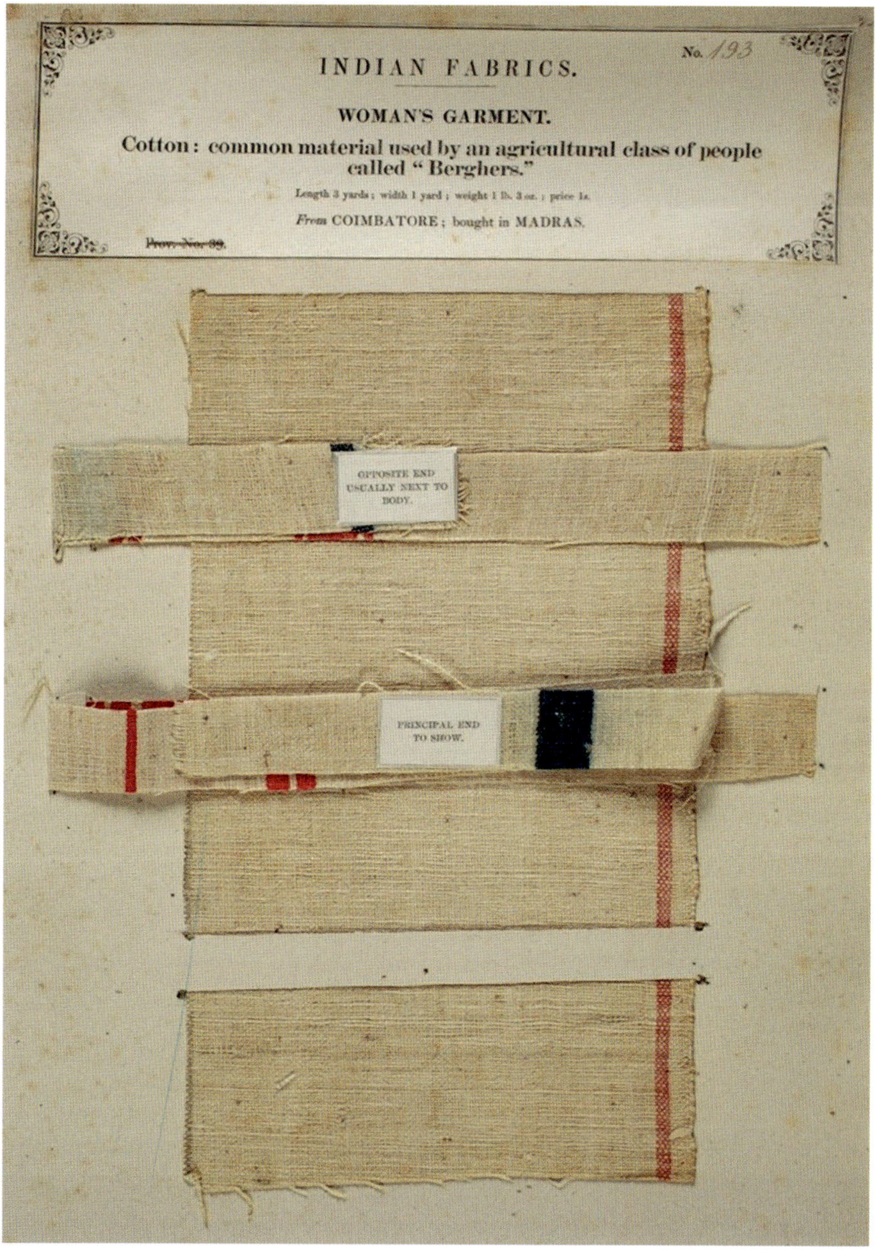

Plate 8

A woman's garment in cotton. The material is coarse and plain, with a thin red border along the length of the cloth. One of the ends is blue. Much smaller than a normal sari. Made of 'common material' and 'used by [an] agricultural class of people called "Berghers"'. The length is only 3 yards; width, 1 yard; weight 1 lb. 3 oz. Price: 1 shilling. Made in Coimbatore. No. 193, Forbes Watson collection.

Plate 9

A woman's garment (sari) in fine cotton interwoven with silk at one end (called the pallu: this shows uppermost when the garment is worn). It has a large border with a fairly intricate design. The length is 7 yards and 27 inches; width, 1 yard and 2 inches; weight, 1 lb. and 7 oz. Price: 12 shillings. Made in Cuddalore. No. 179, Forbes Watson collection.

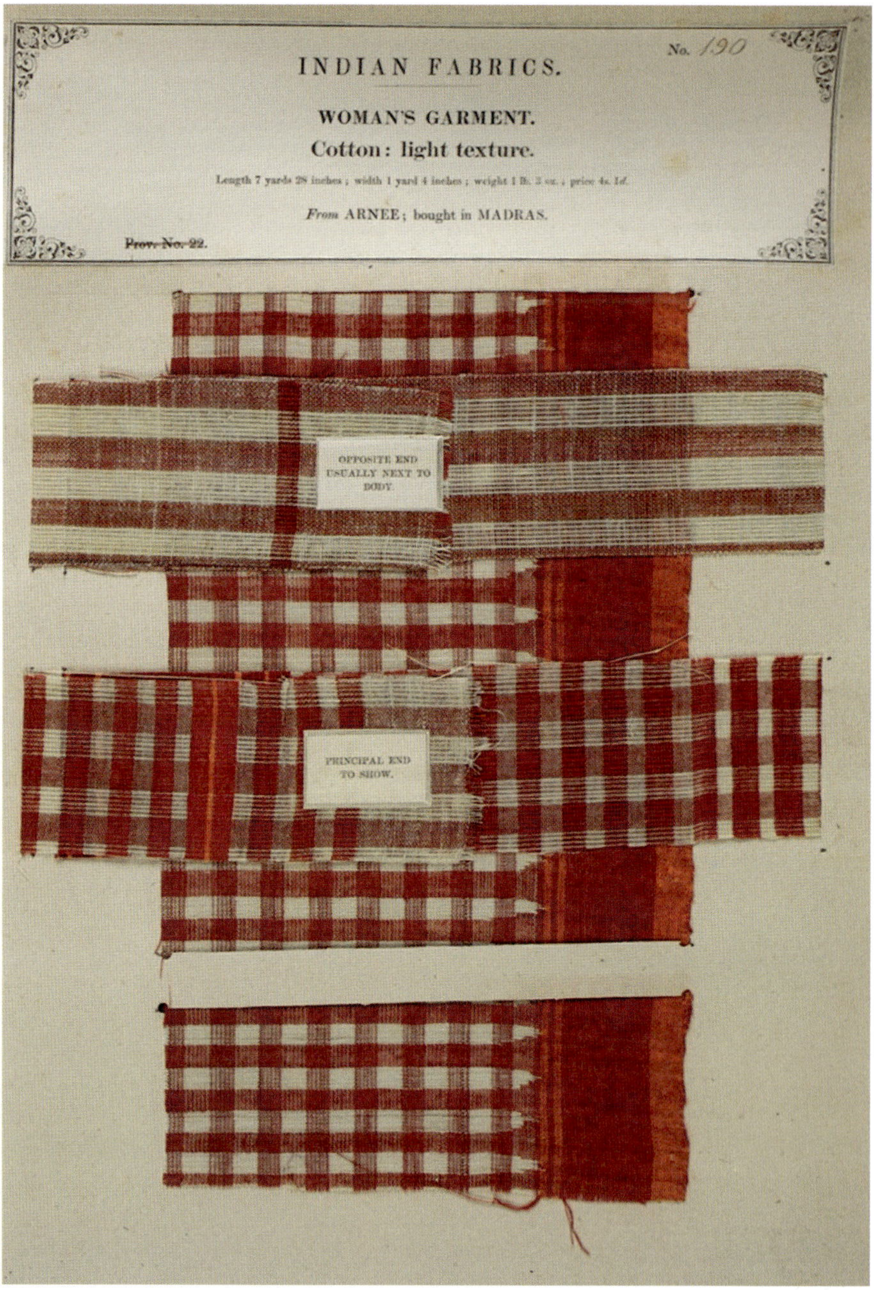

Plate 10

A woman's garment (sari) in cotton. Of moderate quality. Woven in a chequered pattern with a simple border. Described as light in texture (or loosely woven). The length is 7 yards and 28 inches; width, 1 yard and 4 inches; weight, 1 lb. and 3 oz. Price: 4 shillings and 1 penny. Made in Arani. No. 190, Forbes Watson collection.

Plate 11

A woman's garment (sari) in cotton. Made in a striped pattern with a solid border and fairly densely woven. The length is 7 yards; width, 1 yard; weight, 1 lb. and 10 oz. Price: 2 shillings and 3 pence. Made in Bellary. No. 187, Forbes Watson collection.

Plate 12

A very fine cotton sari from Madurai, dyed in distinctive dark red, using a tie and dye technique that produced a pattern of neat spots. Zari (gold wire) is used in the borders and at one end (the pallu). Patterns: rudraksh and gopuram. Price: 1 pound and 14 shillings. IS. 1780–1883, © Victoria and Albert Museum, London.

Plate 13

A fine cotton turban, with some silk used at one end, and a border in zari (gold wire) neatly woven in the rudraksh pattern. The length is 3 yards and 18 inches; width, 3 yards and 9 inches; weight, 1 lb. and 11 oz. Price: 2 pounds, 15 shillings and 3 pence. Made in Coimbatore. No. 39, Forbes Watson collection.

Plate 14

Piece goods. A coarse, plain, densely woven cloth called 'dungary'. This had many uses. The length is 11 yards; width, 23 inches; weight, 2 lbs. and 6 oz. Price: 2 shillings. Made in Salem. No. 474, Forbes Watson collection.

Plate 15

Piece goods. A cotton cloth of fine texture, printed in black and red, with contrasting colour and pattern at one end. Possibly for use as a turban or handkerchief. The length is 4 yards and 18 inches; width, 1 yard; weight, 15 oz. Price: 4 shillings. Made in Madras. No. 371, Forbes Watson collection.

Plate 16

Piece goods. Cotton neck kerchief used to cover the head and shoulders. Of fine texture with a glaze created by rubbing "chank" shells over the cloth. The length is 1 yard; width, 1 yard; weight, 3 oz. Price: 7 and a half pence. Made in Ventapollum. No. 363, Forbes Watson collection.

of red cotton yarn, was imported *into* the Coimbatore region.[47] Yarn from Bellary and Kadapa was sold in the southern Deccan, especially the region around Bangalore.[48] However, it was mostly coarser yarn that was transported in this fashion; fine yarn was usually bought from local spinners.[49] Thread from distant places was sold by merchants in weekly markets.[50]

Earnings from spinning

Wendt calculates the value added by spinners to a finished piece of cloth: most of them were paid in cash and their labour contribution formed the largest part by value of the finished product. Value added in converting cleaned cotton into thread was 63.4 per cent of the final price for coarse to middling cloths and 87.6 per cent for fine cloths.[51] The cost of yarn formed by far the weaver's biggest outlay and the most significant element of the final price of *any* piece of cloth. This does not imply that spinners earned high wages: payments were low and spread out, for it took several spinners to produce enough yarn for a single weaver.

Wages varied largely by fineness of thread. Wendt puts together data from different sources to arrive at some averages: during the seventeenth and eighteenth centuries, workers spinning coarse thread full-time earned 0.44 pagodas a month on average and those making fine thread earned 0.73 pagodas.[52] Women might earn 5.5 pagodas or 20 rupees a year; they contributed anywhere between a third to a half of a household's annual income. Households headed by women (mostly widows) were often reliant wholly upon spinning. These earnings were critical especially during times of dearth or famine, even for those who spun part-time. The importance of spinning for farming households is confirmed by Munro: 'It is from

[47] Buchanan, *A Journey from Madras*, vol. 2, p. 263.
[48] Buchanan, *A Journey from Madras*, vol. 1, pp. 198, 213.
[49] Wendt, 'The Social Fabric', pp. 177–9.
[50] Buchanan, *A Journey from Madras*, vol. 1, p. 213.
[51] This is calculated by subtracting the value of cotton and wastage from the value of the thread produced. Ian Wendt, 'Four Centuries of Decline? Understanding the Changing Structure of the South Indian Textile Industry', in Giorgio Riello and Tirthankar Roy (eds), *How India Clothed the World* (Leiden, Brill, 2009), pp. 193–215; also Wendt, 'The Social Fabric', pp. 144–57.
[52] Wendt, 'The Social Fabric', pp. 155–6.

the produce of their grain *and thread* chiefly that they are enabled to pay their rent.'[53]

To sum up: cloth making involved not just weavers but a very large number of spinners and farmers. In the United States, the cultivation and processing of cotton was intensive and exclusive—it was grown on plantations utilising slave labour or full-time workers. In South India, it formed part of a diversified agricultural cycle and everyday work rhythms. A very large proportion of this work was done by women; whether unpaid or underpaid, it made a significant contribution to the household's income, for spinning was a key stage in the making of cloth, where the greatest value was added.

A supposedly external transformation was to have a decisive impact on the world of weaving in the Indian subcontinent. It has been argued that the labour-intensive nature of spinning represented a bottleneck in the production process and was the trigger for technological innovation in Britain's mill industry.[54] Robert Allen argues that a generalised rise in spinners' wages provided a key incentive for mechanisation. However, John Styles, in his fascinating analysis of cotton weaving in the Lancashire region when the spinning jenny was invented, attributes mechanisation to a local convergence of several factors: a growing demand for Blackburn greys (a plain cloth made with linen warp and cotton weft); the nature of the putting out system and the organisation of household labour; a shortage of spinners for cotton; and the dependence upon long-staple cotton from the Americas rather than cotton from the Levant.[55] This local convergence was embedded in the rhythms of global capitalism dominated by the trade in textiles. In turn, it meshed with colonialism to produce cascading effects on every single aspect of cloth production—from cotton cultivation to spinning and weaving—in India.

[53] *The Baramahal Records*, Section VII: Imposts, p. 28. Italics mine.

[54] See John Styles, 'Fibres, Yarns and the Invention of the Spinning Jenny', paper presented at the World Economic History Congress, Boston, MA, 29 July–3 August 2018.

[55] Styles, 'Fibres, Yarns'. To sum up: Blackburn greys were made with cotton, not wool or linen; the cotton was imported from America (therefore long-staple); there was a shortage of cotton spinners (because local spinners favoured wool, which paid better); therefore the weft thread had to be spun by women and children in the weaver's household. Together, they offered ample incentives for a mechanised solution represented by the spinning jenny. Originally, this was a machine designed to improve the productivity of household labour. Later, it fed into mechanisation on a very different scale.

Changes in cotton cultivation and marketing: the early period

The 'improvement' and expansion of cotton cultivation

As early as the eighteenth century, when the focus of the EIC was on exporting cloth from India, anxieties about the supply of cotton began to be expressed. The objective was to gain firmer control over the supply of cotton and yarn, and some attempts towards this were made at the time. The rise of Britain's mill industry altered the situation and led to a sharp decline in profits from textile exports; the EIC's focus gradually shifted from exporting cloth to exporting cotton. The result was a concerted attempt to intervene in the growing of the crop itself.

From roughly the turn of the century, the EIC had been exporting raw cotton to China.[56] There were expectations that India might become a supplier of cotton to the mill industries of Lancashire and Manchester as well. The major obstacle lay in the fact that nearly all the cotton grown in India was short in staple. Machines in British factories had been designed to spin long-staple cotton; they were less efficient in processing short-staple varieties.[57] In addition, Indian cotton contained various impurities and its natural colour was considered less desirable than that of American cotton. Mill owners sought suitable improvements in Indian cotton in order to reduce their dependence upon American imports—partly as a result of their representations, the Indian government began taking a keener interest in cotton cultivation. The basic idea was to encourage varieties of cotton suited for export to Britain.

Calls for state intervention fluctuated, reaching a peak whenever supplies from the American market were threatened. In 1834–5, the American crop failed; the result was an increase in the demand for Indian cotton.[58] Demands for intervention peaked just before and during the American Civil War, when English mills were abruptly cut off from their main source of supply (the so-called cotton famine of the 1860s). Representations called for

[56] Tan Chung, 'The Britain–China–India Trade Triangle (1771–1840)', *The Indian Economic and Social History Review*, 11(4) (1974), 411–31.

[57] The spinning jenny was successful with long-stapled American cotton, but not with short-stapled cotton from the Levant. See Styles, 'Fibres, Yarns'. Shambu Prasad and Bilgrami also note that mill machinery was designed for long-stapled American cotton; mill owners rejected short-stapled cotton as inferior, ignoring its other qualities like greater strength and absorbency. Length of staple was seen as the sole measure of quality. Prasad, 'Suicide Deaths'; Menon and Bilgrami, *A Frayed History*, pp. 27–80.

[58] Sarada Raju, *Economic Conditions in the Madras Presidency 1800–1850* (Madras, University of Madras, 1941), p. 211.

changes in land tenure and land revenue, improved public works (railways and roads), better irrigation and legal backing for contract enforcement: all in the interests of exporting cotton to Britain.[59]

Measures to 'improve' cotton also involved the introduction of exotic varieties. This attempt formed part of a much larger process of collecting information about local crops and production processes in order to find ways of tapping into them and generating revenues. Many of the EIC's administrators, especially in the medical service, were naturalists with a personal interest in investigating new crops and products: they joined this process enthusiastically or were recruited into it.[60] Dr. Anderson, a surgeon, promoted all manner of industrial crops including cotton. As early as the 1790s, he was distributing cotton seeds from Malta and Mauritius to cultivators in the Madras Presidency.[61]

In the first decade of the nineteenth century, a private merchant by the name of Hughes successfully introduced Bourbon cotton into Tirunelveli district. This came to be called Hughes' Tinnevelly cotton; much of it was exported to China and Britain. Bourbon cotton also took root in the Coimbatore region. In the beginning, it enjoyed little favour with farmers; the oil content of the seed was low, which meant it could not be used as fodder, and the fibre was too fine for local spinners, who were used to cotton of coarser texture.[62] Export demand fluctuated widely and export prices were not much more remunerative than those for indigenous cotton. The main advantage of Bourbon cotton lay in its higher yields, and in the end it came to be cultivated over a considerable acreage. By the 1840s, it had hybridised with local varieties.

Experimental cotton farms were first set up in 1819, and again between 1840 and 1853, with the aim of growing exotic varieties and encouraging

[59] John Dickinson, *Address to the Members of the House of Commons on the Relation between the Cotton Crisis and Public Works in India* (London, P. S. King, 1862), pp. 5–6. For an analysis of the pressure exerted by Manchester factory owners and the responses of governments in Britain and India, see Peter Harnetty, 'India and British Commercial Enterprise: the Case of the Manchester Cotton Company, 1860–64', *The Indian Economic and Social History Review*, 3(4) (1966), 396–421.

[60] Maxine Berg, following Joel Mokyr, argues that these attempts formed part of a process of creating 'useful knowledge' that gained momentum during the eighteenth century; it embodied the convergence of commercial interests with the curiosity and personal interests of naturalists. Maxine Berg, 'Passionate Projectors: Savants and Silk on the Coromandel Coast, 1780–98', *Journal of Colonialism and Colonial History*, 14(3) (2013), https://muse.jhu.edu/article/524454, (accessed 27 May 2020).

[61] Wheeler, *Madras versus America*, p. 28

[62] Cotton Report of 1847, HCPP, p. 52.

farmers to adopt them.[63] The first attempts were unsuccessful; the American cotton plant was not suited to the black cotton soils of the subcontinent (although it took time for American planters, hired to run these farms, to realise this).[64] When grown in red soils, it proved more vulnerable to drought and disease than indigenous varieties.[65] Its shallow roots could not cope with prolonged dry spells; local varieties, albeit more stunted, had deeper roots that allowed them to survive during times of drought. American cotton also attracted more pests.[66]

Yields from American seeds were higher, but so were the chances of crop failure. Farmers preferred smaller, more reliable harvests to bumper crops with a high ratio of failure. Despite these handicaps, and principally because of their yield advantage, American varieties gained popularity in some districts like Coimbatore and Dharwar, and gradually became acclimatised to Indian conditions.[67] It was this acclimatised seed stock that was to be taken up for widespread propagation.

Attempts to promote American cotton during this period also failed for structural reasons. Cotton cultivation was labour and capital intensive; it depleted the soil and its harvests were unpredictable. Cotton was not much more profitable than grain to grow; however, unlike grain, it provided cash earnings and additional employment (from spinning). This produced a complex structure of incentives and disincentives. Farmers preferred to grow it as part of a diversified crop mix and local methods of cultivation took shape in this context.

American cotton required new methods: frequent, deep ploughing with heavy ploughs that needed larger oxen to pull them, more intensive weeding and careful picking at regular intervals. Taken together they involved a considerable increase in farming costs (four to five times greater than average, according to one estimate).[68] Lacking a dependable market, uncertain of getting a higher price and faced with the spectre of crop

[63] See Wheeler, *Madras versus America*, for reports on these experiments. Also, Seth Leacock and David G. Mandelbaum, 'A Nineteenth Century Development Project in India: the Cotton Improvement Program', *Economic Development and Cultural Change*, 3(4) (July 1955), 334–51.

[64] Cotton Report of 1847, HCPP, p. 390; Wheeler, *Madras versus America*, p. 64.

[65] Wheeler, *Madras versus America*, p. 51.

[66] Cotton Report of 1847, HCPP, p. 363.

[67] Select Committee Report, HCPP, pp. 60–1.

[68] Cotton Report of 1847, HCPP, pp. 369, 372; Wheeler, *Madras versus America*, p. 42. Some American planters opined that traditional methods were well suited to indigenous cotton; there was no need to teach farmers new ones. Wheeler, *Madras versus America*, p. 34.

failure, farmers proved unwilling to bear these costs in order to obtain bigger yields.[69]

British mills favoured American cotton, buying Indian cotton only when it was in short supply. Export prices of Indian cotton (and American varieties grown in India) were linked to those of American cotton and fluctuated widely.[70] Observers pointed out that there was little difference in the export prices of indigenous and foreign varieties or indeed between clean and dirty cotton. Thus, the Indian farmer had little incentive to grow foreign varieties or clean cotton more effectively.[71]

American cotton found few buyers in the domestic market, adding to its risks. Local spinners found it unsuitable for hand spinning; weavers asserted that it did not produce strong, durable cloth.[72] It could not be cleaned using the churkha or the foot roller, for the seeds were softer and got crushed during the process. The farmer was forced to sell raw cotton with the seed; nothing could be kept back for household consumption.[73] The seeds were regarded as unsuitable for fodder.[74]

Attempts to introduce new technologies for cleaning were made, but the American saw gin proved unsuitable for indigenous varieties of cotton.[75] It required a large investment that paid for itself only when the machine was worked continuously. The cost was beyond the reach of the ordinary farmer in contrast to the churkha, a simple tool found in almost every rural household. Transporting cotton with the seed to a ginning factory was three times more expensive than carrying de-seeded cotton to market.[76] It took several decades and many experiments before gins suitable for indigenous cotton could be fabricated.[77]

[69] Cotton Report of 1847, HCPP, p. 413. Some planters declared there was nothing they could teach farmers about growing indigenous varieties. It took others years to appreciate the utility of traditional cotton cultivation. Wheeler, *Madras versus America*, p. 63; Cotton Report of 1847, HCPP, p. 408.

[70] Select Committee Report, HCPP, pp. 25, 72–3.

[71] Wheeler, *Madras versus America*, pp. 31–2.

[72] Cotton Report of 1857, HCPP, pp. 233, 238–9; Wheeler, *Madras versus America*, p. 196.

[73] Cotton Report of 1857, HCPP, pp. 238–9.

[74] Cotton Report of 1857, HCPP, pp. 77–8, 86; Wheeler, *Madras versus America*, p. 207.

[75] Cotton Report of 1847, HCPP, p. 6; Cotton Report of 1857, HCPP, p. 193.

[76] Wheeler *Madras versus America*, pp. 57, 207. An American planter pointed out that where cotton was grown and cleaned using slave labour, time was money and it made sense to invest in time-saving, capital-intensive machinery. In India, there were plenty of workers idle for several months of the year: investing in a gin or paying money to get cotton ginned made little economic sense under the circumstances.

[77] See Wheeler, *Madras versus America*, for details of some of these attempts.

Mill owners in Britain complained constantly about the dirt adhering to Indian cotton. For cotton to remain clean, it had to be picked as soon as the pod broke. This necessitated frequent picking (with household or hired labour) and raised costs of production. Indian farmers preferred to pick at longer intervals, letting the pods remain on the plant until a large number had broken.

Domestic cloth production was adapted to local methods of cultivation and processing. Where cotton was spun in the farmer's household, it was handled carefully to prevent too much dirt from getting mixed with it. When spinners (or professional cleaners) performed the second stage of cleaning, they did not expect the cotton to be very clean when it reached them—the main requirement was that it should be de-seeded.[78] By contrast, cotton for export had to be baled and compressed; dirt, dried leaves and other impurities were crushed and mixed with it during the process, making later cleaning more difficult. Cultivators had no particular incentive to handle cotton carefully, for cleaner cotton did not fetch a higher price. In any case, most adulteration (the mixing of different varieties) and dirtying of cotton occurred *after* it had been bought by brokers or merchants and stored for export.[79]

To sum up: in the first half of the nineteenth century, following the collapse of textile exports, the EIC turned to the trade in cotton. Around this time, Lancashire industrialists became interested in Indian cotton as an insurance against the disruption of their usual supply chains. The colonial state sought to encourage American varieties of cotton along with new methods of cultivation and processing. After many experiments, a few American varieties became acclimatised to Indian conditions; more significantly a mechanised infrastructure for cleaning cotton (the cotton gin) began to take shape in tandem with exports.

[78] Cotton Report of 1857, HCPP, Part I, p. 39; EIC, *Report on Cotton-wool*, p. 294.

[79] Wheeler, *Madras versus America*, p. 125. According to a planter, cotton sold on the domestic market was quite clean; adulteration occurred in cotton set aside for export and was the work of brokers. Wheeler, *Madras versus America*, p. 136.

Slow change: from the 1850s to the 1950s

The Lancashire cotton famine and its aftermath

The onset of the American Civil War triggered significant changes in every aspect of cotton cultivation and processing in India. They stemmed from the sudden drying up of American cotton supplies to Lancashire. Exports of raw cotton rose sharply as mill owners sought to make up the shortfall by buying Indian cotton—much of this came from the Bombay Presidency, but Madras also benefited. Raw cotton exports rose from 38.7 million lbs in 1858–9 to 82.5 million lbs in 1859–60, reaching a peak of 120 million lbs in 1865–6 (a rise of 210 per cent over 1858–9). With the end of the Civil War, exports plummeted to 24 million lbs in 1866–7 before stabilising at an average of 65.5 million lbs (the annual average of the five years between 1871 and 1875). This figure represents an increase of 69.4 per cent over the baseline of 1858–9 (see Figure 3.1). From then on, there is considerable variation in exports from year to year, depending on demand: this, in turn, depended on the size of the harvest and the price of cotton in the American market.

The end of the war saw a rapid increase in cotton consumption by *Indian* mills. From only 60,000 bales in 1864–5, this rose to 888,864 bales in 1889, an increase of 1,381 per cent in 22 years.[80] Indian mills consumed only 4.06 per cent of all cotton produced in the country between 1862–3 and 1866–7; this figure rose to 20.94 per cent between 1877–8 and 1881–2 and 36.85 per cent in 1888–9 alone.[81] By the late 1920s, about one third of the cotton grown in the Madras Presidency went to local mills; this had risen to two thirds by the end of the 1930s.[82] Cotton was also exported to China and Japan. Land under cotton increased from 797,504 acres in 1855–6 to 1,766,312 in 1863–4 (an increase of 121 per cent). By 1910–11 this had risen to 2,317,045 acres (an increase of 31 per cent).[83] After this, it was to remain in this range, with a noticeable decline at the end of the Second World War, following an official campaign to grow more food.[84]

[80] F. M. W. Schofield, *Note on Indian Cotton* (Simla, Government Press, 1888), p. 31.

[81] Schofield, *Note on Indian Cotton*, p. 32.

[82] Baker, *An Indian Rural Economy*, p. 274.

[83] Season and Crop reports (Annual) (Madras, Government Press).

[84] *Memoirs of the Department of Agriculture, Madras* (Madras, Government Press, 1954), p. 482; S. M. Sikka, Arjan Singh, Avtar Singh, P. D. Gadkari, R. Balasubrahmanyan, N. K. Iyengar, K. Sawhney, V. K. Bederker, G. B. Patel, P. S. Pandya, V. N. Paranjpe and N. S. Panigrahi, *Cotton in India: a Monograph* (Bombay, ICCC, 1961), p. 186.

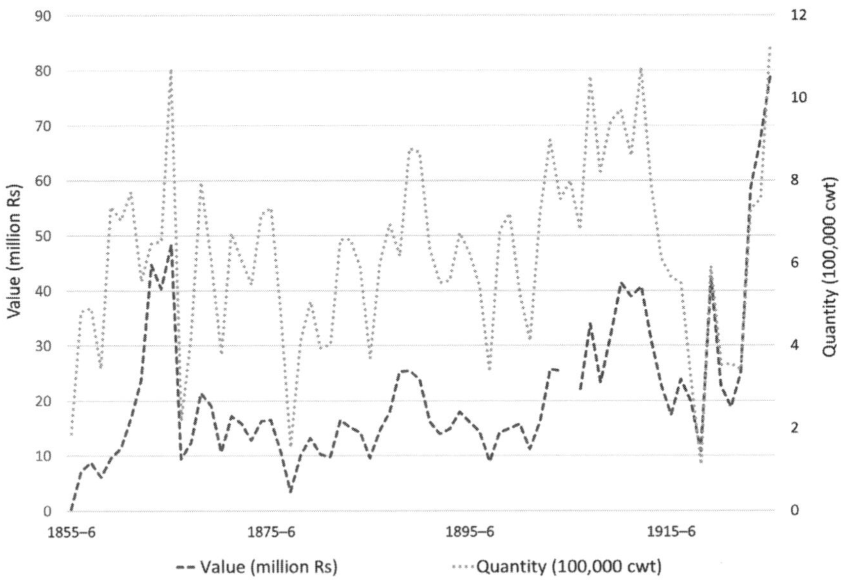

Figure 3.1: Quantity and value of raw cotton exports from the Madras Presidency

Sources: Specker, *Weber in Wettbewerb*, p. 113; *Annual Volume of the Sea-borne Trade*.

The American Civil War produced familiar representations from Lancashire and Manchester asking the Indian government to facilitate exports and make India a long-term supplier of cotton.[85] Despite some objections to state interference in the name of laissez-faire, the colonial government took active measures to promote cotton cultivation. Experimental farms were restarted under a specially appointed Cotton Commissioner before being transferred to provincial governments.[86] New ports were opened, roads improved, railways extended; laws against the adulteration and mixing of cotton varieties were introduced.[87] British firms and agents became involved in the procurement of cotton. All these developments eroded older, labour-intensive methods and encouraged mechanised solutions.

[85] G. R. Haywood, *India as a Source for the Supply of Cotton: Report Addressed to the Executive Committee of Directors of the Manchester Cotton Company* (Manchester, J. J. Sale, 1862).

[86] Schofield, *Note on Indian Cotton*, p. 2.

[87] The first law against fraudulent practices in the cotton trade was passed in Bombay in 1829 (the Bombay Regulation III of 1829) and modified in 1851. This had no mechanism of enforcement. A new Act passed in 1863 (Act IX of 1863) mandated licensing of cotton presses and created an inspecting establishment. This was modified in 1878 and repealed in 1882. Revenue papers 1880, Cotton Frauds Legislation, IOR L/E/6/6, File 236. These early laws were restricted to Bombay from where the bulk of cotton was exported; later legislation covered the whole country.

This boom in cotton cultivation was accompanied by renewed efforts to introduce hybrid and improved seeds. The diversity of indigenous varieties was the outcome of selection over many generations. Seeds were selected for adaptability to local conditions (a long hot season or frost in the cold season required plants with different maturities) or fineness, colour or strength of fibre. Some varieties of cotton were used for making specialised cloth. If weavers stopped making a certain kind of cloth, the cotton grown for it might disappear as well.

The expansion of cotton exports in the 1860s led to a rapid extension of cultivation; paradoxically it also promoted the cultivation of short-staple cotton considered commercially undesirable. Short-staple varieties spread in Gujarat, Khandesh and Central Provinces.[88] Despite attempts to encourage long-staple cotton seeds, farmers preferred to grow varieties with shorter staple but lower chances of failure, for the price difference between them was low. They also grew a mixture of long- and short-staple cotton to balance cost with yield.[89]

In 1863, a Cotton Commissioner for the Central Provinces was appointed in order to set up experimental farms; these were handed over to the agricultural department in 1883.[90] In the Madras Presidency, unsuccessful attempts to grow American and Brazilian cotton at Saidapet were made between 1878 and 1890.[91] Most experiments focused on exotic varieties although some efforts to improve local varieties were also made. In 1917, the Indian Cotton Committee was set up to identify and oversee efforts to increase and improve the cultivation of cotton in India. Its task was to find ways of addressing the 'growing imperial need for cotton'.[92]

[88] *Report of the Indian Cotton Committee* (Calcutta, Government Printing Press, 1919), pp. 60–1, 95–6. Attempts to suppress the cultivation of inferior Kandesh varieties in Berar involved heavy fines for offenders. Revenue papers 1880, Cotton Frauds Legislation, IOR L/E/6/6, File 236, p. 5.

[89] For example, Uppam and Karunganni were grown in the southern districts of the Madras Presidency; Karunganni for its longer staple, Uppam for its greater yield and resistance to droughts. *Memoirs of the Department of Agriculture*, p. 505. Another variety called Pulichai, considered somewhat inferior, was also grown for its ability to survive dry spells. It was often mixed with Karunganni. 'Proceedings of the Legislative Council of the Governor of Madras, Official Report', vol. 61, no. 11, 23 March (Madras, Government Press, 1932), p. 79. For examples from Central India, see *Annual Report of the ICCC for the Year Ending 31 August 1939* (Bombay, The British India Press, 1940), pp. 15–16. Experiments by the agricultural department showed that mixtures often did better than pure varieties. *Annual Report of the ICCC for the Year Ending 31 August 1940* (Bombay, The British India Press, 1941), p. 17.

[90] *Report of the Indian Cotton Committee*, pp. 62, 100.

[91] *Memoirs of the Department of Agriculture*, p. 489.

[92] *Report of the Indian Cotton Committee*, pp. 1–3.

By this time, an increasing proportion of cotton grown in America was consumed domestically, leaving less for export. For this reason, it was felt that Britain should seek cotton supplies from within the empire. In 1923, the Committee became a permanent body, funded by a cess on cotton. Along with provincial agricultural departments, it came to play an important role in shaping the direction of research and policymaking with respect to cotton cultivation.

The primary objective of the cotton improvement programme was the development and propagation of long-stapled cotton. In practice, it promoted American or indigenous varieties of long-staple cotton.[93] In order to maintain the purity of these strains, it was necessary to prevent the cultivation of other varieties in the vicinity and prevent mixing of seeds, especially while ginning. Several laws were introduced to facilitate this.[94]

During the first few decades of the twentieth century, in response to repeated failures in cultivating exotics, the stress shifted to improving native varieties.[95] But experiments continued; from the 1940s the focus shifted back to American and Egyptian varieties, and the development of hybrids.[96] Acclimatised American varieties introduced during the nineteenth century were chosen for selection and propagation.[97] Dharwad American was one of the high-yielding strains that emerged from this process.[98] Another was an American variety, acclimatised in Cambodia and introduced to the Tirunelveli

[93] *Report of the Indian Cotton Committee*, pp. 491, 515, 519. The exclusive focus on long-staple cotton was not without its detractors. In the 1930s, some observers argued that India would never be able to compete successfully with other countries in growing long-staple cotton; they advocated improving its short-staple varieties, for which there was a specialised demand and where it had a natural advantage. In the long run, it was the proponents of long-staple varieties who won. Indian Central Cotton Committee, *Cotton Improvement in India* (Bombay, G. Claridge and Co., 1931), pp. 12, 15.

[94] The Cotton Transport Act was introduced in 1923 to restrict transport of inferior varieties into areas growing better varieties. In Madras, the Madras Cotton Control Bill was passed amidst considerable opposition: it penalised the growing of a variety of cotton called Pulichai. 'Proceedings of the Legislative Council', pp. 796–815. In 1925, the Cotton Ginning and Pressing Factories Act was passed to control fraud. M. A. Dhantwala, *A Hundred Years of Indian Cotton* (Bombay, Orient Longmans, 1948), pp. 55–6.

[95] *Report of the Indian Cotton Committee*, pp. 123–4; *East India Cotton: Correspondence Relating to the Improvement in Indian Cotton*, HCPP (Command Papers), 1904, pp. 4, 18–22.

[96] Sethi and Dharmarajulu, *Indian Cotton*, pp. 12–20, 52. As late as 1940, the Punjab region grew only native varieties of cotton; by 1960, 60 per cent of the crop consisted of American varieties. Sikka *et al.*, *Cotton in India*.

[97] *East India Cotton*, HCPP (Command Papers), 1904, p. 20.

[98] Indian Central Cotton Committee, *The Present Position of the Research Schemes of the Indian Central Cotton Committee* (Bombay, G. Claridge and Co., 1930), p. 7.

region by an employee of the Harvey company.[99] Over the years, improved strains of this were developed and subsidies granted to encourage its cultivation.

Whether improved local varieties or hybridised exotics, the overriding objective was to encourage the cultivation of long-staple cotton, preferably as a monoculture in order to maintain the purity of the strain. The proportion of cotton with staple length higher than 7/8 inches rose from 26 per cent in the quinquennium 1917–22 to 38 per cent in 1937–42 and to 64 per cent in 1942–7. By 1955–6, the area under improved varieties had increased to 67 per cent.[100]

The reorganisation of cotton markets

The export boom produced by the American Civil War was short-lived, but it had important effects on cotton cultivation and marketing in the long term. Export firms, hitherto on the margins of the cotton market, began to crowd out their competitors. Nineteenth-century discussions about cotton cultivation pointed to the absence of a reliable market *and* the failure of export firms to get involved in cotton procurement and cleaning. This began to change in the 1860s. In response to falling demand after the war, many export firms built ginning factories to process their cotton in order to (re)gain the international market. The largest firm in the Madras Presidency was A&F Harvey, which came to dominate the cotton trade in the region around Tirunelveli and Madurai.[101]

The involvement of large firms reshaped the ways in which cotton was sold.[102] In Khandesh (in the Central Provinces), by now a major cotton producing region, it ceased to be taken to fairs and weekly markets from the 1860s. Instead, a separate channel developed, connecting individual peasants to European firms through intermediaries, called kapas (cotton) dealers.[103] In the Madras Presidency, forward contracts became prevalent:

[99] *Memoirs of the Department of Agriculture*, p. 489.

[100] Sethi and Dharmarajulu, *Indian Cotton*, pp. 9–10.

[101] Baker, *An Indian Rural Economy*, p. 254.

[102] I do not discuss the impact of these changes on the farmer. For that, see Sumit Guha, *The Agrarian Economy of the Bombay Deccan, 1818–1941* (Delhi, Oxford University Press, 1987), pp. 129–32; Baker, *An Indian Rural Economy*, and Sabyasachi Bhattacharya, Sumit Guha, Raman Mahadevan, Sakti Padhi, D. Rajasekhar and G. N. Rao. (eds), *The South Indian Economy: Agrarian Change, Industrial Structure and State Policy, c. 1914–1947* (Delhi, Oxford University Press, 1991).

[103] Douglas E. Haynes, 'Market Formation in Khandesh, *c.*1820–1930', *The Indian Economic and Social History Review*, 36(3) (1999), 287–8.

European firms used them to bypass local markets. They bought the cotton with the seed and ginned it themselves or paid for ginning. Four clusters of ginning factories in the Tirunelveli-Madurai region 'became virtually the sole centres of the cotton trade until the First World War'. Cultivation continued to be financed by local moneylenders and village dealers, but they sold the crop in the village to agents of cotton dealers. Almost all the cotton grown in these two districts was bought by Harveys.

In the 1920s, smaller players emerged, but the years following the Great Depression saw large firms regain their prominence.[104] In the Coimbatore region, the cotton market worked in a slightly different way, without much forward contracting, but the ultimate buyers remained textile mills and Bombay merchants.[105] The Depression saw the exit of many intermediate agents and the market came to be dominated by twelve gin-owners. Some wealthy farmers also set up mills.[106]

Traditional methods of cleaning cotton, geared towards retail sale in small quantities, rapidly became obsolete. Cotton gins and ginning monopolies dominated the landscape by virtue of their capacity to buy, store and clean cotton in the volumes demanded by spinning mills and exporters. As demand rose, the potential profits from growing cotton increased in proportion: prosperous farmers were prepared to take previously unacceptable risks in order to obtain larger yields. Mills became their main customers; the demand for long-staple cotton, promoted by the state, recast traditional patterns of cultivation.

The changing story of yarn

The substitution of machine-made yarn for hand-spun yarn represented a fundamental shift in the handloom industry of South India. Imports of mill yarn into the Madras Presidency remained low until the middle of the nineteenth century. After this, they witnessed a steady rise that accelerated after the American Civil War (see Figure 3.2). In the beginning, imported yarn was limited to coastal districts; it reached inland somewhat later, with the building of the railways and improvements in roads.

[104] Baker examines cotton markets during this period; this and the previous paragraph are based on his findings. Baker, *An Indian Rural Economy*, pp. 254–7, 264.

[105] Baker, *An Indian Rural Economy*, pp. 269–70. In Coimbatore, many gins were set up by prosperous farmers; cultivators usually sold cotton after getting it ginned in these facilities.

[106] Baker, *An Indian Rural Economy*, pp. 271–3.

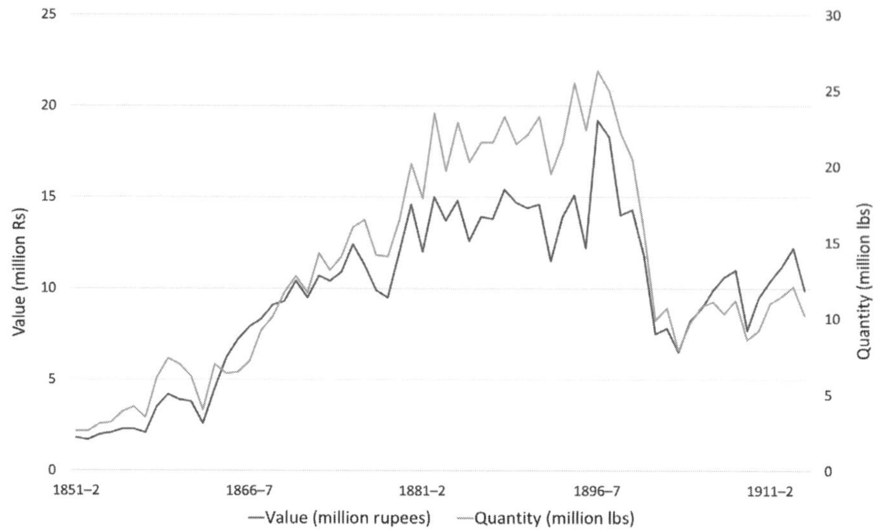

Figure 3.2: Quantity and value of yarn imports by sea into the Madras Presidency

Sources: Specker, *Weber in Wettbewerb*, p. 157; *Annual Volume of the Sea-borne Trade*.

The first effects were on hand-spun yarn of medium thickness and fine yarn: imports crowded out domestic spinners in both cases. Coarser varieties continued to be hand-spun for somewhat longer. Observers attributed this phenomenon to the widespread belief that hand-spun yarn was stronger and more durable than mill yarn. It was also used to make special varieties of cloth. In 1855, weaving centres like Ventapollam in Guntur obtained fine 'country thread' from spinners in Cumbum district for their coloured cloth. The use of English twist for 'the finer description of goods' had become common by this time; however, it was considered inferior to 'country' thread in that it did not absorb red dye to the same degree.[107]

The process of substitution accelerated sharply during the 1860s. Specker shows that the sharp rise in raw cotton exports during the American Civil War was not accompanied by a corresponding increase in cotton acreage. The amount available for local consumption shrank as more and more was diverted to the export market: the result was a steady rise in the domestic price of cotton.[108] In 1863, weavers were reported to be in distress

[107] See the section on Guntur in the *Official and Descriptive Catalogue of the Madras Exhibition, 1855* (Madras, Government Press, 1855).

[108] Specker, *Weber in Wettbewerb*, pp. 121–4. Between 1958–9 and 1965–6, cotton exports increased by 210 per cent, but acreage under cotton rose by roughly 40 per cent.

because of this.[109] We have already seen that many spinners bought cotton for spinning: most of them were poor, without access to capital, and any steep rise in price would have had the temporary effect of driving them out of the market. Imports of yarn did not rise noticeably during this period, but there was a spurt just after the end of the Civil War, followed by an increase in subsequent years (see Figure 3.2).[110]

In the Central Provinces, there were widespread shortages of cotton, yarn and cloth (both local and imported) during the 'cotton famine' of the 1860s. Most of the fall was in the output of coarse yarn and cloth. The spinning of fine yarn and the weaving of fine cloth, by contrast, remained largely unaffected. When cotton was dear, only spinners making fine yarn (which sold for a higher price) were able to continue working; besides, fine yarn also used up less cotton than coarse yarn for the same length of thread. On the demand side, the cotton boom may have generated greater demand for fine cloth, as some farmers grew rich.[111] This conclusion is also echoed by Sumit Guha.[112]

In the Gangetic plain, Borpujari finds no evidence that spinners and weavers of fine cloth fared better than others during this period. Loom numbers fell steeply, especially in districts where cotton was not grown. In cotton-growing districts, the practice of weaving coarse cloth to order, using yarn provided by the cultivator's family, increased. There, the widespread scarcity of cotton and yarn affected the production and sale of cloth in general.[113]

There is general agreement among scholars that spinners suffered disproportionately from the rise in cotton prices. Although the scarcity of cotton ended with the end of the American Civil War, its price remained higher than pre-war levels. This rise in threshold price contributed to the erosion of hand spinning during a period when spinners had to compete

[109] Distress was especially acute in the Central Provinces from where most of the cotton was exported. Cotton Report of 1863, HCPP, p. 329.

[110] Annual yarn imports rose from an average of 3.6 million lbs between 1853–4 and 1857–8 to 6.1 million lbs between 1858–9 and 1862–3, and to 7.26 million lbs in the subsequent five-year period. Between 1868–9 and 1872–312.12 million lbs was imported on an average annually, 20.8 million lbs between 1880–1 and 1884–5, 21.7 million lbs between 1885–6 and 1889–90, and 22.4 million lbs in the next five years, and 23.28 million lbs between 1895–6 and 1889–90. From the turn of the twentieth century, yarn imports declined, being replaced by domestic yarn (largely transported by rail from Bombay).

[111] Harnetty, 'Deindustrialization Revisited', 466.

[112] Guha, 'The Handloom Industry of Central India', 300.

[113] Jitendra G. Borpujari, 'Indian Cottons and the Cotton Famine, 1860–65', *The Indian Economic and Social History Review*, 10 (1973), 37–49.

with increasing quantities of mill yarn, both imported *and* domestic. At first, they were restricted to making coarse thread; this last market was extinguished by the proliferation of domestic mills producing yarn of lower counts and imported yarn from Japan.

In 1869–70, it was estimated the Madras Presidency consumed 31.4 million lbs of yarn, of which 11.7 million lbs was imported and all the remainder, 19.7 million lbs, was country-made or hand-spun.[114] Thus, hand spinners produced roughly 63 per cent of yarn for weaving while imports contributed 37 per cent. Imported yarn was restricted to a few districts—predominantly Chengalpattu, North Arcot, South Arcot, Salem, Canara and Malabar, probably because of their proximity to ports.[115] Relatively little was consumed in the inland cotton-producing belt.

In 1869–70, 73 per cent of imported thread was between 33 and 42 counts; 16 per cent was between 16 and 32 counts. Yarn of counts below 16 (very coarse) was not imported; neither was yarn of counts above 100 (very fine).[116] It seems clear that weavers producing cloths of middling quality were already dependent upon mill yarn; very coarse cloth and very fine cloth was still made from hand-spun yarn. This pattern gradually spread as improvements in infrastructure enabled imported yarn to reach inland markets.

Between 1869–70 and 1882–3 (when Havell made his tour of the Presidency), imports of yarn doubled. By 1882, the use of imported yarn was widespread: 'machine cotton is universally used in the manufacture of all but the coarsest kind of cloth and in cotton carpets'.[117] This coarse yarn was spun primarily for home consumption (and some for carpet weaving).[118] In a few centres, very fine muslins continued to be made with hand-spun yarn known as 'silk-weaver's cotton', said to be as fine as English yarn of 150 counts.[119] It was spun by

> a class of people living in some localities in the Godavari, Vizagapatam and Ganjam districts. They do not belong to the silk-weaver's caste, so the name is probably derived from the fineness of the cotton. The thread is not generally made finer than fine imported thread, but it speaks much for its durability that people are willing to give as much as Rs.15 for a plain cloth (for ordinary

[114] Board of Revenue Proceedings, 28 June 1871, TNSA, p. 4730.
[115] Specker, 'Madras Handlooms', 160–1.
[116] PBR, 28 June 1871, p. 4726, TNSA.
[117] Havell, *Reports Submitted*, p. 7.
[118] Havell, *Reports Submitted*, pp. 6, 7, 19.
[119] Havell, *Reports Submitted*, pp. 20, 49.

> wear) woven with it when they can buy a similar cloth (also hand woven) of machine-spun thread for about half the price ... Formerly it is said that the demand for it was large so that it formed a separate industry in which whole families were engaged. Now only females are occupied in spinning, while the men have become weavers.[120]

Cloth made from fine, hand-spun yarn was also woven in some villages in Chengalpattu.[121] It was bought by wealthy buyers who considered it more durable than cloth made with English thread.

Coarse cloth made with hand-spun yarn was still produced in substantial quantities. In 1889, it was estimated that 42 per cent of yarn used in handloom weaving was hand-spun; 34.5 million lbs of yarn were imported and only 1 million lbs were produced by local mills.[122] Spinning mills were set up comparatively late in the Madras Presidency: the first one was established in 1874. By 1900, there were eleven mills in all: two were composite mills, making cloth as well as thread.[123] By 1923–34, there were 17 mills; meanwhile, many of the older mills had also augmented their capacity.[124] Thread of finer counts was imported; domestic mills concentrated on making yarn of low counts, bringing them into direct competition with hand spinners.

The period between 1890 and 1920 witnessed the almost complete substitution of hand-spun yarn by mill yarn in the Madras Presidency. In 1889, slightly less than half of all yarn was hand-spun and most of it was used to make coarse cloth. The poor kept spinning for as long as they could, if only to meet their own needs. This was especially true of cotton-producing regions, where farmers continued to keep back some cotton for their own use and preferred to pay labourers in kind rather than cash. Imports of yarn by sea remained fairly steady during the 1890s before declining from 1900, when more and more yarn was shipped to Madras from Bombay by rail.[125] The First World War provided a fresh impetus to the expansion of mills and sounded the final death knell of hand spinning.

[120] Havell, *Reports Submitted*, p. 20.

[121] Havell, *Reports Submitted*, p. 20; Letter by Thiagaraya Chetty in Havell, *Reports Submitted*, p. 48.

[122] Raghavaiyangar, *Memorandum*, p. cxii.

[123] Baker, *An Indian Rural Economy*, p. 339; *Papers Relating to the Industrial Conference Held at Ootacamund in September 1908* (Madras, Government Press, 1908).

[124] *Report: Indian Economic Enquiry Committee, 1925*, vol. 2, Minutes of Evidence, part II (Calcutta, Government Press, 1926), p. 281.

[125] *Annual Volumes of the Sea-borne Trade and Navigation of the Madras Presidency and of its Chief Port and each of the Subordinate Ports for the Year 1897–98* (Madras, Government Press, 1898), p. 11.

The closing decades of the nineteenth century saw substantial improvements in physical infrastructure. Hand-spun yarn was a retail business, with a multitude of sellers and buyers congregating in local markets to deal in small volumes. Mill yarn was a bulk commodity transported over long distances: the increasing sophistication of road and rail networks reduced transport costs—and the retail price of mill yarn—enabling mill owners to flood the market.

Studies conducted in select villages in 1917 reported the gradual extinction of hand spinning over two decades.[126] By 1923–4, D. M. Amalsad, textile expert to the Madras government, could work on the assumption that all yarn used by weavers was machine-made.[127] In a survey of cottage industries conducted in 1928, Narayana Rao noted that hand spinning was practically dead but for a small number of spinners in cotton-producing districts and a few places where the efforts of the All India Spinners Association set up by Gandhi had yielded some fruit.[128]

The disappearance of hand spinning and its effects on thousands of women workers finds little mention in the literature on deindustrialisation, as Wendt pointed out.[129] The references are cursory; Tirthankar Roy argues that spinners were so poorly paid that it had no significant economic impact. This argument divorces wages from the wider economic and social context in which households operate; by the same reasoning, a great many weavers were so poorly paid by the mid-twentieth century that there was no economic justification for their existence.

Spinners made a significant contribution to household incomes. During the 1877 famine, missionaries in Krishna district distributed cotton to poor women to spin on the grounds that

> though spinning in the country is at all times very poorly paying work, the cotton is being taken most eagerly and joyfully by these people at present. It gives employment to those members of the family who have for a long time not been able to get any work.[130]

[126] Slater, *Some South Indian Villages*, pp. 66, 115. Respondents in one village said that hand spinning used to be widespread 25 years ago (the 1890s), but had now (1917) disappeared completely. In another village, they reported that hand spinning used to be practised by women from 'low' castes until 10 years ago (1907).

[127] *Report: Economic Enquiry Committee, 1925*, p. 287.

[128] Rao, *Madras Presidency*, pp. 53, 61, 223–7.

[129] Wendt, 'Four Centuries of Decline?', pp. 193–216.

[130] William Digby, *The Famine Campaign in Southern India, 1876–1878*, vol. II (London, Longmans, Green and Co., 1878), p. 351.

After examining the impact of mechanisation on hand spinners in Britain, Jane Humphries and Benjamin Schneider come to a similar conclusion: although badly paid, spinning made a crucial contribution to family incomes, gave women a degree of independence and enabled single women to survive without aid, albeit in very straitened circumstances. Its loss exacerbated poverty, especially in low-wage agricultural areas. Spinners thrown out of work failed to find employment in mills, for these were located in urban centres and their work rhythms were strange and unfamiliar. The victims of mechanisation were those already pushed to the margins.[131]

In South India, the burden fell disproportionately on Pariar spinners. Spinning fine thread involved skills handed down through generations. It seems reasonable to assume that they carried some social value; fine spinning also brought in higher wages. At the very least, Pariar spinners and weavers enjoyed greater autonomy than their counterparts forced to rely exclusively upon agricultural labour for survival.

A large proportion of hand spinners were Pariars; an even larger proportion were women. Both categories found themselves shut out from mills. In the nineteenth century, very few women workers were employed in them. Their numbers increased during the course of the twentieth century but, in the Madras Presidency at least, women were restricted to badly paid jobs, working as reelers, winders and waste pickers. The so-called skilled spinners were all men and were much better paid. Despite this disparity, women had to work for 14 hours a day and were among the first to be dismissed when factories were laying workers off.[132]

Changes in the distribution and sale of yarn

Hand-spun yarn reached the weaver in many different ways: the usual practice was to buy it from spinners, but it could also be obtained from yarn dealers and merchants. When yarn was scarce, weavers might visit several spinners or make the rounds of many weekly markets before obtaining enough of it. The price fluctuated seasonally and was exposed to vagaries of supply. The principal advantages were ease of access, the ability to negotiate directly with the supplier, and buy (or order) the precise quality and quantity

[131] Jane Humphries and Benjamin Schneider, 'Stranded Spinsters', *British Academy Review*, 34 (Autumn 2018), pp. 32–5.

[132] Shobana Warrier, 'Class and Gender: a Study of Women Workers in Cotton Textile Mills of Madras, Madurai and Coimbatore', PhD thesis (Jawaharlal Nehru University, 1993).

required. The production and sale of thread were decentralised, with many sources of supply; this was especially true of cotton-producing regions.

Mechanisation cut off the weaver from cotton and yarn. The distribution of yarn became much more centralised and the power of intermediaries increased. By 1930, four merchants were reported to control the entire supply of medium to fine yarn (60 counts and above) in the city of Madurai. It was imported from Manchester by two firms; the merchants bought the yarn from them and sold it to weavers.[133] Venkatraman describes the distribution system of local mills in the 1930s as follows:

> The local mills have their sole agents for each territorial area and all sales must be effected through them alone. The agents are mainly large capitalists. They get 2 percent commission in the case of local mill yarn and 1 percent in the case of Bombay mill yarn and also a month's credit. The sales to the agents are secured by the guaranteeing brokers, who get 5 anna and 4 pies for every bale of yarn sold to agents.[134]

Master weavers represented yet another layer of intermediaries. In urban centres, where yarn merchants competed with each other, prices might remain competitive during periods of abundance, but in remote villages and weekly markets (where only a few merchants came) they tended to remain inelastic. In the districts of Salem and Coimbatore, yarn cost 1 to 3 annas more per pound in villages than in large towns.[135]

Reconfiguring the web of production

Mechanisation centralised access to yarn but lowered its price relative to the price of cotton. Yarn could be spun much, much faster from a given quantity of cotton by machine than by hand—this gave mill yarn a competitive advantage over hand-spun yarn, especially after the 1860s, when cotton prices stayed high. Its cheapness was one of the chief factors that enabled handlooms compete with mill-made cloth. During the nineteenth century, this competition was largely with imports and mill cloth from *other* provinces. Until the First World War, mills and handlooms in the Madras Presidency

[133] *The Madras Provincial Banking Enquiry Commission*, vol. IV: Oral Evidence (Madras, Government Press, 1930), p. 297.

[134] Venkatraman, *The Handloom Industry*, p. 81.

[135] Venkatraman, *The Handloom Industry*, p. 83.

complemented each other to a large degree. Local mills produced thread but little cloth, and most of this thread was sold to weavers.[136]

Economic historians from Morris D. Morris onwards argue that it was the supply of cheap mill yarn that drove the revival of the handloom industry in India, allowing it cut costs and reduce prices in order to compete with mill-made cloth.[137] Handloom weavers also used imported silk yarn (and somewhat later, artificial yarns) to make new varieties of cloth. Meanwhile, new technologies like the fly-shuttle drove down costs by improving productivity.

The positive effects of mill yarn have received a good deal of attention, but the mechanisation of spinning affected the lives of weavers in other, less positive ways. The once-common practice of weaving cloth with thread supplied by the customer vanished: poor weavers were disproportionately involved in this kind of work. The dependence upon mill yarn became one of the principal causes of trade and price instability experienced by ordinary weavers during the twentieth century. Any significant disruption in the supply of yarn had the potential of throwing thousands of weavers out of work. One of the many committees appointed to examine conditions in the handloom industry during this period pointed out that 'the real weakness of the position in regard to the handlooms was the unsteadiness of the supply of yarn in abnormal times'.[138] Mills held the upper hand in determining supply and price. As more composite mills were set up, the balance between selling yarn and selling cloth tilted to the weaver's disadvantage—more of it was used to make cloth, less went on sale, especially when profits were high.

Even in normal times, mills stood accused of selling sub-standard yarn and of dual pricing. A missionary in Ahmedabad observed that 'the mills usually have two classes of spindles, one producing yarn for their own use and the other for the market. The handloom weaver gets a poor quality of yarn or can get a proper quality only at a prohibitive price.'[139] The Fact Finding Committee set out a long list of malpractices by mills: lower counts of thread were sold as higher, hanks were often short in length; weak yarn suitable only for weft was passed off as warp yarn, factory rejections were put on the market and so on.[140] In the 1930s, a textile expert employed by

136 Baker, *An Indian Rural Economy*, pp. 339–41.

137 Morris D. Morris, 'Towards a Re-interpretation of Nineteenth-Century Indian Economic History', *Indian Economic and Social History Review*, 5 (1) (1968), 9; Roy, *De-industrialisation*, p. 1443; Haynes, *Small Town Capitalism*, pp. 48–50.

138 *Fact Finding Committee*, p. 9.

139 Quoted in Venkatraman, *The Handloom Industry*, p. 44.

140 *Fact Finding Committee*, p. 97.

the Madras government noted that the selling price of some kinds of cloth produced by mills was lower than the market price of yarn used to make them (this was true of some imports as well). This meant either that they were making a loss or, and this was more plausible, selling yarn at a price much higher than the cost of production.[141]

Once tariffs protecting them from yarn imports were introduced, local mills enjoyed even greater freedom in setting prices. The outcome was a rise across the board in the price of imported *and* Indian yarn.[142] We have already seen that mills could sell cloth more cheaply than handlooms because they made yarn themselves and could factor its input cost at cost price. This meant that the market price of cloth did not rise as much as that of yarn: handloom weavers bought yarn at higher prices, but were unable to increase the price of cloth proportionately (for they had to compete with mill cloth). The only way to cut costs was by reducing wages.

This was the state of affairs during normal times. During periods of economic crisis, mills were able to manipulate conditions to even greater advantage. During the First World War, cloth imports fell sharply: mills promptly increased cloth production to take advantage of high prices and sold less yarn on the market. During the Second World War, yarn prices shot through the roof. Between 1939 and 1943, the price of cotton increased by 200 per cent but the price of yarn rose by 600 to 700 per cent.[143] Mill owners made huge profits during the war years and were openly accused of hoarding and speculation.[144] Three factors contributed to this: a rise in the price of cotton, the cessation of imports, and, most importantly, the ability and willingness of mills to take advantage of the consequent shortage of yarn by putting prices up.

Mills ramped up cloth production; the result was a chronic shortage of yarn. Price controls and rationing were introduced, but the chief effect was to create a black market in yarn; meanwhile, influential yarn dealers and master weavers siphoned supplies by registering false looms. 'Termites attack looms; "Mangamma" offerings for yarn; Weavers hungry!' reads a headline from the period in the weekly *Janasakthi*. The reference is to

[141] Venkatraman, *The Handloom Industry*, p. 243.

[142] Development Department, G.O. no. 1218, 12 September 1932, TNSA.

[143] Development Department, G.O. no. 1268, 26 June 1943, TNSA.

[144] Murarji Mill in Bombay with an investment of 1,800,000 rupees made a profit of 3,500,000 rupees in 1942, 7,300,000 rupees in 1943 and 10,300,000 rupees in 1944. *Janasakthi*, 4 April 1945. Madras mills also made huge profits. See Baker, *An Indian Rural Economy*, p. 365.

the bribes required to obtain yarn on the black market: Mangamma was a Nayaka queen famous for her generosity.[145]

Fluctuations in the price and availability of yarn produced chronic uncertainty for ordinary weavers.[146] Substantial distress was reported alongside reports of high wages. Those who managed to obtain yarn prospered, but those who did not suffered unemployment and hunger. Many weavers migrated to towns in search of work and many incidents of rioting and begging were reported.[147] The crisis continued even after the end of the war: mills cut back yarn production by about a fourth in the Madras Presidency alone.[148] Narayanaswami Naidu, conducting an enquiry into labour conditions in 1948, reported that some weavers had failed to obtain yarn for more than a month.[149]

Conclusion

Only a nuanced understanding of traditional methods of growing cotton and making yarn at the beginning of the nineteenth century will allow us to appreciate the sheer scale of change during the next 100 years. Cotton was a cash crop; each stage in the process of growing, cleaning and turning it into yarn was complex and diversified. Cleaning and spinning were labour-intensive and decentralised operations, integrated into the work rhythms of agriculture: they involved household labour and were performed predominantly by women. Earnings and wages derived from them, though low, made a significant contribution to household incomes. Even where cotton and yarn passed through the hands of merchants, they were sold in small quantities to spinners who participated in retail markets.

These complex chains were ruptured and restructured during the second half of the nineteenth century, beginning with the American Civil War.[150] Cotton cultivation, cleaning and marketing became oriented towards the needs and technical requirements of spinning mills (first foreign and later

[145] *Janasakthi*, 20 December 1944.
[146] Development Department, G.O. no. 1129, 14 March 1944, TNSA.
[147] *Janasakthi*, 24 January 1945; 20 December 1944. Also Baker, *An Indian Rural Economy*, p. 402.
[148] Baker, *An Indian Rural Economy*, pp. 366–7.
[149] B. V. Narayanaswami Naidu, *Report of the Court of Enquiry into Labour Conditions in the Handloom Industry* (Madras, Government Press, 1948), p. 11.
[150] See Figure 3.3 for a schematic diagram of the chain of production for Madras handkerchiefs in the early twentieth century, illustrating this restructuring and centralisation.

domestic). This led to a fundamental shift in the way cotton was grown, its varieties and seed stock; indigenous varieties of short-staple cotton were replaced with acclimatised exotics or hybrids. Gins centralised cotton cleaning and the production of yarn was centralised in mills. Traditional methods of processing cotton and spinning yarn had disappeared by the first quarter of the twentieth century; plebeian and part-time weavers, reliant on local supplies of hand-spun yarn, found themselves unable to compete with mill-made cloth. These twin processes of mechanisation and centralisation affected the organisation of weaving itself, as we shall see.

A deliberate attempt at centralisation was first made during the late eighteenth century when the EIC tried to provide yarn in lieu of cash advances: this policy met with strong resistance from weavers.[151] Access to yarn was seen by them as a matter of central importance; yarn markets often served as sites of protest. Angry weavers would shut them down in order to air their grievances.[152] With the displacement of yarn production to mills, this direct access was curtailed once and for all.

Tessie P. Liu shows how a similar erosion of access led to centralisation of control in the handloom industry of Choletais in nineteenth-century France. In the beginning, merchants enjoyed no inherent advantage over weavers in cloth production and trade. Weavers with access to raw material and working capital could easily undercut the putter-out (merchant). Thus 'controlling the yarn supply was essential to any putting-out strategy' in Choletais; for the weavers, 'preserving open access to a source of yarn was crucial to maintaining the independence of the small-scale producer'.[153] Shifts in structures of yarn supply played a critical role in tilting class struggles over cloth production in favour of merchants. In the early nineteenth century, merchants oversaw a shift from linen to cotton, eroding weavers' access to yarn (since cotton was not available locally).[154] Then they mechanised spinning by investing in spinning mills in order to cement control over yarn supply. Their position was strengthened during the cotton famine of the 1860s, when lack of access to raw cotton and yarn left weavers more vulnerable than before.[155]

In South India, the restructuring of production was driven by new forces of global capitalism, abetted by the colonial state. The shrill demands of English mill owners for a secure supply of raw cotton and unhampered access

[151] Wendt, 'The Social Fabric', pp. 185–7; Parthasarathi, *The Transition to a Colonial Economy*, pp. 87–8.
[152] Wendt, 'The Social Fabric', pp. 186–7.
[153] Liu, *The Weaver's Knot*, p. 64.
[154] Liu, *The Weaver's Knot*, pp. 87–8.
[155] Liu, *The Weaver's Knot*, pp. 128–35.

to the Indian market were decisive elements of this process. The colonial state, both in its mercantilist and free-trade phases, aggressively promoted and protected their interests.[156] We have already examined the reconfiguration of cotton processing and spinning; the structures of handloom weaving were also transformed, as we shall see in the next chapter.

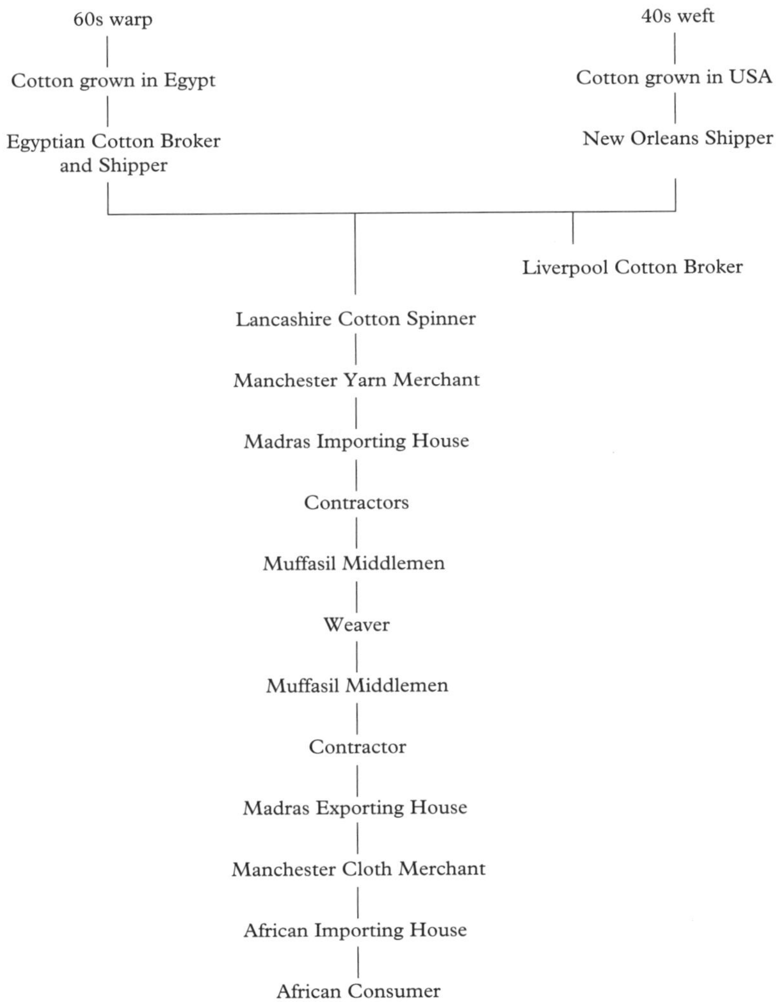

Figure 3.3: Chain of production in the manufacture of Madras handkerchiefs as described by D. M. Amalsad in 1926

Source: Amalsad, 'Development of the Madras Handkerchief'.

[156] This theme will be explored in greater detail in Chapter 7.

4

Weaving

Changing Structures

The household played a central role in weaving. Men usually worked the loom, though there is no evidence of any active taboo forbidding women to do this.[1] The preparatory stages of warping, sizing, winding weft spindles, and so on were performed mostly by women, assisted by children and older members of the household. Warping involved walking between pegs stuck into the ground: it was done under the shade of trees or in a grove.[2] The yarn used for wefts was spun on spindles, usually by old women.

The weaver's family formed a single working unit. The larger community was involved in some tasks, for processes like sizing required more labour than the family could mobilise. These were accomplished through exchanges of labour (paid or unpaid). Warping and sizing were carried out in public spaces like streets and groves. While the weaver was working, the rest of the family prepared the warp for the next piece of cloth. Wages for these preparatory processes were included in his payment. If workers were hired to do the warping and sizing, they had to be paid in cash.[3]

[1] There is evidence for some women weavers during the early twentieth century, but it is not clear whether this was an old practice or a new one. Rao, *Preliminary Report on the Survey of Cottage Industries in the Madura, Ramnad, Trichinopoly and Tinnevelly Districts*, p. 8.

[2] Warping involves laying threads of equal length parallel to each other across the proposed width and length of the cloth. One method was to fix sticks into the ground, fastening one end of the yarn to the first stick and unreeling it: this was wound around the sticks until the last stick was reached, when the course was repeated backwards. Each thread was separated from its neighbour by a cross (called a lease) between each pair of sticks. Edgar Thurston, *Cotton Fabric Industry of Madras Presidency* (Madras, Government Press, 1897), p. 3.

[3] Parthasarathi, *The Transition to a Colonial Economy*, pp. 13–14.

Systems of cloth production in the nineteenth century

The merchant as intermediary

Studies of the handloom industry during the seventeenth and eighteenth centuries focus on the Coromandel coast and production organised by merchants.[4] Some historians argue that it was impossible for weavers to work independently. The outlay on yarn was so large that they could not buy it themselves; only a cash advance by a financier enabled them to do this. In order to be sure of uninterrupted work, the preparatory process (warping) for the next piece of cloth had to be completed while the weaver was working on the loom. Thus, at any time, he had to have a stock of yarn sufficient for at least two pieces of cloth. Since its cost made up the largest part of the cost price (far more than his wages), a substantial outlay of capital was required. According to this argument, weavers needed capital equivalent to several months' income in order to work continuously. Since few weaving households had so much money, they were dependent upon credit provided by merchants.[5]

This advance was, in most cases, a *cash* advance: with it, weavers purchased yarn and carried out preparatory processes such as warping and sizing. This system differed from putting out, where raw materials were advanced, and meant that the merchant exercised little or no control over the production process. It is described by Sinnapah Arasaratnam as follows:

> while in Europe the goods produced belonged to the financier and the payment made to the producer consisted solely of the wages of his labour, in India the weaver appears to have retained his independence and his control over his produce, though his freedom to fix the price of his goods was not unrestricted. Often he only secured a money advance, not raw materials, had control over his tools and thus was master of the produced goods till they changed hands. There seems to have been a general agreement, though, that his creditor had the first call on his goods as long as the money was unpaid.[6]

[4] Parthasarathi, *The Transition to a Colonial Economy*, pp. 12–14; Swarnalatha, *The World of the Weaver*, pp. 73–102; Wendt, *The Social Fabric*, pp. 248–55; Arasaratnam, 'Weavers, Merchants and Company'; Brennig, 'Textile Producers and Production'. All these studies discuss cloth production and procurement systems for export (by different European companies). Douglas Haynes also lays stress on production organised by merchants and argues that little cloth was made outside this system (although weaving with yarn provided by the cultivator was said to be 'common' in the southern Maratha region). Haynes, *Small Town Capitalism*, pp. 31–6, 46.

[5] Parthasarathi, *The Transition to a Colonial Economy*, p. 14; Wendt, 'The Social Fabric', pp. 183, 248.

[6] Arasaratnam, 'Weavers, Merchants and Company', 259.

In the beginning, the EIC obtained cloth from merchants through this system. But as it gained political power, the company's representatives sought to exercise greater control over production. The first step was to cut out the merchant and provide advances through its own employees (called cobdars and head weavers). The EIC also tried to replace cash advances with yarn advances and introduced a strict system of quality control. Its dual position as employer and state gave its representatives a range of coercive and legal powers. Weavers employed by the EIC therefore found themselves in a much weaker position than weavers employed by other merchants. However, its attempts to control production met with sustained and cohesive opposition at different times and places.[7]

Merchants were involved in cloth production in inland regions as well. A close reading of the sources indicates that advances were more common in the production of fine cloths and those meant for distant markets. When making cloth for local markets, the weaver usually operated on his own. The same set of weavers might alternate between both these systems. In Bangalore, the Puttegar (Pattunoolkarar) made fine cloth from cotton and silk. According to Buchanan,

> when the goods are in much demand, it is customary for the merchant to advance one half, or even the whole, of the price of the goods which he commissions; but when the demand is small, the manufacturers [weavers] borrow money from the bankers at two per cent a month and make goods, which they sell to the merchants of the place. They never carry them to the public market.[8]

Very fine cloths (in silk with gold thread) were woven only on commission, with a cash advance.[9] Other weavers—Devangars, Padmasales, Shayanagaru and Billi Muggas—also took advances from merchants or borrowed money to weave cloth on their own account: advances were provided for pieces destined for distant markets.[10] Merchants also advanced money to make coarse cloth in considerable demand. Silagutta in the Mysore country was an export centre for coarse cloth made by the Whalliaru in its hinterland: 'when any considerable quantity is wanted, advances are made by merchants:

[7] See Parthasarathi, *The Transition to a Colonial Economy*, pp. 78–100; Swarnalatha, *The World of the Weaver*, pp. 73–102. Relations between weavers and the EIC are examined in Chapter 5.

[8] Buchanan, *A Journey from Madras*, vol. 1, p. 212.

[9] Buchanan, *A Journey from Madras*, vol. 1, pp. 208, 219; PBR vol. 907, no. 29, 28 February 1822, pp. 2043–5, TNSA.

[10] Buchanan, *A Journey from Madras*, vol. 1, p. 218; PBR vol. 1066, no. 33, 5 June 1826, p. 5600, TNSA; Buchanan, *A Journey from Madras*, vol. 2, p. 239.

but more than the price of one piece at a time is never given in advance. There are no intermediate agents between the merchant and the weaver.'[11]

The independent weaver

Weaving organised by merchants dominated the export sector. But even in the Coromandel coast, weavers making cloth for *local* consumption often worked on their own account, selling cloth in weekly bazaars. In 1803, weavers of 'bazaar cloth' in Rajamundhry objected to an assault by a customs official on one of their members who had gone to get his goods stamped to sell in the market. They disrupted several weekly markets in support of their demand to abolish the stamp duty on bazaar cloth.[12] In 1838, the collector of Nellore described different categories of weavers in his district: some spent their own money to buy raw materials; others borrowed to weave on their own account; some wove partly on their own account and partly for hire; and some worked only for hire.[13] The system of giving yarn to a weaver to get it made into cloth was also widespread.

Buchanan described several systems of cloth production during his journey in Mysore. The weavers of Waluru produced cloth for 'country' or local use and also for export: 'The coarse cloths for the former purpose, they sell at the weekly fairs. The finer kinds they either weave on their own account, selling them to traders at the same places, or they receive advances from merchants to enable them to purchase thread.'[14]

In Sirja-pura (Sarjapur), a manufacturing town near Bangalore, 'the merchants ... act[ed] merely as brokers and the weavers frequently carry their own goods for sale to Bangalore. Purchases are made here by traders from Seringapatam, Sira, Chatrakal etc.'[15] Weavers borrowed from merchants or moneylenders in order to buy yarn, returning the loan once the cloth was sold in a regular cycle of credit.[16]

[11] Buchanan, *A Journey from Madras*, vol. 1, p. 327.
[12] PBR vol. 376, no. 17, 23 April 1804, pp. 3363–71, TNSA.
[13] PBR vol. 1641, no. 42, 24 December 1838, pp. 17253–9, TNSA.
[14] Buchanan, *A Journey from Madras*, vol. 1, p. 40.
[15] Buchanan, *A Journey from Madras*, vol. 1, pp. 271–2 and Buchanan, *A Journey from Madras*, vol. 2, p. 217.
[16] Buchanan, *A Journey from Madras*, vol. 2, p. 218.

Weaving for the consumer

The purest example of self-sufficiency comes from the tribal areas of Vizagapatam (Visakhapatnam) district, where Gadaba women wove a narrow cloth on the most 'primitive looms': its warp consisted of the hand-spun fibres of jungle shrubs and the weft was cotton, dyed with indigo and *Morinda citrifolia*, making stripes of red, blue and white.[17] Another tribe, the Savara, had specialist weavers called the Arisi, who made cloth for them.[18] In both cases, weaving was a subsistence occupation, divorced from markets or market transactions other than rudimentary exchange.

In cotton-producing regions, it was common for cultivators and labourers to spin thread at home—women usually did this work—and give it to a weaver to make into cloth in return for a wage that included his family's labour in warping and sizing. This practice is referred to as 'home consumption' in the records. Around Bangalore, the Togataru, who specialised in coarse, thick cotton cloth with red borders, were too poor to weave on their own account; they did not take (or were not given) advances from merchants either. Instead, 'they in general receive the thread from the women in the neighbourhood and work it up into cloth, for hire'.[19] This practice was also followed in many coastal villages. Around Ingeram, for example, quantities of cloth, called 'bazaar cloth', were woven in this manner: 'It is common practice among inhabitants of villages to furnish the weaver with thread, which he weaves into the cloth required, at so much per cosid [*sic*].'[20]

This practice is discussed in a cluster of reports made by district collectors to the Board of Revenue in connection with new duties on cloth during the early decades of the nineteenth century. In some districts, it was customary to exempt cloth woven by a weaver for his family's use from tax. The exemption also applied to cloth woven to order for a farmer's household (from cotton grown on his land).[21] In 1824, this concession was extended to the whole Presidency: all cloth made for personal use and to order was exempted from duty. The Board of Revenue raised objections on the ground that this would involve a large loss of revenue. It was argued that

[17] Francis, *Vizagapatam District Gazetteer*, p. 97.
[18] Francis, *Vizagapatam District Gazetteer*, p. 95.
[19] Buchanan, *A Journey from Madras*, vol. 1, p. 218.
[20] PBR vol. 438, 26 April 1804, p. 3487, TNSA. Weavers were vehemently opposed to stamp duty on this variety of cloth; its value was estimated to be less than 3 rupees per piece.
[21] PBR vol. 984, no. 20, 24 May 1824, p. 4358, TNSA; PBR vol. 1554, no. 18, 10 April 1837, p. 1850, TNSA; PBR vol. 1567, no. 38, 3 August 1837, pp. 8773–5, TNSA.

cloth manufactured to order by supplying thread could not be defined as 'home made', and duties on it were reimposed.

The reports indicate that this system was widespread, *especially among the poor*. The collector of Kadapa reported that 'the practice of supplying the material and getting cloths made for home use obtains to a great extent in this district'.[22] The collector of North Arcot wrote that he 'was inclined to grant (exemption of duties) to the lower orders of cultivators only, who in their families were in the habit of preparing the thread, getting the cloths made for their own use…'[23] The same system prevailed in other districts.[24] The collector of Chengalpattu reported that 'it is by those whose monthly earnings vary from 2 to 5 rupees that cloth valued at from one to two rupees is chiefly used. Cloths of this description are made by the commoner classes of weavers, on their own account and that of others, who make their own thread, and pay the hire of weaving it into cloth.'[25]

In Kadapa,

> [a]t present the thread used for the hand shuttle is spun by the Mala women from ordinary cotton produced in the district. The Mala weavers do not provide their own cotton for the clothes they weave, but the Kapus give them the cotton from their own fields, pay the women a few annas for spinning it, and then pay the men a regular wage for weaving it into cloth.[26]

Moreover, 'each weaver has his own customers, and very often one family of Malas will have weaved for one family of sudras for generations'.[27]

A servant of the Dutch East India Company touring the Kaveri delta reported that Pariar weavers used yarn spun by the women and children of their households.[28] This might be used to make cloth for personal use or coarse cloth for sale. It was common for labourers picking cotton to be paid in kind; this cotton was cleaned and spun by their families. The Dhers of the Berar region in the Central Provinces cleaned cotton, spun their own yarn and wove it into cloth.[29]

22 PBR vol. 1494, no. 16, 7 March 1836, p. 4088, TNSA.
23 PBR vol. 989, no. 25, 22 July 1824, p. 6341, TNSA.
24 Rajhamundry, Coimbatore, Vizagapatam and North Arcot. PBR vol. 984, no. 42, 17 May 1824, pp. 4439–40, TNSA; PBR vol. 380, no. 7, 31 May 1804, p. 4499, TNSA; PBR vol. 984, no. 42, 17 May 1824, pp. 4439–40, TNSA; Francis, *Vizagapatam District Gazetteer*, p. 123; PBR vol. 989, no. 25, 22 July 1824, p. 6341, TNSA.
25 PBR vol. 1583, no. 23, 23 November 1837, p. 15070, TNSA.
26 Thurston, *Castes and Tribes*, vol. 4, p. 351. The Mala were the social equivalent of the Pariar.
27 Thurston, *Castes and Tribes*, vol. 4, p. 350.
28 Wendt, 'The Social Fabric', p. 219.
29 House of Commons Parliamentary Papers, East India (Cotton), *Report of Rivett-Carnac*, p. 18.

The independent or semi-independent weaver working for a wage formed a significant element of the world of weaving during the early nineteenth century. Many hailed from 'untouchable' castes; their customers were mostly poor to middling peasants or fieldworkers. The system had obvious advantages: the peasant or labourer did not pay for the yarn (the labour of spinning it was concealed and not subject to calculation). The weaver obtained his raw material free of cost, and was free, in theory at least, to negotiate his wage (including preparatory processes carried out in the household). In fact, the hierarchy of caste ensured that the wages of 'untouchable' weavers remained low.

Weaving for hire: the numbers and the evidence

During the seventeenth and eighteenth centuries, most weavers owned their own looms; 'weavers with a single loom were by far the predominant group'.[30] But there were also weavers who owned more than one loom and hired others to work for them. In one village surveyed by the Dutch, 10 per cent of weaving households owned two looms.[31] Arani, an important weaving centre, had 90 weaver households and 9 hired workers.[32] In 1796, the central division of Baramahal was inhabited by 1,378 weavers owning 1,627 looms, a ratio of 1:1.2.[33] In the southern division, 3,019 families owned 3,749 looms, an average of 1.24 looms to a family. Weavers from specialist weaving castes making fine cloth (like the Pattunoolkarar, Seniyar and Saliar) usually had more looms than did those from castes making coarse cloth (like the Kaikolar and Pariar).[34] Weaving centres like Rasipur and Salem (where fine cloth weavers were concentrated) had a higher ratio of looms to households.

There were more looms than weavers almost everywhere in the Presidency.[35] Detailed figures are available for some districts: they show

[30] Wendt, 'The Social Fabric', p. 220.

[31] Brennig, 'Textile Producers and Production', p. 350. A household might have more than one weaver.

[32] Wendt, 'The Social Fabric', p. 235.

[33] *The Baramahal Records*, Section VII: Imposts, pp. 27, 69. Conversely, a list from 1794 shows 1,606 weavers owning 1,551 looms (more weavers than looms). The confusion is probably the result of counting weaving households in some cases and individual weavers in others.

[34] *The Baramahal Records*, Section VII: Imposts, p. 71. See Table 2.5.

[35] In Bellary district, the ratio of weavers to looms was 1:1.5. PBR vol. 1925, no. 42, 8 August 1844, p. 10288, TNSA. In Rajamundhry the ratio of houses to looms was 1:1.1. PBR vol. 1953, no. 26, 27 January 1845, p. 1147, TNSA. Buchanan also says that some weavers owned more than one loom. Buchanan, *A Journey from Madras*, vol. 1, p. 222.

that most weavers owned only one loom, but a small minority owned two or three, and in very rare cases, more. These extra looms were usually worked by members of the extended family (as when brothers lived together, for example) or relatives.[36]

In Nellore district, some weavers employed assistants. They were usually family members, but could also be hired hands.[37] To make cloth with intricate patterns, weavers needed assistance and this was usually provided by a boy who helped to pass an extra shuttle through the warp. Sometimes workers were hired to operate a second loom. Buchanan reports that Puttuegar weavers in Bangalore had 'two to five servants, who are paid by the piece'.[38] The Shayanagaru (a relatively prosperous group) also hired 'servants'. Among the Padma Shalay, by contrast, few servants were employed: all the males of a family lived together and worked in the same house, 'very seldom engaging themselves to work out for hire'.[39] On the whole, the available evidence indicates that only a small minority of weavers owned more than one loom.[40]

The production process

Despite the diversity of production systems, the weaver remained in control of the production process and, to some extent, the product itself. We have seen that most weavers owned their own looms and worked from home. They bought the yarn and undertook all the preparatory processes. They set their own work rhythms. They sold the cloth in local markets or took it to a merchant. Even when bound to a merchant, they retained the right to sell elsewhere as long as they returned his advance.

The merchant exercised little control over production. Studies of weaving during the seventeenth and eighteenth centuries stress the weaver's autonomy of action, especially in the matter of yarn.[41] If the advance (and the final price) offered for a piece of cloth was low, weavers would use less yarn or yarn of inferior quality to make it. Company officials constantly

[36] PBR vol. 1446, no. 11, 25 March 1835, pp. 3156–61, TNSA
[37] PBR vol. 1641, no. 42, 24 December 1838, pp. 17253–5, TNSA.
[38] Buchanan, *A Journey from Madras*, vol. 1, p. 212.
[39] Buchanan, *A Journey from Madras*, vol. 1, p. 217.
[40] Haynes suggests that master weavers were common in western India during the nineteenth century. Haynes, *Small Town Capitalism*, pp. 131–2.
[41] Brennig, 'Textile Producers and Production', pp. 351–2. Haynes comes to the same conclusion. Haynes, *Small Town Capitalism*, pp. 31–6.

complained about the quality of cloth.[42] When the EIC sought to replace cash advances with yarn advances, it faced sustained protests. Weavers also objected to replacing damaged combs, for this forced them to use more yarn and was viewed as an interference in the production process.[43]

Prasannan Parthasarathi argues that their control over the production process placed weavers on a more or less equal footing with merchants before the nineteenth century. In the Coromandel, weavers were free to sell their cloth to a different buyer provided they returned the original advance. This was perfectly feasible in a period when demand outstripped supply and several buyers (including European trading companies) competed with each other to obtain cloth for export. Merchants found it more difficult to terminate contracts; the advance remained at risk until the cloth was delivered or the weaver returned the money.[44] Replacing cash advances with yarn advances had the effect of reversing the situation.

But not all weavers occupied the same level, economically or socially. They were divided into the prosperous and the poor; into groups higher up the caste hierarchy and those at the bottom. Specialist weavers making fine cloth earned more money and ranked higher in terms of social status: the Pattunoolkarar outranked the Kaikolar. A missionary, describing the Pattunoolkarar weavers of Paramakudi in 1856, noted that

> the houses of these weavers are the best I have yet met with anywhere in the interior, they are lofty, built with burnt brick, the roof of almost every house is covered with tiles. The inhabitants are in good circumstances, the women were the best dressed of any village I have yet been to.

In Tirunelveli district, the Pattunoolkarar were said to be better placed (more prosperous) than other groups.[45] Pariar weavers were usually described as the poorest of all. In terms of earnings, there was a clear divide between weavers making fine and coarse cloth. In Coimbatore in 1944, the annual income of a Pattunoolkarar weaver was estimated to be double that of a Kaikolar who made cloth of middling quality, and 70 per cent more than that of a Jadar. Pariars and Kaikolars weaving coarse cloth were estimated

[42] Wendt, 'The Social Fabric', pp. 191–2; Parthasarathi, *The Transition to a Colonial Economy*, pp. 25–6. Also see Arasaratnam, 'Weavers, Merchants and Company', 268.

[43] Parthasarathi, *The Transition to a Colonial Economy*, pp. 85–8, 94–6, 103–5.

[44] Parthasarathi, *The Transition to a Colonial Economy*, pp. 26–7. PBR vol. 364, no. 40, 24 November 1803, p. 13298, TNSA, discusses new legislation to prevent weavers contracted to the EIC from selling cloth to other merchants. This was a frequent practice that earlier regulations had not been able to stamp out.

[45] PBR vol. 1937, nos. 48–9, 7 November 1844, p. 14955, TNSA.

to earn only a third of this.[46] In Bellary, the earnings of fine cloth weavers were roughly double of those making cloth that sold at half that price.[47] In Baramahal, the Jadar and Pattunoolkarar earned more than any other group of weavers; they made cloth of higher value and paid a higher loom tax.[48]

Weavers belonging to different communities normally made different kinds of cloth, but there was also a measure of internal differentiation. A small minority owning more than one loom and employing hired workers was more prosperous than ordinary weavers of the same caste. Wherever merchants were involved, there were some individuals who acted as intermediaries, earning a commission on each weaver who made cloth to order. Prosperous weavers sometimes became merchants.[49] This process of internal differentiation was magnified many times over by the reorganisation of the industry during the course of the nineteenth century.

Changes in production

Production systems changed dramatically during the late nineteenth and early twentieth century. Roy infers a clear trend towards greater centralisation and employment of wage labour, while Haynes argues against any unilinear replacement of one system by another. In his view, a number of systems coexisted side by side. Let us examine the evidence from South India.

The independent weaver

By the second decade of the twentieth century, the practice of making cloth with yarn supplied by the customer had all but vanished. In Kadapa, once home to the largest concentration of Mala weavers in the Presidency, it was reported that

> nowadays very little yarn is home spun and if the ryot still patronizes home-made stuffs he buys his yarn in the bazaars of the bigger villages and towns which get their supply from the spinning mills in Madras and elsewhere. Meanwhile the cotton that he grows finds a ready market in the ginning and

[46] PBR vol. 1942, no. 49, 25 November 1844, p. 16129, TNSA.
[47] PBR vol. 1925, no. 42, 8 August 1844, p. 10295, TNSA.
[48] *Baramahal Records*, Section VII: Imposts, p. 115.
[49] Arasaratnam, 'Weavers, Merchants and Company', 267; *Baramahal Records*, Section VII: Imposts, pp. 25, 41.

> pressing factories of Tadpatri and Prodattur. It is the country cloths worn by the women of the black cotton country that are now mostly manufactured by the Malas. They are sometimes coloured but mostly white with red or black borders. The threads for these cloths is bought ready dyed.[50]

Weaving for home consumption continued on a very small scale in remote pockets. The hill people in the tracts of Visakhapatnam and Ganjam still made clothes for their own use.[51] In some parts of Nellore, Chittoor, Kadapa, Kurnool and Guntur, Malas continued to make cloth in this fashion in the late 1920s.[52] By the 1940s, however, 'home consumption' finds no mention in the records.

The situation of the independent weaver began to change once mill-made yarn captured the market. This had to be bought from intermediaries (the cloth itself might be sold on the open market or to the merchant who supplied yarn).[53] Many late nineteenth-century observers describe weavers working for merchants as well as independent weavers selling their wares in local markets. In 1925–6, 15 per cent of weavers in Adoni (Kadapa district) and 10 per cent of those in and around Kurnool were said to be 'independent'.[54] In Chirala and Perala (Guntur district), they comprised 30 per cent of all weavers.[55] In 1935, Venkatraman noted weavers bringing cloth for sale to weekly markets (where they also came to buy yarn).[56] Independent weavers supplied local markets in the districts of Chengalpattu, Salem and Madurai, but when making silk cloth, kailis and saris for export, they invariably worked for merchants.[57] Data collected by the Textile Enquiry Committee in 1954 supports this picture.[58]

Yarn was bought on cash or credit: those who could pay in cash enjoyed a considerable advantage. The weavers of Mansapuram in Madurai district wove white towels sold in the weekly market and used the proceeds to buy

[50] Brackenbury, *Cuddapah District Gazetteer*, p. 61. In Anantapur, men's clothing was made in this way. W. Francis, *Madras District Gazetteers: Anantapur* (Madras, Addison and Company, 1905), p. 63. By 1927–8, it was a dying practice, found only in some Deccan districts. Rao, *Madras Presidency*, p. 17.

[51] Havell, *Reports Submitted*, p. 20.

[52] Rao, *Chittoor District*, p. 2; Rao, *Cuddapah District*, p. 7; Rao, *Nellore District*, pp. 4, 15; Rao, *District of Guntur*, p. 2.

[53] Roy classifies this relationship as a 'price-contract'. Roy, *Artisans and Industrialization*, p. 75.

[54] Ranga, *The Economics of Handlooms*, pp. 10, 18.

[55] New master weavers employing workers were often counted as 'independent' weavers. Ranga, *The Economics of Handlooms*, p. 39.

[56] Venkatraman, *The Handloom Industry*, p. 90.

[57] Ranga, *The Economics of Handlooms*, pp. 40–7, 54–5, 124–6, 132, 139, 147.

[58] *Textile Enquiry Committee, 1954.*

yarn from merchants.[59] Weavers who bought on credit were dependent upon merchants or moneylenders; besides, yarn provided on credit usually cost more than the market rate.[60] In Tirunelveli district, yarn dealers charged an excess of 4 to 8 annas a bundle (and sometimes one rupee) over the market rate for credit sales.[61] Weavers buying on credit were often forced to sell cloth to their sowcars (merchants).[62]

Many observers noted that the number of independent weavers was falling; despite this, they remained a significant category until the 1940s. In 1942, it was estimated that 28 per cent of weavers in the Madras Presidency were 'independent'.[63] Nor was the transition from an independent weaver to contract or coolie weaver inevitable. In Bhatriprolu, a weaving centre for kailis on the east coast, a sequence of good trading years enabled many weavers to break free from merchants; after this, they shifted to making dhotis for local sale.[64] In 1946, when yarn controls were introduced and weavers were issued ration cards for yarn, the number of 'independent' weavers increased, but this rise cannot be taken at face value, for many of them were fronts for master weavers to whom they surrendered their cards.

Those who managed to save some money set up extra looms and employed workers: master weavers emerged from this process of accumulation. In Berhampore, noted for its silk cloths, most weavers worked under merchants as piece-rate workers: 'Those who have any capital and have developed thrifty habits find it more profitable to employ two or three workers also and to produce more cloth for the merchant-employers than it is to work by themselves.'[65]

Weavers and merchants

Merchants continued to play a key role, especially where cloth was produced for export. In 1882, Havell reported that all the export trade was in the hands of sowcars, who 'supply the workmen with materials and pay them at fixed rates for each cloth and carpet etc.'.[66] The Fact Finding Committee of

[59] Rao, *Madura, Ramnad, Trichinopoly and Tinnevelly Districts*, p. 11.
[60] Rao, *Madura, Ramnad, Trichinopoly and Tinnevelly Districts*, p. 17. In Ellore, weavers buying on credit were charged 12 per cent interest. Ranga, *The Economics of Handlooms*, p. 43.
[61] Rao, *Madura, Ramnad, Trichinopoly and Tinnevelly Districts*, p. 19.
[62] *Madras Provincial Banking Enquiry Commission*, vol. 4: Oral Evidence, p. 297.
[63] *Fact Finding Committee*, p. 71.
[64] Ranga, *The Economics of Handlooms*, p. 41.
[65] Ranga, *The Economics of Handlooms*, pp. 39, 56.
[66] Havell, *Reports Submitted*, p. 27.

1942 and the Court of Enquiry of 1948 found that wherever production was geared towards export, merchants exercised much tighter control through cash or yarn advances, or both.[67] These were often recorded as 'sale' of material, the cloth being 'bought' back. In Thiruchirapalli, silk weavers bought yarn from sowcars; the 'bulk of the finished articles is handed over to the sowcars from whom the supply of raw silk is obtained on credit while a portion is consumed in Trichinopoly town and the rest is exported to Madras, the Ceded districts and Chettinad'.[68]

In Jayankondasholapuram in Thiruchirapalli, a market for saris, merchants from 'Tanjore and other parts bring with them yarns and exchange them for the finished products with weavers'.[69] The system whereby merchants 'sold' yarn to the weavers and 'bought' cloth has been defined as a price-contract.[70]

The putting-out or 'oppandum' system

By the 1930s, a very large number of weavers were involved in putting out: 46.5 per cent according to a survey in 1939; 60 per cent according to the Fact Finding Committee in 1942.[71] They were supplied with yarn and other raw materials and paid a fixed wage even when they worked on their own looms at home. This system came to be called the 'oppandum' system (oppandum means agreement or contract in Tamil). Let us look at a few descriptions from different parts of the Madras Presidency.

In South Arcot, in 1906, most weavers were reported to be 'in the hands of capitalists (usually Komatis or Nattukottai Chetties) who supply them with the thread, pay them piecework wages, and themselves arrange for the sale and export of the finished article'.[72] In Coimbatore, 'except a few middlemen, every weaver is always attached to a trader. He gets a fixed amount of yarn or silk and gold thread from his trader, and, on turning them into finished articles, gets his wages.'[73] As warping mills emerged in

[67] *Fact Finding Committee*, p. 70; Naidu, *Report of the Court of Enquiry*, p. 9.

[68] Narayana Rao, *Survey of Cottage Industries*, p. 15; Rao, *Madura, Ramnad, Trichinopoly and Tinnevelly Districts*, p. 15.

[69] Rao, *Madura, Ramnad, Trichinopoly and Tinnevelly Districts*, p. 16.

[70] Roy, *Artisans and Industrialisation*, pp. 74–5.

[71] Development Department, G.O. no. 2058, 21 August 1939, TNSA; *Fact Finding Committee*, p. 71.

[72] Francis, *South Arcot*, p. 155. Marwadi merchants oversaw a similar system in Anantapur district. Francis, *Anantapur District Gazetteer*, p. 64.

[73] *The Madras Provincial Banking Enquiry Commission*, vol. 4: Oral Evidence, p. 305.

the 1920s and '30s, some merchants began supplying weavers with warped yarn. In other places, weavers continued to warp and size the yarn (with the help of their families), the payment being included in their wage.[74]

The system was common in the production of fine cloths (where costs were high) and cloth for distant markets.[75] Narayana Rao noted the prevalence of oppandums for fine rumals, saris and lace upper cloths made for export to North India in Madurai, Dindigul and Coimbatore. In Coimbatore, 40 to 50 sowcars were said to own from 20 to as many as 300 looms.[76] The Fact Finding Committee of 1940 described a weaver-merchant of the Kaikolar (Senguntha Mudaliar) caste who supplied yarn to 1,000 weavers scattered across several villages: 'his whole establishment is going on like a well-organized factory, although all the employees are working in their own homes'.[77]

In some regions, a three-tier system developed, with the merchant at the top. Under him were master weavers, who employed ordinary weavers. The production of kailis for export involved all these layers.[78] In Salem, cloth dealers advanced yarn to middlemen, paying them on a piece-rate basis, and these middlemen gave yarn to weavers and paid their wages (at piece-rates), charging a commission.[79] Around Kurnool, Bellary and Tadpatri, this was called the 'munganni' system.[80]

> The capitalist advances yarn at the market rate to the employer and sometimes lends him some money. The latter agrees in return to sell the cloth of equivalent weight to the same capitalist at the market rate prevalent on the day of delivery. This employer engages one to ten workers to work for him. Some workers are allowed to work in their own homes, while others are obliged to work in the employer's workshop.[81]

These merchants usually hailed from weaving or trading castes. In Coimbatore, they were local Chetties and Marwaris from Bombay, who

[74] Rao, *Madura, Ramnad, Trichinopoly and Tinnevelly Districts*, pp. 7, 9.

[75] My analysis contradicts Baker's contention that fine cloth for export was associated with 'independent' weavers. Baker, *An Indian Rural Economy*, pp. 398–9.

[76] D. Narayana Rao, *Report on the Survey of Cottage Industries*, pp. 14, 18; Rao, *Madura, Ramnad, Trichinopoly and Tinnevelly Districts*, p. 9; For more examples, see Ranga, *The Economics of Handlooms*, pp. 8–9, 34–6; Brackenbury, *Cuddapah District Gazetteer*, p. 195; *Fact Finding Committee*, pp. 72, 75.

[77] *Fact Finding Committee*, p. 72.

[78] *Fact Finding Committee*, p. 75.

[79] Venkatraman, *The Handloom Industry*, p. 65.

[80] Ranga, *The Economics of Handlooms*, pp. 15–16.

[81] Ranga, *The Economics of Handlooms*, p. 16. For the munganni system, see pp. 20–1.

sent most of the cloth to markets in western and northern India.[82] In the Ramnad region, they were Muslims: Marakayar traders had a long-standing involvement in commerce with East Asia. Now they contracted with Lubbay weavers, also Muslims, to make lungis for export.[83] In Madurai and Salem, most merchants hailed from the Saurashtra community (as did a very large number of weavers in Madurai town).[84] Kaikolars and Devangars acted as yarn merchants in Salem district.[85] In the Tirunelveli region, many of them were Kaikolars (who began calling themselves Senguntha Mudaliars around this time).[86] In Kadapa district, Marwari or Vaishya merchants monopolised the yarn trade.[87] In Chirala and Perala, most yarn merchants were Vaishyas, but there were also some merchants from weaving castes operating on a smaller scale.[88]

Some weavers from specialist weaving castes accumulated capital by acting as intermediaries. Pre-existing economic inequalities became intensified in the new conditions created by global capitalism. Merchants emerged in prosperous and economically differentiated groups like the Saurashtra and Devangar from relatively early on. For the Kaikolar, the process occurred somewhat later. In 1925, some prosperous Mudaliars in Tirunelveli district tried but failed to displace Brahmin merchants who controlled the trade in yarn; by the 1940s, a large number of Mudaliar yarn merchants were active in the district.

At the heart of the oppundum system was the advance given to the weaver *in addition* to yarn.[89] The capitalist saw this as a means of tying him down in the absence of other mechanisms of labour control. For the weaver, cash advances were essential in order to meet expenses; during good times, they became a bargaining point. Their size depended on the state of the market. When the demand for cloth was good, weavers sought large advances by threatening to shift allegiance to some other merchant. During hard times, they were forced to work for merchants to whom they were bound.[90] It is noteworthy that the coolie weavers of Adoni (who did

[82] Indian Industrial Commission (Evidence), vol. 3, p. 445.

[83] Development Department, G.O. no. 618, 14 March 1940, TNSA.

[84] Ranga, *The Economics of Handlooms*, p. 132; *The Madras Provincial Banking Enquiry Commission*, vol. 4, Oral Evidence, p. 297.

[85] Ranga, *The Economics of Handlooms*, pp. 137, 139.

[86] Indian Industrial Commission (Evidence), vol. 3, pp. 447, 484; Venkatraman, *The Handloom Industry*, pp. 70–1.

[87] Ranga, *The Economics of Handlooms*, pp. 8, 19.

[88] Ranga, *The Economics of Handlooms*, p. 36.

[89] *Fact Finding Committee*, p. 73; Ranga, *The Economics of Handlooms*, p. 9.

[90] Geert de Neve and Douglas Haynes have studied the role of advances in the handloom

not even own their looms) never got large advances but only just enough for subsistence.[91]

Master weavers and yarn merchants also took recourse to legal action. In Oravakondah town (Anantapur), 'it had been a common practice ... for the employers to invoke the aid of the "Breaches of Contract Act", which was happily repealed in April 1925, to bring back the workers who run away from time to time to other places because they (the workers) could not pay back the advances to them.'[92] In Salem, 'it was not uncommon for employers to take action against weavers for "breach of contract" for not paying their advances and running away'.[93] In Maharashtra, the family of a migrant weaver who wanted to visit his village was sometimes made to stay back in order to prevent him from absconding.[94]

Coolie weavers

Coolie weavers were workers who made cloth on looms supplied by their employer. They were found in small numbers during the eighteenth and early nineteenth centuries, and up until the third decade of the twentieth century, they appear to have been rare.[95] By 1917, some weaving households in Coimbatore had begun hiring workers because there were not enough family members to work their looms.[96] The same phenomenon can be observed in Kanchipuram and Salem.[97]

By the 1920s, small establishments resembling workshops could be seen in the homes of prosperous weavers and the practice of employing coolie weavers was becoming more widespread. In 1928, Narayana Rao observed master-weaver workshops in several districts.[98] Ranga also describes small

industry. Geert de Neve, *The Everyday Politics of Labour: Working Lives in India's Informal Economy* (Delhi, Social Science Press, 2005). According to most of the weavers I interviewed, satisfactory advances were offered only when the industry was doing well. During market slumps (one coincided with my fieldwork), small advances were offered only to workers who had been with an employer for some time.

[91] Ranga, *The Economics of Handlooms*, p. 11.

[92] Ranga, *The Economics of Handlooms*, p. 14.

[93] Ranga, *The Economics of Handlooms*, p. 133.

[94] Haynes, *Small Town Capitalism*, p. 155.

[95] In western India, karkhanas or small workshops emerged during the nineteenth century. Haynes, *Small Town Capitalism*, p. 132.

[96] Indian Industrial Commission (Evidence), vol. 3, p. 445.

[97] Indian Industrial Commission (Evidence), vol. 3, p. 185; *Salem District Gazetteer*, p. 263.

[98] Rao, *Madura, Ramnad, Trichinopoly and Tinnevelly Districts*, pp. 8–9; Rao, *Cuddapah District*, pp. 8–9.

workshops employing five to ten weavers.[99] Their owners were usually tied to merchants who supplied them with yarn and bought their cloth. The smaller ones were organised around family labour, with workers being employed on extra looms. Two out of four looms owned by a weaver in Chirala were operated by wage workers, but all the preparatory work was performed by the women of the household.[100]

Most workshops were owned by weavers who had accumulated some capital.[101] They used a mix of family labour and hired hands. Most coolie weavers were migrants from villages gravitating to urban centres in search of work. Local weavers were less likely to join workshops; they preferred working from home.[102] Those without looms might end up as hired workers in the same village.[103] Caste and kinship ties played an important role in workshops, for many coolie weavers were bachelors who stayed in the master weaver's house, paying a fixed sum for boarding and lodging.[104] Others lived in rented rooms and worked in their employer's home-workshop for smaller advances and lower wages than weavers who owned their own looms.[105]

The wage differential was considerable.[106] In Chirala, an employer was estimated to make 16.8.0 rupees per month from each worker employed in his house (who also boarded there); the coolie weaver made only 8.8.0 rupees.[107] The rent of the loom was deducted from their wages.[108] To Narayanaswami Naidu in 1948, coolie weavers seemed by far the worst off among all the groups he had observed.[109] In 1935, they dominated the silk-weaving industry of Kanchipuram and the carpet-weaving industry in Salem.[110] By 1939, as many as 30.5 per cent of all weavers were hired workers.[111]

[99] Ranga, *The Economics of Handlooms*, pp. 9, 17–18, 20–1.
[100] Ranga, *The Economics of Handlooms*, p. 57.
[101] By contrast, most factories on the west coast were owned by entrepreneurs from non-weaving castes. Venkatraman, *The Handloom Industry*, p. 72.
[102] Some of these issues will be examined in subsequent chapters.
[103] In Chirala and Salem. Ranga, *The Economics of Handlooms*, p. 82.
[104] Ranga, *The Economics of Handlooms*, p. 82.
[105] Ranga, *The Economics of Handlooms*, pp. 11, 74, 91–2, 145–6.
[106] Ranga, *The Economics of Handlooms*, p. 44.
[107] Ranga, *The Economics of Handlooms*, p. 92.
[108] Venkatraman, *The Handloom Industry*, p. 68; Ranga, *The Economics of Handlooms*, p. 18.
[109] Naidu, *Report of the Court of Enquiry*, p. 10.
[110] Venkatraman, *The Handloom Industry*, p. 68.
[111] Development Department, G.O. no. 2058, 21 August 1939, TNSA.

Factories and cooperatives

In 1844, the Basel Mission set up the first handloom factory (as opposed to home-workshop) in Malabar, but similar attempts in other parts of the Madras Presidency proved unsuccessful.[112] These included a factory in Madurai; one established by one Thigaraya Chetty in Tondiarpet, Madras; one set up by some Nattukottai Chetties; and one by the Department of Industries in Salem.[113] Only in the 1940s is it possible to speak of a handloom factory system. Most factories were small in size and owned by individuals; a handful involved substantial amounts of invested capital.[114] Preparatory processes took place inside the factory or in separate establishments specialising in warping and sizing. This system was associated with migrant workers. In Madurai, the first factories were established in the late 1940s and most of their workers were immigrants from the Tirunelveli-Ramnad region.[115]

Weavers' cooperatives, on the other hand, emerged through state initiatives. Before independence there was much talk about cooperation, but this was viewed largely as a voluntary movement. Early attempts to set up cooperatives failed in the absence of fiscal support, even though sympathetic officials recommended active promotion and state backing. In 1934, the Government of India rejected the Madras government's proposal for a cess on Indian mill yarn in order to raise money to support the handloom industry; instead, it provided a grant to the provinces for this purpose. Madras used this money to set up a Provincial Co-operative Society to coordinate and develop the activities of primary weavers' societies.[116]

During the war years, cooperative societies were restructured to help weavers in distress. Member societies were brought under the effective control of the Provincial Weavers Society. Orders for cloth were placed with them, arrangements were made with mills to provide yarn through forward contracts, cooperative dyeing factories were established and limited financial assistance was provided.[117] Cooperative societies became an important

[112] Indian Industrial Commission (Evidence), vol. 3, pp. 184–5, 484.

[113] *Fact Finding Committee*, pp. 76–7.

[114] In western India, karkhanas expanded in the 1930s; their owners employed loomless weavers coming from places where no work could be found (the Telugu districts of the Madras Presidency and the United Provinces). Haynes, *Small Town Capitalism*, pp. 146–57.

[115] Interview with P. M. Kumar, Madurai, 27 January 2009 and interview with the owner of Saraswathy Textiles handloom factory in Sellur, Madurai, 1 February 2009.

[116] Development Department, G.O. no. 2468, 23 November 1942, TNSA.

[117] Development Department, G.O. no. 366, 19 February 1942, TNSA; Development Department, G.O. no. (M-241) 1723, 19 August 1942, TNSA; Development Department,

channel for the distribution of yarn. There were only 50 societies in 1936 (of which 20 were dormant); the number rose to 336 in 1946 (with 40,000 looms) and 980 in 1960 (with 190,000 looms).[118] After independence, financial assistance helped to strengthen and expand the cooperative sector in the south.[119]

Officials played an active role in encouraging cooperatives, but there was also a significant impetus from below. In the 1930s and '40s, unions called upon the state to protect the handloom industry. The most successful cooperatives were formed as a result of popular mobilisation.[120] Societies created by influential individuals had higher rates of failure. The limits to expansion were set by state funding; the transformation of the handloom industry into a network of cooperatives was never even envisaged.

To sum up: by the mid-twentieth century, the practice of weaving with yarn supplied by the customer had disappeared. The number of independent weavers had fallen considerably. Merchants and master weavers now played a central role in the production process. They provided the weaver with raw materials and paid him a wage; the weaver owned his loom and worked from home (this gave him some control over work rhythms and space). At the same time, there was a rapid increase in the number of loomless or coolie weavers employed in home workshops and small factories.

These production systems fall into a geographical pattern. Weaving for home consumption persisted longer in cotton producing areas, where imports had penetrated to a lesser extent. Along the Coromandel coast (and especially in Telugu-speaking districts), a large number of independent weavers still made dhotis and saris for the local market.[121] They did well wherever local demand for was high and they could tap an independent source of capital.[122] Elsewhere, they faced considerable uncertainty.[123] The

---

G.O. no. 418, 26 February 1942, TNSA; Development Department, G.O. no. 723, 1 April 1942, TNSA.

[118] B. S. Baliga, *Compendium on History of the Handloom Industry in Madras* (Madras, Government Press, 1960), p. 73;

[119] *Census of India 1961*, pp. 24–8.

[120] Yvonne J. Arterburn, *The Silk Weavers of Kanchipuram: a Case Study of the Indian Co-operative Movement* (Delhi, Hindustan Publishing, 1982).

[121] Ranga, *The Economics of Handlooms*, pp. 43, 47, 48, 54, 55, 96, 138.

[122] Weavers in Ellore borrowed from rice mill owners instead of yarn merchants; this gave them freedom in selling and allowed them to shift production more freely. When local demand was low, they wove kailis for merchants; when it was high, they borrowed money from rice millers to make dhotis and saris. Ranga, *The Economics of Handlooms*, pp. 43–4.

[123] Rao, *Survey of Cottage Industries*, p. 83.

weaving of kailis and Madras handkerchiefs for export was organised by merchants and master weavers.[124]

Urbanisation and spatial concentration mark this shift.[125] Madurai town became a much bigger centre of production. In 1891, it contained approximately 5,000 weavers, but by 1917, there were 10,000 weavers in Madurai.[126] This rise outstripped population growth by a considerable margin; in the 1920s, Saunders noted that 'in all the stations the industry is said to be declining so much so that weavers from these places come up to Madurai for employment and overcrowd the market'.[127]

In 1935, Venkatraman noted that 80 per cent of looms in Salem district were concentrated in four taluks near the town: 'scattered artisans are now coming to towns or semi-urban centres'.[128] Every observer of handlooms during this period lays stress on the urbanisation of production. The Fact Finding Committee noted that the handloom industry had become urbanised: in 1940, 39 per cent of looms in the Presidency were located in towns.[129] The dependence upon mill yarn played a key role in this shift.

The production process

Wherever weavers worked from home, the family continued to play a central role. As we have seen, even in workshops the preparatory processes were usually carried out by the master weaver's family, with the help of workers. Much of this work was done by women although weaving remained largely a male preserve.[130] Technological advances brought significant alterations in the division of labour. The fly-shuttle increased loom productivity by anywhere between 25 to 100 per cent.[131] This meant that the warp and weft

[124] Ranga, *The Economics of Handlooms*, pp. 47, 48, 52, 77, 96, 125, 126.

[125] Baker, *An Indian Rural Economy*, p. 405; Roy, *Artisans and Industrialization*, pp. 5–6. I discuss this phenomenon in Chapter 5.

[126] Raghavaiyangar, *Memorandum*, Appendix cxxv–vii: a Note by V. Rajagopalachariar, District Registrar; Indian Industrial Commission (Evidence), vol. 3, p. 483.

[127] Saunders, *The Saurashtra Community in Madura*, p. 116.

[128] Venkatraman, The *Handloom Industry*, pp. 271, 276.

[129] *Fact Finding Committee*, p. 67.

[130] The exception was sizing, usually done by men. There are scattered references to women weavers in the Fact Finding Commission and the sample surveys of the Textile Enquiry Committee in 1954.

[131] Venkatraman, *The Handloom Industry*, p. 53.

had to be readied much faster, and the weaver's family was unable to keep up with the speed of the loom.[132]

Warping mills were established to solve this problem. They involved a significant outlay of capital and were profitable only if operated continuously. At first, warping machines had to be imported (and were therefore expensive), but cheaper indigenous machines were soon fabricated. Warping ceased to be a household affair; it was carried out by specialist warpers (mostly from weaving castes) who invested in these machines.[133] Small-scale warping mills used a mixture of family labour and hired workers, usually women.[134] However, bobbin winding remained a preserve of female workers.[135]

In this way, several processes moved out of the weaver's home. This affected household incomes during a period of transition. In 1954, the Textile Enquiry Committee expressed surprise that in Sholapur (a modernised weaving centre), weavers still preferred to carry out preparatory process at home; for them, this was a way of earning more money.[136] Some observers argued that women displaced from this kind of work could be gainfully employed (and earn more) by weaving, and there is scattered evidence of women taking up weaving during this period.[137] But, on the whole, they continued to perform the worst-paid jobs like bobbin winding. The mass entry of women into weaving took place somewhat later, when men began to move out of it.[138]

Weavers clung to remnants of their old autonomy by refusing to join handloom factories. Observers ascribed this to an aversion to discipline and lack of any sense of time; in other words, they preferred to set their own work rhythms.[139] Skilled weavers, in particular, preferred working from home despite attempts to keep a closer watch on them.[140] But this could not make up for the loss of control, first over raw materials, and later over patterns and designs.

[132] In 1929, Narayana Rao met weavers doubtful about the fly-shuttle for this reason (some had gone back to the throw-shuttle). Rao, *Survey of Cottage Industries*, p. 86.

[133] Venkatraman, *The Handloom Industry*, pp. 128–30.

[134] Naidu, *Report of the Court of Enquiry*, p. 17.

[135] Naidu, *Report of the Court of Enquiry*, p. 15.

[136] *Textile Enquiry Committee*, p. 16; *Fact Finding Committee*, p. 133.

[137] Rao, *Madura, Ramnad, Trichinopoly and Tinnevelly Districts*, p. 8.

[138] de Neve, *The Everyday Politics*, p. 87.

[139] *Papers Relating to the Industrial Conference, 1908*, p. 158; Indian Industrial Commission (Evidence), vol. 3, pp. 177, 184; Saunders, *The Saurashtra Community in Madura*, p. 63.

[140] Ranga, *The Economics of Handlooms*, pp. 76, 132.

The question of stability: working conditions in the mid-twentieth century

Roy argues that the capitalist system of production based on wage-labour that emerged by the mid-twentieth century provided ordinary weavers with greater stability of employment and wages; the risks of market fluctuations were shifted to the capitalist, especially in the case of factories.[141] But this claim is not borne out by the evidence. The most frequent observation about handloom weavers in government reports, independent investigations and newspaper accounts indicates precisely the opposite, namely the *absence* of assured work.

There were not many handloom factory workers in the Madras Presidency, but even in their case, market fluctuations invariably led to unemployment and wage-cuts.[142] *Relative* stability in the factory system evolved only in the 1960s and '70s and was an outcome of state legislation and years of workers' agitations. Even after legislation, working conditions continued to be precarious: owners resisted regularising workers and extending benefits to them. They argued that 'no weaver attached himself to any particular factory, that remuneration was on a piece-rate basis, that there was no continuity or permanency of service'. According to them, weavers, even in factories, were not permanent employees and could not claim the rights and benefits of permanent workers, beginning with continuous, assured employment.[143]

Weavers working for merchants or master weavers certainly did not enjoy security of employment or wages. According to contemporary reports, during downturns, employers found little difficulty in reducing wages and stopping the supply of yarn. A member of the Madurai-Ramnad Chamber of Commerce (a body of factory owners and merchants), surely an authoritative source, observed that the merchant 'commands supplies and hence controls the plight of weavers to whom he dictates lower weaving charges under threat of withholding yarn supplies'.[144] Even when inquiries

[141] Tirthankar Roy, 'Relations of Production in Handloom Weaving in the Mid-Thirties', Working Paper no. 223 (Trivandrum: Centre for Development Studies, 1987), pp. 7, 10, 11.
[142] In 1941, factory weavers comprised 8 per cent of weavers in India as a whole. The percentage was even lower in the Madras Presidency. *Fact Finding Committee*, p. 71. In 1955, there were approximately 700 handloom factories in Madras state (37 per cent in Malabar and South Canara), employing 25,000 weavers. By contrast, the total number of looms in the Presidency were 479,444. ILO, *Handloom Weaving Industry in India*, p. 50.
[143] Development Department, G.O. no. 5973, 20 December 1949, TNSA.
[144] Development Department, G.O. no. 618, 14 March 1940, TNSA.

revealed the payment of fixed wages, master weavers argued that their relationship to weavers was not that of employer to employee, but buyer to seller.[145]

During market slumps, merchants would simply stop supplying weavers with yarn. In 1936, a report from Coimbatore noted that 'they [the sowcars] are not giving work to the weavers and are in fact only waiting to recover their dues from them the moment the looms begin to ply. Many of the sowcars have turned their attention to other trades and some have invested money in the film industry and mill cloth trade.'[146]

Similar stoppages were reported from Madurai in 1939 and 1942; the collector reported that 'the master-weavers are reluctant to spend money on further supplies'.[147] According to another official, 'the truth of the matter is that the Madurai merchants are unwilling to take even slight risks for the sake of weavers from whose toil they have profited all these days'.[148]

Reducing wages was another method of shifting market risks. During times of crisis, weavers were threatened with unemployment in order to drive wages down. In 1940, weavers of Madras handkerchiefs and lungis were told to accept a reduction or cease working.[149] The director of the industries department reported that

> the wages for weaving different classes of cloths have been reduced to some extent. The daily earnings of a weaver now range from Rs 0-6-6 to Rs 0-7-0. But the weavers do not have continuity of employment ... The merchants who act as middlemen are said to be not encouraging the manufacture of Madras handkerchiefs and lungis, unless the weavers are willing for their wages to be reduced further...[150]

In May–June 1945, weavers in Coimbatore complained of wage cuts.[151] In 1948, wages were reduced in many weaving centres.[152] It was not stability

[145] Development Department, G.O. no. 4755, 21 September 1949, TNSA; Development Department, G.O. no. 2566, 14 May 1949, TNSA.
[146] Development Department, G.O. no. 618, 14 March 1940, TNSA.
[147] Development Department, G.O. no. 618, 14 March 1940, TNSA; Development Department, G.O. no. 998 (M-15) MS, 1 May 1942, TNSA.
[148] Development Department, G.O. no. 998 (M-15) MS, 1 May 1942, TNSA. For another instance, see Development Department, G.O. no. 618, 14 March 1940, TNSA.
[149] Development Department, G.O. no. 618, 14 March 1940, TNSA; Development Department, G.O. no. 998 (M-15) MS, 1 May 1942, TNSA.
[150] Development Department, G.O. no. 618, 14 March 1940, TNSA.
[151] *Janasakthi*, 30 May 1945, TNSA.
[152] Development Department, G.O. no. 781, 17 February 1949, TNSA; G.O. no. 1312–13, 14 March 1949, TNSA; Development Department, G.O. no. 4208, 13 August 1948, TNSA; Development Department, G.O. no. 2566, 14 May 1949, TNSA.

but instability that was to become a permanent feature of the handloom industry in the twentieth century. In 1947 and 1954, when wide-ranging surveys were carried out, the most common complaint was lack of continuous employment. Weaving had always been marked by monthly fluctuations, with some periods of intense work (the marriage and festival seasons) and others of low production; the new structures of production magnified unemployment caused by market turbulence.[153]

Data on wage rates is sparse and unreliable, especially for the nineteenth century. Wages for making different kinds of cloth varied widely. Weavers were paid on a piece-rate basis; converting these payments to daily wages or monthly earnings is difficult without ancillary data (such as the time taken to weave different kinds of cloth and the number of pieces woven in a day or week). Wage data for other skilled workers is also scarce. Despite these problems, I have tried to arrive at some provisional figures.

After comparing food consumed by different occupational groups during the eighteenth century, Parthasarathi concludes that weavers were better off in this respect than agriculturalists and village artisans like potters.[154] My data from the late nineteenth century suggests that daily wages (or earnings) from weaving were, on the whole, lower than those from other skilled trades. In the 1890s, the daily wage of carpenters, blacksmiths, bricklayers and goldsmiths ranged from 6 to 10 annas. In comparison, weavers earned between 2.5 to 10 annas a day (but there is only one example of a weaver earning 10 annas). This trend continues into the twentieth century. In the 1930s, the wages of carpenters and smiths varied from 12 to 16 annas a day; those of weavers varied from 2 to 12 annas, depending upon the cloth woven and the contractual relationship.[155] Venkatraman, writing in 1936, estimated that a silk weaver earned 12 annas, a skilled weaver 10 annas and someone weaving ordinary varieties of cloth only 6 annas.[156]

Skilled weavers earned wages similar to (or slightly more than) those of other skilled workers. The wages of ordinary weavers, on the other hand,

[153] Douglas Haynes comes to a very similar conclusion for western India. Haynes, *Small Town Capitalism*, pp. 159–62.

[154] He also argues that their earnings were comparable to those of weavers in Britain. Prasannan Parthasarathi, 'Rethinking Wages and Competitiveness in the Eighteenth Century: Britain and South India', *Past and Present*, 158(1) (1998), 79–109; Prasannan Parthasarathi, 'Historical Issues of Deindustrialisation in Nineteenth-Century South India', in Giorgio Riello and Tirthankar Roy (eds), *How India Clothed the World: the World of South Asian Textiles, 1500–1850* (Leiden: Brill, 2009), pp. 415–35.

[155] See Table 4.1.

[156] Venkatraman, *The Handloom Industry*, p. 184.

were well below this level. Weavers making coarse cloth usually earned about as much as an agricultural worker. A survey of cottage industries published in 1929 compiled wage rates across the Madras Presidency. Daily wages ranged from 5 annas to 16 annas, but in 49 per cent of the cases they were below 8 annas and in only one case did they reach 16 annas.[157] In the 1920s, N. G. Ranga estimated that the daily diet of most weavers was only a little better than agricultural labourers and worse than that of prisoners.[158] Haynes arrives at much the same conclusions for western India.[159]

During the Second World War, wages rose sharply, thanks to increases in the cost of living and a steady rise in cloth prices. However, not all weavers benefited. The war years were marked by scarcity of yarn, which made it impossible to obtain full-time work. In 1946, Narayanaswami Naidu reported that many weavers were working for only 10 to 12 days a month on average; some had not obtained yarn for 6 weeks.[160] Those who had uninterrupted access to yarn made huge profits. Wages varied by place, kind of cloth and market conditions. Lungi weavers, earning high wages in the early 1950s, found themselves near the bottom of the scale by 1960.

Data on monthly earnings reveals considerable differences, with most weavers placed at the lower range of the scale. A sample survey in 1948 concluded that 18.1 per cent of weavers had a household or family income of less than 35 rupees; 54.8 per cent earned 35 to 75 rupees; and 25 per cent earned more than 75 rupees. The highest monthly income was 130 rupees.[161] Table 4.2 summarises the results of the 1948 survey: it shows that coolie weavers earned less (on average) than dependent weavers, who, in turn, earned less than independent weavers. Weavers in cooperatives had the highest average income.[162]

Growing internal differentiation within weaving castes was a feature of the twentieth century. Income data for master weavers is scarce, but we have some figures for weavers owning more than one loom. In 1925, the average income of an ordinary weaver in Madurai was 20 rupees, but that of a weaver owning three looms was 50 rupees.[163] In Tadpatri, the monthly income of a hired weaver was 12 rupees, while a weaver owning four looms

157 Narayana Rao, *Survey of Cottage Industries*, pp. 228–9.
158 Ranga, *The Economics of Handlooms*, pp. 170–1.
159 Haynes, *Small Town Capitalism*, pp. 159–92.
160 Naidu, *Report of the Court of Enquiry*, p. 19.
161 Naidu, *Report of the Court of Enquiry*, p. 20.
162 Naidu, *Report of the Court of Enquiry*, p. 28.
163 *Report: Indian Economic Enquiry Committee, 1925*, p. 284.

(two operated by hired workers) made 41 rupees.[164] Thus, a weaver with three looms, employing two workers, earned two or three times as much as an ordinary weaver with only one loom. A weaver employing a coolie worker on an extra loom earned 12 rupees profit (over costs) from that loom.[165] According to Ranga, master weavers earned much more than the vast majority of their compatriots, who were poor and indebted.[166] Some of them had hundreds of weavers under their control and the difference in earnings increased rapidly, especially during the Second World War.

The modern 'master weaver' versus the 'head weaver' of the eighteenth century

The master weaver emerged as a key figure in the organisation of production during the first half of the twentieth century. Let us examine his role more closely. The designation is derived from European history and many scholars have tried to transplant not just the term, but also the concept to an Indian context. But, as we have seen, the putting-out and workshop systems were uncommon in the Madras Presidency before the twentieth century; this indicates that the role of master weavers in South India was different from that in Europe.

Vijaya Ramaswamy argues that the master weaver first emerged during the Vijayanagara period, which was marked by increased urbanisation and a growing demand for textiles driven by changes in style and fashion. Carding, twisting, winding and spinning became independent professions around this time, and large merchant corporations began to control the trade in cotton, yarn and cloth (as well as the production of cloth). Weavers were subordinated to the master weaver, who 'sometimes emerged from the ranks of the artisans ... [but] more often from the merchants directly controlling textile production'.[167]

Ramaswamy's account of internal differentiation is convincing, but the evidence cited for centralisation of production remains slender at best. Scholarly studies of weaving during the seventeenth and eighteenth centuries stress the fact of *autonomy*: weavers had free access to raw materials and a fair

[164] Ranga, *The Economics of Handlooms*, p. 64.
[165] Ranga, *The Economics of Handlooms*, p. 57.
[166] Ranga, *The Economics of Handlooms*, pp. 179–81.
[167] Vijaya Ramaswamy, 'The Genesis and Historical Role of the Master-weavers in South Indian Textile Production', *Journal of Economic and Social History of the Orient*, 28(3) (1985), 300–13.

degree of control over the final product. The problem lies in Ramaswamy's conflation of two distinct terms and functions. The designations of head weaver and principal weaver occur frequently in Company records: both figures are interpreted as being identical to master weavers.

Arasaratnam points out that Company officials misunderstood the position of the head weaver: in the beginning, they took him to be 'the master craftsman of medieval Europe who employed a number of journeymen who were the "cooly weavers".'[168] Later they discovered that he exercised little control over the production process. Even when the EIC began using head weavers as intermediaries, they did not behave like European 'putters out', refusing to take responsibility for cash advances or cloth deliveries.

The term head weaver reflects a social rather than economic designation. According to Arasaratnam,

> the head weavers appear to have exercised a paternal control over a particular group of weavers but had no economic control over the fruits of their labour. They generally looked after the interests of the weavers in their negotiations with merchants and, of course, got something in return from both the merchants and the weavers for their trouble ... the head weaver was there as the 'big brother', intervening on behalf of an aggrieved weaver or interceding between a merchant and a recalcitrant weaver.[169]

Known as Nattars in some places, they appear to have been elected by consensus. Ananda Ranga Pillai's diary, cited by Mizushima Tsukasa, shows that the traditional headmen of the Kaikolar were selected by an assembly.[170] Head weavers mediated between weavers and the state by collecting the loom tax in return for certain concessions.[171] They also arbitrated internal disputes over caste regulations.[172]

Clearly, they were more prosperous and powerful than ordinary weavers. When the EIC began dealing directly with weavers, cutting out merchants and other intermediaries, head weavers assumed the role of brokers, distributing advances and delivering cloth.[173] But they had little control

[168] Arasaratnam, 'Weavers, Merchants and Company', 276.

[169] Arasaratnam, 'Weavers, Merchants and Company', 265–6. He distinguishes the head weaver from intermediaries like cobdars or careedars in the northern Coromandel: these usually belonged to weaving castes, but could also be banias acting as brokers. Wendt uses head weaver, cobdar and careedar interchangeably. Wendt, 'The Social Fabric', p. 220. It is possible that some head weavers gradually assumed the role of brokers.

[170] Mizushima Tsukasa, *Nattar and the Socio-economic Change in South India in the 18th–19th Centuries* (Tokyo, ILCAA, 1986), pp. 140, 142.

[171] PBR vol. 1359, no. 22, 11 April 1833, pp. 3506–7, TNSA.

[172] Tsukasa, *Nattar and the Socio-economic Change*, p. 143.

[173] Arasaratnam points out that they were not very successful in this. The experiment led to

over production and refused to take responsibility for outstanding balances. Even when they became successful intermediaries, their allegiance was tilted towards the weaver rather than the EIC; head weavers played a leading role in many agitations and negotiations.[174] Those who took the EIC's side came under challenge from their communities.[175]

Other intermediaries like cobdars and careedars also emerged in the coastal districts of Rajamundhry, Visakhapatnam and Masulipatnam. These were brokers from weaving or mercantile castes mediating on behalf of the merchant (or the EIC) in return for a commission. Some distributed advances while others bought cloth from weavers to supply to merchants. After the EIC began buying cloth directly, it appointed head weavers as cobdars. These appointees also supplied advances and collected or bought cloth. Their authority increased over time, but it did not pass unchallenged by ordinary weavers. These intermediaries may have been precursors of the master weaver, but neither their roles or their functions were identical with his.

Modern master weavers, by contrast, were not community leaders, but *capitalist entrepreneurs*. They emerged from a new process acting upon pre-existing differences. In 1917, Alfred Chatterton referred to them as a recent phenomenon.[176] In the sources, the term is used to describe very different kinds of people: big merchants from weaving castes controlling hundreds of looms, weavers owning a few extra looms, and intermediaries between large merchants and weavers. Master weavers have been described as 'weaver-capitalists' and celebrated as architects of the handloom revival.[177] In touch with markets and familiar with the workings of the industry from the inside, they were well placed to make significant innovations. But they also exploited ordinary weavers and contributed to their hardships.

Traditionally, yarn and cloth merchants belonged to mercantile castes like Marwaris, Vaishyas and Chetties. But, during the nineteenth and twentieth centuries, an increasing number of master weavers and yarn merchants emerged from specialist weaving castes. Economic differentiation divided those who controlled markets from those who did the actual work

huge arrears as head weavers refused to take responsibility for balances; the EIC found that they had little property that could be confiscated to make up for these debts. Arasaratnam, 'Weavers, Merchants and Company', 276.

174 Arasaratnam, 'Weavers, Merchants and Company', 276–7; Parthasarathi, *The Transition to a Colonial Economy*, pp. 104–18. This phenomenon is examined in Chapter 6.

175 Parthasarathi, *The Transition to a Colonial Economy*, pp. 117–18.

176 Indian Industrial Commission (Evidence), vol. 3, p. 185.

177 Roy, *Artisans and Industrialization*, pp. 72–104; Haynes, *Small Town Capitalism*, p. 14.

of weaving. Master weavers had two inherent advantages over merchants from trading or mercantile castes: an intimate knowledge of the production process and the ability to control workers through networks of kinship and patronage.[178] At the same time, many of them occupied an insecure position, for their access to raw materials and markets was limited by their resources.

This inherent uncertainty is described in Ranga's study of the 'munganni' system in 1925–6:

> The capitalist always tries to sell a box of yarn at a higher price than the market rate and he can do so, because the employer [master weaver] is in dire need of supplies of yarn to carry on his work and to keep his employees working. The employer on the other hand attempts to sell the cloth, manufactured from the yarn so advanced, to other merchants when prices are much higher than those which his own capitalist is ready to offer. It is evident that such employers have to bear the brunt of fluctuations in both yarn and cloth market; for a fall in the price of cloth, when no compensating factors are present, is enough to ruin them. At the same time this system creates chances for hundreds of pushful artisans to rise from the ranks through thrift, organizing capacity and skill in risk taking. But employers of ordinary skill quickly lose their places and descend to the ranks of employees again.[179]

This process of internal differentiation accelerated during the Second World War, when those with access to yarn accumulated substantial property, including cars and palatial houses. In 1946, one Mariappa Mudaliar and his brothers, owners of several handloom workshops and factories in the town of Karur, had several buildings, two cars, many jutkas (horse carriages), two horses and a stable.[180] The Tamil novel *Panjum Pasiyum*, set in the Tirunelveli region in the 1950s, shows prosperous master weavers alongside struggling weavers faced with unemployment and low wages.

Despite this heterogeneity, master weavers were an economic and not a social category. They were primarily entrepreneurs, although their social position played a key role in their rise and gave them great influence within their communities. One index of this difference is that master weavers, unlike head weavers, rarely led agitations. Instead, they were the targets of popular disaffection.

[178] Haynes, *Small Town Capitalism*, pp. 15–16.

[179] Ranga, *The Economics of Handlooms*, pp. 16, 22.

[180] Madras High Court, *Subbaratnam and Others vs Unknown*, 18 August 1948 (1949 CriLJ 950).

The search for causes

In South India, there was a noticeable shift towards more centralised, capitalist forms of production during the twentieth century. Roy describes this as a decline in 'less productive and less efficient organizations such as household industry' and the expansion of 'more efficient and more productive organizations such as units employing wage labour'.[181] In his view, the shift from price to wage contracts encouraged labour rationalisation and increased productivity. Douglas Haynes agrees that wage labour increased sharply, but not that a 'capitalist' form of production organisation became dominant. Independent and contractual weavers were not replaced *en masse* by coolie weavers in western India.[182] This is also true for South India: production systems remained diverse, but a clear shift to centralisation in terms of control over raw materials, cloth markets and the production process can be observed.

Roy holds that the driving force behind this transition was a process of 'commercialisation' that commenced in the late nineteenth century: this involved '(i) a shift away from production for one's own use, or for use as gifts and tributes, to production for the market, especially the non-local market, (ii) a shift from local to long-distance trade and (iii) the creation of infrastructure and institutions which aid such shifts.'[183] The opening up of trade placed a premium on knowledge and working capital. These resources were harnessed by capitalist entrepreneurs who rationalised the production process in order to remain competitive.[184]

This teleological explanation is not wholly convincing. It is quite true that a large proportion of cloth production in South India was for local markets; some of it did not enter the market at all. But this does not imply that these textiles were 'gifts or tributes' or 'for one's own consumption'. On the contrary, cloth production involved commercial transactions at different levels and scales; some of them may have been in kind rather than cash. Nor was production for distant markets an exclusively modern phenomenon, as Douglas Haynes points out.[185] Indian textiles were sold in three continents (Asia, Europe and Africa) for many centuries. Studies of weaving in the

[181] Roy, 'De-industrialization', 1445.
[182] Haynes argues that capital–labour relationships were not of any 'typical' kind; instead, they were shaped by what he calls 'the politics of the workplace and locality'. Haynes, *Small Town Capitalism*, p. 129.
[183] Roy, *Traditional Industry*, p. 25.
[184] Roy, *Traditional Industry*, p. 25.
[185] Haynes, *Small Town Capitalism*, p. 10.

seventeenth and eighteenth centuries focus almost exclusively on the export market; merchants supplying them invested large amounts of capital in textile production. There was nothing new about commercialisation as such.

In South India, cloth production was organised in many different ways during the early nineteenth century: merchants were intimately involved in the making of fine cloth and textiles for distant markets. The argument that commercialisation was the principal cause of structural change does not explain the vast difference between eighteenth-century structures of production on the Coromandel coast and those developing across India in the early twentieth century. Every stage of production from cotton to cloth (not to mention the relationship of merchants to weavers) was utterly different even when the export sector (encompassing trans-peninsular markets) is considered in isolation.

We must look for a different explanation for the wholesale restructuring of the handloom industry during this period. In South India, the process was triggered by industrial capitalism. Its catalyst was the rapid centralisation of yarn production. By the twentieth century, mills had become the sole suppliers of yarn. The consequences spread outward like ripples in a pond. Before this, cloth and yarn merchants had been distinct.[186] The first group advanced money for making cloth, the second sold yarn to weavers. In the twentieth century, the two functions were fused into one. The Fact Finding Committee commented that the yarn dealer 'in his triple capacity (of yarn dealer, financier and cloth-seller) had rendered himself almost impregnable against possible reformist assaults'.[187]

Technological change also contributed to the transformation. In the eighteenth and early nineteenth centuries, looms were simple and cheap. Their owners could dismantle them and migrate elsewhere.[188] The improved looms of the twentieth century were much more expensive: a frame loom fitted with a fly-shuttle cost approximately 30 rupees in 1936.[189] Fly-shuttles could be attached to an ordinary pit loom for much less (10 rupees according to one estimate).[190] Weavers were forced to make these investments to compete with mills. Narayana Rao recommended state support for hire and purchase to enable poor weavers to install improved

186 Wendt, 'The Social Fabric', pp. 141–2, 177–8.

187 *Fact Finding Committee*, p. 89.

188 Parthasarathi, *The Transition to a Colonial Economy*, p. 12.

189 Development Department, G.O. no. 806, 3 April 1937, TNSA.

190 Venkatraman, *The Handloom Industry*, p. 153.

looms.[191] Increased productivity drove the mechanisation of preparatory processes, but, as we have seen, new machines like warping mills required fairly substantial capital investments.

Without improving productivity, weavers could not hope to survive in the market conditions of the early twentieth century; those unable to invest in new or modified looms sank to the status of coolie weavers. Pariar weavers lacked the money (and social networks) to make these investments, buy mill yarn on the market and pay for warping.[192] When missionaries tried to introduce the fly-shuttle in Kadapa, they found that it did not work well with hand-spun yarn. There was an integral relationship between hand-spun yarn, the traditional loom and subsistence weaving:

> At present the thread used for the hand shuttle is spun by the Mala women from ordinary cotton produced in the district. The Mala weavers do not provide their own cotton for the clothes they weave, but the kapus give them the cotton from their own fields, pay the women a few annas for spinning it, and then pay the men a regular wage for weaving it into cloth. But the cotton spun in the district is not strong enough for the fly shuttle which can only profitably be worked with mill made thread. The result is that if the fly-shuttle were generally adopted, it would leave no market for the native cotton, throw the women out of work, upset the whole system on which the weavers work, and in fact produce widespread misery and confusion.[193]

Roy argues that the adoption of labour-saving devices enabled the handloom industry to modernise, survive and expand. But these devices also created new *systems* of production that excluded many weavers.

The global forces of industrial capitalism drove the restructuring of the handloom industry: yarn supplies were centralised, new technologies introduced and consumer markets reshaped. At the same time, these forces were mediated and modified by different sets of actors. The adoption (or rejection) of technology, and the relations between merchants, master weavers and ordinary weavers were determined by social structures, state policies and a complex mixture of individual and collective choices. A close examination of these factors forms the subject of the remaining chapters.

[191] Rao, *Survey of Cottage Industries*, p. 86.
[192] Chapter 5 looks at the disappearance of the Pariar weaver.
[193] Thurston, *Castes and Tribes,* vol. 4, p. 351; quoted from a note by Bishop Whitehead.

5

Caste and Work

Specialist weaving castes dominate scholarly discussions of the handloom industry: the most significant are the Kaikolar, Devangar, Saliar and Seniyar.[1] Just as the preoccupation with the role of the merchant obscures other forms of production organisation—including weaving for subsistence—the exclusive focus on specialist weaving castes obscures a wide diversity of producers. Among part-time weavers, by far the largest group were the Pariar. Their contribution to the handloom industry of South India has been discussed already; by the twentieth century, they had largely abandoned weaving as an occupation. The decline of the Pariar weaver runs parallel to the emergence of so-called weaver-capitalists from specialist weaving castes. This chapter contrasts the fate of Pariar weavers to that of the Saurashtras, who successfully made the transition to new forms of production. My purpose is to uncover the role played by caste in shaping divergent outcomes to the same set of external circumstances.

Pariar weavers: the historiography and the background

Part-time weavers—including Pariars—have crept into some scholarly works, for their presence in the sources cannot easily be set aside. But they are presented only to be dismissed in the same breath, so to speak, as anomalies and exceptions. Ian Wendt mentions many weaving castes, noting accurately that four dominate scholarly discussion despite 'there being no strong rationale for excluding the others'.[2] Nevertheless, he stresses the distinction between professional full-time weavers (supposedly from core weaving groups) and non-professional weavers from 'various agrarian groups and "Pariahs" from different low castes'. His list of professional weavers is largely restricted to groups identified as 'specialist' weaving

[1] Parthasarathi, *The Transition to a Colonial Economy*, p. 11.
[2] Wendt, 'The Social Fabric', p. 216.

castes.[3] Swarnalatha notes the presence of Pariar weavers in many districts of the Coromandel coast—by her own account, they formed a majority in parts of Masulipatnam and Guntur—but calls them 'non-traditional'.[4]

In the medieval period, castes in South India were divided into two hierarchically integrated groups called the Left-Hand and Right-Hand castes. The Left-Hand group consisted predominantly of non-agricultural castes (mainly artisans and merchants); the Right-Hand group predominantly of agricultural castes. Specialist weaving castes were counted as Left-Hand. Mattison Mines, in a study that focuses chiefly on the Kaikolar, argues that weavers usually lived in their own settlements and took no part in cultivation.[5] Vijaya Ramaswamy, in her study of the textile industry in medieval South India, regards weaving as a preserve of castes like the Saliar and Kaikolar: in her estimation, medieval weavers remained outside the village community (unlike other service castes like carpenters, blacksmiths and potters who were integrated through the jajmani system).[6]

These writings equate caste with occupation, sometimes in strikingly literal fashion: Ramaswamy defines weavers as 'professional caste groups' and treats all inscriptional references to the Kaikolar, Devangar and Saliar, even when there is no mention of textiles or looms in them, as references to weavers:

> [I]t must be noted that in the inscriptions the caste name and the professional name were considered synonymous. If the inscription mentioned 'Banajiga' or 'Chetti' it could be assumed automatically that the reference was to a merchant, and if it mentioned 'Saliya' or 'Kaikkola' it would be quite natural to assume that the reference was to a weaver.[7]

This procedure is inherently problematic, for Kaikolars are often described as soldiers; we have already seen that some of them owned land as well.

In much the same way, Pariars are equated with 'menials' or agricultural labourers.[8] Weaving has never been regarded as a 'polluting' occupation or a menial one; this translates into the assumption that it could not have been practised by 'untouchable' castes. Their absence from the world of weaving in recent times, combined with the supposed link between 'untouchable' castes and 'polluting' work, impels scholars to explain their 'entry' into

[3] Wendt, 'The Social Fabric', p. 216.

[4] Swarnalatha, *The World of the Weaver*, p. 31.

[5] Mattison Mines, *The Warrior Merchants: Textiles, Trade and Territory in South India* (Cambridge, Cambridge University Press, 1984), pp. 3–10, 18, 37–8, 41, 151.

[6] Ramaswamy, *Textiles and Weavers*, p. 36.

[7] Ramaswamy, *Textiles and Weavers*, p. 15.

[8] Ramaswamy, *Textiles and Weavers*, p. 37.

weaving as a special development. Swarnalatha traces their emergence to the egalitarian spirit of the Bhakti and Virasaiva movements of the twelfth and thirteenth centuries that made the caste system more flexible.[9] Washbrook argues that the eighteenth century, marked by political chaos and commercial expansion, provided opportunities for Pariars to enter new occupations like soldiering and weaving; some even became landholders and petty merchants. But this topsy-turvy world was soon turned right-side-up again; 'the golden age of the pariah' ended with the tightening of colonial rule and the end of textile exports.[10]

But there is no reason to assume that 'untouchable' weavers were exclusively an eighteenth-century phenomenon. Stray references attest to their presence from a much earlier period: an eleventh-century Chola inscription speaks of 'nesavu paraiyans' or weaving Pariars; another inscription dating from 1522 in Dharmavaram taluk refers to four important communities associated with weaving, including Malas. Pariar weavers find mention in the records of the Dutch East India Company.[11] More research is needed to establish the extent of their involvement in weaving and the impact of the political and economic changes of the seventeenth and eighteenth centuries on them.[12]

For the nineteenth century, we have a mass of evidence for supposedly 'untouchable' castes—the Pariar, Koliar, Manniwar and Mala—weaving on a very large scale. According to some missionary accounts, the Pariar had two sub-divisions, the Nesavu (weaving) and the Uzhavu (ploughing).[13] The historic connection of Malas to weaving finds expression in legends associated with the community—one tells the story of Laxmi, the goddess of wealth, who disturbs a Mala busy at his loom. She curses him when he spurns her.[14] It is also reflected in social customs: during her wedding

[9] Swarnalatha, *The World of the Weaver*, pp. 39–44.

[10] David Washbrook, 'Land and Labour in Late Eighteenth-century South India: the Golden Age of the Pariah?', in Peter Robb (ed.), *Dalit Movements and the Meanings of Labour in India* (Delhi, Oxford University Press, 1993), pp. 73, 81.

[11] Swarnalatha, *The World of the Weaver*, pp. 39–40; quoted in Wendt, 'The Social Fabric', p. 219.

[12] Ravi Ahuja argues that labour scarcity in the eighteenth century created favourable conditions for social, occupational and spatial mobility. Ravi Ahuja, 'Labour Relations in an Early Colonial Context: Madras, *c.* 1750–1800', *Modern Asian Studies*, 36(4) (2002), 793–826, at 795.

[13] Rev. A. C. Clayton, 'The Paraiyan and the Legend of Nandan', quoted in Raj Sekhar Basu, *Nandanar's Children: the Paraiyan's Tryst with Destiny, Tamilnadu 1850–1956* (New Delhi, Sage Publications, 2011), p. 21.

[14] Thurston, *Castes and Tribes*, vol. 4, p. 363.

ceremony, the Mala bride places her foot on the weaver's beam and the groom places his foot on hers.[15]

In the early nineteenth century, 'untouchables' formed a quarter of weavers in the Madras Presidency (rising to half in some districts). Most of them lived in the dry inland where the agricultural season was short (and especially in cotton-producing regions with easy access to cotton and yarn): this hypothesis is borne out by the sources for Kadapa, Kurnool, Guntur, Coimbatore, Baramahal (Salem) and Madurai districts. It also fits the theory that the bondage of 'untouchable' castes was harshest in zones of *irrigated* agriculture.[16] Even in the textile centres of the Coromandel coast, Pariars wove cloth for local consumption in some districts and, as specialist spinners, played a prominent role in the handloom industry as a whole.

The Pariar weaver in the early nineteenth century

The vast majority of 'untouchable' weavers made coarse cloth—one reason why many scholars dismiss them as unskilled and unworthy of attention. But most people wore coarse cloth and many 'professional' weavers made it too. Weaving groups in every region tended to specialise: Pariars were noted for making strong, white cloth called parkalla or khadi.[17] It had different degrees of fineness and resembled cloth made by Togatarus and Kaikolars, who were 'professional' or 'specialist' weavers.[18]

Some 'untouchable' weavers also produced fine cloth. The Koliar of Baramahal made fine parkallas (described as long cloth or fine, white cloth).[19] Manniwars were reported to 'weave the finest kinds of turbans, and none of the other cloths of the Jadars, but all those made by the Kaikolars. Their manufacture excels in fineness that of all other castes of weavers.'[20] A servant of the Dutch East India Company noted the presence of many Pariar weavers making 'very good textiles' in some villages of the Kaveri delta.[21]

Most 'untouchable' weavers also worked part-time—this contributes to their neglect, for it is assumed that their 'actual' or 'real' occupation was

[15] Thurston, *Castes and Tribes*, vol. 4, p. 361.
[16] Kumar, *Land and Caste*, p. 35.
[17] Buchanan, *A Journey from Madras*, vol. 1, p. 218.
[18] Buchanan, *A Journey from Madras*, vol. 1, pp. 217–18, 355; *The Baramahal Records*, Section VII: Imposts, pp. 27, 64, 65.
[19] *The Baramahal Records*, Section VII: Imposts, pp. 64, 108
[20] *The Baramahal Records*, Section VII: Imposts, p. 27.
[21] Quoted in Wendt, 'The Social Fabric', p. 219.

distinct from weaving. But we have seen that a very considerable quantity of cloth was made by part-time weavers who also worked as fishermen, cultivators, petty traders or agricultural labourers. Many members of specialist weaving castes had other sources of income too, notably in the form of land and cattle. It has been pointed out that the monsoon was a slack time for weaving in general: the climate hampered work (especially warping, which had to be done out of doors) and yarn was in short supply, for most spinners were busy with agricultural work.

Pariars practised a variety of occupations in regions of rain-fed agriculture. In the late eighteenth and early nineteenth centuries, they are described as smelting iron, weaving and soldiering, apart from working in the fields. Weaving was usually combined with agricultural labour. The time spent on each occupation fluctuated from year to year, depending upon the availability of work and raw materials. According to Thurston, many Malas made cloth for eight months in a year.[22] In Baramahal, Munro seems to assume that the Koliar—apart from Totties and Taliars, who also worked as village servants—were full-time weavers.[23]

In weaving for subsistence, the customer usually supplied the weaver with thread (or cotton).[24] This was a common practice, and not just in the case of Pariar weavers. They also made cloth with yarn spun in their own households or bought in local markets.[25] Some Pariar weavers were also hired by merchants and different European companies to weave cloth.[26] This was a relatively uncommon occurrence, if only because they were usually poor and merchants were chary of giving them advances.[27] In any case, they did not take part in the jajmani system of reciprocal obligations: they were not given a proportion of the harvest in return for weaving.

There are (unreliable) estimates of incomes of different groups of weavers: Pariars occupy the bottom of this scale, although it should be stressed that their earnings were not very different from those of poor weavers from specialist weaving castes.[28] They often paid the lowest rate of loom tax,[29] which bore a rough relation to the quality of cloth and the

[22] Thurston, *Castes and Tribes*, vol. 4, p. 350.
[23] *The Baramahal Records*, Section VII: Imposts, p. 115.
[24] This has already been discussed in earlier chapters.
[25] Havell, *Reports Submitted*, p. 19.
[26] *The Baramahal Records*, Section VII: Imposts, p. 22.
[27] *The Baramahal Records*, Section VII: Imposts, p. 22.
[28] PBR vol. 1942, no. 49, 25 November 1844, p. 16129, TNSA.
[29] PBR vol. 1325, no. 47, 24 May 1832, p. 5011, TNSA; PBR vol. 1942, no. 49, 25 November 1844, p. 16135, TNSA.

income of the producer. It seems reasonable to assume that their social status played some role in depressing their wages.

The disappearance of the Pariar weaver

The process of change that resulted in the expulsion of 'untouchable' weavers has already been discussed. By the third decade of the twentieth century, a few Malas in Kurnool and Cuddapah still made coarse cloth for local consumption.[30] There were Adi Dravida weavers in some pockets of Madurai and Thiruchirapalli.[31] In Ilupur and Aravankurichi (Thiruchirapalli), only 15 out of 100 weaving households remained: some of them were reported to 'have taken to agriculture, some to cooly work and others have migrated to Ceylon and other places in search of work'.[32] They worked on their own looms in their homes.[33] Venkatraman records some Mala weavers in the Telugu country and 'Panchamas' (a term used to describe 'untouchable' castes in general) in the Tamil districts during the early 1930s.[34] In Salem district, there were 225 families of 'Adi Dravida' weavers in areas where weaving was still dispersed: Venkatraman describes them as 'relics of the old village communities'.[35]

Missionaries helped Christian converts to continue weaving for a while. In the districts of Tirunelveli and Ramnad, many Koliars had converted to Christianity during the 1870s. In the 1920s, some Koliar weavers were said to work for Christian middlemen who supplied them with yarn and sold the cloth to an exporting firm in Tirunelveli town.[36] In Tirupur, Pariar

[30] Rao, *Madras Presidency*, p. 17.
[31] Rao, *Survey of Cottage Industries*, pp. 6, 17.
[32] Rao, *Survey of Cottage Industries*, p. 18.
[33] Venkatraman, *The Handloom Industry*, p. 78.
[34] Venkatraman, *The Handloom Industry*, p. 181. According to him, 'non-weaving' castes like 'Vellalas, Mussalmans, Panchamas, Balijas and Malas' comprised approximately 30 per cent of all weavers; workers in handloom factories were 'mainly of "non-weaver" castes, especially in the west coast'. Roy interprets this to mean that they were Panchamas, Muslims, Balijas and Malas. Roy, *Artisans and Industrialization*, p. 84. This is somewhat misleading, for there were hardly any factories in regions where Malas lived (Venkatraman, *The Handloom Industry*, p. 69). In the Tamil speaking districts, Pariars or Panchamas worked from home and not in factories. On the west coast, the first factory weavers were Christian converts from the Basel Mission; their caste is unknown. Evidence for later periods shows that factory weavers, even when they hailed from non-weaving castes, rarely belonged to 'untouchable' castes.
[35] Venkatraman, *The Handloom Industry*, p. 275.
[36] J. S. Ponniah, *Research Studies in the Economic and Social Environment of the Indian Church: an Enquiry into the Economic and Social Problems of the Christian Community in Madura, Ramnad and Tinnevelly Districts* (Madurai, American College, 1938), pp. 104–6.

weavers wove khadi cloth for a khaddar company organised by the Congress Khaddar Board; in Karur, they were members of the Basel Mission and worked in handloom factories set up by it.[37] According to a sample survey carried out in the Tamil-speaking districts of the former Madras state in 1960, 'Harijans' formed only 0.67 per cent of weavers; as many as 185 out of 187 lived in just one district (Tirunelveli).[38]

Men and women from 'non-weaving' castes joined the handloom industry in large numbers during the twentieth century.[39] These included Vellalas and Balijas in some regions.[40] The Fact Finding Committee of 1940 noted that many members of cultivating castes like Gounders, Vanniyars, Reddis and Vellalas had taken to weaving.[41] In 1954, sample surveys conducted by the Textile Enquiry Committee recorded many weavers from agricultural castes.[42] In 1960, the sample survey for the census showed that 11.26 per cent of all weavers came from 'non-weaving' castes (excluding 'untouchables').[43] By 1960, less than 1 per cent of all weavers were from so-called untouchable castes, but over 10 per cent came from castes without any previous association with weaving.[44]

One reason for the disappearance of the 'untouchable' weaver has already been discussed. Weaving for subsistence was predicated on direct access to yarn; with the mechanisation of spinning, the Pariar weaver was cut off from his raw material. He lacked the resources to buy mill yarn and invest in new looms. But this does not explain why he failed to become a wage labourer (like other poor weavers) in handloom factories and workshops. This brings us to the second factor in his exclusion, namely his social status.

[37] Ranga, *The Economics of Handlooms*, pp. 141, 144.

[38] *Census of India 1961*, p. 64. By this time, the Kannada- and Telugu-speaking districts of the former Madras Presidency had been hived off from Madras State. Malas, who continued to weave in some parts of the Deccan, are not recorded in this survey. 'Harijans', literally children of god refers to so-called untouchable castes. The term was introduced by Gandhi and came to be used widely, even in official documents. Individuals from 'untouchable' castes and their political organisations objected to it (as being condescending), popularising the term 'Dalit' instead.

[39] During the early nineteenth century, some members of some cultivating castes made cloth. But new entrants into weaving in the twentieth century usually abandoned agriculture altogether.

[40] Venkatraman, *The Handloom Industry*, p. 181.

[41] *Fact Finding Committee*, Appendix 25.

[42] *Textile Enquiry Committee*, pp. 175, 183, 194, 199, 216.

[43] *Census of India 1961*, p. 63.

[44] *Census of India 1961*, p. 63.

Plate 17

Company painting, gouache on watercolour, dated *c.*1840–50, by an unknown artist from Thanjavur. A pencil inscription in English reads ‘Brass pot makers’. Museum number: IS.1-1990, © Victoria and Albert Museum, London.

Plate 18

Company painting, gouache on watercolour, dated 1830, by an unknown artist from Thanjavur. The inscriptions in Telugu under each couple describe them as carpet weavers (the man carries a carpet under his arm), cloth weavers (the man holds a finished piece of cloth) and tailors respectively. The women carry the tools of their trades. Museum number: IS.39:12-1987, © Victoria and Albert Museum, London.

Plate 19

Company painting, gouache, dated 1770, by an unknown artist from Thanjavur. Part of a series of 36 paintings depicting different castes and occupations. The inscription in English reads 'Pot Maker'. Museum number: AL.9128:30, © Victoria and Albert Museum, London.

Plate 20

Company painting, gouache, dated 1770, by an unknown artist from Thanjavur. Part of a series of 36 paintings depicting different castes and occupations. The inscription at the bottom (in English) reads 'Basket Maker'. Museum number: AL.9128:34, © Victoria and Albert Museum, London.

Plate 21

Company painting, gouache, dated 1790, by an unknown artist from Thanjavur. One of a series of 16 paintings depicting different castes and occupations. The man carries a chicken and a kettle, the woman a fish. The inscription (in English) reads 'An officer's cook'. Museum number: 0925:2/(IS), © Victoria and Albert Museum, London.

Plate 22

Company painting, gouache, dated 1770, by an unknown artist from Thanjavur. Part of a series of 36 paintings depicting different castes and occupations. The English inscription at the bottom reads 'Faqueer cast' [*sic*]. 'Fakir' was the common term for a Muslim ascetic. Museum number: AL.9128:12, © Victoria and Albert Museum, London.

Plate 23

Company painting, gouache, dated 1800, by an unknown artist from Thanjavur. Part of a series of 14 paintings depicting different castes and occupations. An inscription at the back reads 'Komuthy Cash Merchant' in English and Tamil. In all probability, it shows a money lender. Museum number: AL.8940G, © Victoria and Albert Museum, London.

Plate 24

Company painting, gouache on watercolour, dated *c.* 1840–50, by an unknown artist from Thanjavur. Part of a series of 16 paintings depicting various occupations. It shows a woman de-seeding cotton using a churka and another woman fluffing it up with a bow. Museum number: IS.97-1989, © Victoria and Albert Museum, London.

Plate 25

Company painting, gouache on watercolour, dated *c.* 1840–50, by an unknown artist from Thanjavur. Part of a series of 16 paintings depicting various occupations. It shows a woman on a spinning wheel and another woman winding the yarn into hanks. Museum number: IS.100-1989, © Victoria and Albert Museum, London.

Plate 26

Company painting, gouache on watercolour, dated *c*. 1840–50, by an unknown artist from Thanjavur. Part of a series of 16 paintings depicting various occupations. An inscription in pencil reads ‘Malabar wiver cast’ [*sic*]. Museum number: IS.102-1989, 1840-50, © Victoria and Albert Museum, London.

Plate 27

A man operating a warping frame in a hut in Chirala, Andhra Pradesh. Before this, women had to walk up and down between sticks, twisting the thread around them to make the warp. With the warping frame, this became a specialised job: it was no longer performed by the weaver's family but in warping workshops or warping sections of weaving factories. Photograph by *Pankaj Seksharia.*

Plate 28

Women working in a handloom factory in Madurai, Tamil Nadu. They're winding bobbins of thread to be inserted into fly shuttles used to weave the weft. Photograph by *Karuna Dietrich Wielenga*.

Plate 29

A man working a loom fitted with a jacquard at the weaving centre in Kalakshetra, Chennai. The jacquard is the box-like apparatus on the top with cards hanging from it. It consists of a chain of cards, each with a pattern of holes punched into it. They pass over a matrix of pins, activating them. In turn, these pins raise warp threads according to a sequence determined by the punched holes. The jacquard loom allowed weavers to make intricate patterns at much faster speeds. Photograph by *Karuna Dietrich Wielenga*.

Plate 30

A woman weaving on a loom in a handloom factory in Madurai, Tamil Nadu. Her hand holds the cord: when pulled, it propels the shuttle across the beam, through the 'shed' or gap formed by alternating warp threads. The introduction of the fly shuttle speeded up weaving and increased output. Before this, the weaver had to throw the shuttle through the 'shed' with

Plate 31

A newspaper photograph showing some of the volunteers who helped organise a handloom weavers conference in Madurai in 1945. The accompanying article states that there were 500 volunteers in all: 300 handloom weavers, 150 mill workers and 50 women. Source: British Library, Endangered Archives Project, EAP372/9/6/15 Janacakti [11 Apr 1945]. DOI: https://doi.org/10.15130/EAP372.

Plate 32

A warp being wound onto a beam after sizing in Chirala, Andhra Pradesh. This is a Malkha warp (using yarn spun from

In the new structures of handloom production, workers were recruited and controlled through networks of caste and kinship. Pariars had no master weavers in their ranks to employ them. The new workspaces were communal, with workers congregating in factories and workshops; a small workshop might be no more than a room in a master weaver's house. In this kind of setting, social prejudice was allowed full play. It is extremely unlikely that loomless workers from specialist weaving castes (or indeed any other caste) would agree to work in close proximity to an 'untouchable' and their chances of being employed by master weavers from other castes were vanishingly small.

Another obstacle lay in the fact that weaving skills were usually transmitted through an informal system of apprenticeship. In Dharmavaram, the apprenticeship system was as follows:

> If a father has only one son, he himself trains him. If he has three or four boys, he trains one of them and the rest are sent to other weavers to learn work. While under training, these boys are not paid anything for six months, in which period they are expected to learn their trade. After the elapse of the six months, they are paid one rupee each per month until they become good workmen.[45]

Silk and art silk weaving saw something of a boom in the second half of the twentieth century in the Arani region; many men and women from non-weaving castes, especially Vanniyars (who worked as small cultivators or agricultural labourers) became weavers. Pariars were unable to do this because the skills required to make fine saris with solid borders could only be acquired by working as assistants to weavers. These weavers were perfectly willing to take Vanniyars as apprentices, but not somebody from a supposedly 'untouchable' caste.[46]

The factory system displayed social exclusion in its starkest form. Pariar weavers were absent from handloom factories in cities like Madurai, although workers from agricultural castes were freely admitted. Handloom factories were open to new entrants, but closed to 'untouchable' castes.[47] In an analogous way, 'untouchables' were excluded from the spinning sections

[45] Ranga, *The Economics of Handlooms*, pp. 81, 82, 109–10.

[46] D. Jayaraj and K. Nagaraj, *Socio-economic Factors Underlying Growth of Silk-Weaving in the Arani Region – a Preliminary Study*, Themes in Social Sector Research: the S. Guhan Memorial Series, Monograph 5 (Madras, Madras Institute of Development Studies, 2006), p. 31.

[47] Geert de Neve, studying the handloom industry in one South Indian town in the 1980s, found that while there were new entrants into weaving from several castes, Dalits were excluded. He argues that this was because of the sharing of space and food in handloom workshops and factories. de Neve, *The Everyday Politics*, pp. 170–1.

of Bombay's textile mills because the practice of licking broken threads before joining them was held to be 'contaminating' if *they* did it.[48]

The creation of new spaces where workers worked in close proximity to each other played a key role in the disappearance of the 'untouchable' weaver. Before this, he worked in his own home, using his own tools; the cloth made by him carried no stigma as long as he worked in isolation—indeed, it was sought for its durability and strength. But once systems of production and the arrangement of workspaces changed, bringing workers from different castes into close proximity, Pariar weavers were promptly excluded from the industry.

For Tirthankar Roy, this restructuring represents the suppression of its less-skilled and inefficient ('obsolete') or 'backward segments'. In contrast, the 'progressive segments' were able to adapt and restructure production along capitalist lines (by reorganising labour more efficiently).[49] There is another way of looking at the question: the supposedly faceless, inefficient and obsolete parts of the handloom industry consisted of 'untouchable' weavers, women who spun yarn, and poor weavers from specialist weaving castes. In modern Tamil Nadu, the association of Pariars with weaving has vanished entirely and no trace of it remains in the folk memory of even the Pariar themselves. Scholarly works on Pariars (and other Dalit castes) rarely mention their association with weaving.[50]

Discourses around caste and work

What does this association tell us? To begin with, it makes a significant contribution to the evolving discussion on caste. There have been innumerable attempts to explain caste using categories of race, occupation, ritual hierarchy and so on. Since the pioneering work of Louis Dumont, the concept of purity and pollution, opposing 'clean' to 'unclean' work, has come to dominate general accounts and academic theories about caste. Thus, 'untouchable' castes are associated with 'unclean' work such as

[48] Gail Omvedt, *Dalits and the Democratic Revolution: Dr. Ambedkar and the Dalit Movement in Colonial India* (Delhi, Sage Publications, 1994), pp. 141–2.

[49] Roy, *Artisans and Industrialization*, pp. ix, x, 2–5, 73.

[50] Some studies refer to a sub-division of Pariars called 'Necavar Paraiyar' or 'Nesavu Paraiyar', literally 'weaver Pariars'. Robert Deliege, *The Untouchables of India* (Oxford, Berg, 1999), pp. 60, 116–45; David Mosse, 'Idioms of Subordination and Styles of Protest among Christian and Hindu Harijan Castes in Tamilnadu', *Contributions to Indian Sociology*, 28(1) (1994), 67–106; Basu, *Nandanar's Children*, pp. 17, 21.

tanning and scavenging—but not with weaving, which has no connotations of ritual pollution.

By contrast, David Mosse argues that while the purity-pollution binary is important as an idiom of relationships of dominance and dependence in which Dalit castes are involved, it is not definitive of the whole discourse: it is 'the social relationship rather than the impurity of the action [that] defines inferiority. In so far as it is relevant to caste status, the cultural definition of impurity is inseparable from the service relationship of which it is a powerful sign.'[51]

In the light of this explanation, it is striking that weaving outside the jajmani system was practised by so many 'untouchable' castes during the nineteenth century. Is it possible that occupational and income diversity gave its practitioners more flexibility in setting the rules of social engagement? If so, this relative independence was limited in that most 'untouchable' weavers also worked as agricultural labourers. Interestingly, the origin myth of the 'Nesavu Paraiyans' lays claim to their 'true' identity as high-caste weavers (Koliyapillai).[52]

The association of supposedly unclean work with ritual pollution breaks down quite often—there is nothing impure about agricultural work (performed largely but not exclusively by Dalit castes). But it is possible to discern some correspondence between the raw materials of a trade and *relative* status. Within different categories of weavers, as Bayly points out, there existed a hierarchy: weavers of coarse cloth were at the bottom and those making silk at the top. Silk carried connotations of purity and wealth, for it was worn during ritual ceremonies.[53] Among leather workers, those who handled it 'in the raw' were stigmatised more than those who worked it after curing.[54]

The relationship of occupation to social status is complex and contradictory, for relationships of subordination and dependence also come into play. Many examples reveal its elasticity. Vijaya Ramaswamy discusses the changing status of Kaikolars from the medieval period, although their occupation remained unaltered. In the mid-nineteenth century, Saurashtra weavers did not rank particularly high in status terms according to the author of the *Madura Manual*.[55] Some decades later, wealthy Saurashtras began to claim Brahmin status through an organised campaign. Meanwhile the association

[51] Mosse, 'Idioms of Subordination', pp. 71, 87.
[52] Mosse, 'Idioms of Subordination', p. 89.
[53] Bayly, 'The Origins of Swadeshi', p. 294.
[54] Shahana Bhattacharya, 'Labour in the Leather Industry in India, 1870s–1970s', PhD thesis (University of Delhi, 2012), pp. 175–216.
[55] Nelson, *The Madura Country*, pp. 187–8.

of 'untouchability' with certain occupations solidified. Ramnarayan Rawat argues that 'the factor that has contributed most to the continued subordination of Dalits has been the ghettoization of their communities into so-called "traditional" and "ritually impure" occupations.'[56] This process becomes particularly visible from the late nineteenth century on.

Pariar weavers and the census

Nicholas Dirks argues that modern understandings of caste are influenced by the colonial archive and the policies of the colonial state, especially from the late nineteenth century, when anthropological views of Indian society began to be reflected in them.[57] Many colonial observers and Indian intellectuals rejected occupational explanations of caste, citing evidence from the census, but it proved surprisingly durable. Starting with Dumont, ritual purity was conflated with occupational purity: supposedly 'unclean' occupations were associated with supposedly 'untouchable' castes.

But many 'unclean' occupations are not traditional but modern. Tanning as an industry emerged only in the twentieth century, and tannery owners and colonial bureaucrats actively encouraged the recruitment of Pariars *because* they were traditionally associated with the handling of cattle carcasses: their inferior social status was held to qualify them for supposedly 'polluting' work. In actual fact, as Shahana Bhattacharya shows, Pariars were new recruits to the industry.[58] Ramnarayan Rawat argues that the association of Chamars with the ritually 'impure' occupation of leather working was largely constructed during the nineteenth and twentieth centuries through Hindu, colonial and post-colonial representations of untouchability. In the early nineteenth century, Chamars were primarily agriculturists also involved in occupations like weaving and tanning; their subsequent identification with leather work had the effect of reinforcing their 'untouchability'.[59]

Nowadays most scholars would agree that the census did not merely record information about social groups, it also influenced social structure in terms of collective self-representation. Let us examine census data on

[56] Ramnarayan S. Rawat, *Reconsidering Untouchability: Chamars and Dalit History in North India* (Delhi, Permanent Black, 2012), p. 3.

[57] Nicholas B. Dirks, *Castes of Mind: Colonialism and the Making of Modern India* (Delhi, Permanent Black, 2002).

[58] Bhattacharya, 'Labour in the Leather Industry in India', pp. 175–216.

[59] Rawat, *Reconsidering Untouchability*.

Pariar weavers in this light. In the 1871 census, the population of India was divided into 18 broad caste categories taken to be synonymous with different occupations. Thus, in the Madras Presidency, all cultivating castes were enumerated under the head 'Vellalar' (a dominant caste of cultivators); 'low' or labouring castes under the head 'Pariar'; and weaving castes under the head 'Kaikalar' (the Kaikolar being a very large caste of 'specialist' weavers).[60] A similar classification was adopted in the census of 1881 despite the admission that 'the lines of occupation and of caste no longer enclose identical spaces'.[61]

The list of castes grouped under the category of weavers/'Kaikalar' does not contain Malas or Pariars; the Koliar or Koliyan, elsewhere identified as a sub-caste of the Pariar, is the only 'untouchable' caste listed in it. However, only 47.4 per cent of those listed under this head are classified under the occupational category of 'Dress' (that is, those whose occupation was making cloth *and* shoes) while 21.3 per cent are recorded as being engaged in cultivation. On the other hand, most 'untouchable' castes, including the Malas, are listed under the category of labourers/'Pariar', but 26.4 per cent of them are placed under the occupational category of 'Dress', indicating they were involved in the manufacture of cloth or shoes.

Revealingly, the compiler of the final report assumes that all of them were cobblers (an occupation stigmatised because of its association with leather).[62] But they included a great many inhabitants of Kadapa and Nellore, where, as we know, many Mala weavers lived. The 1891 census maintains this discrepancy: the list of castes grouped under 'Kaikolar' retains the Koliar, but omits the Mala and the Pariar. The gap between occupational and caste categories is viewed as a sign of change, the erosion of traditional patterns of employment. In actual fact, these patterns were much more complex than officials assumed.

This discussion should not be taken to imply that caste had no influence on occupation. The caste system was adaptive, not rigid, and changed over time. But jati (caste) had a strong effect on an individual's working life in terms of circumscribing his or her choices and enforcing structural disabilities on groups at the bottom of the social pyramid. This was true of Pariar weavers; their failure to throw up head weavers or merchants is an index of their social subordination. They figure prominently among weavers

[60] William Robert Cornish, *Report on the Census of the Madras Presidency, 1871* (Madras, Government Press, 1874).
[61] *Census of India, 1881: Madras, the Report*, vol. I (Madras, Government Press, 1883), p. 104.
[62] Cornish, *Report on the Census*, p. 170.

who made cloth free of charge for zamindars in exchange for exemption from the loom tax.[63] Merchants in Baramahal, supplying cloth to the EIC, complained that Koliar weavers were too poor to be trusted with advances. From the seventeenth to the nineteenth centuries, weavers from specialist weaving castes came together at regular intervals to demand higher wages or assert control over the production process.[64] The only instance of Pariar weavers acting in this way that I have been able to discover is a petition for reducing the loom tax.[65]

Despite this, weaving offered significant economic benefits and its loss meant a substantial contraction of available opportunities. Its long-term effects are visible in the exclusion of Pariars from the modern textile industry. This was linked to the transfer of concepts of 'pollution' and 'purity' to modern workspaces. This does not imply that Pariar weavers were not stigmatised before this period. However, their exclusion from an occupation that was *not* stigmatised helped to shape the discourse that identified them as practitioners of 'menial' and 'unclean' tasks. The long shadow of this discourse is visible in the treatment of the Pariar weaver in historical and anthropological literature.

Caste and work: the Pattunoolkarar in the nineteenth century

Pattunoolkarars are recorded as living in several districts of the Madras Presidency—Madurai, Thanjavur, Thiruchirapalli, Chengalpattu, Baramahal and Coimbatore—in the nineteenth century. They trace their origin to the region of Saurashtra in Gujarat (hence the appellation Saurashtras). According to ancestral traditions, they migrated to the deep south in slow stages between the sixth and sixteenth centuries. Their language or dialect—a mixture of Gujarati, Marathi, Telugu and Tamil—supports this tradition.[66] Some of them settled in the Deccan (where they were called Puttegars).[67]

[63] PBR vol. 1327, no. 25, 11 June 1832, p. 5352, TNSA.

[64] Parthasarathi, *The Transition to a Colonial Economy*, pp. 101–20; Swarnalatha, *The World of the Weaver*, pp. 123–45.

[65] *The Baramahal Records*, Section VII: Imposts, pp. 115–16. Aparna Balachandran has uncovered petitions by Pariars (not weavers) in the city of Madras: Aparna Balachandran, 'Christ and the Pariah: Colonialism, Religion and Outcaste Labor in South India, 1780–1830', PhD thesis (Columbia University, 2008), pp. 81–144.

[66] K. R. R. Sastry, *The Madura Saurashtra Community: a Study in Applied Economics* (Bangalore, Bangalore Press, 1927), pp. 5–6.

[67] Buchanan, *A Journey from Madras*, vol. 1, p. 208; Thurston, *Castes and Tribes*, vol. VI, pp. 162–3.

It is possible that this migration was completed during the Nayaka period, for they claimed the patronage of many Nayaka rulers.

The literal meaning of Pattunoolkarar in Tamil is 'silk thread people' and they are usually referred to as silk weavers. By the nineteenth century, they were also making fine cotton cloth. In 1792, the Pattunoolkarar of Baramahal were described as weavers of silk and cotton.[68] The Pattunoolkarar of the Bangalore-Mysore region made cloth entirely in silk or a mixture of cotton and silk: this was described as 'very rich, strong fabric' and 'very much varied by the different colours employed, and the different figures woven in the cloth'. Their output 'rarely consist[ed] of plain work'. Gold thread (zari) was also used, but only on commission. The value of their output was reported to be much higher than cloth made by other weavers.[69]

In Madurai, the Pattunoolkarar were famous for red saris and turbans, and white dhotis with intricate borders of red and gold.[70] The saris and turbans used tie and dye, a technique they may have brought with them from Gujarat.[71] They dyed the cloth themselves, with colour extracted from the chay root; Madurai saris were renowned for the quality of their dyeing. The Pattunoolkarar of Baramahal made cloth for export to Thanjavur, Mysore and the Carnatic.[72] From Bangalore, it found its way to 'the country formerly belonging to Tippoo'.[73] Much of their output was for local elites, Crill and Murphy suggest that it was the Maratha rulers of Thanjavur (1675–1853) who popularised tie and dye textiles in the deep south. The Pattunoolkarar settlements of Thiruchirapalli and Kumbakonam probably made textiles for Maratha nobles in the Thanjavur court.[74]

[68] They made striped Kuttanis of cotton and silk used in drawers and petticoats; Korasela, a somewhat coarse red and white gauze silk; Kusamba salla, a coarse gauze for petticoats and gowns; silk and cotton fabric with white and blue or red and yellow stripes; moggisari with blue stripes and silk borders; dorias or striped muslins; charkhanis or cross striped muslins; phuldars or flowered muslins; chadidars or narrow striped muslins; sela or plain muslins; muslins with red borders; jamakalams or cotton carpets striped in blue and red and blue and white. *The Baramahal Records*, Section VII: Imposts, pp. 64–5.

[69] Buchanan, *A Journey from Madras*, vol. 1, pp. 208, 209, 220.

[70] The Forbes Watson Textile Collection has samples of both. Watson, *The Textile Manufactures*, pp. 18, 19; Nelson, *Madura Country*, p. 874; Forbes Watson Textile Collection, Series I, no. 33, 36, 37; *Reports by the Juries*, p. 94.

[71] Murphy and Crill, *Tie-dyed Textiles of India*, pp. 105, 108, 110–11, 115–17.

[72] *The Baramahal Records*, Section VII: Imposts, p. 65.

[73] Buchanan, *A Journey from Madras*, vol. 1, p. 212.

[74] Murphy and Crill, *Tie-dyed Textiles of India*, p. 105.

As weavers of fine cloth, they needed large amounts of working capital, and merchants were involved with them from early on. Buchanan noted that in Bangalore,

> when the goods [of the Puttuegars] are in much demand, it is customary for the merchant to advance one half, or even the whole, of the price of the goods which he commissions; but when the demand is small, the manufacturers borrow money from the bankers at two per cent, a month, and make goods, which they sell to the merchants of the place. They never carry them to the public market.[75]

The purchase of yarn remained the province of the weaver. The Puttuegar of Bangalore kept 'from two to five servants, who were paid by the piece'; along with the Cutterys (who also wove in silk) they were the most prosperous of all weavers.[76] In Madurai, they are described as 'skilful and industrious workmen'. Some had become 'very wealthy': they were 'called "Chetties" or merchants by Tamils, presumably because they themselves retail the cloths which they weave without the intervention of middlemen.'[77]

Change and adaptation

The association of the Pattunoolkarar with fine cloth and silk weaving became even stronger during the course of the twentieth century. In 1920s Madurai, they made fine, white cloth with borders of gold and silver thread.[78] Their tie and dye saris sold in large quantities: by the 1930s, these 'Sungadis' were being exported to North India and Calcutta. Largely because of them, the handloom industry in Madurai city developed a pronounced tilt towards fine cloth production. In the 1920s, less than half the looms in the city used yarn of counts 60 and above; by 1942, as many as 90 per cent were using fine yarn.[79] It was a Saurashtra lawyer, L. K. Tulsiram, who introduced chemical dyes into Madurai in the late nineteenth century and the city soon became famous for combining traditional mordants with modern chemical dyes.[80]

A late nineteenth-century account of the Pattunoolkarar of Madurai reveals considerable economic differentiation. The community included large merchants, petty brokers and coolie weavers. Of the 20,000 to 25,000

[75] Buchanan, *A Journey from Madras*, vol. 1, p. 212.
[76] Buchanan, *A Journey from Madras*, vol. 1, p. 212.
[77] Nelson, *Madura Country*, p. 87.
[78] Saunders, *The Saurashtra Community in Madura*, p. 69.
[79] Yanagisawa, 'The Handloom Industry', 5.
[80] *Papers Relating to the Industrial Conference, 1908*, pp. 200–2.

Pattunoolkarars in the city (including women and children), 10,000 were said to belong to the 'cooly class who earn their living by daily wages'. The income of a coolie weaver was about 5 rupees a month and never rose above 10 rupees. About 400 to 500 families (roughly 2,000 individuals) were said to be 'petty traders'; some 'sell threads purchased in turn from bigger merchants' while others sold lace in retail or advanced 'small sums of money to the holders of looms and order a small supply of cloths and sell them to the richer merchants'. The brokers 'collect cloths manufactured in the town and sell them either to the merchants in the town or abroad'. These were said to be numerous: most of them earned between 5 to 20 rupees a month. There were a few 'capitalists' with very large trading concerns; five or six of them made a profit of 100 rupees or more every month. Larger brokers and merchants employed agents to 'go about the town and watch the progress of cloths entrusted to the labourers' and keep accounts.[81]

By the 1920s, it was common practice 'for a merchant to advance the yarn and receive the finished cloth, for which he pays the weaver a regular rate'.[82] Half the weavers making cotton cloth worked for wages, mostly from home.[83] Attempts to enlist them in handloom factories failed.[84] In 1926, in Paramakudi near Madurai, out of 5,000 Saurashtra families, 500 were reported to be capitalists or 'masters' and another 300 'employers' (smaller master weavers), giving out yarn to be worked into cloth. Many ordinary weavers did not even own their own looms; 'they borrow their looms from capitalists and pay a loom rent of Rs. 8 for weaving one cloth of 45 yards. These people form ten per cent of the total number of weavers.'[85]

In silk weaving, master weavers hired workers for a fixed wage because 'the cloths manufactured are very costly and an artisan needs more than Rs 300 to set up as an independent weaver'. Coolie weavers worked in the master weaver's house 'because he cannot trust them with his materials'.[86] Many Saurashtra women were employed in dyeing factories, tying knots for 2 annas a day. The dyeing industry was in the hands of 'many hundreds of small capitalists each of whom has invested anything from Rs 1000 upwards'. There were about 2,000 factories dyeing cloth in all colours and

[81] Raghavaiyangar, *Memorandum*, Appendix cxxv–vii.
[82] Saunders, *The Sourashtra Community in Madura*, p. 105.
[83] Ranga, *The Economics of Handlooms*, p. 155.
[84] This will be discussed in Chapter 6.
[85] Ranga, *The Economics of Handlooms*, pp. 148–9.
[86] Ranga, *The Economics of Handlooms*, pp. 154–5

2,500 'red' factories (dyeing only in red). These factories employed no more than 20 workers for a few days at a time.[87]

Thus, the Saurashtra community was divided into distinct classes. Wealthy yarn merchants and large master weavers comprised a small minority. As early as 1917, the yarn market of Madurai was said to be controlled by four Saurashtra traders who bought yarn from two firms in Madras. Below this elite were numerous small capitalists (master weavers or dye factory owners). Both groups were active in adapting and promoting new technologies and campaigning for state aid. These technological innovations included new warping techniques, modified jacquards (cheaper than imported ones) and methods of combining traditional mordanting with chemical dyes.[88] In 1921, some of them founded an association, the 'Asu Machine Sangham' 'to encourage the warping industry, to find improved methods of sizing ... to encourage new discoveries and inventions connected with the industry'. A member was reported to have invented a new sizing machine.[89]

But the majority of Saurashtra weavers eked out a bare subsistence. K. R. R. Sastry describes them as living in one-room tenements in narrow and filthy streets with no civic facilities.[90] By his calculation, only 5 per cent of Saurashtras were well-to-do, while 60 per cent were 'leading a hand-to-mouth existence'.[91] Another observer noted that

> most of them are today very poor and miserable, in spite of appearances of prosperity and many writers have mistaken the skill, energy and organising capacity displayed by a few big successes among them for general prosperity. But actual economic conditions do not warrant any such happy conclusions.[92]

By the 1920s, some Saurashtras had diversified into other trades and occupations: there were Saurashtra goldsmiths, carpenters, house-masons, lawyers, doctors, mill owners and so on.[93] Many became landowners although they did not work their holdings personally.[94] According to Ranga,

[87] Ranga, *The Economics of Handlooms*, p. 157.
[88] Sastry, *The Madura Saurashtra Community*, pp. 20–1, 24, 25; Ranga, *The Economics of Handlooms*, p. 152.
[89] Sastry, *The Madura Saurashtra Community*, p. 49.
[90] Sastry, *The Madura Saurashtra Community*, pp. 54, 66.
[91] Sastry, *The Madura Saurashtra Community*, pp. 69–70.
[92] Ranga, *The Economics of Handlooms*, pp. 155–6.
[93] Sastry, *The Madura Saurashtra Community*, p. 36.
[94] Saunders, *The Sourashtra Community in Madura*, p. 26. Ranga reports that the Saurashtras of Madura owned 10,000 acres of wetlands in all, of which roughly 2,000 acres were held by twelve individuals. Ranga, *The Economics of Handlooms*, pp. 155–6.

poor Saurashtra weavers found work as labourers in fields around the city during the agricultural season.[95]

The Saurashtras formed a close-knit community. It was generally believed that they preferred to work with each other and for each other. Saurashtra capitalists usually hired workers from their community;[96] while borrowing money they tapped their compatriots first.[97] The Saurashtra Sabha was established in 1895: its activities included running a school, maintaining the community temple, charity, grants for the upanayanam (sacred thread ceremony) of orphans, promoting the 'social, moral and intellectual advancement of the Saurashtras' and disbursing funds for projects such as digging wells and constructing bathing ghats.[98] It was also active in settling internal disputes.[99]

By the late nineteenth century, wealthy Saurashtras were making a concerted effort to claim Brahmin status. They wrote to the Madras government, asking to be listed under the category of Brahmins in the census. They campaigned for ordinary Saurashtras to return themselves as 'Saurashtra Brahmins'. The Pattunoolkarar returned 54 sub-divisions during the census: a majority described themselves as Saurashtra, some as Brahmin, others as Chetty.[100] Many of them had begun following Brahminical practices: Saunders noted that the incidence of child marriages was increasing, an uncommon practice before this time.[101]

The ambiguous role of community

Roy describes the Saurashtras of Madurai as artisan-capitalists and ascribes their enterprise and growth to a strong sense of community. He takes community to mean '*social organization* which matters to the successful conduct of business' and argues that the Saurashtras actively promoted a sense of community and identity consonant with 'cooperative capitalism'. 'The Saurashtra model of cooperative capitalism had two faces: "benevolence and inwardness", where "benevolence was expressed in social investments and markedly subdued hierarchy", and inwardness in keeping

[95] Ranga, *The Economics of Handlooms*, p. 155.
[96] Sastry, *The Madura Saurashtra Community*, p. 31.
[97] Saunders, *The Saurashtra Community in Madura*, pp. 115–16.
[98] Sastry, *The Madura Saurashtra Community*, pp. 40–1.
[99] Saunders, *The Saurashtra Community in Madura*, p. 118.
[100] *Census of 1891*, vol. 13, Madras Report (Madras, Government Press, 1893), pp. 283–6.
[101] Saunders, *The Saurashtra Community in Madura*, p. 27.

all transactions of business within the community.' He argues that 'the notion of "class" as consciousness or as bargaining group is conspicuous by its absence in *all* sources on Saurashtras, old or new.'[102]

From skilled weavers of fine cloth patronised by ruling elites, the Saurashtras had become a relatively prosperous and economically differentiated group by the late nineteenth century. In subsequent decades, they became divided into a wealthy elite, a somewhat larger 'middle class', and a mass of poor weavers (comprising 80–90 per cent of all Saurashtras). To call this cooperative capitalism and label it the success of an entire community is somewhat misleading. Roy presents it as a *collective* success on the grounds that wealthy Saurashtras invested money for the benefit of the community, especially in education.

But the investment of surplus capital in temples, festivals and educational projects is a fairly common practice. The Nadars of Tirunelveli did it in order to shore up their social position and buttress their claims to higher status. This can only be done by raising it for the *group* as a whole—in the case of the Nadars, this aspiration was driven by a wealthy elite. Nadar merchants invested in schools and scholarships to promote social reform compatible with dominant practices and draw attention away from their traditional occupation of toddy tapping.[103] It is more than likely that Saurashtra merchants acted on the same calculation.

In addition, it was perfectly rational for Saurashtra capitalists to cultivate a benevolent image as a method of gaining ascendancy over their workers. Community networks underpinned new forms of production organisation and played an important role in labour control based on debt and patronage rather than employment contracts.[104] Douglas Haynes and Santosh Rai show how master weavers sought to enhance their position as big men by sponsoring religious festivals, maintaining local temples and arbitrating intra-caste disputes.[105] In the United Provinces, Muslim master weavers used notions of solidarity to tie ordinary weavers to them

[102] Tirthankar Roy, 'Capitalism as Community: a Study of the Madurai Sourashtras', *The Indian Economic and Social History Review*, 34(4) (1997), 447. Emphasis in original.

[103] See Robert Hardgrave, *The Nadars of Tamilnad: the Political Culture of a Community in Change* (Berkeley, University of California Press, 1969).

[104] Haynes shows this very clearly for western India. Haynes, *Small Town Capitalism*, pp. 127–58.

[105] Haynes, *Small Town Capitalism*, pp. 85–9; Santosh Kumar Rai, 'Becoming a Grihasta: Hierarchies of Work among Handloom Weavers in Early Twentieth Century United Provinces, India', in Rana Behal, Alice Mah and Babacar Fall (eds), *Rethinking Work: Global Historical and Sociological Perspectives* (New Delhi, Tulika, 2011), pp. 73–88, at p. 80.

and exclude Hindu merchants.[106] In other words, caste solidarity was used by employers to undercut class solidarity. When weavers formed unions, factory owners sought to dissuade them by stressing the importance of community solidarity.[107]

Community ties were used to strengthen capitalist forms of production. Ordinary weavers were also complicit in this process: we have seen that they preferred borrowing from and working for master weavers and merchants from their own caste. Yet, there were fissures in solidarity. Railway stations had canteens with separate sections for Brahmins and Non-Brahmins; some Saurashtras ate in the Brahmin section while others ate in the Non-Brahmin section, depending upon the 'social status of the individual'.[108]

These fractures occasionally emerged into the open. Roy's contention that the notion of class was absent among the Saurashtras is not quite accurate. Community identity was undercut to some degree by class divisions between workers and capitalists. Saurashtra weavers were among the first to organise themselves into unions and figured prominently in the protests of the 1940s. Some were active in the freedom movement: notable members of the Congress included N. M. R. Subburaman, who came to be known as the 'Madurai Gandhi'. In the 1940s, many Saurashtras, including some former Congressmen, joined the Communists. Among them were R. K. Sandulal and R. V. Siddha, a weaver who played a key role in organising the Handloom Weavers Federation. Before this, he had been active in the campaign to boycott foreign cloth.[109]

An old party member in Madurai explained that on the question of fighting the British and political freedom, the community was largely supportive of the Congress; but when it came to economic issues, they turned to Communist unions.[110] On political and social questions or problems affecting the handloom industry as a whole (such as tariffs), the community preserved a façade of unity, but on issues like wage rates and profiteering by master weavers and yarn merchants, the ordinary Saurashtra weaver adopted other forms of solidarity and collective action.

The fact that their employees belonged to the same caste did not make yarn merchants and master weavers less ruthless in cutting costs

[106] Rai, 'Becoming a Grihasta', pp. 83–5.

[107] *Janasakthi*, 11 April 1945; 6 June 1945.

[108] Saunders, *The Sourashtra Community in Madura*, p. 26.

[109] P. Srinivasan, *Communist Heroes of Tamilnadu* (Part I) (Madras, Marxist Education Society, 2005) (in Tamil), pp. 230, 235.

[110] Interview with Mayandi Barathi, a Communist party worker and one of the editors of *Janasakthi* in the 1940s, Madurai, 18 February 2008.

during downturns. In 1942, the collector of Madurai unsuccessfully tried to persuade them to keep production going in order to avoid large-scale unemployment. An official declared in exasperation that 'the truth of the matter is that the Madurai merchants are unwilling to take even slight risks for the sake of weavers from whose toil they have profited all these days'. Some wealthy Saurashtras set up rice doles for the poor, but made it clear that these would not be continued indefinitely.[111]

Roy argues that the claim to Brahminhood helped Saurashtras 'cement the collectivity which operated behind economic success'. However, this collectivity was a fractured one and its 'success' was restricted to a small minority. Let us look more closely at the attributes of the identity they sought to create. The emphasis on Brahminhood denied the actual work-identity of the vast majority of Saurashtras. In a book entitled *History of the Sourashtras in Southern India*, published by the Sourashtra Literary Society 'for the information of those who are not well acquainted with the origin and history of the Sourashtras' and 'to remove all misunderstandings about the race', it is asserted that the

> Sourashtra Brahmins were originally leading a purely religious life, but now they have begun to do business of different descriptions fitted to their position. Their chief occupation is agriculture, but some are trading, dyeing and weaving; however it can be safely affirmed that their business interferes in no way with their religious creed and ceremonies. The name Putnulgars means *silk weavers,* and is sometimes erroneously applied to the Sourashtras too ... the Sourashtras are now seen as a mercantile community.[112]

Historically, the social status of castes practising weaving fluctuated widely. Some of them laid collective claim to higher social status at different points of time. During the medieval period, these claims were linked to temple service—donations made and privileges obtained during worship, festivals and rituals. The right to blow the conch shell (*sangu*), ride a palanquin and carry a flag in religious processions were sought after symbols of privilege. Conflicts broke out over them during times of social churning as part of the general struggle between Left-Hand and Right-Hand castes.[113]

[111] Development Department, G.O. no. 998 (M-15) MS, 1 May 1942, TNSA. In a parallel example, a Devangar weaver of Vijayanagaram (Visakhapatnam district) remarked that 'our caste Devangars are also as great exploiters of our labour as the Vaishyas. The so-called communal sympathy does not count when economic gain is the goal.'

[112] *History of the Sourashtras in Southern India* (Madras, Sourashtra Literary Society, 1891), pp. 13–14.

[113] Ramaswamy, *Textiles and Weavers*, pp. 54–5.

By the late nineteenth and early twentieth centuries, social claims had been firmly linked to Brahmin, supra-Brahmin or Kshatriya status. Many artisanal castes, and not just weavers, made them; Vishwakarmas (who worked mostly as smiths) asserted they were Brahmins; Kaikolars renamed themselves Senguntha Mudaliars in support of their claim to Kshatriya descent. The key signifier of status shifted from temple endowments to group position in the varnashrama scale. This reflects the importance accorded to classical texts, classical interpretations of hierarchy and their Brahmin interpreters by colonial officials. In this new framework, weaving as an occupation undercut claims to high status. The roots of the negative association between physical labour and social status lie in a Brahminical world view that gained strength during the colonial period.

In this chapter, we looked closely at the trajectories of two different communities whose members practised weaving. With the emergence of new forms of production, Pariar weavers, socially oppressed and poor, were pushed out of the handloom industry. Saurashtra weavers, relatively prosperous and economically differentiated, not only adjusted to these structures but helped to shape them. The vast majority of Saurashtras adapted to a life of insecurity and relative poverty; others entered the middle class; and a small minority made fortunes. These disparate trajectories raise questions about the putative links between caste and work in South India. Work in the sense of physical labour has never held a position of pride in the dominant discourses of Hinduism, but from the late nineteenth century, it becomes possible to discern a much firmer link between work and social status: the Pariar becomes associated with 'ritually impure' occupations like leather work and scavenging, while the Saurashtra elite seeks to disassociate itself from weaving in order to raise its social status.

6

Solidarity and Action

So far, we have examined the process of change in the handloom industry of South India from the early nineteenth century. Its chief elements were a shift towards urbanised production; the emergence of a substantially new and centralised production chain based on new technologies; new actors like the master-weaver cum yarn dealer; and far-reaching alterations in the social composition of the world of weaving.

Weavers responded to this process of change by adapting *and* resisting. Their actions played an important role in shaping the emergent structures of production. Protests and struggles were undertaken to protect collective interests. There were acts of 'everyday resistance' involving choices and practices at an individual level seeking to assert residual control over the production process. Other actions formed part of an ongoing process of adaptation to changing circumstances.

All of them were circumscribed by pre-existing structures of power (political, economic and social). The collective actions of the nineteenth century differed substantially from those of the twentieth century. Each set of responses was shaped by a specific configuration of power, which it attempted to subvert or use. Mobilisation also involved internal structures of solidarity that altered over time. Thus, the trade union as a collective association emerges only in the twentieth century and not before.

Charles Tilly employs the term 'repertoires' to describe what he calls 'claim making routines' adopted by claimant-object pairs. Actions are drawn from an existing repertoire, which, in turn, is shaped by the regime under which the claimants operate (Tilly takes this to be synonymous with the state). Each regime creates a specific environment of political opportunities and threats to which makers of claims necessarily respond. Changes in this environment produce changes in forms of contention. These repertoires are modified slowly over time, alongside changes in the nature of the regime.[1] I make use of this concept to uncover the changing strategies adopted by weavers in South India during the course of the nineteenth and twentieth centuries.

Where Tilly focuses on the state as the primary shaper of repertoires, I extend the analysis to other structures of power, including production systems, caste and the wider political milieu.[2] Changes in forms of organisation and protest were organically linked to changes in the production process, state policies and the larger political context. Internal structures of solidarity played an important role in shaping collective responses; therefore I pay close attention to the process by which they were cemented or fractured.

Collective action is capable of triggering changes in existing power structures. Tilly discusses its ability to challenge political regimes. Haynes and Prakash point out that power is 'constantly being fractured by the struggles of the subordinate'.[3] The setting up of cooperatives and attempts to enact protective legislation in the mid-twentieth century were responses to collective action. It also shaped some aspects of the production process. However, it is important to keep the very unequal balance of power between the contestants in mind while assessing the actual outcomes of popular struggles.

The late eighteenth and early nineteenth century

We have seen that cloth production was organised in many different ways during this period. For those who wove on their own account or with yarn provided by the customer, claim-making was directed towards the state. Weavers working for private merchants also directed their actions against the state by the systematic avoidance of duties on cloth, opposition to the loom tax, and complaints and petitions about yarn and cloth markets. Merchants were the target of less overt, more routine actions: weavers skimped on the quantity and quality of yarn or shifted allegiance from one

[1] Charles Tilly, *Regimes and Repertoires* (Chicago, University of Chicago Press, 2006), pp. 17, 35, 43–4.

[2] Marcel van der Linden points out that Tilly's focus on the state leads him to underplay mode of production, class conflict, and even social and cultural questions. Marcel van der Linden, 'Charles Tilly's Historical Sociology', *International Review of Social History*, 54(2) (2009), 237–74.

[3] Douglas E. Haynes and Gyan Prakash (eds), *Contesting Power: Resistance and Everyday Social Relations in South Asia* (Delhi, Oxford University Press, 1991), pp. 2–3.

employer to another in order to obtain a better price for cloth. Weavers working for the EIC found themselves face-to-face with an entity that acted as employer and political authority, combining commercial and coercive-regulatory functions. It is here, where the two powers merge, that the most overt acts of resistance are visible.

The repertoire of claim-making in the early nineteenth century included individual, group-sanctioned acts (the evasion of duties, the manipulation of yarn); overt yet contained actions such as petitioning and migration; and direct protests involving disruption of yarn and cloth markets, stoppages of work, and mass gatherings. Let us examine each of them in turn.

The most widely documented and possibly the most widespread response to underpayment was a deliberate reduction in the quality and quantity of yarn used to make cloth. Weavers might weave the sides more densely than the middle, or use different kinds of yarn to make the cloth. When market conditions were favourable, they tried to sell cloth to another buyer for a higher price. Both practices were designed to maintain their bargaining position with respect to merchants. In order to obtain cloth of good quality, merchants needed to pay what was recognised as a fair rate (under prevailing conditions), for they exercised little or no control over the production process. For this reason, all attempts by the EIC to intervene in production were deeply resented.[4]

Other forms of resistance included evasion of the stamp duty on cloth and avoidance of the loom tax. These taxes and duties represented a significant burden. After the EIC withdrew from cloth production, it began collecting them with renewed vigour in order to augment its revenues. In 1817, the collector of Madurai wrote to the Board of Revenue about a new system whereby weavers had to provide regular (written) statements informing choukeydars (officers) of the exact quantity of cloth they were in the process of manufacturing. This procedure was introduced to prevent evasion of duties: 'An arrangement of this kind was found necessary as it was discovered that in many villages a very small portion of the cloth which had been woven ever paid duty.'[5] Meanwhile, weavers and merchants in Madurai district found ways to imitate the 'chop' or impress made on the cloth after the duty had been paid.[6]

[4] Parthasarathi, *The Transition to a Colonial Economy*, pp. 101–20; Swarnalatha, *The World of the Weaver*, pp. 123–45.

[5] MDR, vol. 1166, p. 27, TNSA. The EIC brought in new regulations to curb evasion and sought to prosecute and punish offenders. MDR, vol. 1167, pp. 183, 253–4, TNSA.

[6] MDR, vol. 1164, pp. 48–9, TNSA; TDR, vol. 3575, 15 December 1829, TNSA.

As long as the merchant and the state remained distinct, it was possible for weavers to approach the latter for redress against the former. When the two coalesced, little space was left for manoeuvring.[7] Nevertheless they tried, and sometimes succeeded, in taking advantage of departmental differences within the EIC. A favoured method was to approach its commercial residents (responsible for cloth procurement) for support against the demands of revenue officials.

In the late 1790s, in Baramahal, where the EIC had recently opened a factory, weavers and spinners took advantage of different departmental mandates. Those seeking to avoid the loom tax persuaded the commercial resident to support their position against revenue officials demanding payment. The latter complained that many weavers were evading the tax by (falsely) claiming to work for the EIC.[8] The collector of Rajamundhry had this to say:

> The weavers termed company's weavers in this district … have become here the most refractory and troublesome set of inhabitants in the whole country, all authority except that of the commercial resident they set at defiance and instances have occurred that, upon serving the most regular demands for revenue due by them, they have assembled in a body, and driven the peons from their villages.[9]

Weavers also approached revenue authorities to complain about commercial residents forcing them to work for the EIC. The practice of forced work often crops up in the correspondence and there is abundant evidence to show that commercial residents abused their power in many ways.[10] In Baramahal, farmers bringing thread to local markets deposed that they were forced to sell it to Company weavers. Meanwhile, some Company weavers approached Munro with complaints about low payments for cloth.[11]

Weavers living in zamindaris petitioned the EIC against exorbitant taxes or other cesses. Swarnalatha adduces instances where officials intervened to put a stop to exactions and prevent the custom whereby weavers were compelled to buy grain at high prices from zamindars.[12] There

[7] Parthasarathi examines the differences between indigenous states and the EIC with respect to relations with merchants and weavers. Parthasarathi, *The Transition to a Colonial Economy*, pp. 121–48.

[8] Public Department Sundries, vol. 121, no. 27, Commercial Department Consultations, vol. 11, 19 August 1817, p. 1466, TNSA; TDR, vol. 3592, p. 129, TNSA.

[9] TDR, vol. 3594, 3 December 1817, pp. 408–9, TNSA.

[10] MDR, vol. 1190, p. 223, TNSA; PBR vol. 369, 11 January 1804, pp. 667–8, TNSA; PBR vol. 363, 7 November 1803, pp. 12719–20, TNSA.

[11] *The Baramahal Records*, Section VII: Imposts, pp. 14–18, 22–4.

[12] Swarnalatha, *The World of the Weaver*, pp. 124–5.

were incidents of this kind from Tirunelveli and Madurai, where weavers complained against a poligar (anglicised from palayakarar, the Tamil term for a petty ruler or zamindar): his men had looted money and taken cloth without payment for a wedding in his family. Some complained of being flogged and detained, and of having bonds of surety extorted from them.[13] Conversely, some weavers sought protection from poligars against the EIC: this happened in the Etiapoor zamindari.[14] The trade in cloth was an important source of revenue for poligars.[15] The EIC's operations to obtain cloth hurt their interests and many of them were at loggerheads with it for political reasons.

Despite tension between different wings of the EIC, they also worked together. Commercial residents routinely sought the help of revenue officials to collect balances from weavers.[16] Parthasarathi points out that the number (and scale) of weavers' protests reached a peak during the late eighteenth century when the territorial reach of the EIC expanded rapidly. My evidence indicates that this trend continued into the early nineteenth century, until commercial operations were wound up. The EIC used its political authority to prevent weavers from migrating, set revenue officials and military peons to collecting balances, and put down protests by force.

Migration

The phenomenon of mass migration has been widely discussed. It was undertaken for many reasons, ranging from subsistence to tax avoidance, but also as a form of protest. Research on eighteenth-century India has shown that society as a whole was more mobile, less 'fixed' than in the nineteenth century: the inherent unpredictability of the agricultural economy was largely responsible for this.[17] Sometimes weavers were pushed out by famine or war; sometimes they were invited to settle elsewhere on

[13] TDR, vol. 1190, 14 March 1804, pp. 40–1; Letters from Commercial Resident to Acting Collector dated 16 August 1799, 29 October 1799, 9 November 1799, MDR, vol. 1177, p. 50, TNSA. Other examples are in MDR, vol. 1190, p. 55, TNSA.

[14] Extract translation of a message from the Etiapoor gomastah enclosed in a letter from the Commercial Resident to the Acting Collector dated 20 November 1799, vol. 1177, p. 169, TNSA; letter from Commercial Resident to Assistant Collector dated 3 December 1799, vol. 1177, TNSA.

[15] MDR, vol. 1178, pp. 470–1, TNSA; MDR, vol. 1129, p. 163, TNSA.

[16] MDR, vol. 1192, 8 February 1805, pp. 20, 28, 123, TNSA.

[17] Washbrook, 'India in the Early Modern World Economy', 93–5.

better terms; sometimes they migrated in order to obtain better market conditions.

Let us take *necessity* first. One reason for migration was the decline of established centres of power and the consequent drying up of livelihoods. The Pattunoolkarar migrated in stages from Gujarat to the deep south. They settled for a while in the territories of the Vijayanagara empire; after its decline, they moved southwards into the new Nayaka kingdoms.[18] Other groups of weavers in the Tamil region—like the Devangar of Salem and Coimbatore—speak Kannada or Telugu, indicating an analogous process of migration.

Wars also impelled weavers to migrate, sometimes into the victor's domain. After Hyder Ali invaded the EIC's territories, weavers from the Chengalpattu region moved to the Mysore country. A reverse movement was recorded in 1793 when one Triverback Sumbajee approached the collector of Chengalpattu to ask for land to establish a village for the 'accommodation of some artificers said by him to have come from foreign countries'. The immigrants included silk and fine cloth weavers, and lace makers from regions formerly ruled by Tipu and the Marathas: they had left because of 'the dearness of rice and the want of means of procuring a livelihood'.[19]

During famines or near famines, cultivators, weavers and labourers moved to adjoining regions, where food and work could be found. Part-time weavers moved between occupations during hard times. But the nineteenth century also produced a novel kind of migration, driven by the erosion of traditional occupations. Many of the indentured labourers who migrated to Mauritius, Natal and other places had been erstwhile weavers. Pariars unable to earn a living from weaving swelled these numbers.[20]

Migration was also a strategy of *avoidance*. Some weavers would migrate from Tirunelveli to the neighbouring district of Madurai (where the loom tax had been abolished) every year, at the time of assessment, in order to evade it.[21] Weavers in Ganjam moved regularly between zamindari and government villages to avoid the loom tax.[22]

[18] Douglas E. Haynes and Tirthankar Roy, 'Conceiving Mobility: Weavers' Migrations in Pre-colonial and Colonial India', *Indian Economic and Social History Review*, 36(1) (1999), 35–67, at 44.

[19] Chingelput District Records, vol. 445, p. 141, TNSA.

[20] Kumar, *Land and Caste*, pp. 130–1, 139.

[21] PBR vol. 1903, no. 34, 12 February 1844, p. 2578, TNSA.

[22] PBR vol. 1369, no. 8, 20 June 1833, p. 7574, TNSA.

Finally, migration also served as a form of *protest*. In the medieval period, there are instances of weavers leaving a kingdom in protest against high taxes—these might be reduced subsequently to induce them to return.[23] In the seventeenth and eighteenth centuries, they would dismantle their looms and leave (without returning cash advances) in response to what they saw as unfair treatment. Often, this involved moving to a place outside the ruler's control and bargaining with him to facilitate their return.[24]

Ravi Ahuja shows that migration or 'collective withdrawal' was a mode of protest widely used by agrarian labourers as well as rural and urban artisans during the early modern period. He sees this 'ultimate resource against oppression' as part of a regional political culture shared by different groups. In his view, it was particularly effective in the seventeenth and eighteenth centuries, a time of great spatial and social mobility caused by militarisation and commercialisation.[25]

As a form of protest, migration declines and all but disappears during the nineteenth century. What were the reasons for this? The consolidation of power by a single political entity reduced its effectiveness, for it depended upon the existence of many centres of power. Once the hegemony of the EIC had been established, it ceased to work. Its decline was also driven by changes in the nature and exercise of state authority. Prasannan Parthasarathi argues that the EIC represented a normative break with the political practices of previous rulers.[26] In my view, his depiction of the paternalism of pre-colonial polities requires more empirical substantiation, but the argument for a basic shift in regulatory regimes is convincing. The EIC made concerted efforts to enact new rules, including pursuing weavers into neighbouring territories to enforce contracts.[27]

Revenues obtained from trade were critical to the finances of pre-colonial states. Rulers encouraged weavers and other artisans to settle in their territories by giving them tax exemptions. The EIC was forced to

[23] Ramaswamy, *Textiles and Weavers*, p. 34.

[24] Ravi Ahuja, 'Labour Unsettled: Mobility and Protest in the Madras Region, 1750–1800', *The Indian Economic and Social History Review*, 35(4) (1998), 394–5; Parthasarathi, *The Transition to a Colonial Economy*, pp. 106–8, 126.

[25] Ahuja, 'Labour Unsettled', 381–404; Jon E. Wilson, '"A Thousand Countries to Go to": Peasants and Rulers in Eighteenth-Century Bengal', *Past and Present*, 189(1) (2005), 81–109.

[26] Parthasarathi, *The Transition to a Colonial Economy*, pp. 121–48.

[27] Parthasarathi, *The Transition to a Colonial Economy*, p. 93; Karuna, 'Weaving Histories', pp. 207–8.

adopt this practice in order to compete successfully with them.[28] However it never ceased to resent it—its officials argued against these exemptions, and this view gathered strength as its involvement in the textile trade waned.[29] At the same time, the EIC enacted procedures and regulations derived from English jurisprudence, modified to suit a colonial context.[30] The written contract and its enforcement became central to this new system of jurisprudence. Collective withdrawal was viewed as a breach of contract, deserving of punishment, rather than as a legitimate form of protest, to be resolved by negotiations. In the final analysis, its effectiveness depended upon the willingness of the state to recognise its legitimacy and engage with its practitioners—this the colonial state refused to do.[31]

Methods of protest: conflicts over the loom tax and duties on cloth

A closer look at the conflicts over the loom tax and cloth duties reveals a whole repertoire of claim-making, including avoidance, migration, petitioning, mass assemblies and even threats of violence. The drive to increase revenue collections combined with theories of political economy made officials reluctant to relinquish the loom tax. Meanwhile, the introduction of cloth duties led to widespread discontent.[32] A common response was evasion and petitioning.[33] Throughout the first half of the nineteenth century, weavers in

[28] MDR, vol. 1146, 20 December 1803, p. 72, TNSA; MDR, vol. 1187, 22 March 1803, p. 41, TNSA; MDR, vol. 1178 II, 12 July 1802, p. 368, TNSA; PBR vol. 356, no. 7, 22 August 1803, pp. 9682–5, TNSA.

[29] PBR vol. 455, no. 7, 9 November 1807, p. 8790, TNSA; consultation dated 28 February 1856 in India Revenue Consultations, 5 January to 28 March 1856, P/193/39, IOR, London.

[30] For the late eighteenth century, see Ravi Ahuja, 'The Origins of Labour Policy in Late Eighteenth-Century Madras', *The International Review of Social History*, 44(2) (1999), 159–95; Prabhu Mohapatra shows that criminalisation of breach of contract lay at the core of colonial jurisprudence in the nineteenth century. Mohapatra, 'Regulated Informality'.

[31] This does not imply that pre-colonial states were 'benevolent', only that they recognised collective withdrawal as a legitimate method of protest. They also lacked the coercive capacity to force weavers to return. For a discussion of the limits of power in pre-colonial polities, see Shashank Kela, *A Rogue and Peasant Slave: Adivasi Resistance 1800–2000* (New Delhi, Navayana, 2012), pp. 19–45.

[32] Buchanan writes about weavers complaining against taxes in Salem district. Buchanan, *A Journey from Madras*, vol. 1, pp. 241–2, 264–5. In Rajamundhry, they objected to peons 'entering their houses at all times to stamp goods in the looms'. PBR vol. 380, no. 7, 31 May 1804, p. 4499, TNSA.

[33] Petitioning was probably employed in earlier periods as well. The extent of its use awaits further research. For Rajasthan, see Nandita Prasad Sahai, *Politics of Patronage and Protest the State, Society, and Artisans in Early Modern Rajasthan* (New Delhi, Oxford University Press, 2006); for petitioning in eighteenth-century Madras, see Ahuja, 'Labour Unsettled'.

many different regions objected to the loom tax on the grounds that it was too high, too unequal or against 'custom'. Requests for exemption poured in.[34] So did petitions for reduction or abolition.[35]

Some groups threatened non-cooperation or violence to reinforce their demands. In 1839, weavers in Madurai rose in opposition and 'refused to render any assistance to the collector'. It was felt that any recourse to 'compulsory measures ... would be attended by the closing of the shops, temporary cessation of traffic and general disgust'.[36] After this popular outburst, the loom tax was allowed to lapse in the district. In Salem, weavers went on strike in 1832 to demand abolition of the tax. The collector reported that the 'combination is general throughout this district but owes its rise ... to the weavers of Coimbatore and some other districts, most of whom are taxed much higher than the weavers of this zillah.'[37]

Protests erupted in Rajamundhry when a weaver on his way to sell cloth was stopped and flogged for evasion. Weavers from neighbouring villages 'assembled and stopped the markets of Peddapore, Cautraulapilly, Yalaswaram, etc'. It was thought that their leaders were planning to call an assembly to draw up a petition against duties. In this episode—as in many others—there were reports of groups moving about convincing (or forcing) more cautious weavers to join them.[38]

The longest, most sustained struggle against the loom tax was conducted by the weavers of Kanchipuram, who claimed that they had been exempted from it back in the 1780s.[39] From 1834, they began writing a stream of petitions to the Board of Revenue, the Government of India and even to the Court of Directors in London. These efforts failed and in 1843 they were ordered to pay the tax.[40]

[34] For Thiruchirapalli and Cuddalore, see PBR vol. 358, no. 37, 15 September 1803, p. 10796, TNSA; PBR vol. 1430, no. 120, 24 November 1834, pp. 13197–8, TNSA.
[35] PBR vol. 1374, no. 67, 25 July 1833, p. 9234, TNSA; PBR vol. 1409, no. 17, 23 June 1834, pp. 5396–7, TNSA; PBR vol. 422, no. 5, 10 February 1806, pp. 950–2, TNSA; PBR vol. 1664, no. 31, 11 July 1839, pp. 8604–5, TNSA; PBR vol. 1976, no. 6, 18 August 1845, p. 10092, TNSA; MDR, vol. 4680, p. 121; TDR, vol. 4711 A, p. 413, TNSA.
[36] PBR vol. 1675, no. 2, 10 October 1839, p. 13589, TNSA.
[37] PBR vol. 1326, no. 38, 7 June 1832, p. 5478, TNSA; PBR vol. 1348, no. 67, 6 December 1832, p. 12857, TNSA; PBR vol. 1312, no. 78, 2 January 1832, p. 238, TNSA.
[38] PBR vol. 376, no. 17, 23 April 1804, pp. 336370. Yarn markets were disrupted to draw the attention of the authorities. PBR vol. 438, 26 April 1804, pp. 3482–92, TNSA. For more examples, see Wendt, 'The Social Fabric', p. 182.
[39] PBR vol. 971, no. 31, 16 November 1820, pp. 9959–60, TNSA.
[40] PBR vol. 1875, no. 12, 14 September 1843, p. 12899, TNSA.

Most weavers in other taluks obeyed, but the Kanchipuram weavers 'in a body still refused to comply with the orders of the government'.[41] When the tahsildar (a revenue officer) tried to attach the properties of some of them, 'they assembled to the number of about 2000 and notwithstanding that the tahsildar had provisions of regulation III of 1831 read over to them, refused to disperse and carried off from him by force the property he had distrained'. Upon this, the collector dispatched the tahsildar with 100 armed peons to arrest the ringleaders and 'commit them to the criminal court for trial'. He was authorised to use force if necessary.

When the tahsildar arrived, he found that 'a body of 6000 weavers had collected armed with sticks and stones and he considered it impracticable to do anything without the aid of troops'.[42] A detachment was sent to deal with them; 'some of the ringleaders having been seized, the rest dispersed'. Subsequently, the 'heads of ... weaving villages' met the collector and agreed to pay the tax.[43]

The weavers of Kanchipuram continued to petition for annulment of the loom tax, even approaching the courts (without success). Partly as a result of their struggle, an investigation into moturpha taxes, including the loom tax, was ordered in 1861. This eventually ended in their abolition.[44]

What were the root causes of this dispersed, yet recurring opposition? For one thing, the burden of the loom tax fell disproportionately upon poor weavers.[45] The collector of Kurnool observed that it had become a real burden after the general decline in weaving caused by English imports.[46] The rates varied widely, some weavers being exempted or assessed at a lower rate, while others paid much more. This fed into the feeling that the tax was arbitrary and added to the perception of injustice.[47]

In some cases, the central issue was not rates, but the right to levy the tax itself.[48] The weavers of Kanchipuram argued that they had been promised exemption when they were invited to settle in the region (after the war with Hyder Ali). In their view, the state was obliged to honour

41 PBR vol. 1887, no. 2, November 1843, p. 16579, TNSA.

42 PBR vol. 1887, no. 2, November 1843, pp. 16580–8, 16815–16, TNSA.

43 PBR vol. 1918, no. 6, 10 June 1844, p. 7793, TNSA.

44 See consultation dated 28 February 1856 in India Revenue Consultations, 5 January to 28 March 1856, P/193/39, IOR, London.

45 Consultation dated 28 February 1856, in India Revenue Consultations, 5 January to 28 March 1856, P/193/39, IOR, London.

46 PBR vol. 1972, no. 18, 30 June 1845, p. 8054, TNSA.

47 PBR vol. 455, no. 7, 9 November 1807, p. 8790, TNSA; PBR vol. 1908, no. 39, 18 March 1844, p. 4715, TNSA.

48 PBR vol. 1918, no. 6, 10 June 1844, p. 7792, TNSA.

its promise. Officials argued that it 'never could have been intended that this relief and indulgence should extend beyond a few years or at most a definitive period'.[49]

According to the collector of Ganjam,

> the moturpha is paid I consider cheerfully by all classes who by custom of the country have been formerly subject to the impost. There is no tax more strenuously resisted or more difficult of collection when endeavoured to be newly enforced on any class who have not previously been subjected to the fiscal screw.[50]

The state reluctantly allowed exemptions as long as the EIC had a direct stake in the production of textiles for export. Once it withdrew from the textile trade, the need for concessions vanished and the logic of increasing revenue at all costs took over. The Madras Board of Revenue remained a staunch defender of the loom tax, maintaining that weavers did not pay 'any [other] contribution in aid of the public resources', and recommended its enhancement and extension.[51]

Caste networks played an important role in conflicts. When new rates were introduced in the Baramahal district, each caste (the Jadar, Kaikolar and Koliar) petitioned the authorities and sent delegations asking for a reduction.[52] When weavers in the town of Salem refused to pay the loom tax, the collector reported that those in other taluks 'declare that, if the people of Salem pay, then they are also willing to do so, but the fear of being turned out of their caste alone prevents them at present'.[53]

It took innumerable petitions and struggles, and several inquiries into living conditions, before moturpha taxes were finally abolished. The immediate cause was an economic depression, particularly acute in the 1830s and 1840s. Revenue collections fell and suggestions for reducing assessments and taxes to revive agriculture and industry were made. Thus ended an important struggle between weavers and the state.

[49] PBR vol. 1873, nos. 14–15, 28 August 1843, p. 12139, TNSA.

[50] PBR vol. 1773, no. 18, 7 July 1845, p. 8361, TNSA.

[51] PBR vol. 455, no. 7, 9 November 1807, p. 8790, TNSA; consultation dated 28 February 1856 in India Revenue Consultations, 5 January to 28 March 1856, P/193/39, IOR, London.

[52] *The Baramahal Records*, Section VII: Imposts, pp. 114–16.

[53] Many collectors expressed this opinion and called for reduction in rates. PBR vol. 1312, no. 78, 2 January 1832, p. 239, TNSA; PBR vol. 438, 26 April 1804, pp. 3482–92, TNSA.

Visakhapatnam district in 1816–17: old forms and new

In July 1816, several thousand men, women and children belonging to weaver families working for the EIC assembled on the hilltop of Samachellum (Simhachalam, a pilgrim centre)[54] near Visakhapatnam 'in the hope of attracting the notice of the company's servants and thereby be enabled to obtain justice'.[55] The commercial resident and assistant magistrate persuaded them to send a delegation to Visakhapatnam to present their grievances. As soon as the delegation reached the town, it was placed under guard and peons were sent to disperse the crowd. Subsequently, the delegates were released and told to put down their grievances in writing. They presented eight petitions (one each for eight mocoums or divisions of weaving villages), but these were returned by the judge on the grounds that they had not been prepared properly.

On this occasion the weavers' complaints were dismissed out of hand. According to the commercial resident, the petitioners were not Company weavers at all, or else were 'ring leaders' and 'notorious' characters. Once the assembly had been dispersed, the state apparatus closed ranks and the Board of Trade in Madras commended the commercial resident for dealing effectively with the situation.[56]

Soon after this, another delegation of weavers was sent from Visakhapatnam to Madras. They stayed there for several months before the Board of Trade finally agreed to set up a commission of inquiry to look into their grievances. It took much effort and more petitions before it was actually formed. Hundreds of weavers and their representatives deposed before it and submitted written material including letters, accounts and cadjams (palm leaf records).

Their main complaints were directed against the brokers (cobdars) appointed by the EIC to make advances. According to the weavers, these cobdars refused to pay the full advance; and insisted on paying in kind (with grain, cotton or yarn, or tobacco) instead of cash. They bought rejected cloth at low prices (to sell on their own account); they also purchased ready-made cloth from non-Company weavers, lending advances saved

[54] Swarnalatha discusses this episode in *The World of the Weaver*, pp. 135–43, using it to draw conclusions about weavers' protests in general and the attitude of the state towards them. I use it here to formulate a different set of arguments about methods of organisation and protest. All my quotations are from archival documents.

[55] Commercial Department Consultations, vol. 13, 14 February 1818, pp. 546–7 (petition), TNSA.

[56] Commercial Department Consultations, vol. 11, 11 August 1817, from p. 1417 on, TNSA.

in this fashion at usurious rates. Those who complained about them were punished and flogged. The head servant of the factory used his influence with the commercial resident to deny the weavers justice.

It should be noted that almost all these complaints pertain to alterations in the *system* of production: the advance of raw materials and supplies instead of cash, tighter control in sorting cloth, the arbitrary distribution of advances, penal punishments for what were commercial disputes.

The EIC sought to dismiss the complaints on technical grounds, by arguing that the weavers had not followed due process. The colonial state arrogated to itself the right to define collective gatherings and stoppages of work as 'insurrections' and declare them 'illegitimate'. Mass protests could not be acknowledged; the Board of Trade could not 'sanction combinations of weavers for the purpose of making general complaints' nor acknowledge 'persons stating themselves to be agents for such combinations'.[57] Weavers were told to seek redress from the competent authority: complaints of ill-treatment had to be addressed to the district magistrate. As for the question of withheld payments, they should 'present their grievance to the Commercial Resident and if further dissatisfied appeal to the zillah [district] court under section XXVI of Regulation I of 1806'.[58]

This episode has many striking aspects. One is the use of collective action to attract attention, followed by a readiness to adapt to prescribed methods of presenting witnesses and submitting documents of proof. In order to meet questions about their legitimacy, leaders obtained documents signed by hundreds of weavers authorising them to act. When a delegation of seven weavers met the commission of inquiry, they were asked how they had 'become constituted chiefs for the whole of the weavers of Vizagapatam district'. They replied that 'the weavers constituted us their agents themselves and assured us of every assistance'.[59] When asked whether they had any written authority to this effect, they answered that it was with their representative in Madras.

Delegations from different mocoums, consisting of six men each (but carrying written authorisations from hundreds more), came before the commission to depose. The separate delegations in turn authorised one

[57] See P. Swarnalatha, 'Revolt, Testimony and Petition: Artisanal Protests in Colonial Andhra', in Lex Heerma van Voss (ed.), *Petitions in Social History*, International Review of Social History, Supplement 9 (Cambridge, Cambridge University Press, 2001), p. 109; Swarnalatha, *The World of the Weaver*, p. 139; Hossain, *The Company Weavers*, pp. 109–23.

[58] Commercial Department Consultations vol. 11, pp. 1422–4, TNSA.

[59] Commercial Department Consultations vol. 13, p. 353, TNSA.

Immandy Ammanah to represent them and give all necessary details.[60] The weavers had, in fact, selected two 'principal agents': the other, Surnumpoody Ramanah, was stationed in Madras along with some other delegates.

The weavers of Visakhapatnam successfully adapted to the procedures of colonial jurisprudence. After assembling in their thousands and selecting representatives, they also produced written documents of authorisation when that proved necessary. In the end, despite declaring that it would not recognise combinations, the state was forced to set up a committee to inquire into their grievances.

A comparison with earlier protests shows how older techniques of confrontation and negotiation were adapted to new circumstances. Parthasarathi points to the importance attached to writing in the preceding period.[61] However, the mass of documentation assembled in this case is of a new and striking kind. Ammanah presented various kinds of supporting evidence: accounts written on cadjams by cobdars, notes instructing weavers to collect grain from a merchant, letters instructing them to provide cloth on private account and so on. He also produced witnesses including Brahmin accountants, ex-cobdars and merchants, and cross-questioned cobdars and the witnesses *they* presented.[62] Responding to questions by the commission, delegates averred that they had followed 'due procedure' in that they had first approached the competent authorities and presented petitions, resorting to collective action only when these attempts failed.[63]

Popular struggles are based on bonds of solidarity. As Parthasarathi points out, these are 'made and remade continuously through work, worship, marriage and politics'.[64] Caste and kinship networks played a central role in them, but different castes also joined together to make demands.[65] Devangar and Saliar weavers came together for this particular struggle.[66] A man of the Janapa caste (associated with gunny-weaving) is reported to have provided some money.[67] The delegations in Madras received funds sent by ordinary weavers, carried by men bringing cloth to the city for sale.[68]

[60] Commercial Department Consultations vol. 13, pp. 398, 400, TNSA.
[61] Parthasarathi, *The Transition to a Colonial Economy*, p. 104.
[62] Commercial Department Consultations vol. 13, pp. 416, 472, 520–1, TNSA.
[63] Commercial Department Consultations vol. 13, pp. 386, 392, 411, TNSA.
[64] Parthasarathi, *The Transition to a Colonial Economy*, p. 111.
[65] Parthasarathi, *The Transition to a Colonial Economy*, pp. 113–14.
[66] Commercial Department Consultations vol. 11, pp. 1430–3, TNSA.
[67] Commercial Department Consultations vol. 11, pp. 1430–3, TNSA.
[68] Commercial Department Consultations vol. 11, pp. 1442–3, TNSA.

There were also internal frictions. The cobdars and the commercial resident managed to get a group of weavers to affirm their satisfaction with the existing arrangements. They also got signed declarations in support of the EIC's operations. In response to this, weavers prepared petitions (with documents of authorisation): their delegates averred that declarations supporting the cobdars had been obtained under duress. However, a simple comparison of the number of weavers who signed these authorisations and those on the EIC's rolls shows that not all weavers joined the protest. The very act of assembling, selecting representatives, drawing up petitions and stopping work created bonds of solidarity.[69] These were probably cemented by the fact that their complaints were directed against 'banyan' cobdars. The head servant of the factory was also a bania (the common term for someone belonging to a mercantile caste).

The delegates asked for the replacement of these cobdars by men from weaving castes. Cobdars acted as brokers between merchants and weavers in some districts of the Madras Presidency. The EIC sought to cut merchants out by working with weavers directly through cobdars. In Visakhapatnam district, the first cobdars, appointed around 1802, came mostly from weaving castes. They were later replaced by banias on grounds of inefficiency (not sorting cloth properly, accepting cloths of low quality, etc.).[70]

The most prominent spokesman of the Vishakhapatnam weavers was Ammanah; Ramanah remained in Madras, lobbying officials and submitting petitions (signed by 'head weavers' and 'weavers'). Along with 18 other delegates, these two men were chosen to present the petitions in Visakhapatnam. They also formed part of the delegation to Madras that communicated regularly with Visakhapatnam through letters.[71] Ammanah belonged to a weaving caste. He had once been a cobdar and was clearly a prosperous and influential man. By the time of the protest, he had ceased to work for the EIC. He probably had a personal interest in the protest insofar as getting rid of bania cobdars would enable men like himself to take their places.

Each mocoum sent six representatives to the commission; 'Head weavers' from every mocoum participated in the protest. During this period—as Parthasarathi, Swarnalatha and Arasaratnam all point out—weavers were usually represented by 'head weavers'.[72] Parthasarathi argues

[69] Parthasarathi, *The Transition to a Colonial Economy*, pp. 101–20.

[70] Swarnalatha, *The World of the Weaver*, pp. 83–4.

[71] Parthasarathi, *The Transition to a Colonial Economy*, pp. 115–16.

[72] Arasaratnam, 'Weavers, Merchants and Company', 276–7; Parthasarathi, *The Transition to a Colonial Economy*, pp. 104–18.

that they played a critical role in the organisation and execution of protests in the late eighteenth century. Towards its end, they became increasingly entrenched in the EIC as brokers and their allegiance gradually shifted. In support of this hypothesis, he cites incidents where weavers came together to challenge their authority.[73]

It is true that relations between head weavers and ordinary weavers became increasingly troubled during this period, but in Visakhapatnam both were on the same side against cobdars who, not coincidentally, belonged to mercantile castes. Head weavers, certainly in this case, were strongly knit with the community and did not (or could not) act independently of it. This was beginning to change as they gained in power and influence, but ordinary weavers were still capable of forcing them to support their demands or,[74] failing that, electing new leaders and agents to represent them.

To sum up: during the early nineteenth century, weavers defended themselves energetically against merchants and the state. Conflicts involved control over the production process, incomes and taxes. Meanwhile, the EIC was creating new structures of regulation by using its power to legislate and redefining legitimate forms of collective action. Stoppage of work, mass assemblies and threats of violence persisted, but this period is marked by the primacy of *petitioning*. Like migration or 'collective withdrawal' in an earlier period, it was used by many different groups. In Europe, the practice is associated with a shift towards more participatory forms of government. Precisely the opposite occurred in India. Aparna Balachandran links petitioning by Pariar communities in the city of Madras to the territorial sovereignty of a colonial state that defined itself as the sole dispenser and adjudicator of justice. In India, petitioning became emblematic of the legal regime of an increasingly *coercive* government that frowned upon other forms of protest.[75]

Weavers learned to petition and assemble documentary evidence in support of their claims. The sheer mass of documentation produced in 1816 is a response to new procedures and expectations. They used fissures in regulatory structures to wage their battles. Attempts by the state to enforce 'legitimate' forms of grievance redressal were challenged and weavers

[73] Parthasarathi, *The Transition to a Colonial Economy*, p. 117.

[74] In one incident, 'about 1000 weavers ... seized the head weavers thereof who were minding the Company's business without joining them'. Quoted in Parthasarathi, *The Transition to a Colonial Economy*, p. 117.

[75] Balachandran, 'Christ and the Pariah', p. 82.

learned to conform to the state's demands with regard to due process *without* eschewing mass protests.

Forms of solidarity drew upon social networks reformulated in specific contexts. Swarnalatha describes weavers marching from village to village, mobilising their fellow caste-men.[76] In some late eighteenth-century protests, different castes formed an alliance or 'samayam'.[77] In 1816, an alliance between the Saliar and Devangar, possibly supported by Janapas, becomes visible. These networks sustained the struggle as it sought to confront the state in faraway Madras.

Its leaders were 'head weavers', but their leadership was reaffirmed through consultation. There were cracks in solidarity, shown by the fact that some weavers were persuaded to support the cobdars. Meanwhile, the role of head weavers was beginning to change. In the very different economic, political and social conditions of the twentieth century, they would cease to play a leading part in protests.

The late nineteenth and early twentieth century: a time of change

As the structures of the handloom industry were transformed, forms of protest and organisation also changed in response. During the conflicts of the early nineteenth century, the state in its dual role of employer and tax collector had been the principal target of protests. By contrast, the struggles of the twentieth century pitted the weaver against the master weaver and yarn dealer (or factory owner). The state presented itself as arbitrator between capital and labour, and weavers sought to put pressure on it to act in *their* interests. Its economic policies had a profound impact upon their livelihoods. In these changed circumstances, they were forced to modify their repertoire and develop new forms of organisation and protest—but these, in turn, drew upon older practices and bonds of solidarity.

Migrants and locals: the emergence of the handloom factory

Migrant workers played an important role in the reorganisation of the handloom industry during this period. Its spatial geography altered as

[76] Swarnalatha, *The World of the Weaver*, pp. 129–30.
[77] Swarnalatha, *The World of the Weaver*, pp. 129–30; Parthasarathi, *The Transition to a Colonial Economy*, pp. 113–14.

production became urbanised, clustering around towns. These were sources of raw materials (yarns and dyes) and provided access to markets. Weavers abandoned rural centres, but many of them lacked the tools and resources to weave on their own account under the new system. Instead, they worked for other weavers, often from the same caste, who had managed to accumulate some capital. These men often provided them with places to stay. The new handloom centres of western India were built by migrant weavers from Telugu speaking districts and the United Provinces.[78] Migration fuelled the growth of Madurai town, transforming it into a major centre of production during this period.[79]

These expanding centres contained a growing number of workshops and factories. In the Madras Presidency, the development of workshop production was slower than in western India. Local weavers, owning their looms, preferred, as far as possible, to work from home. They resisted the pressure to join large-scale factory enterprises. Most of the early factories failed; the usual explanation was that weavers disliked a disciplinary regime and preferred to work at home, where they had some control over work rhythms and space.[80]

According to the superintendent of an experimental factory set up in Salem, 'the ordinary weaver does not like factory life; he does not want to subject himself to any discipline. He can work at home as he likes.'[81] In this factory, 'only the waifs and strays of the community sought admission ... while the better class of weavers who could earn their living were not attracted to it'.[82] The process of reorganising production included an element of compromise and negotiation: weavers resisted factories, but had to submit to increased control by master weavers when working from home.

This is illustrated by the case of Madurai, where the oppundum and workshop systems emerged in tandem. Local weavers (the Pattunoolkarar) work under the oppundum system to this day. When asked why early factories (set up by Pattunoolkarar entrepreneurs) failed, a weaver replied that this was because people like him disliked working in them.[83] The factory system was seen as a form of degradation.[84] During an acute period of crisis in the

[78] Haynes, *Small Town Capitalism*, pp. 74–83.

[79] Raghavaiyangar, *Memorandum*, Appendix C, xxv–vii. In the 1940s, many weavers from Ramnad and Tirunelveli migrated to Madurai to work in factories.

[80] Indian Industrial Commission (Evidence), vol. 3, p. 484.

[81] Indian Industrial Commission (Evidence), vol. 3, p. 185. Other commentators say much the same thing. *Papers Relating to the Industrial Conference, 1908*, p. 158.

[82] Indian Industrial Commission (Evidence), vol. 3, p. 177.

[83] Saunders, *The Saurashtra Community in Madura*, p. 63.

[84] The Saurashtra see themselves as skilled weavers making fine saris and dhotis while factory weavers make towels and bedsheets. In contrast to the factory workers, they own their own

1980s, some Saurashtra weavers sought employment in factories, but left as soon as they could find work once more under the oppundum system.[85] In western India, local weavers refused to work in karkhanas: in the end, owners managed to circumvent this obstacle by employing migrant workers of the same caste as themselves. The availability of a migrant workforce was critical for the workshop system.[86]

In Madurai, the factory cluster that eventually developed in Sellur, a new neighbourhood on the banks of the Vaigai opposite the main town, was dependent upon migrant workers. The first factories had modest beginnings, when weaving households with several looms began employing workers to make cloth on them. They were set up by Saliar and Mudaliar (Kaikolar) weavers, who came to Madurai from Ramnad district. Many of them hailed from a single village, Mandalamanickam. The requisite capital was obtained by selling land in home villages, from money earned abroad (in Burma or Malaysia), or by working as petty traders.[87]

Saraswathy Textiles was originally set up in 1947 by a weaver from Mandalamanickam. His father had migrated to Malaysia, where he ran a grocery store. He came back to India in 1947, moved to Madurai, and set up five looms in his own house. He worked one of them himself for a few years, but, as the number of looms increased, all of them were staffed by hired weavers. In the beginning, he obtained orders from Andhra traders, carrying the finished cloth to their shops in the central part of the city. A very large proportion of weavers in his factory (and other workshops in Sellur) hailed from Ramnad district and Mandalamanickam in particular.[88]

The distaste felt by local weavers for factories is illustrated by an episode from Adoni (Kadapa). In the early 1920s, small workshops employing coolie weavers were set up there. 'Independent' weavers refused to work in them: '[t]hey can get themselves employed but they hate to become employees'. Many of them migrated to Assam instead. In 1924, about a thousand migrants from Adoni found the wages in Assam too low. They wanted to

---

looms. Interview with N. V. Sekar, a Saurashtra weaver, 28 January 2009, Madurai. As a child, and then a young man, he worked with his mother in the handloom factories of Sellur making towels and bedsheets. After 15 years, he set up his own loom with the help of an uncle and learned to weave the fine saris that Saurashtras specialise in. He said this was necessary, for otherwise no one would give him a bride. When he began working in Sellur, fine cloth production was declining and many Saurashtras went there to find work. Once it revived, most of them left; working in factories and weaving coarse cloth was seen as demeaning.

[85] Interview with N. V. Sekar, 28 January 2009.

[86] Haynes, *Small Town Capitalism*, pp. 147–8.

[87] Interview with the owner of Saraswathy Textiles, Sellur, Madurai, 1 February 2009.

[88] Interview with the owner of Saraswathy Textiles.

return to Adoni, but, having no money to go by train, they decided to walk the whole distance. Many of them succumbed on the way to hunger and disease.[89]

The evidence indicates that many weavers resisted proletarianisation as far as possible. But only those with some resources were successful in doing this. In the munganni system of production around Kurnool, hired weavers were graded according to their means and treated accordingly: those 'who have their own houses and are trusted by the employers are allowed to work in [them] with the yarn given out by the employers ... but the other weavers ... are not trusted with the materials and so have to work in the workshops, on the looms supplied by the employers.'[90]

Adaptation

Technological change was a hallmark of this period. In the beginning, innovation met with resistance. There were good reasons for this. Technology imported from Britain was not designed for local methods of production. There were significant differences in yarn quality, the kind of cloth produced, and so on.[91] While the fly-shuttle increased working speed, the time required for preparatory processes (and the size of the market) remained unaltered.[92]

It was only when wealthy individuals took the lead that the fly-shuttle took hold.[93] This occurred in places where large-scale capitalists controlled production and exported a good deal of cloth. Market access gave them an incentive to make the requisite investments in mechanising preparatory processes. Large capitalists on the coast, who controlled the production of kailis for export, promoted the fly-shuttle and its use became widespread from early on in the twentieth century. By contrast, in many of the interior districts, small merchants who controlled the cloth trade were reported

[89] Ranga, *The Economics of Handlooms*, pp. 10, 11.

[90] Ranga, *The Economics of Handlooms*, p. 17.

[91] A complete warping and sizing unit imported from England failed. Baliga, *Compendium*, p. 12; Alfred Chatterton, *Industrial Evolution in India* (Madras, 'The Hindu' Office, 1912), pp. 220–2.

[92] In Nagpur, weavers, after adopting fly-shuttles, burnt them in protest. Their productivity increased, but they could not sell the cloth and the preparatory processes failed to keep up with the speed of weaving. Harnetty, 'Deindustrialization Revisited', 494. For other examples, see Tirthankar Roy, 'Acceptance of Innovation in Early Twentieth-Century Indian Weaving', *The Economic History Review* (New Series), 55(3) (August 2002), 507–32.

[93] Roy, 'Acceptance of Innovation'.

to be against the fly-shuttle; this was one of the reasons cited for its slow diffusion.[94]

We have seen that Mala weavers in the Kadapa region regarded the fly-shuttle as a threat. A missionary noted that it did not work well with hand-spun yarn and predicted that its introduction would lead to the collapse of a system based on access to local cotton and hand-spun yarn. Mala wavers did not have the capital to buy mill yarn. Improved looms and devices like the fly-shuttle, dobby, heald and jacquard required a substantial investment of money and time. In the end, the production of coarse cloth made with hand-spun yarn did collapse except for a few places, where external intervention provided its makers with some support. In Malabar and Karur, the Basel Mission introduced new systems and technologies to make weaving viable, mostly for Christian converts from 'non-weaving' castes.[95]

Meanwhile, modified machines to suit local circumstances were being fabricated by men with a strong presence in the industry. Thiagaraya Chetty, a prosperous weaver-merchant, modified the fly-shuttle to fit traditional pit looms. He also called for experiments in decentralised spinning and the modernisation of traditional dyeing practices.[96] The small elite of weaver merchants in Madurai threw up innovators who devised methods to speed up weaving and its preparatory processes. An 'improved weaving mechanism', resembling the Jacquard loom,[97] was invented by one Kuppusami in Madurai. It 'reduced the cost and time required for weaving lace-bordered fabrics with fancy designs by nearly sixty percent'. Another Saurashtra invented a sizing machine that could be fabricated much more cheaply than those imported or built by the Industries Department.[98] A Kaikolar of Salem invented a modified Jacquard that was cheaper to make.[99] L. K. Tulsiram pioneered the shift from indigenous to chemical dyes; traditional methods of mordanting with natural materials were applied to chemical dyes.[100]

Many leading figures from weaving castes (not themselves weavers) were active in petitioning the Madras government to intervene in support of the handloom industry. A few became members of the Legislative Assembly and raised its problems there. They participated in industrial

[94] Indian Industrial Commission (Evidence), vol. 3, p. 185.
[95] Venkatraman, *The Handloom Industry.*
[96] *Papers Relating to the Industrial Conference, 1908*, pp. 130–1.
[97] *Papers Relating to the Industrial Conference, 1908*, pp. 199–200.
[98] Venkatraman, *The Handloom Industry*, p. 135.
[99] Venkatraman, *The Handloom Industry*, p. 183.
[100] Chatterton, *Industrial Evolution in India*, p. 208.

conferences, parleyed with officials, and wrote pamphlets and books to mobilise public opinion for their ideas. These concerned the introduction of new technologies, the setting up of training centres, state support for the industry and new tariffs to reduce the advantage enjoyed by the mill industry.[101] Sympathetic civil servants like Havell, Chatterton and Amalsad worked closely with these men.

Everyday acts of resistance

The sources offer few glimpses of daily existence.[102] Weavers working at home enjoyed some control over the production process even when working for master weavers. Master weavers provided the raw materials and kept a strict watch on quality, but there are indications that weavers still had a few tricks up their sleeve. Ranga criticises 'bad practices' like using fewer threads in the warp.[103] Haynes describes the pilfering of yarn, the selling of cloth on the side, lack of cooperation when merchants sought to speed up production, the practice of absconding with advances and so on; 'small-scale stratagems designed to give the weaving household some extra breathing space in its efforts to secure its subsistence, leisure and freedom'.[104]

Weavers in workshops fought for autonomy in myriad ways. Owners complained that they took breaks whenever they liked and refused to work fast.[105] To some extent, they could still determine the pace and timing of their work. Women workers reeling bobbins for weavers might wind just enough, take a break to do some household chores and come back to finish the winding.[106]

A union leader related how one of his old colleagues juggled factory work with organising. His work involved winding the warp on to beams, ready to

[101] Members of the Saurashtra Sabha presented a petition asking for a weaving school and for a representative from the weaving community to be appointed to the Legislative Council. *The Third Tour of His Excellency The Hon'ble Sir Arthur Lawley to Madura and Trichinopoly, November 18–20, 1906* (Madras, Government Press, 1909), pp. 35–7. See also, *Papers Relating to the Industrial Conference, 1908.*

[102] Haynes reconstructs 'politics at the site of production' using interviews and studies from the early twentieth century. Haynes, *Small Town Capitalism*, especially pp. 140–58. This reconstruction is not possible for South India, for there are very few studies on the lives of weavers for the period and few people still live who can remember the events of the 1940s and '50s.

[103] Ranga, *The Economics of Handlooms*, p. 40.

[104] Haynes, *Small Town Capitalism*, p. 144.

[105] Haynes, *Small Town Capitalism*, pp. 151–2.

[106] de Neve, *The Everyday Politics*, pp. 97–8.

be transferred to the loom. This was an important job, for production would come to a halt if the beams were not ready on time. He would begin work early, finish his quota of beams and spend the rest of the day doing union work. The factory owner was not happy with this, but could do nothing to stop him.[107] Tea breaks, food breaks and smoking breaks were decided by the workers. Owners tried to enforce a faster pace of work. During times of peak demand, the owner (or overseer) might remove the fly-shuttle from a loom if its occupant was late, denying him or her a day's work. Occasionally, he would allot the loom to someone else.[108]

Advances and debts played a key role in determining relationships between employers and workers. The 'cash advance' was used to control weavers, but it could also be used as a bargaining chip by them. The silk weavers of Adoni, despite being 'economic slaves' of yarn merchants, were 'in a position to threaten their employers that they will leave Adoni for the Assam plantations or some other distant place and coerce them into advancing more money from time to time, because the latter are unwilling to lose their employees and the advances.'[109]

The coolie weavers of Kurnool were 'poor, heavily indebted and devoid of all credit'. Around 1925, they were described as

> very mobile, impatient of any control over them and unwilling to pay back the advances given to them. Being devoid of all sense of honour, having no property, possessing no good name to lose, these workers are becoming very untrustworthy, and the employers find it quite impossible to carry on their trade under this Mungani organisation.[110]

Many weavers ran away without returning their advances. In the early twentieth century, they participated actively in food riots.[111] Later, they joined nationalist agitations against imported mill cloth.

The 1930s and 1940s: new forms of organisation

Collective problems affecting the industry as a whole (non-availability of yarn, competition from mills, demands for state intervention) were

[107] Interview with Mr. Murugan, secretary of the Sellur Handloom Workers Union, CITU, Madurai, 3 February 2009.
[108] Interview with P. Valli, Madurai, 24 January 2009.
[109] Ranga, *The Economics of Handlooms*, pp. 9–10.
[110] Ranga, The *Economics of Handlooms*, p. 18.
[111] David Arnold, 'Looting, Grain Riots and Government Policy in South India 1918', *Past and Present*, 84(1) (1979), 133–4.

articulated by community leaders, but when it came to wages, bonuses and working conditions, sharp divisions emerged between master weavers or yarn dealers and ordinary weavers.

Unionisation among handloom weavers in South India began in the 1930s and became widespread in the 1940s. The first unions were small and local, often comprising workers from a single caste. Compromises with master weavers (or merchants) were brokered by government representatives or community leaders. In February 1938, a dispute over wages was reported from Arupukottai (Ramnad district), where 'large bodies of workers made representations to the master weavers'.[112] The circle inspector of police intervened and master weavers gave a formal undertaking not to reduce wages. Later, in 1939, an unregistered union was formed with about a thousand members, all Devangars. It wrote to the collector complaining of continuing unemployment and the refusal of merchants to advance yarn to weavers.[113]

Unions rapidly grew in number and strength during the war years. Their growth was aided by rampant profiteering by yarn dealers and master weavers. Inequality and exploitation became much starker.[114] The war period was marked by endemic shortages of yarn. Mills sold less yarn, using it to make cloth instead. But shortages also stemmed from hoarding as mill owners took advantage of the absence of imports to push prices up and earn windfall profits. This situation was exacerbated by inflation; soon yarn prices ceased to bear any relation to the actual costs of production.[115] When yarn controls and yarn rationing were introduced, yarn dealers and master weavers combined to make huge profits on the black market. The open accumulation of wealth during a period of distress sharpened divisions between ordinary weavers and master weavers, with most agitations revolving around the supply of yarn and a growing black market.

The state set up Textile Control Boards dominated by mill owners and big capitalists. District advisory boards to oversee yarn quotas were packed with master weavers and yarn dealers. These boards were responsible for counting the number of looms and estimating the amount of yarn required. Their members overstated the number of looms under their control in order to corner yarn, which they sold on the black market. Yarn dealers also made

[112] Development Department, G.O. no. 618, 14 March 1939, TNSA.
[113] Development Department, G.O. no. 618, 14 March 1939, TNSA.
[114] One of the chief organisers of the Tamilnadu Handloom Workers Federation explicitly stated that it was black marketeering and profiteering by yarn dealers and master weavers that led to the proliferation of unions. *Janasakthi*, 14 February 1945.
[115] Development Department, G.O. no. 1268, 26 June 1943, TNSA.

large profits.[116] A weaver in Kanchipuram testified that the official list of looms (above 5,000) was based on inflated figures provided by a few master weavers; in actual fact only 2,000 looms existed.[117] Some master weavers supplied yarn on condition that weavers deposit their ration cards with them. Many were forced to agree and future supplies of yarn to that card went to the master weaver.[118] False looms were registered in order to sell yarn on the black market.[119]

Unions were active in exposing these practices and enforcing rationing in cities. The practice of issuing ration cards for the supply of yarn was instituted partly through their efforts. They also demanded representation in the Textile Control Commission and District Advisory Boards. Where unions were strong, the black market was curbed to a certain degree and weavers were able to obtain some yarn. They succeeded in getting representation in many district boards, providing a check on the issue of ration cards. In some places, they succeeded in getting the right to distribute yarn themselves rather than through master weavers.[120] These successes were counterbalanced by failures in other places.[121]

Karur, a small town with approximately 70 weaving workshops, illustrates the rising inequality of the period and the backlash provoked by it. Weavers, mobilised by two unions, demanded the distribution of yarn to individual weavers (and not factory owners)—many weavers were being denied work and black-marketeering was rampant. The textile commissioner refused, but yarn distribution had to be stopped after 2,000 weavers marched to the house of the sub-divisional magistrate, demanding a postponement until they could appeal to authorities in Madras. Meanwhile, master weavers and factory owners were also coming together to form their own associations.

[116] Development Department, G.O. no. 2484–90, 9 June 1944, TNSA; Development Department, G O. no. 2231, 24 May 1944, TNSA; Development Department, G.O. no. 5108, 16 October 1948, TNSA; Naidu, *Report of the Court of Enquiry*, pp. 14–15. Also see *Janasakthi*, 14 March 1945; 18 July 1945; 20 December 1944; 9 May 1945; 25 July 1945; 30 May 1945.

[117] *Janasakthi*, 9 May 1945.

[118] *Janasakthi*, 11 July 1945; Development Department, G.O. no. 4755, 21 September 1949, TNSA; Development Department, G.O. no. 2566, 14 May 1949, TNSA; Naidu, *Report of the Court of Enquiry*, p. 15.

[119] *Janasakthi*, 18 July 1945; 20 December 1944.

[120] In Madurai, the president of the yarn dealers' association was the head of the district advisory committee and its secretary was the president of the weavers' union. Both signed ration cards that were issued to weavers and master weavers. *Janasakthi*, 18 July 1945; 25 July 1945, ;30 May 1945; 8 August 1945; 14 February 1945; Srinivasan, *Communist Heroes*, p. 299.

[121] *Janasakthi*, 6 June 1945.

Another attempt to distribute yarn a few days later failed when the weavers convened a general strike. Coolies and hand-cart pullers also struck work in support. In the end, the authorities decided to give yarn to factory owners under police protection in the police station. In response, weavers picketed the shops of a few owners, and men and women lay down at the entrance to prevent yarn from being carried in. They were forcibly removed and beaten with batons to make them disperse. Violence erupted in several places, the properties of two owners were looted, and a factory and two cars burnt.[122]

After the war, conflict continued unabated, this time over wages. In 1945, struggles broke out in Coimbatore, Karaikudi, Auruppukotai, Sankarankoil and other centres. In Bhuvanagiri (South Arcot), 2,000 weavers went on strike after petitions to the factory owners association to increase their wages failed to elicit any response. A compromise was brokered after a week and they got a raise.[123] In January 1948, coolie weavers in Chengalpattu district 'refused to work under their master weavers in protest against the reduction of their wages from 10 to 9 rupees per piece'. The dispute was 'satisfactorily' settled and work resumed.[124] In April 1948, the master weavers of Thiruchirapalli signed an agreement with the handloom workers union, but broke it after a fortnight. The Commissioner of Labour tried to mediate, but the workshop owners refused to rescind wage reductions and the dispute was referred to the Industrial Tribunal.[125] Higher wages became a recurrent demand of agitations.[126] Weavers petitioned master-weaver associations, struck work and took out rallies, sometimes under union leadership and sometimes alone.

Popular mobilisation was not confined to weavers. The 1930s and '40s were an active phase of unionisation in the Madras Presidency. Coimbatore and Madurai witnessed protests by handloom weavers and mill workers. Unions were formed in 'informal' industries like tanneries and beedi making, and in the service sector (by hotel employees and transport workers).[127] Their demands were broadly similar: wage increases, better working conditions, paid leave, continuous employment and bonuses.

[122] *Subbaratnam and Others vs Unknown.*

[123] *Janasakthi*, 30 May 1945.

[124] Development Department, G.O. no. 781, 17 February 1949, TNSA.

[125] Development Department, G.O. no. 4208, 13 August 1948, TNSA.

[126] *Janasakthi*, 30 May 1945; Development Department, G.O. no. 4208, 13 August 1948, TNSA; Development Department, G.O. no. 781, 17 February 1949, TNSA.

[127] Ravi Ahuja points out that unions emerged in almost all trades, industries and services during this period, without distinction between 'formal' and informal' sectors. Ravi Ahuja (ed.), *Working Lives and Worker Militancy: the Politics of Labour in Colonial India* (Delhi, Tulika Books, 2013), p. xv.

Labour laws and union strategies

Unions demanded that the state regulate working conditions in handloom factories (and other small industries) by extending labour laws to them. The same phenomenon is visible in western Maharashtra.[128] The Madras Non-Power Factories (NPF) Act was passed in response to labour mobilisation in small industries. By the mid-1940s, this and other laws became a reference point for union agitations.[129] Once the Industrial Disputes Act was passed, unions began approaching Industrial Disputes Tribunals as well. Shop-floor disputes were now examined under legal constructs. The legal framework for small industries was shaped partly by labour mobilisation, but almost immediately it began to act back upon union strategies.

Weavers had campaigned for legal rights and protection; instead, they found themselves caught up in labyrinthine laws and institutions designed to keep them out of the ambit of regulation (as we shall see in the next chapter). In order to claim formal rights, they were faced with the task of satisfying the legal definitions of 'employee' and 'worker' set out in various laws. These were vague and imprecise, and their contentions were constantly challenged by factory owners with deep pockets and access to the best lawyers. By dragging legal proceedings out and appealing at every possible stage, they usually succeeded in tiring unions out.

Even where weavers managed to establish their status as employees, the struggle to obtain basic rights (a minimum wage, continuity of employment, bonuses and welfare measures) was prolonged and difficult. Industrial tribunals often ruled that weavers were not entitled to bonuses, continuous employment or any other welfare measures *even when their status as workers was established*. The reason cited was that master weavers and factory owners could not afford these luxuries![130] Even when the awards were favourable, weavers were forced to wage yet another struggle to get them implemented in the face of delaying tactics and official indifference.[131]

[128] Haynes, *Small Town Capitalism*, pp. 265–302.

[129] These were enacted in response to agitations in several small-scale industries calling for some form of state regulation. Development Department, G.O. no. 382, 26 January 1949, TNSA; Development Department, G.O. no. 1312–13, 14 March 1949, TNSA.

[130] Development Department, G.O. nos. 5190, 25 October 1949; Development Department, G.O. no. 5973, 20 December 1949, TNSA.

[131] For a detailed discussion of labour laws during this period, see Dietrich Wielenga, 'Emergence of the Informal Sector'.

The state exhorted workers to eschew strikes and protests in favour of legal channels, and to negotiate with employers and resolve grievances by mutual agreement. At the same time, legal avenues were gradually rendered defunct or inaccessible. In the end, unions failed to obtain legal protection for weavers. However, struggles for better wages and bonuses continued in some regions. It was only in the 1970s that weavers in Tamil Nadu managed to claim a cash bonus. Until then they were gifted some cloth (if the owner was willing) at Deepavali.[132] Their strongest weapon was a strike during the peak season, just before the major festivals. Unions usually came up with a long list of demands, with wage and bonus rates at the top, and regularisation of employment, dearness allowance and other benefits at the bottom. Agitations generally ended with a compromise over wage rates (without discussing permanent benefits).[133] These negotiations were usually facilitated by the local labour officer.

Mobilisation also succeeded in forcing the state to expand the cooperative sector and provide it with support. The strongest cooperatives were formed in areas where unions were strong. In Kanchipuram, the Kamakshiamman Silk Weavers' Cooperative was established after a prolonged agitation (including a 15-day strike). In 1954, when the master weavers of Kanchipuram decided to reduce wages, the union collected signatures from 6,000 weavers and presented a memorandum and notice of strike to the Minister of Labour. The Commissioner of Labour intervened, but no compromise could be effected. The weavers struck work. Their demands included the restoration of wage rates, allocation of state funds to set up a cooperative and a separate Cess Fund for a silk weavers' cooperative; all of them were gained in the end.[134]

Structures of solidarity

Unions were male preserves, though women are visible from time to time, participating in protests and strikes. They played a prominent part in the large gathering at the Vaigai (see below in this section) and the protests against yarn distribution in Karur.[135] Union demands focused on the male

[132] Interview with Mr. Murugan; de Neve, *Everyday Politics*, p. 144.

[133] Interview with Mr. Murugan.

[134] Yvonne J. Arterburn, *The Loom of Interdependence: Silk Weaving Cooperatives in Kanchipuram* (Delhi, Hindustan Publishing, 1982), p. 100. Cooperatives also became channels of political patronage. Arterburn, *The Loom of Interdependence*, pp. 128–49.

[135] This was the case as late as the 1980s in handloom unions around Erode. de Neve, *Everyday Politics*, pp. 137–68.

weaver, who was the beneficiary of state policies and laws. Even though they performed most of the ancillary tasks associated with weaving, women did not even figure in conflicts and debates over the definition of 'worker'. They were largely excluded from union membership despite playing an active part in agitations.

Caste played a key role in mobilisation. We have seen that many of the early unions were organised along caste lines. But cross-caste alliances soon began to emerge. A very large show of strength was organised by the Tamil Nadu Handloom Weavers Federation at its first Provincial Conference in Madurai in 1945, when many independent unions joined the Federation. Some 18 weavers' unions with 14,000 members attended from Tirunelveli district. There were 67 handloom weavers' unions from Chengalpattu.[136]

The gathering, held in the dry bed of the Vaigai, where an enormous tent had been set up, is described in newspaper reports and eyewitness accounts. Around 50,000 weavers and workers came to the conference. Thousands of women—10,000, according to one estimate—attended, many of them with children in tow. Meena Krishnaswamy, a party activist, recounts that one part of the pandals (tents) was filled with cradles (thottils) in which babies slept.[137] Muslim weavers from Ramnad, Devangars from Coimbatore and Kaikolars from Tirunelveli attended in large numbers. Different flags—the red of the Communists, the green of the Muslim League and the tricoloured Congress flag—were hung from the main tent.[138]

Two kinds of unions emerged in the city of Madurai. Some concentrated on organising skilled Saurashtra weavers while others worked with weavers in handloom factories.[139] They functioned independently even when allied under the banner of the All India Trade Union Congress (AITUC). This duality reflected a difference in production systems: the Saurashtras wove fine cloth (mostly from home) while factory workers in Sellur made towels and bedsheets. But caste identity also played a prominent part. Some unions were dominated by Saurashtras, while those in factories had weavers from many castes (Kaikolar, Saliar, Moopanar). Caste and kinship played an important role in mobilising weavers, but solidarities created on the shop floor and in the neighbourhood also cut across caste identities.[140]

[136] *Janasakthi*, 14 February 1945, 28 February 1945.

[137] Interview with Meena Krishnaswamy, member of the Communist Party of India, Chennai, 8 February 2008; *Janasakthi*, 11 April 1945.

[138] *Janasakthi*, 11 April 1945.

[139] They were formed by the Communists, the Congress and the Dravidian parties.

[140] Sellur came to be crowded with factories and workshops, with coolie weavers in every lane. Each lane was originally occupied by members of one caste, but gradually became more

Caste and class solidarity could reinforce or undercut each other at different times and conjunctures. Caste was a key element of labour recruitment and control.[141] It cemented vertical ties between factory owners and master weavers on the one hand, and workers or coolie weavers on the other. Master weavers argued that unions would end up destroying community bonds and group unity, and used this as an argument to dissuade weavers from joining them.[142] But caste also played a cementing role in early unions even though collective action might be aimed at an employer of the same caste. Union organisers described the individualism of master weavers and yarn dealers as a betrayal of community for profit and called for class solidarity in response. But this did not prevent them from calling on master weavers to respond to the plight of ordinary weavers as *patrons*, on the basis of caste solidarity.[143]

Negotiations between employers and unions were usually mediated by community leaders or government representatives. In all these instances, caste, kinship, and gradations of economic and social status played a significant role in determining outcomes. A dispute between the weavers and master weavers of Erumalainayakkanpatti (Madurai) over black marketeering ended in a compromise brokered by the local Congress Committee treasurer.[144] In 1925, in Chirala and Perala, there was a 'Weaving Committee' where weavers and employers were equally represented and to which 'every dispute which is not settled by mutual agreement is referred for final settlement'.[145]

The novel *Panchum Pasiyum*, set in the early 1950s among the Kaikolar ofTirunelveli, contains an episode that illustrates the complicated interplay of caste and class. It begins with ordinary weavers asking for an increase in wages. Some master weavers are sympathetic to their demands while others are not (both poor and rich weavers are Kaikolars). A meeting is called in the temple of the caste deity to deal with this problem and other matters to do with the temple. In the beginning, master weavers and

---

mixed. A solidarity of shared spaces emerged—barbers worked without payment and tea shop owners provided tea on loan during strikes (other historians have described the same phenomenon in mill strikes). Described to me in various interviews.

[141] See Haynes, *Small Town Capitalism*, pp. 146–57, for a discussion.

[142] This argument was used by the master weavers of Erumalainayakkanpatti. *Janasakthi*, 4 July 1945.

[143] Songs criticising the greed of master weavers are collected in Pandit S. Sivaprakasam, *Puduvai Nesavu Thozhil: Ezhaiyar Ezhuchi Paattu (Pondicherry Handloom Industry: Songs of Inspiration for the Poor)* (Pondicherry, Kalanidhi Press, 1932).

[144] *Janasakthi*, 1 August 1945.

[145] Ranga, *The Economics of Handlooms*, p. 40.

factory owners discuss wage rates while ordinary weavers wait outside. A few express support for the workers, but the majority refuse to give in. After some discussion, a compromise is reached. All those waiting outside are called in and informed of the decision. The meeting then proceeds to discuss problems relating to the upkeep of the deity.

The author explains that since temple matters concern the whole community, all weavers, rich or poor, have the right to voice their opinion and all have an equal say in the matter. But this does not apply to wage rates, which can only be decided by the owners. Subsequently, the workers organise themselves into a union; one of the smaller master weavers faces bankruptcy, deserted by his wealthy fellows.[146]

This episode and other motifs in the novel illustrate fault lines within the notion of community. On certain matters, all members are notionally equal. However, in any economic conflict between employers and employees, ordinary weavers are subservient to master weavers. Even here the community has a role to play. Appeals are made on the basis of group membership—master weavers are implored to treat their fellows fairly—and discussions are held inside the community temple.

Class differentiation *within* weaving communities strengthened class-based forms of solidarity. This is displayed in the coming together of the Tamil Nadu Handloom Weavers Federation. Meanwhile, master weavers and yarn merchants formed their own associations to negotiate with unions and lobby the state. In Erumalainayakkanpatti (Madurai), the association threatened to stop giving yarn to any weaver who joined the union. Union members were asked to pay their debts immediately, some were assaulted and rallies were blocked. The master weavers association got the police to threaten weavers and arrest some of them.[147] Yet, even in the midst of conflict, the dividing line between weavers and master weavers was not entirely fixed. One union leader declared that 'there are … 10 master weavers. Among them only 3–4 of them are harassing us … These are the rulers of the black market.'[148]

Small master weavers were precariously placed. A union leader remarked that it was the big players who called the shots. Weavers would congregate before the houses of large owners in an attempt to shame them. After a compromise was reached, smaller master weavers generally acted upon

[146] T. M. Chidambara Ragunathan, *Panchum Pasiyum (Cotton and Hunger)*, 15th edn (Chennai, New Century Book House, 2005).
[147] *Janasakthi*, 11 April 1945; 6 June 1945.
[148] *Janasakthi*, 6 June 1945.

it.[149] In *Panchum Pasiyum*, some of them show sympathy for the plight of ordinary weavers.[150] Several owners supported the union's demands during the Karur strike.

The relationship was marked by conflict and patronage; caste and class were intertwined. A union song addresses the capitalist, saying, 'You are witness to the cultivator feeding his bullock in times when there is no cultivation; isn't it your responsibility to feed the worker during times of unemployment?' In this way, it appeals to his role as patron. At the same time, it deplores the accumulation of wealth by master weavers at the expense of ordinary weavers and describes their relationship as that between capitalist and worker.[151] Both these elements played a significant role in determining everyday relationships and conflicts. As de Neve points out, caste, class, kinship and religion should not be essentialised—they were in constant interaction with each other in the context of concrete acts of resistance and mobilisation.[152]

Conclusion

Weavers played an active part in their own history by defending their position against merchants and employers. Their actions and strategies (repertoires of resistance) altered in response to changing structures of state authority. Nineteenth-century struggles sought to retain control over the production process. Migration as a form of protest disappeared once the EIC consolidated its power and petitioning became prevalent. It was supplemented by other strategies ranging from tax evasion to mass assemblies and the disruption of yarn markets.

By the early twentieth century, handloom weavers were embedded in new structures of production in which migrant workers played a significant rolc. Methods of claim making displayed both change and continuity. There was slow adaptation to technological change even as everyday acts of resistance continued.

Community leaders no longer represented weavers as a whole. Prominent and wealthy individuals (not necessarily the traditional heads of castes) raised industry-wide concerns and called for state intervention.

[149] Interview with Mr. Murugan.
[150] Ragunathan, *Panchum Pasiyum*.
[151] Sivaprakasam, *Puduvai Nesavu Thozhil*.
[152] de Neve, *Everyday Politics*, pp. 12–13, 21–2, 84.

In the hands of these 'big men', petitioning was transformed into active lobbying—they were active inside and outside the legislative assembly, in state sponsored conferences and in the mass media.

Ordinary weavers turned to new methods of organising, based on new forms of solidarity. These were built upon caste and kinship, but also came to incorporate bonds of class emerging on the shop floor and in the neighbourhood. From the late 1930s, unions became the main vehicles of protest. Their methods encompassed petitioning, bargaining, strikes and mass assemblies. None of these was new; all were adapted to fit new structures of authority and power. The discourse (and legal framework) of workers' rights was adopted by unions.

Acts of resistance emerged out of changing circumstances, but they also helped to alter structures of power and regulation. The institution of yarn controls and ration cards during the war years was an outcome of popular agitations. Collective resistance forced employers to make alterations in production regimes; the state was compelled to legislate on workers' rights. The legal framework for labour relations in small industries and union agitations exercised a reciprocal influence on each other. The NPF Act emerged in response to demands for legal protection for workers in small industries.

The shortcomings of labour legislation and the state's bias in adjudicating disputes influenced union strategies. From the 1950s, a clear tendency to focus on short-term questions rather than tackling structural problems (such as security of employment, working conditions and statutory benefits) becomes visible. The prolonged battle for legal protection proved largely unsuccessful; cooperatives were the only tangible achievement weavers were able to wrest from the state. The shifting contours of their interaction is the subject of my concluding chapter.

7

The State and the Weaver

Historians of the nationalist school blamed the colonial state for the decline of the handloom industry. Most revisionist writings ignore or minimise its role: in them, the market, not the state, is seen as the principal catalyst of change.[1] It is quite true that ascribing all change to the state is limiting and deterministic, but ignoring its power to direct and influence the process of change would appear to be equally reductionist. State policies played an important role in the transformation of the handloom industry in South India. Here, instead of treating it as a monolithic entity, I propose to uncover different voices within the state and the external influences that prodded it into action. This analysis also takes in the policies of the Indian state after 1947, for these had their roots in the colonial period, especially after the passage of the Government of India Act of 1935.

State power played a critical role in the emergence of global capitalism. Patrick O'Brien stresses the geopolitical context in which the textile industry was mechanised and reorganised in Britain and elsewhere. He argues that theories of cultural exceptionalism developed to explain technological innovation fail to account for the emergence of the cotton mill industry in Britain. Its colonial possessions and naval supremacy were crucial in securing supplies of raw materials—especially cotton from the Americas, grown with slave labour. Colonial expansion also allowed it to capture export markets for cloth. Without these two factors, large-scale mechanisation would not have been feasible.[2] In an analogous way, Charles Sabel argues that choices between forms of production (craft-based or factory-based) were not neutral, but influenced by state policies.[3]

[1] Tirthankar Roy, 'Traditional Industry in Colonial India', *Economic and Political Weekly*, 35(48) (25 November 2000), 4287.

[2] Patrick O'Brien, 'The Geopolitics of a Global Industry: Eurasian Divergence and the Mechanization of Cotton Textile Production in England', in Giorgio Riello and Prasannan Parthasarathi (eds), *The Spinning World: a Global History of Cotton Textiles, 1200–1850* (Delhi, Primus Books, 2012), pp. 351–65.

[3] Piore and Sabel, *Second Industrial Divide*.

Technological expansion requires economies of scale; without them, it cannot be sustained. The state played a key role in creating markets through colonialism. Technological innovation and expansion must be understood in the context of state power supporting mercantilism through government policy and force of arms. This provided the indispensable context in which market demands, private enterprise, and natural and cultural endowments acted.

In India (and South India), state power acted upon the handloom industry in two ways. The economic and trade policies of the colonial state had a direct effect on cloth prices and capital investments. It also shaped capital–labour relationships by providing a legal framework for labour control.

State policy during the nineteenth century

In the beginning, the domestic textile industry in Britain was protected from Indian competition by very high tariffs on cloth imports from India. Between 1800 and 1819, the import duty in England on plain and flowered muslins, and flowered calicoes increased from 30 per cent to 44 per cent ad valorem. The duties on plain calicoes rose from 21 per cent in 1800 to 85 per cent in 1813.[4] In sharp contrast, early nineteenth-century imports of British textiles into India were taxed at nominal rates. British textiles paid an import duty of 2.5 per cent ad valorem and raw cotton paid an export duty of 2.5 per cent ad valorem, with a drawback when exported to Britain.[5] Thus Britain protected its domestic textile industry with high tariff walls and opened up the Indian market by lowering tariffs in India. The country was the most important market for Lancashire, taking roughly 40 per cent of Britain's cotton piece goods exports in the period between 1880 and 1913.[6]

Meanwhile, the transit duty system in British India acted against the interests of local manufacturers and trade, and facilitated the import of British goods—cloth in particular. Borpujari shows that, in comparison to the duties paid by British yarn and cloth imported into India, yarn and cloth manufactured locally paid a duty of 7.5 per cent ad valorem up

[4] Raju, *Economic Conditions*, p. 208.
[5] Borpujari, 'Impact of the Transit Duty System', 221.
[6] B. R. Tomlinson, 'India and the British Empire 1880–1935', *The Indian Economic and Social History Review*, 12(4) (1975), 337–80, at 340.

until 1823. In 1823, the duty on finished cloth was reduced to 2.5 per cent, but separate duties still continued to be levied at different stages of production, greatly increasing the price of the final product.[7] Town duties were an additional burden.[8]

The transit duty was a flat rate levied on all goods, irrespective of the distance they travelled, harming short-distance and local trade in particular.[9] In the pre-British system, the amount varied according to distance, for duties had to be paid only when goods passed through a check post. Borpujari looks at Bengal, but his analysis holds good for Madras as well.[10] The consistent opposition of weavers and cultivators to stamp duties on transit and sale stemmed from their effects on the production of coarse cloth for local consumption, which was largely untaxed before this. Under the colonial regime, any cloth found unstamped, even after being sold, could be confiscated.[11] Many kinds of cloth that had previously been untaxed were brought into the net.[12] Separate taxes were levied at every stage of production: there were taxes on raw cotton, yarn, cloth and dyed cloth. The cumulative tax burden on a piece of finished cloth could rise to as much as 20 per cent in Bengal and 17.5 per cent in the Madras Presidency.[13]

An administrator critical of the transit duty system in Madras remarked that

> [e]nough has already been said to convince the supreme government that the trade of India has been depressed and all classes of people harassed and discouraged by our mode of taxing the inland traffic. But so long as its continuance is considered preferable (as a measure of finance) to any other mode of raising the requisite funds for the purposes of government it is useless to repeat the evidence on which it has been most justly condemned.[14]

A general improvement in weaving and trade was reported from several districts after they had been abolished.[15] The advantage to British

[7] Borpujari, 'Impact of the Transit Duty System', 231.
[8] Raju, *Economic Conditions*, pp. 252–3.
[9] Raju, *Economic Conditions*, p. 222.
[10] See, for example, PBR vol. 986, no. 8, 7 June 1824, pp. 4992–9, TNSA; PBR vol. 966, no. 34, 23 October 1823, pp. 9125–6, TNSA.
[11] TDR, vol. 4711, pp. 45–50, TNSA; PBR vol. 984, no. 20, 24 May 1824, pp. 4538–9, TNSA.
[12] PBR vol. 984, no. 20, 24 May 1824, p. 4538, TNSA; PBR vol. 966, no. 34, 23 October 1823, pp. 9125–6, TNSA.
[13] Borpujari, 'Impact of the Transit Duty System', 224; Raju, *Economic Conditions*, p. 209. Also, PBR vol. 872, no. 62, 30 November 1820, pp. 10280–1, TNSA.
[14] PBR vol. 1849, 6 March 1843, p. 3405, TNSA.
[15] PBR vol. 1974, no. 31, 14 July 1845, p. 8627, TNSA.

manufactures and trade from unequal domestic taxation in Britain and India (and favourable tariffs for British imports) were explicitly acknowledged and justified. The desirability of the country acting as a supplier of raw materials and a captive market for British manufactures was widely expressed and held to be an advantage to the Indian public and to Britain.[16]

The period from 1813 to 1880 is generally viewed as one in which 'free trade' was adopted, with mercantilist policies taking a back seat. However, several historians, beginning with John Gallagher and Ronald Robinson, have shown that state policy continued to favour British industry, enabling it to capture export markets and obtain cheap raw materials.[17] According to Sabyasachi Bhattacharya, the influence of laissez-faire should not be exaggerated, for most policy decisions were based on pragmatism, not theory. The economic interests of Britain, the strength of parliamentary lobbies and the influence exercised by chambers of commerce played a key role in determining policy.[18] There was much lobbying, both inside and outside Parliament, through the press and pamphlets.

In 1859 and 1860, the government of India raised import duties on British cloth and yarn (in response to a huge fiscal deficit) equalising it for all imports, irrespective of their origin. The measure was strongly opposed by mill owners in Lancashire and Manchester.[19] Over the next few years, the authorities, both in Britain and in India, faced calls to reduce or abolish all tariffs on yarn and cloth imported into India. Free-traders argued that import duties protected Indian spinners and weavers (and domestic spinning mills)—they acted against 'general wellbeing' by diverting capital into industries India was not 'endowed for'. The net effect was to raise the cost of cloth for the ordinary consumer, who would get imported cloth at cheaper prices if the duties were abolished.[20] Predictably, duties on imported yarn and cloth were reduced gradually, and finally abolished in 1882.[21] In

[16] Borpujari, 'Impact of the Transit Duty System', 239; Peter Harnetty, *Imperialism and Free Trade: Lancashire and India in the Mid-Nineteenth Century* (Vancouver: University of British Columbia Press, 1972), p. 6.

[17] John Gallagher and Ronald Robinson, 'The Imperialism of Free Trade', *Economic History Review*, 2nd series, 6(1) (1953), 1–15.

[18] Sabyasachi Bhattacharya, 'Laissez Faire in India', *The Indian Economic and Social History Review*, 2(1) (January 1965), 1–23.

[19] Harnetty, *Imperialism and Free Trade*, pp. 12–14.

[20] See the petition from the inhabitants of the borough of Preston, Lancashire, to the principal secretary of state and similar petitions in IOR L/E/7/68. Also, Harnetty, *Imperialism and Free Trade*, p. 22.

[21] Harnetty, *Imperialism and Free Trade*, p. 34.

1877, Sir John Strachey, announcing the decision of the Home government to repeal duties on cotton goods, said that

> we are often told that it is the duty of the government of India to think of Indian interests alone, and that if the interests of Manchester suffer, it is no affair of ours. For my part, I utterly repudiate such doctrines. I have not ceased to be an Englishman because I have passed the greater part of my life in India and have become a member of the Indian government. The interests of Manchester, at which foolish people sneer, are the interests not only of the great and intelligent population engaged directly in the trade in cotton, but of millions of Englishmen. I am not ashamed to say that while I hope that I feel as strongly as any man the duties which I owe to India, there is no higher duty in my estimate than that which I owe to my own country. I believe that our countrymen have a real and very serious grievance and that it is no imaginary injury against which they complain.[22]

Demands to promote the cultivation of long-staple cotton suitable for English mills have already been discussed; their fiscal burden was considerable. The Indian government spent large amounts in order to encourage exotic varieties of cotton. By 1858, the Court of Directors had used up £100,000 in setting up and running experimental farms.[23] With the onset of the American Civil War, the demand for state intervention to ensure a reliable supply of cotton for Lancashire and Manchester became stronger and shriller. Ironically, the argument that the state should abstain from interfering with private enterprise (by taxing British imports) coexisted with calls for much greater state intervention in favour of British firms in order to encourage the cultivation of long-staple cotton and to expend huge sums of money on transport and ancillary infrastructure to promote its export.[24]

The Indian government responded by investing in railways and roads (called 'cotton roads') and appointed Cotton Commissioners to oversee experimental farms and promote exotics in different parts of the country. It also passed laws to prevent the adulteration of cotton.[25] Short-staple varieties continued to be grown in the short-term, but the effort to promote long-staple hybrids bore fruit in the end.[26]

[22] R. Knight, *Manchester and India: a Protest Against Sir John Strachey's Financial Statement in the Legislative Council of India Dated 15 March 1877* (Calcutta, Thacker Spink and Co., 1877), pp. 4–5.
[23] *Speech of Col. Sykes in the House of Commons on Thursday, February 18, 1858 on the Proposed India Bill* (London, Smith Elder and Co., 1858).
[24] Harnetty, *Imperialism and Free Trade*, p. 37.
[25] Harnetty, *Imperialism and Free Trade*, pp. 55, 62–5. For the expansion of public works in response to British commercial interests, see Bhattacharya, 'Laissez Faire in India', 1–23.
[26] Indian Industrial Commission (1916–18): Appendices to the Report (Calcutta, Government Press, 1919), pp. 319–40.

British mill owners lobbied energetically, both in London and Calcutta, for new land revenue arrangements to encourage private capital to invest in Indian agriculture. They demanded grants of land in perpetuity: as long as land tenures were insecure, private capital would hesitate to invest in cotton cultivation. They asked for freehold tenures and regulations allowing the redemption of land revenue in order to encourage farmers to cultivate cotton in larger quantities.[27] In 1861, the Government of India sanctioned the granting of waste lands and allowed the redemption of land revenue.[28]

Arguments of laissez-faire were cited to reject tariff protection, but set aside when it came to intervening in the cultivation of cotton or building transport infrastructure.[29] Meanwhile, free trade as a doctrine began to lose its influence during the late nineteenth century as the colonial state moved towards a more interventionist role in the economy, partly in response to demands by Indian nationalists.

Artisan workers

The EIC's complicated relationship with weavers forms an important context for the evolution of labour control during the colonial period. New concepts of jurisprudence, especially in the enforcement of contracts and the repayment of debts, were introduced. Merchants (who, until then, enjoyed limited *legal* means of enforcing contracts) were supported through the power of the state in their attempts to force weavers to fulfil contracts and repay debts.[30] The expanding power of the Company-state made it increasingly difficult for weavers to escape its reach.

According to regulations introduced in 1806, written agreements were taken from weavers, spelling out contracts in detail. Those who failed to fulfil the clauses could be prosecuted in the courts. Delays in delivery were punished by placing peons over the weavers or by forced repayment of advances. Regulations governed the sorting and rejection of cloth that failed to meet stipulated standards. Rules for grievance redressal allowed

[27] Haywood was sent to India by the Manchester Cotton Company in 1862 to explore the possibilities of improving and expanding cotton cultivation in India. Haywood, *India as a Source*. Also, Bhattacharya, 'Laissez Faire in India', pp. 8–9.

[28] Bhattacharya, 'Laissez Faire in India', p. 9.

[29] Bhattacharya, 'Laissez Faire in India', pp. 25–6.

[30] See Parthasarathi's work for a detailed discussion. Parthasarathi, *The Transition to a Colonial Economy*, pp. 83–100.

individual weavers to approach the commercial resident, the collector and the courts, but mass complaints were not to be entertained.[31]

Ravi Ahuja shows that, during the early nineteenth century, the colonial state took ideas derived from English jurisprudence, adapted to a colonial context, in order to enact legislation to control labour. Disciplining workers and restricting mobility were key concerns. Breaches of contract were penalised. Unlike England, corporal punishment was prominent in Indian regulations.[32] Commercial residents had judicial powers to restrain and punish Company weavers.[33] Flogging was routine. The EIC used coercion to compel weavers to work for it. In one case, the collector of Chengalpattu gave orders to his subordinate that 'Taulatah Yagapah Chitty having contracted for the Hon'ble Company's investment, you will therefore notify by beat of tom throughout your district prohibiting the weavers from weaving any other cloth until the investment be completed'.[34] Force was also used to collect the loom tax. Specker records several cases where corporal punishment was inflicted upon those who failed to pay it.[35]

In 1859, the Workman's Breach of Contract Act was introduced. It came to be used by employers in a wide range of sectors, from plantations to small industry, to control workers. The legislation specified punishment under criminal law for breach of contract by workers, but breach of contract by employers incurred only civil damages. Any offender could be fined or imprisoned for three months (with hard labour) on a magistrate's order.[36] Factory owners in many handloom centres invoked it to discipline workers and bring back weavers who had run away with advances.[37]

State policy during the twentieth century

The colonial state did not formulate an official policy for handlooms or industrial development in India. Instead, its actions were determined by various debates within government.

[31] Swarnalatha, *The World of the Weaver*, pp. 97–9.
[32] Ahuja, 'The Origins of Labour Policy'.
[33] PBR vol. 364, 24 November 1803, p. 13299, TNSA.
[34] Extract of Court's Revenue Letter to Fort St. George, 5 May 1796, IOR/F/4/35/927, London.
[35] Specker, *Weber in Wettbewerb*, pp. 270–1.
[36] Michael Anderson, 'India 1858–1930: the Illusion of Free Labour', in Douglas Hay and Paul Craven (eds), *Masters, Servants and Magistrates in Britain and the Empire, 1562–1955* (London, University of North Carolina Press, 2004), p. 431.
[37] Ranga, *The Economics of Handlooms*, pp. 14, 133.

Handlooms versus mills

From roughly the mid-nineteenth century, the handloom industry faced competition from British and Indian mills. State policies had variable effects on the handloom sector and domestic mills. The countervailing excise duty imposed on mill-made cloth (in response to pressure from British manufacturers opposing protection to Indian industry) worked to the advantage of handloom producers (exempt from this duty). The absence of tariffs on imported yarn had the same effect.[38] Both were unintended consequences of the refusal to protect the Indian mill industry.

But as time went on, the colonial state was forced to look to the condition of the Indian economy, and domestic industries in particular. Growing public criticism fuelled demands for the state to play an active role in developing indigenous industries. These calls grew in strength as legislative participation became broader based. A countervailing current opposing any government intervention developed among some groups of officials and the influential lobby of English commercial interests in India.[39]

By the early twentieth century, the Indian government was faced with a financial crisis. Its revenue collections were less than its increasing expenditures (including remittances to London) and tariffs on imports came to be seen as a way of improving revenues.[40] In 1917, the import duty on cloth was increased to 7.5 per cent; in deference to the interests of Lancashire mill owners, the countervailing excise duty on Indian mills was not removed (but not increased either). But pressure for its abolition was building up.[41] A severe crisis in the early 1920s encouraged Bombay mill owners to launch a strong campaign for the abolition of excise duty. Strikes and agitations by workers also put pressure on the government. In 1925, the countervailing excise duty on domestic mill cloth was finally withdrawn.[42]

Meanwhile, the import duty on cloth rose to 11 per cent in 1921 and 15 per cent in 1930. By 1934, duties on cotton piece goods imported

[38] Amalsad in G.O. no. 806, 3 April 1937, TNSA.

[39] Padmini Swaminathan, 'State Intervention in Industrialisation: a Case Study of the Madras Presidency', *Indian Economic and Social History Review,* 29(4) (1992), 479–506.

[40] Tomlinson, 'India and the British Empire', 344–5.

[41] Basudev Chatterji, 'The Abolition of the Cotton Excise, 1925: a Study in Imperial Priorities', *The Indian Economic and Social History Review,* 17(4) (1980), 355–79, at 360.

[42] See Chatterji, 'The Abolition of the Cotton Excise', for the sustained agitation to withdraw the countervailing cess. In the end, the wishes of Lancashire had to be set aside to satisfy the domestic mill industry.

from Britain stood at 25 per cent while imports from other countries paid 35 to 50 per cent (giving British goods a competitive advantage).[43] These policies, emerging from pressures within and outside India, worked against the handloom industry. Domestic mills were now insulated from foreign competition. This left them free to compete more aggressively with handlooms using their newfound advantage.[44]

Tariffs provided protection to the domestic mill industry. The abolition of excise duties allowed them to sell cheaply, forcing down handloom prices. The selling price of yarn was now governed by the price of imported yarn rather than the actual cost of production. High tariff walls allowed mills to make large profits by keeping yarn prices high. Higher counts of yarn had to be imported (for few domestic mills made them); here again tariffs were a handicap to weavers. They found themselves squeezed from both sides as yarn prices increased and cloth prices fell. The effect was particularly damaging during the Depression, when the price of cloth fell steeply, but the price of yarn remained relatively high.[45]

In response, the 'big men' of the handloom industry demanded some protection from competition by domestic mills. In 1928, a conference on textiles was convened after a resolution in the Legislative Council. The conference called for the abolition of duties on imported yarn (for counts above 40) and legislation to compel mills to provide good-quality yarn of proper length and count.[46] The state rejected both proposals. Demands that certain types of cloth be reserved for handlooms (by forbidding mills to make them) were also raised. In 1932, the Tariff Board opined that this proposal was not practicable. Instead, it appealed to mills to 'refrain from entering into unfair competition with the handloom industry'.[47]

The government contented itself with passing resolutions on 'the influence of education and co-operative spirit'. It also set up a small fund to encourage cooperatives. Amalsad was particularly scathing in his attack

[43] B. S. Baliga, *Compendium on History of Handloom Industry in Madras* (Madras, Government Press, 1960), p. 35.

[44] In addition, an import duty of 5 per cent ad valorem on yarn was introduced in 1927 and increased to 6.5 per cent in 1931. Baliga, *Compendium*, p. 35.

[45] Development Department, G.O. no. 806, 3 April 1937, TNSA. This was acknowledged by various committees, including the Tariff Board. Development Department, G.O. no. 868, 9 May 1941, TNSA. In 1939, the Congress government in Madras supported the abolition of import duty on yarn above 50 counts to protect the handloom industry. This proposal was rejected by the Government of India. Baliga, *Compendium*, pp. 41–2.

[46] Development Department, G.O. no. 1519, 20 June 1938, TNSA; Baliga, *Compendium*, p. 22.

[47] Baliga, *Compendium*, p. 45.

on this policy. He pointed out that while the mill industry was protected by tariff walls, handlooms were only provided a puny subsidy: 'a large body of articulate interests are benefiting at the expense of a larger, but inarticulate community'. Even this subsidy was merely 'a rebate or money refunded out of the duty collected on imported yarn consumed by the handloom weavers themselves. It represents a tax levied on the handloom weaver at one end and partially (not wholly) refunded at the other.'[48] He calculated that nearly 100,000 rupees had been collected from weavers in the Madras Presidency (in the form of increased yarn duties), while a sum of 59,500 rupees was returned to them through the subsidy.

Education and training

Some historians have noted a marked tendency on the part of the Madras government to support greater state intervention in order to promote industrial development.[49] Administrators like Havell, Chatterton and Amalsad took an energetic interest in the handloom industry. But the doctrine of laissez-faire (under attack in Britain after the success of protectionist policies enacted by Germany and the USA) was cited to avoid direct intervention in industrial matters. Until 1923, proposals emanating from Madras were usually rejected by the government of India.[50]

Early interventions came principally in the field of education, for Delhi ruled against any attempt to promote specific industries. The focus on technical education commenced in the nineteenth century. It was brought into focus by the Report of the Royal Commission on Technical Education in 1884. Meanwhile, demands from an increasingly vocal middle class for better educational facilities grew. As a result, several technical and engineering institutes were founded, including the Imperial Institute of Science at Bangalore (funded by the Tatas). However, most of them were starved of funds and resources.[51]

There was much discussion on the kind of education that should be imparted—whether scientific and technical education of a high standard or practical industrial education, oriented towards employment. This discussion extended to the social background of prospective students—should they be candidates from the already educated (largely Brahmin)

[48] Development Department, G.O. no. 806, 3 April 1937, TNSA.
[49] Swaminathan, 'State Intervention', 505.
[50] Swaminathan, 'State Intervention', 479–508.
[51] *Papers Relating to the Industrial Conference, 1908*, p. 94.

minority or from artisanal communities? The early focus (from 1886 on) was on proficiency in technical subjects. Later, official evaluations found that it was mostly Brahmin students who sat for these exams while 'the great mass of the industrial population' were 'practically left unaffected'. Most of the students who passed these courses had no intention of entering industrial employment in order to earn a livelihood.[52]

In the early part of the twentieth century, advocates of training candidates from artisanal and working-class backgrounds gained ground. Chatterton argued that the existing system was designed to produce administrators, not practitioners.[53] Several industrial institutes were opened during this period, including weaving schools in Madras and Madurai. The one in Madurai failed to take off. The expert appointed to run it was dismissed after a few months and the school itself closed down after some years.[54] The Madras Institute proved more successful. It provided two courses, one for supervisors and the other for artisans. It also manufactured various appliances and sold them to weavers. But the school was wound up after 1926.[55] From the 1930s, the emphasis shifted back to teaching students subjects like management and design, and efforts to train the ordinary workman were abandoned.[56]

As head of the Madras School of Arts, Chatterton set up an experimental weaving department with different looms, held weaving competitions and tried to find technological solutions for warping and sizing. From 1902, experiments were conducted in the weaving department to find ways of adapting the fly-shuttle loom to Indian conditions.[57] Chatterton persuaded the Madras government to set up a handloom weaving factory in Salem in order to experiment with new kinds of looms, preparatory mechanisms and a factory-based system of production, and to demonstrate the use of these methods and processes to weavers in general.[58] The Madras Chamber of Commerce, dominated by British capital (which was opposed to any form

[52] *Papers Relating to the Industrial Conference 1908*, pp. 14–15.

[53] Alfred Chatterton, *Rural Economics in India*, The Russell Lecture 1926 (London, Oxford University Press, 1927), p. 6.

[54] Baliga, *Compendium*, p. 13.

[55] Baliga, *Compendium*, p. 20.

[56] See Padmini Swaminathan, 'Technical Education and Industrial Development in Madras Presidency: Illusions of a Policy in the Making', *Economic and Political Weekly*, 27(30) (1992), 1611–22.

[57] *Department of Industries Bulletins*, Bulletin no. 4, IOR/V/25/600/151, British Library.

[58] Swaminathan, 'State Intervention', 494–5.

of protection for Indian industry), consistently criticised the programme and the government of India ordered its closure in 1910.[59]

After the imperial government ruled against model factories, it was decided to propagate and popularise the advantages of the fly-shuttle through peripatetic demonstration parties. These generally consisted of a superintendent, accompanied by five weavers, who carried various appliances such as a warping mill, beaming frame, frame loom, fly-shuttle, dobbies and jacquards, demonstrating their use in villages.[60] These travelling groups were revived by Amalsad in the early 1920s before being finally abolished in 1932.[61] They played an important role in the adoption of the fly-shuttle.

Contrasting approaches: E. B. Havell and Alfred Chatterton

There were substantial differences of opinion over policies and methods to promote the handloom industry both within government and outside. We have seen that Madras and Delhi diverged on the basic question of state intervention. Within the provincial government, there were varying opinions about what could or should be done. Two prominent individuals (and their associates) laid out competing intellectual justifications for state action.

During the late nineteenth century, some colonial administrators with a keen interest in the artistic and artisanal heritage of India began looking for ways to revive it. Some of them, notably E. B. Havell and George Birdwood, were associated with the Arts and Crafts Movement in England. The first steps to preserve and develop artisanal traditions were the fruit of individual initiative. The School of Arts in Madras was founded by Dr. Hunter, a surgeon of Black Town (Madras), in 1850 at his own expense. It was subsequently taken over by the government, but Hunter continued as superintendent until 1874.[62] His successor E. B. Havell was strongly influenced by William Morris.

Members of this group called upon the government to make active efforts to preserve Indian arts and artisanal culture. Forbes Royle rather patronisingly argued that India should not be seen merely as 'a farm from

[59] Baliga, *Compendium*, p. 13.

[60] *Indian Industrial Commission*, Minutes of Evidence (1916–17), vol. 3, Madras and Bangalore (Calcutta, Government Press, 1918), p. 185.

[61] Baliga, *Compendium*, pp. 19, 28.

[62] *Papers Relating to the Industrial Conference 1908*, p. 15.

which to draw our supplies of raw produce … or as a field which we have to cover with our manufactures', but rather 'as an estate we have to improve'.[63] He emphasised the antiquity of its arts and manufactures, and the skill of Indian artisans. All that was necessary was the 'modification of some of their simple and though rude-looking, yet efficient tools'.[64] This school of thought argued against any attempt to replicate industrialisation. Havell was critical of the Swadeshi movement for 'being content to follow behind commercial Europe'. He argued instead for a revival of Indian arts and handicrafts.[65]

> Those who believe that hand labour in manufacture is becoming a thing of the past are entertaining a delusion fatal to real progress in India. … Hand manufactures can be developed and improved quite as much as mechanical industry. A country like India, which possesses hundreds of thousands of skilled handicraftsmen, and where the cost of living is many times cheaper than it is in Europe, possesses a source of potential wealth capable of almost indefinite expansion. It is the most suicidal and fatuous policy to assume that the skilled handicraftsman must be turned into a cooly minding a machine.[66]

The idea was to preserve the traditional arts and crafts of India without 'contaminating' them with 'modern' or 'western' ideas. Another proponent of this approach, Thomas Wardle, was sent to India to study the silk industry.[67] Some of these men worked with the authorities to organise exhibitions to promote the commercial products of India. They also founded a journal with state support that survived for a decade with the stated aim of documenting and preserving Indian art.

This school of thought laid emphasis on artistic sense rather than the nature of the work. For them, art was related to everyday life: the weaving of coarse cloth was true art as much as miniature painting.[68] George Birdwood wrote that 'in India you cannot yet draw a distinction between art and industry. … Everything … is hand wrought and everything down to the

[63] J. Forbes Royle, 'The Arts and Manufactures of India', in *Lectures on the Results of the Exhibition Delivered Before the Society of Arts and Manufactures and Commerce* (London, David Bogue, 1852), p. 334.
[64] Royle, 'The Arts and Manufactures of India', pp. 334, 394.
[65] E. B. Havell, 'Preface', *Essays on Indian Art, Industry and Education* (Madras, G. A. Natesan and Co., n.d.); E. B. Havell, *The Basis for Artistic and Industrial Revival in India* (Madras, The Theosophist Office, 1912), pp. 135–40.
[66] Havell, *Essays on Indian Art*, p. 30.
[67] Thomas Wardle, 'The Indian Silk Culture Court at the Colonial and Indian Exhibition', *Journal of Indian Art*, 1 (1886), 123.
[68] Article on Art and Politics in MSS EUR D. 736/5, IOR, London.

cheapest toys and earthen vessels is therefore more or less a work of art.'[69] Thomas Wardle opined that 'even if their work lacks mechanical regularity, they have down to today managed, somehow or the other, if they have had a pattern to weave, to put, so to speak, soul into it, and to raise it above the commonplace fabrics so often produced in modern Europe'.[70]

For all its sympathy, this was essentially a romantic picture of the pre-modern Indian artisan who 'took pleasure in his work'. Even if he had 'fewer political rights, less pay and less comfort', as far as work was concerned, he 'was intellectually free'.[71] It formed part and parcel of the romantic view of the caste system that regarded it as having preserved and reproduced craft skills, and united Indian society.[72]

For Havell, the industrial regeneration of India was 'first and last a moral and intellectual problem, not a technical one'.[73] He was critical of Chatterton's argument that village industries should be reorganised on capitalist principles. Havell argued that by forcing the weaver to leave the village for a factory he (Chatterton),

> would thus sweep away entirely all the artistic traditions of the famous Indian industry and reduce the weavers to the condition of day labourers under the control of individual capitalists who have no other qualifications than their knowledge of up to date mechanical appliances and no other ideal than that of filling their own pockets.[74]

Instead, he favoured cooperatives (to eliminate the sowcar) and improved technology. He argued that 'the principle of co-operation will do even more for that organisation [the traditional organisation of village handicrafts] than the factory system can ever do'.[75]

[69] George Birdwood, *Paris Universal Exhibition of 1878: Handbook to the British Indian Section* (London, Offices of the Royal Commission, 1878), pp. 55–6.

[70] Wardle, 'The Indian Silk Culture Court', p. 117.

[71] E. B. Havell, 'Art, Economics and Politics', *The Calcutta Review* (September 1925), MSS EUR D. 73615, IOR. Havell was critical of capitalist industrial development and political democracy. He disliked non-cooperation (though he approved of Gandhi's efforts to develop and popularise khadi) and called it 'an inartistic political concept which can breed only ill will and strife'. He admired Mussolini's Italy for sparking a revival of art and creativity: 'Fascism under Mussolini's inspiration has altered the whole spiritual and moral outlook of the Italian people. … His programme covers all branches of art and every kind of activity. … Fascism is art, for it too is an original movement of the spirit and is not a deduction but a creation and even in action it relies on a seminal inspiration rather than a conclusion closely drawn of reasoning.'

[72] Havell, *Basis*, p. 152; George Birdwood, *Two Letters on the Industrial Arts of India* (London, Whittingham and Co., 1879), pp. 8, 21.

[73] Havell, *Basis*, p. 134.

[74] Havell, *Essays on Indian Art*, pp. 72–5, 80. Also, Havell, *Basis*, pp. 183–5.

[75] Havell, *Basis*, p. 185.

> Each weaving community [should] have a central establishment under its own control which would arrange the purchase of materials at whole sale rates, prepare warps for the weavers' looms and organize the sale of the finished products. The actual weaving would be carried on as at present in the weavers' houses by the master weavers and their apprentices. A system of this kind would retain the economic advantages of the factory system and eliminate its many evils.[76]

He advocated a policy of providing improved appliances free of cost to poor weavers at their doorsteps (instead of relying upon exhibitions, demonstrations and schools) and criticised the government for failing to support them effectively. [77]

Alfred Chatterton, active in Madras from the turn of the century, used a different set of arguments. Arriving in India in 1888 as professor of engineering in the College of Engineering in Madras, he became increasingly influential after 1900, when he was appointed superintendent of the School of Arts. He was a key figure in the introduction and spread of the fly-shuttle in South India.

Chatterton was an advocate of small industries in opposition to the 'hideous concentration of human life and human activity in smoke-begrimed cities, with unparalleled luxury for the few and squalor for the many'.[78] He favoured 'a judicious combination of the man with the machine' against 'mindless mechanisation, which set aside India's greatest asset, abundant and cheap labour', and called for increases in efficiency and productivity through capital investments, technical improvements and sub-division of labour.[79]

> The day has gone by when each artisan family can be considered a complete industrial unit, and if any improvement is to be effected in the status of the indigenous industries it must follow on the lines on which industrial development has proceeded in almost all industries all over the world. All modern progress is in the direction of a minuter sub-division of labour and the introduction of automatic appliances which render production less dependent upon manual skill and dexterity.[80]

At first, he saw cooperatives as a possible method of reorganising weaving, but soon abandoned this view in favour of the factory system:

[76] Havell, *Essays on Indian Art*, p. 83.
[77] Havell, *Basis*, pp. 176–7.
[78] Chatterton, *Industrial Evolution in India*, p. 27.
[79] Alfred Chatterton, *Weaving in India* (Allahabad, Indian Press, 1907), p. 3.
[80] Chatterton, *Weaving in India*, p. 5.

> That any improvement can be affected by working along cooperative lines is very doubtful and it is even still more certain that the individual weaver can never hope to better his present condition. The handloom weaving factory is the only direction in which progress seems possible. The weavers themselves are helpless and the organisation and capital which are necessary to put the industry on a better footing must come from outside.[81]

His pessimism derived from a belief that the individual weaver was hopelessly indolent and lazy. For this he blamed the climate and the caste system.[82] This 'hopeless attitude of mind' rendered the weaver averse to any change.[83] Therefore, the artisan's daily work had to be 'directed by men who have received a special training to fit them to exercise efficient control over considerable number of hand-workers'.[84] After expressing some criticisms of the sowcar in the beginning, he came to defend his role.

> In the weaving industry [the sowcar] is really an entrepreneur, a middleman between the weaver and the general public. He provides finance and gives employment. He is the master and they are the workmen, often tied to him by debt. The weavers are ignorant, improvident, untrustworthy and need to be coerced. The sowcar knows them and is able to keep them under control.[85]

Any successful intervention would have to work through the sowcar, who was 'the natural head of the weavers'.[86]

Chatterton's vision for the weaving industry was

> groups of fifty to two hundred weavers centred around a warping and dressing plant. This will supply warps to the weavers, who may either be collected in a shed or will work in their own homes. The trade will be in the hands of those who run the warping plant and on them will mainly fall the work of introducing improved looms and methods among the hand weavers ... The part which the government should play in this movement is to supply the skilled technical knowledge required to devise the equipment and when that step has been taken to start demonstration factories and trade schools for the instruction of those who want to become foremen and master weavers.[87]

While setting himself against large-scale enterprises and wholesale mechanisation, he was a firm supporter of capitalist development in general. His vision is essentially a smaller version of the factory as a private

[81] Chatterton, *Industrial Evolution in India*, p. 254.
[82] Chatterton, *Industrial Evolution in India*, p. 14.
[83] Chatterton, *Industrial Evolution in India*, p. 251.
[84] Chatterton, *Industrial Evolution in India*, p. 210.
[85] IOR/R/2/20/133, p. 11, London.
[86] IOR/R/2/20/133, p. 11, London.
[87] Chatterton, *Industrial Evolution in India*, p. 33.

enterprise, with the state intervening only in cases where there was no possibility of private investment. Chatterton was opposed to any form of tariff protection.[88] In his view, India needed a more 'paternal' form of state intervention, direct but limited, the cost of which could be accurately determined. This could be done by providing technical education and setting up new industries to be handed over to private enterprise after some time.[89]

Both these views are full of contradictions and inconsistencies. Havell romanticised the handloom weaver, exalted his artistic sense and skill, but sought to insulate him from technology and denied the need for India to industrialise at all. Some of its political implications are revealed in his admiration for Mussolini and Italian fascism. Nevertheless, Havell's sympathy for weavers was real and tangible, and his advocacy of cooperatives as an effective means of safeguarding their interests proved both original and far-reaching.

Chatterton, by contrast, saw the weaver as a cog in a machine and stressed the desirability of turning him into a worker governed by 'enlightened' factory owners and sowcars for the greater good. This view was linked to a firm belief in technology, capitalism and private enterprise. Practically speaking, Chatterton played a key role in introducing technological innovations in small industries such as handlooms and tanning. These competing views were echoed in policy debates in the public sphere and within government.

Artisan futures: cooperatives vs factories

Despite these debates, the government did nothing much to promote the interests of the handloom industry until the Second World War. Many forums, including the Industrial Commission, and individuals writing on industrial policy drew attention to large industries while paying lip service to the importance of small and 'cottage' industries. In the case of cottage industries, two lines of argument gradually developed. One advocated cooperatives; the other favoured organising them into small factories.[90] The Fact Finding Committee on handlooms and mills was in favour of cooperatives, but opined that 'sowcar merchants will have to be taken into

[88] Chatterton, *Industrial Evolution in India*, p. 13.
[89] Chatterton, *Industrial Evolution in India*, pp. 60, 212.
[90] Indian Industrial Commission (1916–18), pp. 196, 200–3.

confidence and not antagonized'.[91] It recommended that 'where there are middlemen their services should be utilised and where there are none, a network of co-operative institutions and perhaps joint stock organizations may be formed'.[92]

There was much talk of cooperatives as the most effective solution to the problems of the weaver. In official circles, this was viewed as a voluntary movement in which weavers would come together and raise capital to start cooperatives.[93] But this could only be done by prosperous weavers, who would, in the nature of things, prefer becoming master weavers instead. Without fiscal support from the state, cooperatives could not succeed: this was borne out by the failure of most of the early experiments.[94] Sympathetic officials recommended state support, but concrete action was slow and halting.[95]

In 1928, as public pressure built up, a conference was organised to chart a plan for government initiatives in the textile sector. It called for a network of cooperatives to be set up. The official response, predictably, was lukewarm: 'the prospects of success in this direction they felt were not encouraging in view of the improvident and intemperate habits of the weaver'. Instead, it was decided that the Co-operative Department would be asked to 'pay special attention to the development of weavers' societies on the lines suggested by the Conference'.[96] Amalsad, the textile expert in the industries department, was a strong votary of cooperation.

It was only from 1935 that weavers' cooperatives obtained some help from the government. In 1933, at an Industrial Conference in Shimla, the Madras government proposed a cess on Indian mill yarn with a countervailing duty on Indian and imported cloth. The proceeds were to be applied to a proper organisation for handlooms. The proposed cess was rejected, but the government of India, while passing the Tariff Protection (Amendment) Act of 1934, provided a grant to the handloom industry not exceeding the proceeds of an import duty of a quarter anna per pound on imported yarn (up to counts of 50).[97] This grant, distributed to the provinces,

[91] *Fact Finding Committee*, p. 214.

[92] Quoted in Baliga, *Compendium*, p. 35.

[93] Baliga, *Compendium*, pp. 16–18.

[94] Baliga, *Compendium*, pp. 15–18.

[95] Amalsad was a strong advocate of cooperatives and his exasperation with state inaction is visible in his reports. Development Department, G.O. no. 806, 3 April 1937, TNSA; Development Department, G.O. no. 1519, 20 June 1938, TNSA.

[96] Baliga, *Compendium*, pp. 24–6.

[97] Baliga, *Compendium*, p. 26.

was used in Madras to organise a Provincial Co-operative Society, which was to coordinate and develop the activities of primary weavers' societies.[98]

In general, the Madras government proved more sympathetic to handloom weavers than Delhi (or other provincial governments). The Madras Congress had influential members from weaving communities in its ranks and a strong support base within them. In 1939, the Congress government in Madras called for the withdrawal of import duties on yarn above counts of 50. It also suggested an excise duty on mill-made cloth and a law to prohibit mills from producing certain kinds of cloths.[99] These suggestions were rejected by Delhi. During the Second World War, fresh differences emerged. Madras was keen to include handlooms in the state programme for producing 'standard cloths'. Pointing to widespread weaver distress (and rioting), it protested against 'any scheme calculated to increase the weaving capacity of the mills without at the same time ensuring that the handlooms do not remain idle'.[100]

Concrete steps to aid cooperatives were taken: the government provided more financial assistance, negotiated with mills to ensure yarn supply, and increased the share capital of primary and provincial cooperative societies.[101] Wartime conditions were regarded as an opportunity to promote state intervention. Advocates of cooperatives suggested directing state support towards the expansion of the cooperative network.

State-sponsored weaving centres were set up to provide unemployed weavers with relief, and weave cloth for war supplies. It was planned to convert them into cooperative societies later on.[102] Ailing societies were given financial assistance.[103] Assistance to indemnify cooperative central banks against business losses in their transactions with societies undertaking relief schemes was provided.[104] The Madras Handloom Weavers Provincial Cooperative opened two dye houses at Madurai and Salem to supply dyed yarn to cooperative societies.[105]

It is no coincidence that cooperatives began to obtain state support at a time when weaver protests and unionisation were rising to a peak.

[98] Development Department, G.O. no. 1519, 20 June 1938, TNSA.

[99] Baliga, *Compendium*, pp. 44–6, 49.

[100] Development Department, G.O. no. 1942, 12 September 1942, TNSA.

[101] Development Department, G.O. no. 2468, 23 November 1942, TNSA; Baliga, *Compendium*, pp. 61–2.

[102] *Census of India 1961*, p. 18.

[103] Development Department, G.O. no. (M-241)1723, 19 August 1942, TNSA.

[104] Baliga, *Compendium*, p. 62.

[105] Development Department, G.O. no. 366, 19 February 1942, TNSA.

State aid for cooperatives was a recurring theme of agitations. Successful cooperatives were formed under the leadership of unions.[106] For its part, the state probably viewed them as a method of diffusing popular anger in a difficult situation created by its obdurate refusal to 'interfere' with private enterprise and the free market.[107]

In 1949, amid widespread unemployment, the Madras government encouraged weavers to join cooperatives; an advance of 25 rupees per person was provided to remit the capital for this. In 1950, a State Handloom Committee was formed to advise the government on the handloom industry.[108] In 1953, there was another crisis of unemployment. Weavers from the Tirunelveli region decided to march to Madras to demand protection for handlooms and greater support for cooperatives: this came to be called the march of the Hungry Battalion. An All-India Handloom Board was set up and a cess levied on mill cloth was set aside for the development of khadi and handlooms.[109] In 1953–4, loans repayable in two years were given to weavers buying shares in cooperative societies.[110]

The number of cooperatives rose from only 50 societies in 1936 (out of which 20 were dormant), to 659 societies with a total of 86,000 looms in 1947, to 980 societies with 190,000 looms in 1960.[111] Measures like the reservation of certain varieties of cloth for handlooms that had been rejected earlier were finally enacted.[112] The 1950s and '60s were the heyday of the cooperative sector. But not long afterwards, handloom cooperatives were transformed into channels of political patronage and many of them collapsed as a result of systematic mismanagement.[113]

From the very beginning, it was clear that the state had limited funds for the cooperative sector. The transformation of the handloom industry into a network of cooperatives was never envisaged. There is little doubt that cooperatives gave some security to weavers enrolled in them. At the same

[106] In Salem, cooperative societies were set up under the leadership of Kandasamy, K. K. Ramdas and other members of the AITUC. Subbiah of the Communist Party of India played a leading role in organising handloom workers in Tirunelveli district and building cooperatives during the 1940s. Srinivasan, *Communist Heroes*, pp. 299, 319.

[107] In the beginning, the state was hesitant to introduce measures interfering with markets. But by 1942–3, it was decided to regulate the textile industry to ensure supplies for the war. Development Department, G.O. no. 1268, 26 June 1943, TNSA.

[108] *Census of India 1961*, pp. 23–4.

[109] *Census of India 1961*, p. 29.

[110] *Census of India 1961*, p. 29.

[111] ILO, *Handloom Weaving Industry in India*, p. 56.

[112] *Census of India 1961*, p. 24.

[113] See Mines, *The Warrior Merchants*, pp. 121–42; Arterburn, *The Loom of Interdependence*.

time, they allowed the state to evade larger problems of labour regulation. A dual structure developed: a small proportion of weavers obtained work in the regulated structure of cooperatives (with some economic and social protection), while the rest, excluded from labour regulation, were left without any security of work or wages.[114]

The state and private capital

We have seen that some voices within government favoured cooperatives as a lasting solution to the problems of the handloom industry. This view coexisted with a strong emphasis on leaving private enterprise and the market to do their work. During the Second World War, when extraordinary measures were taken, the stress on maintaining 'normal' trade channels and protecting private enterprise remained unaffected.

Faced with chronic shortages and very large increases in the price of yarn, the Madras government decided to introduce yarn control measures and organise the production of 'standard cloths'. It was decided that yarn distribution should be 'through normal trade channels' and not the government. Wholesale distributors were licensed and allowed a fixed margin of profit while retail prices were placed under 'government supervision'.[115] We have already discussed the profiteering encouraged by this system.

Relief measures included the production and sale of Handloom Standard Cloth through master weavers and merchants. Master weavers were given licenses to make cloth and the government bought it from them at a fixed price.[116] It was argued that relief through weavers' centres and cooperatives would reach only a limited number of weavers; therefore limiting yarn supply at concessional rates to 'approved' organisations was not considered desirable.[117]

Yarn control measures were reintroduced in 1948 after being suspended for a brief period. There was considerable debate over how to organise supply this time around. There were indications that the government was considering distributing yarn and cloth through cooperatives. The question

[114] See Babu P. Remesh, *Organisational Structure, Labour Relations and Employment in Kancheepuram Silk Weaving* (Noida, V. V. Giri National Labour Institute, 2001).
[115] Development Department no. 1942, 12 September 1942, TNSA.
[116] Baliga, *Compendium*, p. 68.
[117] Development Department, G.O. no. 1129, 14 March 1944, TNSA.

was raised in the legislative assembly where most members came out against the prospect. It was argued that the market could not be blamed for the illegal actions of a few traders, and that yarn and cloth distribution should be done through normal trade channels. Only a few members argued in favour of cooperatives.[118] In the end, the Madras government decided to distribute yarn through cooperatives as well as private dealers and master weavers. Many of the dealers had been active in the black market in previous years and, because of their political influence, these 'black-market men' managed to obtain licences again.[119]

An industrial policy for the future

The relationship of the state to private capital in the handloom industry must be viewed in the context of wider industrial policies. Formally at least, the colonial state maintained a position of non-interference in the economic realm in the face of growing demands for state support. From 1937, Congress ministries in the provinces started developing industrial policies and economic plans for the future, when India would become independent. The process was marked by significant disagreements. Some Congressmen supported greater state control of industry; others advocated leaving it to private enterprise. The former were more influential in the beginning, but it was the latter who prevailed in the end.[120]

Within the Congress, there were influential advocates of large-scale industry, while others favoured decentralised, small-scale or cottage industries as being peculiarly suited to the Indian context. A compromise was reached by agreeing to demarcate the domains of large-scale and cottage industries, and to minimise conflict through planning.[121] Industries were a concurrent subject under the Government of India Act of 1935. It was decided that the central government should focus on large industries

[118] Madras Legislative Assembly Debates, Official Report, vol. 14, nos 1–12, August–September (Madras, Government Press, 1948), pp. 658–789.

[119] Development Department, G.O. no. 5108, 16 October 1948, TNSA.

[120] Vivek Chibber, *Locked in Place: State-building and Late Industrialisation in India* (Delhi, Tulika Books, 2004).

[121] Cottage industries were prominent in the first note (1937) issued by the National Planning Committee for the guidance of sub-committees. In a new note issued in 1945, they were relegated to the end, with a reference to protection. A special note by the chairman of the Planning Committee clarified that although Congress policy was to encourage cottage industries, it could not ignore large-scale industry and would be failing in its duty if it did so. K. T. Shah (ed.), *Report: National Planning Committee* (Bombay, Vora and Co. Publishers, 1949), pp. 35–7, 41, 46, 53, 97.

and the key sectors of the economy while provincial governments would deal with the rest.[122]

In accordance with this policy, small-scale and cottage industries were largely ignored in the first five-year plan. This changed substantially by the time of the second plan (1956). It had become clear that large-scale industry was not expanding as fast or as much as expected. The second plan stressed the importance of small-scale industry in terms of generating employment. Since the sector required lower capital investments and used existing resources of capital, labour and raw materials, it was decided to promote it by discouraging large-scale enterprises in basic consumer goods, reserving them for the small-scale sector instead.[123]

In this way, support for small-scale industry came to be integrated into national policy. Its supporters were much more prominent at the provincial level. During debates in the legislative assembly, Madras state was described as the land of cottage industries.[124] Large-scale textile mills emerged late in South India compared to other parts of the country and handlooms played a larger role in the economy. The Madras government insisted on including them in yarn allocations during the war years.

In practice, support for small industries translated into support for the small entrepreneur or factory owner—this was especially evident in discussions about labour legislation.

The state and labour legislation

Legislation to protect workers in factories developed gradually, after sustained struggles and a series of official inquiries into labour conditions. The general excuse was that Indian workers had not matured and were not efficient or productive enough to warrant protection. Prejudice with respect to workers in the unorganised sector was even stronger.

[122] In response to a question about government support for cottage industries in the Constituent Assembly in 1948, the Minister of Industries replied that the development of cottage industries was primarily the responsibility of provincial governments. Much the same view was expressed at the Industries Conference of 1947. Shah, *Report*, p. 272.

[123] Planning Commission, *Report of the Village and Small Scale Industries Committee (Second Five Year Plan)* (Delhi, Government Press, October 1955), pp. 1, 3, 7, 8, 15–17.

[124] See discussions in the Madras Legislative Assembly Debates: Official Report, vol. 5, nos 1–14, March–April (Madras, Government Press, 1947), pp. 1039–40; Madras Legislative Assembly Debates: Official Report, vol. 7, nos 1–15, October–December (Madras, Government Press, 1947), pp. 332–5, 562–73.

In his study of early labour legislation, Aditya Sarkar points out that officials were well aware that working conditions in small-scale industries were often worse than in large factories.[125] The Royal Commission on Labour noted this fact and suggested separate legislation for unregulated and non-power factories.[126] However, attempts in this direction never took off at the national level.

In Madras, the first attempt at labour legislation came in 1932 through two private member bills. Ganala Ramamurti, a nominated, non-official member of the Legislative Council from the Vishwakarma caste, introduced two bills, the Artisans' Protection Bill and the Beedi Factories Bill, with the limited aim of curbing child labour in workshops. However, he was forced to withdraw them after the government declared that it did not have the resources to appoint inspectors for the purpose.[127]

In 1937, the first Congress government in Madras considered regulating small-scale, non-power factories, but no concrete action was taken. In 1942, large tanneries and beedi factories were brought under the Factories Act, but this order was withdrawn on grounds of difficulty in implementation and non-cooperation by employers. In 1944, the Commissioner of Labour recommended the extension of the provisions of the Factories Act to other small establishments, but the suggestion was set aside on the pretext of eliciting public opinion and weighing its consequences. The Madras government decided to postpone the measure until after the war, as part of the post-war reconstruction of the economy.[128]

With the end of the war, the proposal was taken up again, and the NPF Act passed in 1947. This regulated working conditions in small factories and workshops, including working hours, holidays, health and safety, and conditions for dismissal. Its provisions did not include wage rates or collective bargaining. It was enacted alongside the Madras Shops and Establishments (MSE) Act, which regulated shops and commercial establishments in urban municipalities and large panchayats.

The debates around the Artisans Protection Bill, the NPF Act and MSE Act reveal two opposing viewpoints. Their proponents (mostly labour leaders) pointed to the terrible conditions of work in home- and workshop-based industries. Their opponents saw them as a threat to the very existence

[125] Aditya Sarkar, *Trouble at the Mill: Factory Law and the Emergence of the Labour Question in Late Nineteenth-century Bombay* (New Delhi, Oxford University Press, 2018), pp. 129–75.
[126] *Main Report of the Labour Investigation Committee* (Delhi, Government Press, 1946), p. 48.
[127] IOR: L/E/8/868 and 'Proceedings of the Legislative Council of the Governor of Madras', 63(1), 31 October (Madras, Government Press, 1932), pp. 82–90.
[128] Development Department, G.O. no. 2120, 27 April 1948, TNSA.

of small industries and petty traders. Instead, they called upon the state to protect the 'small people': entrepreneurs and traders, the 'backbone' of the economy.[129] One legislator declared that

> they are the real backbone of trade, they are the entrepreneurs, they are the agencies of industry and commerce of our Province. They are men of self-reliance and self-effort. I do not know why the government instead of coming to their rescue should propose measures restricting the scope of industry...[130]

It was argued that any attempt to regulate labour in small industries would increase costs for employers and render them uncompetitive. Support for the small entrepreneur formed part of a larger narrative—according to this view, industry in India was taking its first steps and could not afford luxuries like labour legislation, for this would only place it under a crippling burden. The fitness of workers to obtain paid leave, notice before dismissal and so on were also questioned.[131]

The NPF Act applied only to establishments with a minimum of ten workers. In addition, a worker had to prove continuous employment (of six months) to avail many of its provisions.[132] The bills did not regulate wages, bonuses or social security (such as provident fund and maternity benefits). When new laws were passed to codify these benefits, definitions of employee and worker restricted their application to workers in large industries.

Handloom factory owners and their associations argued that implementation of the NPF Act would render their factories uncompetitive.[133] A newspaper article pointed out that cottage industries enjoyed considerable political patronage. The author expressed doubt that the law would be successfully applied, for the officials charged with enforcing it worked under the same political leaders.[134] Events justified this apprehension. The NPF Act was dismantled within months of its passage on the excuse that the new Factories Act of 1947 (passed by the central government) superseded it.[135]

[129] MLA Debates, vol. 5 (nos 1–14), pp. 1036–40; MLA Debates, vol. 7 (nos 1–15), pp. 333–74, 562–9.

[130] MLA Debates, vol. 7 (nos 1–15), p. 374.

[131] Dietrich Wielenga, 'Emergence of the Informal Sector'.

[132] Dietrich Wielenga, 'Emergence of the Informal Sector'.

[133] Development Department, G.O. no. 2120, 27 April 1948, TNSA.

[134] Development Department, G.O. no. 2120, 27 April 1948, TNSA.

[135] The NPF Act covered establishments employing ten or more workers while the Factories Act applied only to establishments employing 20 or more workers (if they did not use powered machines). It was argued that the Madras government could use powers granted in the Act

Lobbying, political pressure and court challenges kept handloom factories out of the purview of regulation. The town of Karur had 50 small handloom factories, employing between 20 and 100 weavers each. The Karur Weaving and Knitting Factory Owners Association lobbied for blanket exemption from the Factories Act. They argued that their establishments were cottage industries, mere extensions of private residences, and could not be expected to comply with its provisions. The state duly exempted them.[136] When some factory inspectors tried to enforce the Factories Act and the Employees Provident Fund Act, the courts ruled that Karur's workshops could not be defined as factories.[137] Even though these workshops employed more than 20 workers, the court accepted the contention of the owners that there was no employer–employee relationship because they had no 'control' over the work the weavers did. The Factories Act was applied very inconsistently to handloom factories until in the end they were exempted from it.[138]

Master-weaver associations lobbied for exemption from the MSE Act as well, arguing that it increased their costs. Independent weavers and establishments employing family members were the first to be exempted.[139] Petitions for exemptions poured in from different parts of the state and the Member of the Legislative Assembly from Udipi made a representation in the Assembly. Master weavers argued that a weekly holiday reduced the income of workers on piece-rates. The Commissioner of Labour objected that the encouragement to industry should not be at the cost of workers employed in it. The outcome of this lobbying was the exemption of all piece-rate workers (not just weavers) from the MSE Act.[140]

to extend its application to establishments with more than ten workers (removing the need for a separate law). Owners promptly challenged this power: the High Court ruled that the government could not declare a whole class of establishments as factories; it could only notify individual establishments. Development Department, G.O. no. 2210, 22 April 1949, TNSA; Dietrich Wielenga, 'Emergence of the Informal Sector'.

[136] Industry, Labour and Co-operation (ILC) Department, G.O. no. 3203, 15 November 1954, TNSA.

[137] Madras High Court, *M. Ratnaswami Mudaliar vs Unknown*, 24 September 1958 (AIR 1959 Mad 203, 1959 CriLJ 614); Madras High Court, *S. Palanaiappa Mudaliar vs Additional First Class Magistrate*, 17 April 1958 ((1958) 2 MLJ 346).

[138] It is not clear when this exemption was granted. ILC Department, G.O. no. 603, 2 February 1965, TNSA.

[139] Development Department, G.O. no. 4817, 31 October 1953, TNSA.

[140] Development Department, G.O. no. 4817, 31 October 1953, TNSA.

Is a weaver a 'worker'?

The definition of worker/workman/employee became a key question in the interpretation of labour laws: the NPF Act, the MSE Act, the Factory Act, the Industrial Disputes Act, the Employees Provident Fund Act and the Employees State Insurance Act. Each bill incorporated a different definition: all of them were vague and ambiguous and therefore open to challenge. Weavers had to fit the definition of worker in order to make claims under the law. It was only the male weaver who figured in these legal debates. Ancillary workers, and women in particular, were rendered invisible once again.

The first step by master weavers and merchants was to claim that the weavers working for them were *not* their employees. Their mutual relationship was described as being that of buyer and seller: as sellers (instead of workers) they could not argue for protection under the law. This line of argument was employed in *every* dispute that came before the state. From the beginning, the decisions or awards of the quasi-judicial Industrial Tribunals set up to hear them were strikingly inconsistent. Some tribunals ruled that an employer–employee relationship existed, others denied it.[141]

As these disputes moved into the courts (along with similar disputes in industries like beedi making and tanning) the argument became more sophisticated. Workshop and factory owners contended that their relationship with coolie weavers was not that of master and servant because the piece-work contract between each individual worker and the firm was a contract for services (and not of service). Legally, for an employer–employee relationship to exist, the contract had to be 'of service' and not 'for service'. Various Supreme Court and High Court judgments laid out tests for determining whether a particular work arrangement was a 'contract of service'. The crucial test was held to be whether the control exercised by an employer extended, not just over the work to be done, but also *how* it was done. Supervision and complete control over the production process came to be defined as the determining features of an employer–employee relationship.[142]

[141] Development Department, G.O. no. 5190, 25 October 1949, TNSA; Development Department, G.O. no. 2566, 14 May 1949, TNSA; Development Department, G.O. no. 1421, 10 April 1950, TNSA.

[142] *S. Palaniappa Mudaliar vs Additional First Class Magistrate; Ratnaswami Mudaliar vs Unknown*; Madras High Court, *Annamalai Mudaliar and Bros vs Regional Provident Fund*, 20 January 1955 (AIR (1955) Mad 387 and (1955) ILLJ 674 Mad).

A number of disputes in the handloom factories of Karur made their way to the Madras High Court. The owners argued that weavers were not their employees even though the looms belonged to the factory owners, the weavers worked in the factory premises and were supplied with yarn by them. The argument was that despite this the owners exercised no control over the time of the weavers, who came and went as they pleased, and that the weavers could quit if and when they so desired. The judgment accepted this argument, ruling that people working on the premises of a factory (for wages or otherwise) could not be defined as workers for that reason alone; there needed to be a master–servant relationship to show that they were 'employed'. This and this alone made them 'employees'. Supervision and control over time was defined as a crucial element of this relationship. Since weavers had flexible hours (or so it was claimed) and did not come under direct supervision, they were only providing a contract for service and not a contract of service. Therefore they could not be considered employees: without this status, they were not entitled to make claims under laws applying to workers and employees.[143]

In this way, the courts set benchmarks for determining the definition of workers and employees. Ambiguity persisted since the interpretation of evidence by individual judges varied considerably. In other cases under identical circumstances, judges ruled that direct supervision existed and so did a master–servant relationship; those weavers were treated as employees.[144] The tussle over legal definitions continued to remain at the centre of struggles to gain better wages, working conditions and social benefits.[145]

Establishing their status as workers proved to be only the first of many stumbling blocks. Even when this was established, demands for better wages, bonuses or social security measures were rejected out of hand by labour officers and heads of labour tribunals. The justifications cited included the argument that the handloom industry was 'not sufficiently organised'.[146]

[143] *Annamalai Mudaliar vs Regional Provident Fund.*

[144] Madras High Court, *Kamarajan Textiles vs Employees State Insurance*, 24 August 1976 ((1977) 2 MLJ 296); Madras High Court, *Kandaswami Weaving vs Regional Director, Employees State Insurance Fund*, 6 December 1967 ((1968) 2 MLJ 436); Madras High Court, *Madurai General Workers Union vs Brinda Textiles Handloom Factory*, 24 March 1967 ((1968) IILLJ 101 Mad). In this case, the High Court reversed the judgment of the labour court by ruling that supervision existed and therefore they were workmen.

[145] ILC Department, G.O. no. 603 and 604, 2 February 1965, TNSA; ILC Department, G.O. no. 644, 19 February 1957, TNSA; ILC Department, G.O. no. 3553, 3 August 1956, TNSA; ILC Department, G.O. no. 603, 2 February 1965, TNSA; ILC Department, G.O. no. 4974, 11 October 1962, TNSA.

[146] Development Department, G.O. no. 5190, 25 October 1949, TNSA.

Tribunals allowed wage reductions, irregularity of employment and non-payment of dearness allowance on the grounds that factory owners and master weavers had to cope with the vagaries of the market and could not afford to provide fixed wages or employment.[147]

The faulty architecture of labour laws combined with chronic and deliberate inconsistency of implementation excluded the majority of workers in small industries from their ambit. The laws were weak, imprecise and limited in effect. They had glaring loopholes built into them from the very beginning. Employers subverted and weakened them through systematic lobbying and legal challenges. The handloom industry was officially exempted from the purview of some laws; factory owners took care to keep their establishments below the threshold of the Factories Act or sub-contracted production.[148] In this way, the handloom industry, although organised along capitalist lines, came to occupy a central position in the 'informal' sector of the Indian economy.

Conclusion

State policies affected the handloom industry of South India throughout the nineteenth and twentieth centuries. Tariffs and domestic duties determined its competitiveness with respect to domestic and foreign mills. Laws and enactments to regulate labour shaped its internal structures. These policies and laws emerged through a complex process of negotiation within and outside government. Administrators and experts (notably Havell, Chatterton and Amalsad), Lancashire mill owners, British business interests in India, Indian businessmen, weaver organisations and trade unions sought to influence the state and determine the direction of policy and legislation with varying degrees of success. Political and fiscal imperatives also played a role in this process.

In the nineteenth century, pressures from Lancashire (and British capital in general) were strong: they helped to transform India from an exporter of handlooms to very large export market for British cloth. In the twentieth century, the colonial government was forced to respond

[147] Development Department, G.O. no. 5190, 25 October 1949, TNSA; Development Department, G.O. no. 4755, 21 September 1949, TNSA.

[148] Some factory owners in western India divided their factories with makeshift partitions to 'show' separate establishments and avoid the Factories Act. Haynes, *Small Town Capitalism*, pp. 285–7.

to growing demands to protect Indian mills and safeguard its own fiscal interests. Although handlooms received little direct attention (more in Madras than elsewhere) the industry was affected by all these decisions.

The industrial policy of independent India was also shaped by competing interests. In the beginning, small-scale and cottage industries were removed from the ambit of centralised planning; later, they were seen as a key sector in terms of generating employment. They were always prominent in political and economic negotiations at the provincial level. In the handloom industry, the emergence of a small cooperative sector alongside tens of thousands of unregulated small-scale private enterprises reflects an unstable attempt to balance competing interests.

Much the same clash of interests is visible in the legal framework of labour regulation that emerged during the middle decades of the twentieth century. These laws were drafted and implemented in such a way as to exclude handloom weavers (and workers in many small industries) from legal protection. They played an important role in shaping the internal structures of the handloom industry and its place in the larger economy. Small workshops and factories (in which the vast majority of weavers were employed) became part of what came to be called the 'informal' sector, organised on capitalist principles, with high levels of self-exploitation and external exploitation. A much smaller proportion of weavers found employment in the cooperative sector, with somewhat better conditions of work.

Conclusion

The handloom industry of South India was transformed during the course of the nineteenth and twentieth centuries. This book began by reconstructing the world of weaving in the first decades of the nineteenth century—its spatial geography, varieties of cloth, the stages of converting cotton into yarn and cloth, methods of organising production, market networks, and the social composition of weavers—before tracing the process of change that affected all of them.

Geographically, the distribution of weaving fell into two broad patterns. Durable and coarse cloth, comprising the bulk of production, was woven by weavers scattered throughout the countryside. Many of them wove part-time and relied upon other sources of income to supplement their livelihood. A large proportion belonged to 'untouchable' castes and up until now they have never been accorded their proper place in the historiography of handlooms. The weaving of fine and patterned cloth was concentrated in relatively few towns and villages.

Cotton was grown in large quantities in inland districts, wherever conditions favoured its cultivation. Elsewhere, it was planted in small quantities for local consumption. Raw cotton travelled long distances, passing through many hands and markets. It was sold in dispersed retail markets to hand spinners. Their yarn, in turn, reached the weaver through different channels.

Cloth production was organised in many different ways. Making cloth from yarn provided by customers was a common practice, especially in cotton-growing districts. Other weavers bought yarn on their own account and sold the cloth in local markets. In general, merchants advanced money to weavers for fine varieties or for cloth of middling to coarse quality sold in distant markets. European trading companies fitted themselves into this system. The EIC bought cloth through merchants for a long time. It was only towards the end of the eighteenth century that it began advancing money to weavers through intermediaries.

In general, weavers exercised considerable control over the production process. Even when working for merchants, they received cash advances to buy yarn and worked on their own looms at home. A small proportion were loomless. Some prosperous weavers owned several looms and a few made the transition to becoming merchants themselves. This economic differentiation was especially visible among fine cloth weavers like the Devangar, Saliar and Pattunoolkarar.

When the EIC tried to replace cash advances with yarn, or interfered in the production process in the interests of quality, it faced resistance and protests in many places. It was a common practice to use less yarn if a fair price for cloth was not forthcoming. Migration across territorial jurisdictions was another form of protest early on, while evasion of taxes, petitioning, mass assemblies and disruption of markets became more common as time passed. There were other uncertainties (both natural and man-made) that affected the demand for cloth and the availability of cotton and yarn.

During the first half of the nineteenth century, the export sector suffered by the withdrawal of the EIC from the textile trade while weavers making fine cloth (for domestic consumption) faced competition from British mills. During the second half of the century, weavers making coarse cloth had to compete with mill cloth, but the export sector saw a small revival and the production of fine cloth recovered to some degree. The complex stages of converting cotton into cloth were ruptured and restructured. Social hierarchies, state policies and pragmatic adaptations affected this process, but the ultimate result was a reorganisation of production systems from top to bottom.

Cleaning was mechanised. Cotton was routed to mills to be converted into yarn (and exported in greater quantities). Hand spinning vanished. Once mill yarn replaced hand-spun yarn—a process almost completed by the first decade of the twentieth century—weavers could no longer obtain it in direct, face-to-face transactions. Access to working capital to buy yarn and install fly-shuttles became increasingly vital. Changes in fashion and competition from mill cloth also affected the industry. Many weavers making coarse cloth (including the vast majority of Pariar weavers) were forced to abandon weaving altogether. The remainder were faced with stagnant or shrinking sales.

Specialist weavers shifted to making new kinds of cloth for niche and export markets. The process involved much greater centralisation of production and a shift towards wage-contracts. Weavers became dependent upon merchants who assumed the functions of financiers, yarn suppliers and cloth sellers rolled into one. Most of them hailed from mercantile castes, but, as time passed, some weavers from specialist weaving castes also became successful entrepreneurs or 'weaver-capitalists'. They accumulated wealth, experimented with new technologies and succeeded in capturing some markets.

Ordinary weavers were forced to accept new relationships of production in which the last vestiges of autonomy were eroded. The process was not without friction. Many groups, especially those with some social standing and a strong local presence, refused to enter the workshop or factory system, preferring to work from home albeit tied to master weavers as wage workers. Others became loomless wage workers in workshops and factories, where new forms of solidarity developed.

This restructuring was marked by chronic instability. There were recurrent bouts of unemployment and wage reductions driven by fluctuations in the availability of mill yarn and disruptions in consumer markets. When the price of cloth was high, domestic mills sold less yarn on the market, using it to make cloth instead. Acute shortages were caused by import disruptions (this happened during both world wars) and there was a good deal of naked profiteering by yarn merchants and master weavers. Even during normal times, the supply and price of yarn were controlled by mill owners and large yarn dealers. Recurrent crises had the effect of throwing thousands of weavers out of work and reducing wages. This chronic instability can be read as flexibility from capital's point of view—flexibility in hiring and firing workers and flexibility of wages. Its constant reproduction became central to the internal accumulation of capital in the handloom industry and drove its expansion.

Weavers were forced to adapt traditional strategies of resistance to changed circumstances throughout this period. In the nineteenth century, we see them modifying methods of protest by conforming to the state's demands for due process. From the 1940s, they joined trade unions in large numbers. The methods adopted by these unions (petitioning, bargaining and negotiations, strikes, mass assemblies) were not new, but had to be adapted to new structures and relationships. Their targets were capitalists organised into master-weaver and yarn-merchant associations. The state recast itself as a neutral arbitrator between capital and labour (while tilting in practice on the side of employers): its legal framework became the reference point of union struggles.

The tripartite interaction between unions, the state and capital played a key role in modifying the structures of the handloom industry in the 1940s and 1950s. Cooperatives were formed with state sanction and state aid—they existed side by side with home-based weaving organised by master weavers and handloom factories. State policy supported (or refused to disturb) flexible arrangements of work in these places. As a result, the handloom industry outside the small cooperative sector was subsumed into the informal economy. State policies were oriented towards the mill industry and small capitalists in the small-scale sector; they helped maintain an uneasy status quo in which employers enjoyed a decisive advantage. A combination of state intervention, individual adaptation and collective action shaped the modern structures of the handloom industry in South India.

Divisions of caste, class and gender played a key role in this process. In the early nineteenth century, work within the weaver's household was demarcated by gender. Spinning was largely a female occupation. Other preparatory processes such as warping were also performed by women while weaving remained a male preserve. By the early twentieth century, women had been wholly displaced from spinning. In weaving, they continued to be relegated to the preparatory processes. It was only after warping became mechanised that they took to weaving in large numbers.

In the early nineteenth century, weaving was the full-time or part-time occupation of people from many castes. Each group maintained its cohesiveness through caste and kinship networks. Leaders were expected to act in ways that ensured the well-being of the community as a whole (this tendency is particularly evident in the case of specialist weaving castes). Transmission of knowledge and skills was familial. Actions of solidarity and protest were organised through caste networks (with inter-caste alliances playing a subsidiary role). The uses of caste changed during the twentieth century when it became central to the twin processes of labour recruitment and control. The exclusion of Pariar weavers from the new structures of the handloom industry is an example of its efficacy. Caste also shaped relationships between capital and labour. Most master weavers employed workers of the same caste and labour recruitment was enmeshed in patron–client relationships based on debt.

But class solidarities also developed during efforts at collective self-assertion vis-à-vis master weavers. They are evident during the high-water mark of unionisation in the 1940s. However, we should guard against the reductionist notion that class replaced caste in framing capital–labour relationships. The two were not exclusive. During times of conflict, weavers spoke the language of class—of the 'mudalali' or capitalist exploiting the 'thozhilazhi' or labourer—*and* the language of caste by calling upon the 'mudalali' to remember his responsibilities as patron to his clients.

Thus, the transformation of the handloom industry in South India involved different arenas, from the global (the mechanisation of spinning, the pressure exerted by British mill owners) to the regional (the specific configuration of the mill and handloom industries in Madras as well as the socio-political constellation of power) to the local (the trajectory of the Pattunoolkarar in the Madurai region, for example), all the way down to the shop floor.

Postscript

This complex interaction continued to shape the contours of the handloom industry after 1960. Handloom weavers accepted the transition to decentralised powerlooms in some places, but resisted it in others. Some state governments (notably Tamil Nadu and Andhra Pradesh) provided greater support to the handloom industry while others (like Maharashtra) actively championed the shift to powerlooms.

At the national level, the larger narrative (or 'master frame') of poverty reduction saw employment generation as a key objective of economic policy.[1] Government policy leaned towards 'protecting' the handloom industry in limited ways. Provincial governments supported cooperatives, reserved some categories of cloth for the handloom sector and tried to regulate yarn supplies. These policies varied significantly from state to state. Collective mobilisation by weavers also focused on issues and demands affecting the industry as a whole (subsidies, yarn supply, reservation of products) rather than wage rates.

This trajectory changed from the 1980s as neo-liberalisation took hold. The New Textile Policy of 1985 reflected this shift by advocating free markets and private enterprise as remedies for the problems faced by the textile industry. The state's partial withdrawal left a space that was filled by NGOs. They worked with weavers, helping them to stay afloat through interventions in production and marketing (within the dominant framework of free markets and developing entrepreneurship).

These interventions stress the importance of preserving traditional skills and cultural traditions linked to them. Cheap mill cloth made from artificial fibres has displaced handlooms in the mass market. Handlooms are increasingly seen as products for an aspirational, culturally confident middle class. The view that handwoven cloth embodies the cultural heritage of India is not new. Along with khadi and handicrafts, it played a key role

[1] Raka Ray and Mary Katzenstein employ the term 'master frame'; see the 'Introduction', in Raka Rai and Mary Katzenstein (eds), *Social Movements in India: Poverty, Power and Politics* (Lanham, MD, Rowman and Littlefield, 2005), pp. 1–32.

in shaping cultural ideas about the nation in the 1950s.[2] In recent years, a new ecological narrative that sees handlooms and handicrafts as sustainable products with a low carbon footprint has also developed, echoing an older Gandhian narrative of self-sufficiency and sustainability.

In this narrative, the product (the beauty of design, its cultural meanings and ecological footprint) becomes the focus of attention while its producer is reduced to a footnote. This is particularly apparent in advertisements for fashion brands and designer wear. The stress remains firmly on the material (organic, locally sourced) and the design (unique to some community or locality). The relationships of production and exchange in which artisans are embedded find no mention.

All these narratives are imbued with nostalgia: they hark back to an imaginary past where crafts and skills were supposedly embedded in self-sustaining and reciprocal social relationships. But this ignores the hierarchical context in which they were practised. Handicrafts are also regarded as more humane and less exploitative than machine-based industries. Quite apart from the problems inherent in romanticising the past, these narratives ignore the capitalist transformation of the handloom industry during the nineteenth and twentieth centuries.

The growing focus on markets, designs, techniques and productivity fits the neo-liberal emphasis on entrepreneurship. NGO initiatives may be useful in helping weavers and artisans obtain a better deal, but it is vital to look beyond them to *production relations*. The continued relevance of handlooms depend upon attempts to imagine and create more egalitarian structures of production. For this, it is important to grasp the transformation of production relations and the position of handloom weavers with respect to workers in the informal sector as a whole.

The handloom industry and India's informal economy

The transformation of the handloom industry must be understood, not in isolation, but as part and parcel of the slow capitalist transformation of the Indian economy. In handlooms, this involved production for distant markets; growing control of capital over inputs, output and markets (even when weavers retained the means of production); higher rates of capital

[2] McGowan, *Crafting the Nation*; Lisa Trivedi, *Clothing Gandhi's Nation: Homespun and Modern India* (Bloomington, Indiana University Press, 2007); Ramagundam, *Gandhi's Khadi*; and Tarlo, *Clothing Matters.*

accumulation; and the predominance of wage labour. This process was shaped by intersecting forces of change. Similar (though not identical) developments were occurring in other 'traditional' industries (like tanning), new ones (like beedi manufacturing), and many service sectors (transport, hotels and shops). Together with diverse modes of self-employment, they came to form the vast 'informal' sector of the Indian economy.

The definition of informality has been the subject of much debate. Its principal element is held to be the absence of state regulation in three fields: capital accumulation, the labour market and capital–labour relationships. Earlier definitions treated the formal and the informal sectors as watertight compartments and drew attention to the nature of business enterprises (whether registered or not). More recent definitions recognise that the two are intertwined.[3] The focus has shifted to the *nature* of the relationship between capital and labour and the extent of state regulation. Nowadays, many scholars view the 'informal' sector as an integral part of capitalism in the Indian context.[4]

Recent scholarship has deepened our understanding of the informal sector and its relationship to the wider economy, but we still know very little about its origins. Its presence is taken for granted by scholars from different disciplines. In India, its expansion is usually traced to the adoption of neo-liberal economic policies in the late 1980s and '90s.[5] However, the trajectory of the handloom industry outlined in this book shows that the informal sector assumed its modern shape long before this period. A nuanced understanding of its emergence is essential to any evaluation of contemporary capitalism. This can only be done through historical studies of individual industries and services.

In the transformation of the handloom industry in South India, the 1940s and 1950s represent a watershed, when an economic boom (followed by a slump) and political battles intersected with long-term forces to shape the contours of the wider economy. It was a period when, as Ravi Ahuja notes, labour first made its presence felt as a political force.[6] And while labour

[3] In an early conceptual formulation of the formal–informal divide, Holmstorm likened the formal sector to a citadel surrounded by a large and sprawling informal sector. Later, he compared it to a gradual slope, without clear boundaries. Jan Breman likens the informal sector to a sea with the formal sector sticking out of it like small islands.

[4] For a summary of the debate over definitions, see Basile and Harriss-White, 'Introduction'.

[5] Rohini Hensman ascribes the expansion of the informal sector to state policy and legislation from the mid-1970s. See Rohini Hensman, *Workers, Unions and Global Capitalism: Lessons from India* (Delhi, Tulika Books, 2011), pp. 63–85.

[6] Ravi Ahuja, '"Produce or Perish": the Crisis of the Late 1940s and the Place of Labour in Postcolonial India', *Modern Asian Studies* (2019), 1–72.

mobilisation was stronger and more effective in large factories, there exists a growing body of evidence to show that it was also widespread across many small industries and services.[7] It was during this period that the economic policies of independent India were debated and formulated, with various social groups jostling for power and influence.

Historical studies of this period of transition are finally emerging. It saw a realignment and consolidation of social and political forces that is critical to a proper understanding of contemporary India. Some scholars have examined the influence of big capital on policy-making.[8] Others have shown how Gandhism was relegated to the fringes of economic policy.[9] However, very little is known about the emergence (and influence) of small capital in India's industrial landscape. Following the Polish economist Michał Kalecki and drawing on the work of P. S. Jha, Barbara Harriss-White points to the crucial role played by the 'intermediate classes' in the actual functioning of the informal economy.[10] The emergence of weaver-capitalists forms part of a historical process that raised the profile and influence of this social category.

By the 1960s, political voices in favour of giving more freedom to small capitalists and small industry had gained a decisive ascendancy over unions advocating protection for workers. Labour legislation came to exclude the vast majority of workers in small industries and agriculture. In combination with economic policies that encouraged small-scale industry (by exempting it from regulation), it precipitated the division of the Indian economy into two intertwined sectors, with the formal sector taking advantage of informal mechanisms in many ways.[11] This had profound consequences, not just for the handloom industry, but the Indian economy as a whole.

[7] See, for example, Ahuja, *Working Lives and Worker Militancy*.

[8] See Chibber, *Locked in Place*. Also, Nasir Tyabji, *Forging Capitalism in Nehru's India: Neo-colonialism and the State, c. 1940–1970* (Delhi, Oxford University Press, 2015).

[9] See Govindhu and Malghan, *The Web of Freedom*.

[10] Barbara Harriss-White, *India Working: Essays on Society and Economy* (Delhi, Cambridge University Press, 2004); P. S. Jha, *The Political Economy of Stagnation* (Delhi, Oxford University Press, 1980).

[11] For labour legislation and its role in the emergence of the informal sector in India, see Dietrich Wielenga, 'Emergence of the Informal Sector'.

Divergent paths of economic development

The transformation of the handloom industry in South India supports the thesis of diverse paths to industrialisation. It also places a question mark over the assumption that mechanisation or industrialisation is inevitable and only the routes to this goal vary. Handlooms did not disappear under competition from mills or become reorganised into factories or decentralised powerlooms. At a wider level, it is clear that India did not follow the same path to industrialisation as the West. Nehruvian dreams of large-scale industrialisation did not materialise; but neither did Gandhian dreams of self-sufficient villages. What took shape was an economy still dependent upon agriculture and an industrial sector dominated by small-scale industries, with low levels of mechanisation. Today we are faced with the inherent limits of technological solutions and a far-reaching threat to the very existence of the planet embodied in climate change. Increasing rates of technological unemployment and rapid resource depletion make it clear that large-scale industrialisation is not a model that can be replicated infinitely in every continent and country.

My hypothesis that outcomes are shaped by *conjunctures* (long- and short-term, local and global) is illustrated by the divergent trajectories of the handloom industries of western and southern India. The emergence of large factories was arrested in both regions, but cooperatives came to occupy a much larger space in the South; this is probably the chief reason why handlooms held out for longer there. In western India, where the karkhana or workshop model of production had become much more widespread in the 1940s, small-scale and dispersed powerlooms ended by swamping the handloom industry.

By the 1940s, the workshops or karkhanas of western Maharashtra were recruiting migrant weavers from fairly distant regions. Douglas Haynes shows that labour recruitment and control were based on caste networks and patronage, with loomless migrants being far more dependent on workshop owners than local weavers.[12] More capital could be accumulated through the workshop model, for owners exercised much greater control over labour and the means of production—combined with a readily available mass of dependent workers, this made the transition to powerlooms attractive and easy. In the South, by contrast, there was much more resistance to workshops and home-based production dominated the landscape. Co-operatives, where

[12] Haynes, *Small Town Capitalism*, pp. 146–57.

members owned their looms and worked at home, were seen as an attractive alternative by ordinary weavers. Replacing handlooms with powerlooms in a home-based industry proved inherently difficult, for it was predicated on a substantial number of weavers investing in relatively expensive machines.

Differences in state policy also contributed to this divergence. In the 1950s, the central government began to encourage mechanisation with the eventual goal of replacing handlooms with decentralised powerlooms.[13] The Bombay government promoted this policy, but it met with resistance in Madras. The Madras government favoured expansion of the cooperative sector to defuse large-scale protests caused by widespread unemployment. Powerlooms were seen as a threat to jobs at a time when thousands of weavers were already unemployed. A few years later, it was felt that keeping powerlooms out would mean losing production to other states where they were gaining ground. The state government outlined plans for introducing them in handloom cooperatives, but these were soon abandoned.[14] It took decades for powerlooms to gain ground in Tamil Nadu: their real expansion occurred after 1985, when the government actively began promoting them.[15]

Yet another reason for divergence can be traced to the arena of politics. In the 1940s and '50s, trade unions took the lead in demanding state support for handlooms. Although master-weaver associations managed to block labour legislation, this mobilisation played an important role in state support for cooperatives and other incentives for the handloom industry. There were shop-floor struggles against powerlooms as well. According to an old union leader in Madurai, some master weavers who were trying to mechanise in the sixties faced opposition from trade unions.[16] In Maharashtra, by contrast, the unions were defeated and many weaver-capitalists embraced mechanisation.

All over India, handlooms became an integral part of the informal sector in an economy dominated by small-scale enterprises. Was there any alternative trajectory open to them? Two aborted lines of development can be traced to the 1930s. During this period, there was a faint possibility that handloom factories might become the dominant mode of production. Some karkhandars or workshop owners in Maharashtra tried to scale up their

[13] This was a key recommendation of the Textile Enquiry Committee set up to make policy recommendations for the textile industry. *Textile Enquiry Committee*, p. 28.

[14] ILC Department, G.O. no. 2375, 17 July 1957, TNSA.

[15] Tirthankar Roy, 'Growth and Recession in Small-scale Industry: a Study of Tamil Nadu Powerlooms', *Economic and Political Weekly*, 34(44) (30 October–5 November 1999), 3137–45.

[16] Interview with P. M. Kumar.

units. But this trend was aborted and very soon owners began sub-dividing their units to avoid labour legislation and undermine union mobilisation.[17]

In the Madras Presidency, a more sympathetic response to the demands of workers (in the shape of effective labour legislation) might have encouraged a degree of formalisation in the 1940s. Another possibility opened up briefly in the 1950s, when a large number of cooperatives were formed. With greater state support and proper regulation of working conditions, cooperatives might have become the dominant mode of cloth production in Tamil Nadu. However, this would have required a very different configuration of forces in the political sphere.

India's economic trajectory stands in stark contrast, not just to Britain, but also to the experience of East Asian economies like Japan and South Korea that encouraged large-scale industrialisation and economies of scale. In East Asia, the vast informal sector that is typical of India was not allowed to develop. In Vivek Chibber's view, this divergence can be attributed to the effectiveness of the state's apparatus in those countries. By contrast, the institutional structures of independent India left little power in the hands of the state to direct private capital.[18]

However, this argument does not address the federal nature of India's political system in which state governments enjoy a significant degree of autonomy in creating social infrastructure (education and healthcare) and setting economic policy.[19] The degree of industrialisation achieved by different states (Bihar compared to Tamil Nadu) varied significantly. The very different trajectory of the handloom industry in Maharashtra and Tamil Nadu reveals that state intervention was capable of influencing lines of future development. In this study, I have tried to show that the interplay between capital, state power and workers' rights must be investigated at the regional level to uncover the specific conjunctures that shaped India's economic trajectory.

History reveals the existence of diverse paths of development and industrialisation. This implies that the future will throw up varied possibilities as well. What does this mean for handlooms in particular? Will

[17] Haynes, *Small Town Capitalism*, pp. 243–4, 287.

[18] Chibber, *Locked in Place*.

[19] For the wider effects of federalism, see Francine R. Frankel, *India's Political Economy 1947–1977: the Gradual Revolution* (New Delhi, Oxford University Press, 1978); Francine R. Frankel and M. S. A. Rao (eds), *Dominance and State Power in Modern India: Decline of a Social Order* (New Delhi, Oxford University Press, 1989); Shashank Kela, 'Federalism and Its Discontents', *The Caravan*, 1 February 2019, https://caravanmagazine.in/literature/doctrine-state-rights-india (accessed 19 April 2020).

they eventually become obsolete in India as they have elsewhere? Perhaps, but, if so, there is nothing inevitable about the process. The fate of the handloom industry depends upon the choices and actions of a diverse array of participants. At the time of writing it is in steep decline, with the number of weavers falling steadily since the 1990s. At the same time, there are few sources of alternative employment that provide any security of wages and work either. The informal sector continues to dominate India's economy, while a looming ecological crisis poses new questions for industrial expansion. It is possible that the handloom industry will acquire fresh relevance, but its survival and health depend, in the final analysis, upon creating better conditions of work for ordinary weavers through effective labour laws and new, more equitable structures of production.

Appendix 1

Tables

Table 1.1: Piece goods of different qualities consumed in the taluks of Lalgudi and Woodiarpollium, in the district of Thiruchirapalli, 1838–9

Description	Quality		Value per corge as inserted in the tariff (rupees.annas.pice)	Consumption in Lalgudi taluk		Consumption in Woodiar-pollium taluk		Total	
				Corge	Pieces	Corge	Pieces	Corge	Pieces
Cloths used by women	Superior quality	1st sort	280.0.0						
		2nd sort	245.0.0						
		3rd sort	183.12.0			2	11	2	11
	Inferior quality	1st sort	131.4.0		2	1	5	1	7
		2nd sort	109.6.0		10	4	15	5	5
		3rd sort	91.14.0		10	2	9¼	2	19¼
		4th sort	75.0.0		2½	9	2½	13	5
		5th sort	52.8.0		1	88	9¾	203	10¾
		6th sort	35.0.0		8¼	493	10¼	649	18½
Silk-bordered men's cloths	Superior quality	1st sort	105.0.0		1½	3	16½	3	18
		2nd sort	87.8.0		2¼	7	11½	7	13¾
		3rd sort	70.0.0	1	2	18	5	19	7
	Inferior quality	1st sort	52.8.0	11	16¾	49	6¼	61	3
		2nd sort	45.0.0	15	10½	55	4	70	14½
		3rd sort	37.8.0	60	16	79	8	140	4
Muslins	Superior quality	1st sort	270.0.0			2	¾	2	¾
		2nd sort	210.0.0			3	14	3	14
		3rd sort	175.0.0			7	16¾	7	16¾
		4th sort	140.0.0			4	10¾	4	10¾

Description	Quality		Value per corge as inserted in the tariff (rupees.annas.pice)	Consumption in Lalgudi taluk		Consumption in Woodiar-pollium taluk		Total	
				Corge	Pieces	Corge	Pieces	Corge	Pieces
Muslins	Inferior quality	1st sort	130.0.0		2	2	10¾	2	10¾
		2nd sort	110.0.0			5	1	5	1
		3rd sort	90.0.0			14	6¾	14	6¾
		4th sort	72.8.0	1	4¾	7	16¼	9	1
Common cloths		1st sort	51.0.0						
		2nd sort	46.0.0		1	2	6	2	7
		3rd sort	27.0.0	25		19	8	44	8
		4th sort	19.4.0	479	16	124	16½	604	12½

Source: PBR vol. 1690, no. 26, 6 January 1840, p. 327, TNSA.

Table 1.2: Number of looms producing different varieties of cloth in the Ceded Districts, 1804

Varieties of cloths		No. of Looms	No. of cloths produced in a year	Value of cloth produced in a year (star pagodas)
White cloths	Dhotar or Brahmin cloths	1,415	73,176	4,373.5.12
	Pautel or women cloths	1,666	101,271	40,159.24.58
	Shelah muslins	1,485	55,115	54,064.27.3
	Turbans	621	29,625	17,595.23.7
	Sunyerkahnah	442	20,849	14,723.7.0
	Rumals	1,010	51,649	35,143.15.32
	Kaudies	7,944	568,433	161,643.25.39
	Mothasaudy or women's coarse cloths	1,500	70,724	25,411.30.15
	Dupattas	109	5,394	5,606.8.60
	Puddum	72	37,739	1,215.0.0
	Doriahs	34	1218	3,802.21.0
	TOTAL	16,298	1,015,193	403,100.27.14

Varieties of cloths		No. of Looms	No. of cloths produced in a year	Value of cloth produced in a year (star pagodas)
Red cloths	Saudies or women's cloths	728	47,801	33,515.17.23
	Karwahs	5	240	122.26.20
	Rumals or handkerchiefs	108	7,830	1,859.3.40
	TOTAL	841	55,871	35,497.5.3
Blue cloths	Saudies	881	60,224	42,326.15.53
	Neely puchodeys	5	720	645.0.0
	TOTAL	886	60,944	42,971.15.53
Silk cloths	Silk cloths	15	366	2,018.41.10
	Cumbayet sowela or women's cloths	4	114	554.19.20
	Men's showelas	6	174	691.31.40
	Poolasa Puchodee	5	60	600.0.0
	Poolasa saudee	10	240	2,033.14.0
	Goddamarri rumals	4	72	240.0.0
	TOTAL	44	1,026	6,138.21.70
Amez Mist	Kumple puchodie	113	5,193	
	Suffade soosey	9	738	179.17.40
	Lawl soosey	391	29,081	9,791.32.30
	Rajamahly soosey	43	2,322	991.21.0
	Saris or women's cloths	933	57,549	49,109.31.40
	Rumals	37	3,355	1,361.36.60
	Kawla Soosey	31	4,140	1,010.0.0
	TOTAL	1,557	102,378	70,080.6.10
GRAND TOTAL		19,626	1,235,412	557,787.33.70

Source: PBR vol. 382, no. 18, 21 June 1804, p. 5078 onwards, TNSA.

Table 2.1: Number of looms in different districts of the Madras Presidency from 1821–2 to 1843–4

Year	S. Arcot[a]	N. Arcot[b]	Chingelput[c]	Guntur[d]	Nellore[e]	Nellore Sub-division	Rajamundhry[f]		Masulipatam[g]
1821–2	8,451	5,051	68		7,783/8,132		4,601		7,575
1822–3	8,712	5,731	97		8,097/8,477		5,311		8,369
1823–4	8,401	5,440	107		8,664/9,025		4,765		8,089
1824–5	6,355	3,308	92		7,757/8,125	3,968	5,708	6,689	8,382
1825–6	6,675	3,406	102		6,880/7,320	3,797	6,267	7,220	8,802
1826–7	9,259	4,034	149		7,421/7,812	4,109	9,465	12,031	8,989
1827–8	9,666	4,353	156		8,045/8,498	4,244	9,824	11,934	9,324
1828–9	10,102	4,674	137		8,608/9,055	4,470	10,443	11,747	9,553
1829–30	10,226	4,990	152		8,963/9,417	4,551	9,758	11,545	9,786
1830–1	9,678	5,327	178 +3,739	12,362	9,423/9,855	4,946	9,128	11,304	9,820
1831–2	10,054	5,379		12,045		4,861		10,500	9,379
1832–3	10,168	5,263	3,867	8,746		4,584		8,910	8,213
1833–4	8,701	4,153		4,406		2,141		7,363	3,688
1834–5	9,368	4,598		4,611		2,705		8,556	4,089
1835–6	10,204	5,232		6,062		3,125		9,817	4,802
1836–7	11,320	5,602		7,421	7,913	3,497		11,347	5,544
1837–8	11,854	5,855		8,297		3,691		11,876	6,050
1838–9	11,983	6,107		7,850		3,804		11,361	6,316
1839–40	11,976	6,187		7,890		3,966		10,694	6,005
1840–1	11,696	6,354		8,119	4,568½ +4,055			10,141	6,277
1841–2	11,800	6,269		8,089	5,538½ +4,077			10,885	6,525
1842–3	12,092	6,309	5,410	7,790	5,584½ +4,014			11,569	6,722
1843–4	11,495		5,306	8,970	9,646			12,016	6,852

Year	Tanjavur[h]	Thiruchrapalli[i]	Madurai[j]	Tirunelveli[k]	Coimbatore[l]	Salem[m]	Bellary[n]	Kadapa[o]
1821–2				7,840			18,474	22,317
1822–3	9,098			8,147			19,174	23,679
1823–4	9,522/ 15,479			7,513			18,183	24,053
1824–5	9,376			7,178			18,071	19,835/ 19,883
1825–6	8,692			7,979			18,946	18,923
1826–7	9,012			8,339			19,027	20,707
1827–8	13,307			9,139			19,196	21,922
1828–9	14,394		12,479	12,070			19,423	23,358
1829–30	14,098			12,618			21,077	25,052
1830–1	13,812		9,302	12,790	19,793		21,006	25,758
1831–2	13,787	7,286					20,955	
1832–3	13,837					15,162	20,533	
1833–4	13,541					10,462	18,380	
1834–5	13,126						17,761	
1835–6	13,449		12,155				18,889	
1836–7	14,414						20,125	
1837–8	14,889		18,898	15,584			22,713	
1838–9	15,355			14,938			22,090	
1839–40	15,714			14,362	1,4814		21,500	
1840–1	16,121			14,813	1,5782		22,352	
1841–2	16,243			14,603	1,7058		23,503	
1842–3	16,417			15,066	1,7675		23,702	
1843–4	15,935	7,826		14,541	1,7774		24,231	27,468

Notes:

a PBR vol. 1376, no. 38, 22 August 1833, pp. 10030–8, TNSA. The increase in the number of looms in 1826–7 comes from one taluk, Cuddalore, where they rose from 170 to 1,899. This probably represents the taxing of existing looms after the EIC ceased operations. Some 430 looms in 1830–1 paid taxes to temples, landlords, etc. Data from 1831–2 onwards is from PBR vol. 1925, no. 19, 5 August 1844, p. 10201, TNSA. The figure for 1843–4 is from PBR vol. 1980, no. 46, 4 September 1845, p. 10844, TNSA.

b PBR vol. 1932, no. 34, 7 October 1844, p. 13004, TNSA; 1833–5 and 1843–4 were famine years.

c PBR vol. 1324, no. 18, 14 May 1832, pp. 4740–5. The small jump in 1826–7 is because some looms in one taluk, hitherto exempt, began paying tax. The figure for total looms is misleading, because 3,739 looms were paying no tax in 1832. The figure for 1830–1 is from PBR vol. 1324, no. 18, 14 May 1832, p. 4746, TNSA. I have added 3,739 looms, exempted before this, making a total of 3,917 looms. The figures for 1832–3 and 1842–3 are from PBR vol. 1906, no. 30, 29 February 1844, p. 3823, TNSA. The figure for 1843–4 is from PBR vol. 1974, no. 31, 14 July 1845, p. 8627, TNSA.

d PBR vol. 1929, no. 29, 5 September 1844, p. 11761, TNSA. The steep decline from 1833–4 was caused by a famine in which nearly half the population of Guntur perished.

e PBR vol. 1931, no. 47, 23 September 1844, pp. 12537, 12543–4, TNSA. The figures in the second column are from a sub-division of Nellore consisting of the taluks of Buddapoody, Davagoodoor, Ongole, Enamananellore and Chendaloor. The increase of approximately 1,000 looms in 1841–2 was the result of the loom tax of three new taluks being brought to the circar account (p. 12521). A slightly different set of figures for the years 1821–2 to 1830–1 are provided in PBR vol. 1334, no. 22, 13 August 1832, pp. 7768–9, TNSA. The figure for 1836–7 is from PBR vol. 1641, no. 42, 24 December 1838, p. 17250, TNSA. The figure for 1843–4 is from PBR vol. 1974, no. 30, 14 July 1845, p. 8610, TNSA.

f PBR vol.1335, no. 17, 20 August 1832, p. 8187, TNSA. The increase in 1826–7 can be explained by the end of the EIC's operations and the levy of the loom tax on its weavers. The numbers in the second column are from PBR vol. 1953, no. 26, 27 January 1845, p. 1147, TNSA. The decline in 1832–3 is because of famine. The increase of 1836 represents the inclusion of the moturpha of Pettapore zamindary.

g PBR vol. 1955, no. 21, 10 February 1845, p. 1852, TNSA. The fall in 1833–4 was caused by famine.

h PBR vol. 1942, no. 66, 28 November 1844, p. 16367, TNSA. The second figure for 1823–4 is from PBR vol. 985, no. 45, 31 May 1824, p. 4829, TNSA. This is an estimate provided by a renter asking for compensation on losses sustained on cloth exempted from duty. It is likely to be exaggerated.

i PBR vol. 1359, no. 40, 15 April 1833, p. 3695, TNSA. Some 2,731 looms were exempted from tax. PBR vol. 1969, no. 48, 2 June 1845, pp. 6867–8, 6871, TNSA.

j PBR vol. 1325, no. 44, 21 May 1832, p. 4901 onwards, TNSA. This number is not reliable for moturpha taxes had been abolished in Madurai, and the list was drawn up during an attempt to reintroduce the tax. The collector notes the absence of popular cooperation during enumeration. It is not clear whether persons or looms are being counted. PBR vol. 1575, no. 78, 28 September 1837, p. 11901, TNSA. This figure is unreliable, for it was calculated in order to reintroduce the loom tax. The figures for 1828–9 and 1837–8 are from PBR vol. 1928, no. 49, 26 August 1844, p. 11353, TNSA.

k PBR vol. 1327, no. 53, 11 June 1832, pp. 5589–90. Some of the figures for 1837–8 onwards are from PBR vol. 1937, no. 80, 7 November 1844, p. 14952, TNSA.

l PBR vol. 1942, no. 49, 25 November 1844, p. 16141, TNSA; PBR vol. 1942, no. 49, 25 November 1844, p. 16140, TNSA.

m PBR vol. 1437, no. 39, 8 January 1835, p. 299, TNSA.

n PBR vol. 1925, no. 42, 8 August 1844, p. 10288, TNSA.

o PBR vol. 1325, no. 46, 24 May 1832, pp. 5005–6, TNSA. The figure for 1843–4 is from a report in PBR vol. 1931, no. 48, 23 September 1844, p. 12547, TNSA.

Table 2.2: Number of looms between 1820–1 and 1843–4 in different districts of the Madras Presidency

District	No. of looms recorded at the beginning of the period	No. of looms after correction	No. of looms at the end of the period	Increase	Decrease	Percentage
S. Arcot	8,451 (1821–2)	11,747	11,495		252	2.1 ↓
N. Arcot	5,051 (1821–2)		6,310	1,259		24.9 ↑
Chengalpet	3,917 (1830–1)		5,410	1,493		38 ↑
Guntur	12,362 (1830–1)		8,970		3,392	27.4 ↓
Nellore	7,783 (1820–1)	9,028	9,599	571		6.3 ↑
Rajamundhry	6,689 (1825–6)	12,174	12,016		158	2.3 ↓
Masulipatam	7,575 (1820–1)		6,852		723	9.5 ↓
Thanjavur	9,098 (1822–3)	13,374	15,935	2,561		19.1 ↑
Thiruchirapalli	7,286 (1831–2)		7,826	540		7.4 ↑
Madurai	9,302 (1830–1)		12,155			30.6 ↑
Tirunelveli	7,840 (1820–1)	10,349	15,066	4,717		45.6 ↑
Coimbatore	19,793 (1830–1)		17,774	2,019		10.2 ↓
Salem						
Bellary	18,474 (1820–1)		24,231	5,757		31.1 ↑
Kadapa	22,317 (1820–1)		27,468	5,151		23.08 ↑

Note on calculations:

For some districts, sudden increases represent existing looms, hitherto exempted from the loom tax. They were usually included when the EIC's factories closed and the weavers employed by it were made to pay the loom tax, or when weavers hitherto subject to zamindars began paying loom tax to the government. These have been calculated as follows:

Increase in South Arcot from 1825–6 to 1826–7 – 38.7%
Increase in Nellore from 1840–1 to 1841–2 – 16.3%
Increase in Rajamundhry from 1825–6 to 1826–7
+ increase from 1835–6 to 1836–7 – 66% + 15.5%
Increase in Thanjavur from 1826–7 to 1827–8 – 47%
Increase in Tirunelveli from 1827–8 to 1828–9 – 32%

The loom figures for all these districts have been modified accordingly.

Table 2.3: Value of piece goods exported from the district of Rajamundhry between 1821–2 and 1843–4 (in rupees)

Year	Total value	To Bengal	To Madras	To England and other coasts
1821–2	974,075	167,908	127,204	678,963
1822–3	653,730	142,525	185,168	326,037
1823–4	597,492	108,890	171,511	317,091
1824–5	703,193	72,675	280,491	350,027
1825–6	880,849	52,781	209,191	618,877
1826–7	546,317	28,028	140,379	377,910
1827–8	357,286	16,028	67,372	273,886
1828–9	352,462	8,303	79,851	264,308
1829–30	376,156	478	117,297	258,381
1830–1	233,392	17,649	81,418	134,325
1831–2	580,506	6,787	74,043	499,676
1832–3	485,564	15,971	86,550	383,043
1833–4	357,550	22,851	179,452	155,247
1834–5	636,501	737	184,026	451,738
1835–6	491,502	429	204,561	286,512
1836–7	437,451	30,640	269,248	137,563
1837–8	408,819	18,844	216,260	173,715
1838–9	226,768	9,184	85,991	131,593
1839–40	194,515	36,731	78,778	79,006
1840–1	211,353	20,448	62,183	128,722
1841–2	167,212	13,408	63,789	90,015
1842–3	159,312	3,913	62,969	92,436
1843–4	107,254	11,323	2,425	93,506

Source: PBR vol. 1953, no. 24, 27 January 1845, p. 1147, TNSA.

Table 2.4: Number of looms in the Madras Presidency between 1840 and 1961

Year	Number of looms	Source
1843–4	165,107	Board of Revenue Proceedings (totalled from Table 2.1). This does not include some districts such as Madurai, Visakhapatnam, Salem, Malabar and Canara.
1856–7 to 1860–1 (avg)	204,623	Board of Revenue Proceedings, 28 June 1871, p. 4725, TNSA. Estimate based on reports sent by collectors.
1869–70	279,220	Board of Revenue Proceedings, 28 June 1871, p. 4725, TNSA. Estimate based on reports sent by collectors.
1889	300,009	Estimate by Board of Revenue (quoted in *Fact Finding Committee*, p. 28).
1901	167,806	Venkatraman, *The Handloom Industry*, pp. 25, 26.
1921	169,403/241,622	First figure from the loom census conducted with the 1921 census; second figure from Statistical Atlas (quoted in Venkatraman, *The Handloom Industry*, pp. 25–6).
1932	225,000	*Fact Finding Committee*, p. 28.
1941	340,451	*Fact Finding Committee*, p. 27.
1945	496,000	Census of looms by Yarn Commissioner (quoted in *Census of India, 1961*, vol. 11-A, 'Handlooms in Madras State', pp. 18–19).
1947	650,000	Census of looms by Yarn Commissioner (quoted in *Census of India, 1961*, pp. 18–19).
1948	541,879	Naidu, *Report of the Court of Enquiry*, p. 5.
1951	507,714	*Census of India, 1961*, pp. 18–19.
1954	461,722	*Census of India, 1961*, pp. 18–19.
1955	418,747	*Census of India, 1961*, pp. 18–19.
1957	435,922	*Census of India, 1961*, pp. 18–19.
1961	508,372	*Census of India, 1961*, pp. 18–19.

Table 2.5: Caste-wise breakdown of looms in the Southern Division of Baramahal, 1796

Districts	Kaikolars		Jadars		Koliyars		Shaliyars		Seniyars		Chamdavars		Silk Weavers		Total	
	No. of looms	No. of families	No. of looms	No. of families	No. of looms	No. of families	No. of looms	No. of families	No. of looms	No. of families	No. of looms	No. of families	No. of looms	No. of families	No. of looms	No. of families
Salem	54	25	257	133	20	13	61	16	74	22			144	62	610	271
Sennagiri	225	179	108	73	2	2									335	254
Belur	15	15	22	22	36	36									73	73
Attur	174	155	73	47	60	61							3	3	310	264
Viraganur	3	2	3	3	72	68							21	21	99	94
Sendamangalam	434	350	190	153	265	244			36	34					925	784
Rasipur	11	11	162	123			64	45	89	57			26	16	352	252
Namakkal	147	140	20	19	112	111			2	2			80	53	361	335
Paramatti	361	370	64	65	62	58					32	32	70	53	589	578
Kattuputtur	64	64			31	32									95	96
Total	1,488	1,341	899	638	660	628	125	61	201	115	32	32	344	204	3,749	3,019

Source: *The Baramahal Records*, Section VII: Imposts, pp. 70–1.

Table 2.6: Caste-wise breakdown of looms in Baramahal district

District	Kaikolars 1793–6			Jadars 1793–6			Silk weavers			Koliyars			Chamdavars[4]			Shaliyars			Seniyars			Manniwars	Kurubar	Janappar	Andis
Southern Division[1]																									
Salem	157	55	54	149	213	257	148	119	144	9	28	20	13	25		23	56	61	55	79	74				2
Attur	122	147	174	42	54	73		2	3	25	45	60				29			7						
Sendamangalam	258	358	434	176	115	190	21			67	147	265				37			79	35	36				
Namakkal	32	118	147	4	5	20	25	72	80	49	145	112							1	4	2				
Paramatti	138	380	361	7	65	64	29	65	70	4	6	62	11	3	32										20
Kattuputtur	37	65	64							11		31													
Sennagiri		141	225		58	108					1	2													
Belur		15	15		22	22					36	36													
Viraganur		3	3			3			21		10	72					21								
Rasipur		11	11		166	162		30	26					10			71	64		96	89				
TOTAL	744	1293	1488	378	698	899	223	288	344	165	418	660	24	38	32	89	148	125	142	214	201				22
Percentage	41.6	41.8	39.7	21.2	22.5	24	12.5	9.2	9.2	9.2	13.4	17.6	1.3	1.2	1	4.9	4.8	3.3	7.9	6.9	5.4				
Central Division[2]																									
Dharmapuri			30/26			22/12																12/12	62/13	8/8	
Adamanakottai						14/14																10/11	72/72	31/31	
Pennagaram			12/12			41/52												16/21				21/21	40/43	18/18	
Durreve			6/6			7/8												10/14				18/18	2/2	2/2	
Murpide																		4/4				10/10	31/26	22/22	
Tenkaraikotai			4/4			12/10																8/8	41/38	4/4	
Nangapalli			52/32			114/127																	3/3		
Tiruchengod			177/177			30/26																12/10			

District	Kaikolars 1793–6	Jadars 1793–6	Silk weavers	Koliyars	Chamdavars[4]	Shaliyars	Seniyars	Manniwars	Kurubar	Janappar	Andis
Eddapadi	171/171	55/50			110/101						
Mallasamudram	81/81	4/3									
Sankaridurg	50/50	80/70						40/32			
Omalur	37/39	65/60						22/20			
TOTAL Percentage	535/505 33.3/32.6%	444/432 27.6/27.9%			110/101 6.8/6.5%	30/39		153/ 142 9.5/ 9.2	249/ 247	85/85	
Northern Division[3] Percentage	20 3.6	50 9.1	40 7.3	10 1.8	60 10.9	10 1.8	20 3.6	211 38.4	78 14.2	50 9.1	

1 The number of looms belonging to each caste is divided into three columns. The first column is from a report dated 31 January 1793, on p. 18; the second column is from a report dated January 1796, on p. 63; and the third column is from a report dated 31 March 1796, on pp. 79–80 of *The Baramahal Records*, Section VII: Imposts.

2 These figures are from a report in *The Baramahal Records,* Section VII: Imposts, p. 27.

3 These figures are from the report of 1796, *The Baramahal Records,* Section VII: Imposts, pp. 64–5.

4 I have listed the Chenniwars reported from the Central division (p. 27 of *The Baramahal Records*, Section VII: Imposts) as Chamdavars as they seem to be the same, with even the numbers matching.

Table 2.7: Caste-wise breakdown of looms in the district of Madurai

Caste	No. of persons/looms	Percentage of total
Weaver (probably Pattunoolkarar)	1,877	20.18
Kaikolar	663	7.13
Pariar	4,476	48.12
Shanier	414	4.45
Shaider	1,502	16.14
Ealoover	29	0.31
Shaulier	217	2.33
Barber	79	0.85
Lubbay	46	0.49
TOTAL	9,302	

Source: PBR vol. 1325, 21 May 1832, no. 44, p. 4901 onwards, TNSA.

Table 2.8: Number of looms belonging to different castes in Coimbatore and loom tax paid by them, 1831–2

Category of weaver	No. of looms	Average tax per loom (in Rs.as.ps)	Amount of tax collected	Percentage of weavers
Silk weavers	63	0.7.13	49.5.0	0.32
Cavoory	25	0.7.5	18.3.0	0.13
Jadars	8,046	0.6.7	5,212.1.1	40.65
Kaikolars	7,216	0.5.14	4,278.8.12	36.46
Saniar	31	0.6.1	18.8	0.16
Satanies	6	0.6.5	3.8	0.03
Saliars	7	0.5.6	3.8	0.04
Besters	109	0.4.3	45.7	0.55
Pariars	3,062	0.3.5	1,026.1.8	15.47
Jamookanahs	105	0.4.1	42.7	0.53
Cumbly weavers	578	0.2.8	145.6.0	2.92
Gunny weavers	234	0.2.15	68.9.8	1.18
Mat weavers	43	0.3.1	13.2.0	0.22
Sundries	268	0.3.14	103.9.0	1.35
TOTAL	19,793		11,031.3.13	

Source: PBR vol. 1325, no. 47, 24 May 1832, p. 5011, TNSA.

Table 2.9: Number of looms belonging to different castes in Coimbatore district, 1833–4

Castes	No. of looms	Tax paid (in Rs.as.ps)	Percentage of caste to total
Pattunoolkarars	47	82.14.5	2
Jadars	7,223	12,811.4.9	40.8
Kaikolars	6,896	11,529.3.1	39
Saniars	39	63.7.1	
Cauverays	26	35.3.10	
Agamoodies, Polavurs and Coravurs	20	25.9.1	
Saliars	14	14.1.6	
Jungawaudies	137	162.3.2	
Sembudavurs	18	24.6.2	
Seveyars	108	131.1.11	
Andies	90	89.13.11	
Pariars	2,240	2,160.2.11	12.6
Arasapully	1	0.14.1	
Satanies	1	0.12.3	
TOTAL	16,860	27,132.2.2	
Cooroomburs	550	396.1.0	
Janapurs	227	166.13.9	
Lubbays	38	34.1.9	
TOTAL	17,675	27,729.2.8	

Source: PBR vol. 1942, no. 49, 25 November 1844, p. 16125, TNSA.

Table 2.10: Distribution of looms among various castes and average loom tax paid by each in Tirunelveli district, 1843–4

Caste	No. of looms	Average tax per loom (Rs.as.ps)
Pattunoolkarar	633	1.10.6
Kaikolar	2,503	4.4.2
Yeloovurs	2,160	2.3.1
Lubbies	4,830	3.5.11
Puttakasalier	905	3.9.11
Saider	679	1.9.9
Puller, Pariar	2,831	1.13.3
TOTAL	14,541	

Source: PBR vol. 1937, no. 80, 7 November 1844, p. 14954, TNSA.

Table 2.11: Number of looms belonging to different categories of weavers in the district of Nellore and loom tax paid by them

Year	Looms of fine cloth weavers		Looms of barbers		Looms of pariars		Looms of gunny makers		Looms of cumbly makers		Looms of tape makers		Looms not taxed	Total looms	Total tax (in Rs.as. ps)
	No.	Tax (in Rs.as.ps)	No.	Tax (in Rs.as. ps)	No.	Tax (in Rs.as.ps)	No.	Tax (in Rs.as. ps)	No.	Tax (in Rs.as.ps)	No.	Tax (in Rs.as. ps)			
1822–3	4,086	7,360.11.3	4	3.0.0	3,534	4,023.5.6	93	77.12.0	60	85.1.0	6	6.4.0	349	8,132	11,556.1.9
1823–4	4,950	8,727.9.10	4	3.8.0	2,989	3,447.10.5	83	67.4.0	70	98.10.0	1	0.8.0	380	8,477	12,345.2.3
1824–5	5,351	9,858.2.2	3	2.8.0	3,116	3,474.6.5	62	63.4.0	132	143.10.0	0		361	9,025	13,541.14.7
1825–6	4,768	8,734.0.5	7	8.12.0	2,772	3,151.9.1	63	64.8.0	143	142.0.0	4	5.0.0	368	8,125	
1826–7	3,760	7,293.4.11	6	6.6.4	2,938	3,436.3.0	128	114.0.0	44	59.2.0	4	5.8.0	440	7,320	
1827–8	4,398	8,001.5.5	5	5.12.0	2,841	3,388.5.1	131	128.4.0	47	61.10.0	7	7.4.0	391	7,812	11,592.8.6
1828–9	4,707	8,488.1.2	5	4.12.0	3,121	3,545.7.1	70	66.8.0	139	133.14.0	3	3.12.0	453	8,498	12,202.6.3
1829–30	4,827	8,567.1.3	6	6.12.0	3,543	3,973.14.9	105	96.8.0	127	131.10.0	0		447	9,055	12,775.14.0
1830–1	4,865	8,702.5.4	6	6.12.0	3,889	4,358.6.2	70	62.4.0	133	134.13.0	0		454	9,417	13,264.8.6
1831–2	5,235	9,872.5.2	6	7.4.0	3,800	4,558.14.6	43	38.8.0	153	168.15.0	186	167.4.0	432	9,855	14,813.2.8
Average	4,695 (54.77%)		5		3,254 (37.9%)									8,571	

Source: PBR vol. 1334, no. 22, 13 August 1832, pp. 7768–9, TNSA.

Table 2.12: Number of looms belonging to different categories of weavers in the district of Nellore

Taluks	Saliar weavers	Jandra weavers	Malaweavers	Togata weavers	Kaikolar weavers	Sautoo weavers	Coorova weavers	Doodakoolah weavers	Linga Balija weavers	Mangala weavers	TOTAL
Survapully	0	209	160	0	0	3	0	0	0	0	372
Cottah	22	41	47	0	16	0	0	0	0	0	126
Nellore	606	373	244	0	7	16	0	0	0	0	1,246
Talamunchy	552	103	153	0	16	0	0	0	0	0	824
Sungum	217	54	210	2	2	27	0	2	0	0	514
Cavely	64	0	146	0	0	0	0	0	0	0	210
Toomalatapoor	87	56	73	4	4	1	0	0	0	0	225
Goondavole	6	0	49	10	0	8	0	0	0	0	73
Ravoor and Varegontapad	65	0	373	30	0	23	0	0	0	0	491
Caleghery and Doothaloor	5	0	210	111	0	0	0	2	0	2	330
Buddapoody	115	0	183	0	0	0	0	0	3	0	301
Davagodoor and Putchavah	6	0	573	0	0	15	0	0	0	3	597
Ongole	195	0	492	0	0	7	0	0	0	0	694
Enamanamellore	0	75	254	0	0	56	6	0	0	0	391
Chendalore	692	619	190	0	0	0	18	0	0	0	1,519
TOTAL	2,632	1,530	3,357	157	45	156	24	4	3	5	7,913

Source: PBR vol. 1641, no. 42, 24 December 1838, pp. 17296–9, TNSA.

Table 2.13: Kinds and qualities of cloth woven in 1961

	Number of looms					
Varieties of cloth produced	**Superfine**	**Fine**	**Medium**	**Coarse**	**Total**	**Percentage**
Sarees	3,309	1,452	880	7	5,648	41.4
Dhoties	740	841	1,411	13	3,005	22.2
Uppers and towels	196	32	224	71	523	3.8
Other utility varieties	29	33	538	1,686	2,286	16.7
Export varieties	350	1,546	268	1	2,165	15.9
Total	4,624	3,904	3,321	1,778	13,627	100.0
Percentage	34.0	28.6	24.4	13.0	100.0	

Source: *Census of India, 1961*, vol. 11-A, Handlooms in Madras State, 1964, p. 62.

Table 4.1: Daily wages of skilled workers compared with those of weavers

Year	Daily wages in annas							Sources
	Carpenter	Blacksmith	Goldsmith	Bricklayer	Male agricultural labourer	Female agricultural labourer	Weaver	
1878	8	8		7	4	1.8		a
1886			10				2.5 to 6	b
1892	7 to 10	6 to 10	6 to 8	6.5 to 10	2.8 to 4	1.6 to 2		c
1893							8 to 10	d
1895							2.5 to 3	e
1898							3.6 to 5	d
1912							4.8 to 8	f
1918	11 to 12	12	12	11 to 13	3 to 8	2 to 4	6 to 12	g
1925							3.8 to 10	h
1929							2.7 to 16	i
1936	16	14	16	14	4 to 4.8	2.8 to 3	2 to 12	j

Sources:

a Moore, *Manual of the Trichinopoly District*, p. 108
b Havell, *Reports Submitted*, p. 30.
c Raghavaiyangar, *Memorandum*, p. 136.
d Saunders, *The Saurashtra Community in Madura*.
e Arthur F. Cox, *Madras District Manual: North Arcot*, vol. 1: (Madras, Government Press, 1895).
f Venkatraman, *The Handloom Industry*, pp. 184–5.
g Slater, *Some South Indian Villages*, pp. 90, 119.
h Ranga, *The Economics of Handlooms*, pp. 44, 45, 66.
i Compiled from Narayana Rao's preliminary and final reports on cottage industries.
j Venkatraman, *The Handloom Industry*, pp. 184–5, and P. J. Thomas and K. C. Ramakrishnan (eds), *Some South Indian Villages: a Resurvey* (Madras, University of Madras, 1940), pp. 95, 96, 198.

Table 4.2: Monthly earnings of different categories of weavers, 1948

Kind of weaver	Average family income (in rupees)	Average income per gainfully occupied weaver
Weaver in a cooperative	78	39
Independent weaver	68	36
Dependent weaver	54	33
Coolie weaver	45	31

Source: Naidu, *Report of the Court of Enquiry*, p. 23.

Appendix 2

Note on the Loom Tax

The loom tax formed part of the moturpha taxes.[1] It was their most important component, making up 32 per cent of total collections under this head.[2] The moturpha tax was ostensibly a tax on the profits of individuals and households (other than cultivators) carrying out different kinds of manufacture. But it proved very difficult to define by reason of its variability. For example, traders were subject to the moturpha tax in some districts of the Madras Presidency, but not others. Cattle were taxed in certain districts; in others, agricultural labourers. In some districts, a tax on each caste was included under the moturpha.[3] In Madurai district, no moturpha tax and therefore no loom tax was levied at all.[4]

The collector of Tirunelveli accurately described the difficulty in defining the moturpha: 'It is difficult if not impossible to define the moturpha tax ... it varies without apparent causes in almost every village both in object and rates of taxation and it is regulated (if that term can be applied to anything so irregular) nominally by local custom.'[5] In other words, the loom tax (like other moturpha taxes) was almost completely arbitrary even though theoretically these taxes were supposed to be in accordance with the 'circumstance of the people and the extent of trade carried on by them'.[6]

[1] A detailed discussion on the loom tax is available in the Consultation dated 28 February 1856, in India Revenue Consultations, 5 January to 28 March 1856, P/193/39, IOR.

[2] And 2 per cent of the total revenue, Consultation dated 28 February 1856, in India Revenue Consultations, 5 January to 28 March 1856, P/193/39, IOR.

[3] PBR vol. 1977, no. 38, 14 August 1845, p. 9966, TNSA.

[4] P/193/39, IOR.

[5] PBR vol. 1820, 29 September 1842, p. 11037, TNSA.

[6] PBR vol. 1977, no. 38, 14 August 1845, p. 9966, TNSA.

In Coimbatore district, for example, the loom tax varied from village to village; even two weavers living in the same village and weaving the same kind of cloth might pay different rates.[7] There was considerable variation in loom tax rates across districts. Kadapa alone had 63 rates, the highest being 14 rupees and 13 annas to a loom, and the lowest 7 annas.[8] Across the Madras Presidency, the highest rates were found in Bellary and Kadapa, followed by Guntur, Salem, Tirunelveli and Coimbatore. The rates in Thiruchirapalli were the lowest.[9] In general, weavers of fine cloth paid a higher tax; but it was not uncommon for prosperous weavers to be charged at a lower rate than poorer ones. Many weavers were exempted from the tax as a privilege granted in the past.[10] Thus, for example, the fine weavers of Thiruchirapalli town were exempted from the loom tax.[11] In Tirunelveli, Saurashtra weavers making fine cloth (and more money) paid less than Kaikolar weavers making coarse cloth.[12]

The loom tax was usually collected through head weavers, and, in some cases, through toties (village servants, mostly Paraiars). Head weavers and toties who collected the tax generally enjoyed an exemption on one or more of their own looms.[13] In some cases, the loom tax was paid to landlords or temples, to whom the looms had been alienated.[14]

[7] PBR vol. 1325, no. 47, 24 May 1832, pp. 5007–8, TNSA.

[8] Consultation dated 28 February 1856, in India Revenue Consultations, 5 January to 28 March 1856, P/193/39, IOR.

[9] Consultation dated 28 February 1856, in India Revenue Consultations, 5 January to 28 March 1856, P/193/39, IOR.

[10] P/193/39, IOR.

[11] PBR vol. 1359, no. 40, 15 April 1833, pp. 3690–2, TNSA.

[12] PBR vol. 1937, no. 80, 7 November 1844, p. 14954, TNSA.

[13] PBR vol. 1325, no. 46, 24 May 1832, p. 5006, TNSA; PBR vol. 1359, no. 40, 15 April 1833, pp. 3690–2, TNSA; PBR vol. 1328, no. 31, 25 June 1832, p. 5952, TNSA.

[14] PBR vol. 1376, no. 38, 22 August 1833, p. 10031, TNSA; PBR vol. 1359, no. 22, 11 April 1833, pp. 3506–7, TNSA.

Glossary

Adi Dravida	literally Original Dravidian. A term used in south India to refer to someone from a Dalit caste
Angavastram	an upper cloth for men, roughly as large as a shawl, draped around the torso
Bania	colloquial term for moneylender or merchant. Also used to refer to mercantile castes in general
Bazaar	market. 'Bazaar cloth' refers to cloth made for sale in local markets, not for the EIC or merchants
Cadjam	palm leaf record
Choukeydar	guard or watchman. Also used for functionaries manning toll gates
Circar	government
Copdar	an intermediary used by the EIC during the early nineteenth century (when it was still exporting cloth) to handle advances, collect cloth and monitor quality
Corge	a unit used to calculate quantities of cloth, especially piece goods. Twenty pieces of cloth made one corge
Cuppisa	a blouse
Deepavali	a major Hindu festival falling in October/November
Dhoti	a cloth for men used to cover the lower body
Dungary	a coarse, plain, tightly woven cloth
Dupatta	a cloth used to cover the upper part of the body
Fanam	a currency used in the Madras Presidency until 1815. A small silver coin divided into 80 copper units called cash. The gold pagoda was worth 42 fanams; the Indian rupee 12 fanams
Jajmani	a hierarchical system under which members of plebeian castes (service and artisanal) in a village provided services to dominant (landowning) caste households in return for fixed shares of the harvest
Kambayam	another name for the lungi or kaili

Khadi	a plain, thick, coarse and durable variety of cloth, mostly unbleached
Langotee	loin cloth
Lungi	a coloured cloth worn by men in South India. Used to cover the lower body and woven in checks
Mothasaudy	a plain, coarse, durable sari (worn by women)
Mundu	another name for the dhoti or veshti
Oppandum	literally, agreement or contract. Under this system, weavers worked at home for a master-weaver (who provided the yarn), making cloth in return for a fixed wage
Pagoda	a unit of currency used in the nineteenth century. One English pagoda was worth three and a half rupees. Pagodas were minted by the French and Danish as well, but their value (in rupees) was less than that of the English pagoda
Palayakarar	later anglicised to ‘poligar’. The feudal title of a class of administrative and military subordinates of the Nayaka rulers in South India (seventeenth century). During the early nineteenth century, many of them still owned large estates covering many villages (whose inhabitants paid taxes to them)
Parkalla	another variety of plain, coarse, durable cloth
Punjams	the number of warp threads in a cloth. Fine cloths had more warp threads, and were therefore of higher punjams
Ravikkei	a blouse
Rumal	kerchief
Sari	a single unstitched piece of cloth worn by women
Tahsildar	administrative officer in charge of a taluk or tahsil
Taluk	an administrative sub-division of a district
Torta	towel
Veshti	the Tamil term for dhoti
Zilla	district

Bibliography

Primary Sources

Unpublished Records

Archives of the SPG, Rhodes House Library, Oxford.
Board of Revenue Proceedings, TNSA.
Chingleput District Records, TNSA.
Collections of the Victoria and Albert Museum, London.
Commercial Department Consultations, TNSA.
Development Department (1921–53), TNSA.
India Office Records and Private Papers, British Library.
Industry, Labour and Co-operation Department, TNSA.
Madura District Records, TNSA.
Proceedings of the Board of Revenue, TNSA.
Public Department Consultations, TNSA.
Revenue Department, TNSA.
Tinnevelly District Records, TNSA.

Census, Gazetteers and Manuals

Brackenbury, C. F., *Cuddapah District Gazetteer* (Madras, Government Press, 1915).

Census of India 1881: Madras, the Report, vol. 1 (Madras, Government Press, 1883).

Census, 1891, vol. 13, Madras Report (Madras, Government Press, 1893).

Census of India 1961, vol. 11-A, Handlooms in Madras State (Delhi, Government Press, 1964).

Chetty, Narahari Gopalakristnamah, *Manual of the District of Kurnool in the Madras Presidency* (Madras, Government Press, 1886).

Cornish, William Robert, *Report on the Census of the Madras Presidency, 1871* (Madras, Government Press, 1874).

Francis, W., *Madras District Gazetteers: Anantapur* (Madras, Addison and Company, 1905).

Francis, W., *South Arcot District Gazetteer* (Madras, Government Press, 1906).

Francis, W., Madras District Gazetteers: *Vizagapatam* (New Delhi, Asian Educational Services, 1992), reprint.

Handloom Census of India, 2009–10 (Delhi, NCAER, 2010).

Joint Census of Handlooms and Powerlooms, 1995–96: Handloom Sector (Delhi, NCAER, 2004).

Le Fanue, H., *A Manual of the Salem District in the Presidency of Madras* (Madras, Government Press, 1883).
Moore, Lewis, *A Manual of the Trichinopoly District in the Presidency of Madras* (Madras, Government Press, 1878).
Nelson, J. H., *The Madura Country: a Manual* (Madras, The Asylum Press, 1868).
Richards, F. J. *Madras District Gazetteers: Salem,* vol. 1, part I (Madras, Government Press, 1918).

Printed Reports (official and semi-official)

Amalsad, D. M., 'The Development of the Madras Handkerchief and Lungi or Kily Industry in the Madras Presidency', Department of Industries Bulletin No. 22 (Madras, Madras Government, 1926).
Annual Volumes of the Sea-borne Trade and Navigation of the Madras Presidency and of its Chief Port and Each of the Subordinate Ports 1874–75 to 1924–25 (Madras, Government Press).
Annual Report of the ICCC for the Year Ending 31 August 1939 (Bombay, The British India Press, 1940).
Annual Report of the ICCC for the Year Ending 31 August 1940 (Bombay, The British India Press, 1941).
Baliga, B. S., *Compendium on History of the Handloom Industry in Madras* (Madras, Government Press, 1960).
Buchanan, Hamilton F., *A Journey from Madras through the Countries of Mysore, Canara and Malabar,* vol. 1 (London, British Library Historical Print Editions, 1807).
Buchanan, Hamilton F., *A Journey from Madras Through the Countries of Mysore, Canara and Malabar,* vol. 2 (London, T. Cadell and W. Davies, 1807).
English East India Company, *Reports and Documents Connected with the Proceedings in Regard to the Culture and Manufacture of Cotton-wool, Raw Silk and Indigo in India* (London, 1836).
English East India Company, *The Baramahal Records*, Section III: Inhabitants (Madras, Government Press, 1907).
English East India Company, *The Baramahal Records*, Section IV: Products (Madras, Government Press, 1912).
English East India Company, *The Baramahal Records*, Section VII: Imposts (Madras, Government Press, 1920).
Hadaway, W. S., *Cotton Painting and Printing in the Madras Presidency* (Madras, Government Press, 1917).
Havell, E. B., *Reports Submitted by Mr. E. B. Havell During the Years 1885–1888 on the Arts and Industries of Certain Districts of the Madras Presidency* (Madras, Government Press, 1909).
Heyne, Benjamin. *Tracts Historical and Statistical on India; Journals of Several Tours through Various Parts of the Peninsula: also an Account of Sumatra, in a Series of Letters* (London: printed for Robert Baldwin; and Black, Parry and Co., 1814).
House of Commons Parliamentary Papers, *A Return of 'Papers in the Possession of the East India Company, Showing what Measures have been Taken since 1836 to Promote the Cultivation of Cotton in India'*, 21 May 1847.

House of Commons Parliamentary Papers, *Report from the Select Committee on the Growth of Cotton in India; together with Minutes of Evidence,* 17 July 1848.
House of Commons Parliamentary Papers (Command Papers), *East India Cotton: Correspondence Relating to the Improvement in Indian Cotton, 1904.*
House of Commons Parliamentary Papers, East India (Cotton), *Return to an Order of the Honourable House of Commons, Dated 24 August 1857 for a Selection of Papers Showing, the Measures Taken since 1847 to Promote the Cultivation of Cotton in India.*
House of Commons Parliamentary Papers, East India (Cotton), *Further Return: Copy of Correspondence between the Secretary of State for India, and the Governor General or Other Persons in India, on the Subject of Cotton Cultivation in India, and the Prospects of Supplies of that Article to this Country during the year 1863.*
House of Commons Parliamentary Papers, East India (Cotton), *A Copy of the Report of Mr. H. Rivett-Carnac, Cotton Commissioner for the Centrap Provinces and Berars, on the Operations of his Department for the Year 1867.*
Indian Central Cotton Committee, *The Present Position of the Research Schemes of the Indian Central Cotton Committee* (Bombay, G. Claridge and Co., 1930).
Indian Central Cotton Committee, *Cotton Improvement in India* (Bombay, G. Claridge and Co., 1931).
Indian Industrial Commission, Minutes of Evidence, 1916–17, vol. 3, Madras and Bangalore (Calcutta, Government Press, 1918).
Indian Industrial Commission (1916–18): Appendices to the Report (Calcutta, Government Press, 1919).
Madras Exhibition of Raw Products, Arts and Manufactures of Southern India, 1855, *Reports by the Juries* (Madras, Government Press, 1856).
Madras Legislative Assembly Debates: Official Report, vol. 5 (Nos. 1–14) (March– April 1947) (Madras, Government Press, 1947).
Madras Legislative Assembly Debates: Official Report, vol. 7 (Nos. 1–15) (October–December 1947) (Madras, Government Press, 1947).
Madras Legislative Assembly Debates, Official Report, vol. 14, No. 1–12 (August–September 1948).
Main Report of the Labour Investigation Committee (Delhi, Government Press, 1946).
Memoirs of the Department of Agriculture, Madras (Madras, Government Press, 1954).
Naidu, B. V. Narayanaswami, *Report of the Court of Enquiry into Labour conditions in the Handloom Industry* (Madras, Government Press, 1948).
Official and Descriptive Catalogue of the Madras Exhibition, 1855 (Madras, Government Press, 1855).
Papers Relating to the Industrial Conference Held at Ootacamund in September 1908 (Madras, Government Press, 1908).
Planning Commission, *Report of the Village and Small Scale Industries Committee (Second Five Year Plan)* (Delhi, Government Press, October 1955).
'Proceedings of the Legislative Council of the Governor of Madras, Official Report', vol. 61, no. 11, 23 March 1932 (Madras, Government Press, 1932).
Raghavaiyangar, S. Srinivasa, *Memorandum on the Progress of the Madras Presidency during the Last Forty Years of British Administration* (Madras, Government Press, 1892).

Rao, D. Narayana, *Preliminary Report on the Survey of Cottage Industries in the Madura, Ramnad, Trichinopoly and Tinnevelly Districts* (Madras, Government Press, 1928).
Rao, D. Narayana, *Preliminary Report on the Survey of Cottage Industries in the Cuddapah District* (Madras, Government Press, 1927).
Rao, D. Narayana, *Preliminary Report on the Survey of Cottage Industries in the Kurnool District* (Madras, Government Press, 1927).
Rao, D. Narayana, *Preliminary Report on the Survey of Cottage Industries in the East Godavari District* (Madras, Government Press, 1929).
Rao, D. Narayana, *Preliminary Report on the Survey of Cottage Industries in the Kistna and West Godavari Districts* (Madras, Government Press, 1929).
Rao, D. Narayana, *Preliminary Report on the Survey of Cottage Industries in the Guntur District* (Madras, Government Press, 1929).
Rao, D. Narayana, *Preliminary Report on the Survey of Cottage Industries in the Nellore District* (Madras, Government Press, 1929).
Rao, D. Narayana, *Preliminary Report on the Survey of Cottage Industries in the North Arcot District* (Madras, Government Press, 1929).
Rao, D. Narayana, *Preliminary Report on the Survey of Cottage Industries in the Salem District* (Madras, Government Press, 1929).
Rao, D. Narayana, *Preliminary Report on the Survey of Cottage Industries in the Tanjore and South Arcot Districts* (Madras, Government Press, 1929).
Rao, D. Narayana, *Report of the Survey of Cottage Industries in the Madras Presidency* (Madras, Government Press, 1929).
Report of the Fact Finding Committee (Handlooms and Mills) (Bombay, Ministry of Commerce, 1942).
Report of the Famine in the Madras Presidency during 1896 and 1897 (Madras, Government Press, 1898).
Report of the Indian Cotton Committee (Calcutta, Government Printing Press, 1919).
Report: Indian Economic Enquiry Committee, 1925, vol. 2, Minutes of Evidence, Part II (Calcutta, Government Press, 1926).
Report of the Textile Enquiry Committee, September 1954 (Delhi, Government of India Press, 1954).
Schofield, F. M. W., *Note on Indian Cotton* (Simla, Government Press, 1888).
The Madras Provincial Banking Enquiry Commission, vol. 4: Oral Evidence (Madras, Government Press, 1930).
The Third Tour of His Excellency The Hon'ble Sir Arthur Lawley to Madura and Trichinopoly, November 18–20, 1906 (Madras, Government Press, 1909).
Thurston, Edgar, *Castes and Tribes of Southern India*, vol. 4 (Madras, Government Press, 1909).
Thurston, Edgar, *Castes and Tribes of Southern India*, vol. 6 (Madras, Government Press, 1909).
Thurston, Edgar, *Cotton Fabric Industry of Madras Presidency* (Madras, Government Press, 1897).
Thurston, Edgar, *Monograph on the Silk Fabric Industry of the Madras Presidency* (Madras, Government Press, 1899).
Watson, J. Forbes, *The Textile Manufactures and the Costumes of the People of India* (London, India Office, 1866).

Other Contemporary Publications

Birdwood, George, *Paris Universal Exhibition of 1878: Handbook to the British Indian Section* (London, Offices of the Royal Commission, 1878).

Birdwood, George, *Two Letters on the Industrial Arts of India* (London, Whittingham and Co., 1879).

Bombay Cotton Annual 1924–25, 6 (Bombay, East India Cotton Association, 1925).

Chatterton, Alfred, *Weaving in India* (Allahabad, Indian Press, 1907).

Chatterton, Alfred, *Industrial Evolution in India* (Madras, The 'Hindu' Press, 1912).

Chatterton, Alfred, *Rural Economics in India*, The Russell Lecture 1926 (London, Oxford University Press, 1922).

Dhantwala, M. A., *A Hundred Years of Indian Cotton* (Bombay, Orient Longmans, 1948).

Dickinson, John, *Address to the Members of the House of Commons on the Relation between the Cotton Crisis and Public Works in India* (London, P. S. King, 1862).

Digby, William, *The Famine Campaign in Southern India, 1876–1878*, vol. 2 (London, Longmans, Green and Co., 1878).

Havell, E. B., *Essays on Indian Art, Industry and Education* (Madras, G. A. Natesan and Co., n.d.).

Havell, E. B., *The Basis for Artistic and Industrial Revival in India* (Madras, The Theosophist Office, 1912).

Haywood, G. R., *India as a Source for the Supply of Cotton: Report Addressed to the Executive Committee of Directors of the Manchester Cotton Company* (Manchester, J. J. Sale, 1862).

History of the Sourashtras in Southern India (Madras, Sourashtra Literary Society, 1891).

Hoole, Elijah, *Madras, Mysore and the South of India: or a Personal Narrative of a Mission to those Countries, 1820–1828*, 2nd edn (London, Longman, Brown, Green and Longmans, 1844).

International Labour Organization (ILO), *Handloom Weaving Industry in India with Special Reference to Madras State* (New Delhi, ILO India Branch, 1960).

Kearns, Rev. James, *Report of the Puthiamputhur Mission*, SPG E2, Missionaries Reports, June 1856, Archives of the Society for the Propagation of the Gospel in Foreign Parts, Rhodes House Library, Oxford.

Knight, R., *Manchester and India: a Protest Against Sir John Strachey's Financial Statement in the Legislative Council of India Dated 15 March 1877* (Calcutta, Thacker Spink and Co., 1877).

Lewis, Edwin, *History of the Telugu Missions of the London Missionary Society in the Ceded Districts* (Madras, Addison and Company, 1879).

Mahta, D. N., 'Cotton Growing in India', in *The Indian Cotton Growing Review*, vols 1–2 (Bombay, The Indian Central Cotton Committee, 1947).

Mullens, Joseph, *Missions in South India: Visited and Described* (London, W. H. Dalton, 1854).

Pascoe, C. F., *Two Hundred Years of the S.P.G.: an Historical Account of the Society for the Propagation of the Gospel in Foreign Parts 1701–1900* (London, SPG, 1901).

Ponniah, J. S., *Research Studies in the Economic and Social Environment of the Indian Church: an Enquiry into the Economic and Social Problems of the Christian Community in Madura, Ramnad and Tinnevelly Districts* (Madurai, American College, 1938).

Ranga, N. G., *The Economics of Handlooms: Being a Study of the Social and Economic Conditions of Handloom Weavers of South India*, Andhra Economic Series No. 3 (Bombay, Taraporewala and sons, 1930).

Royle, Forbes J., 'The Arts and Manufactures of India', in *Lectures on the Results of the Exhibition Delivered Before the Society of Arts and Manufactures and Commerce* (London, David Bogue, 1852).

Sastry, K. R. R., *The Madura Saurashtra Community: a Study in Applied Economics* (Bangalore, Bangalore Press, 1927).

Saunders, Albert James, *The Sourashtra Community in Madura, South India* (Unpublished Manuscript available in the Library of the American College, Madurai, n.d).

Sethi, B. L. and Dharmarajulu, K., *Indian Cotton: Its Past, Present and Future* (Bombay, ICCC, 1957).

Shah, K. T. (ed.), *Report: National Planning Committee* (Bombay, Vora and Co. Publishers, 1949).

Sikka, S. M., *et al.*, *Cotton in India: a Monograph* (Bombay, ICCC, 1961).

Slater, Gilbert (ed.), *Economic Studies*, vol 1: *Some South Indian Villages* (London, Oxford University Press, 1918).

Speech of Col. Sykes in the House of Commons on Thursday, February 18, 1858 on the Proposed India Bill (London, Smith Elder and Co., 1858).

Venkatraman, K. S., *The Handloom Industry in South India*, Supplementary to the Madras University Journal (Madras, Diocesan Press, 1936).

Wardle, Thomas, 'The Indian Silk Culture Court at the Colonial and Indian Exhibition', *Journal of Indian Art*, 1 (1886) 123.

Watson, J. Forbes, *On the Growth of Cotton in India: Its Present State and Future Prospects, with Special Reference to Supplies to Britain*, Reprinted from the *Journal of the Society of Arts* (London, W. Trounge, Machine and General Printer, n.d).

Watt, George, *The Wild and Cultivated Cotton Plant of the World: a Revision of the Genus Gossypium, Framed Primarily with the Object of Aiding Planters and Investigators who may contemplate the systematic improvement of the cotton staple* (London, Longmans, Green & Co., 1907).

Wheeler, James Talboys, *Madras versus America: Handbook to the Cotton Cultivation in the Madras Presidency* (New York, Virtue and Yorston, 1866).

Sources in Tamil

Ragunathan, T. M. Chidambara, *Panchum Pasiyum (Cotton and Hunger)*, 15th edn (Chennai, New Century Book House, 2005).

Sivaprakasam, Pandit S., *Puduvai Nesavu Thozhil: Ezhaiyar Ezhuchi Paattu (Pondicherry Handloom Industry: Songs of Inspiration of the Poor)* (Pondicherry, Kalanidhi Press, 1932).

Srinivasan, P., *Communist Heroes of Tamilnadu*, part I (Madras, Marxist Education Society, 2005).

Newspapers

Janashakti (Tamil weekly)

Secondary Sources

Ahuja, Ravi, 'Labour Unsettled: Mobility and protest in the Madras Region, 1750–1800', *The Indian Economic and Social History Review*, 35(4), (1998), 381–404.

Ahuja, Ravi, 'The Origins of Colonial Labour Policy in Late Eighteenth-Century Madras', *International Review of Social History*, 44(2) (1999), 159–95.

Ahuja, Ravi, 'Labour Relations in an Early Colonial Context: Madras, c. 1750–1800', *Modern Asian Studies*, 36(4) (2002), 793–826.

Ahuja, Ravi (ed.), *Working Lives and Worker Militancy: the Politics of Labour in Colonial India* (Delhi, Tulika Books, 2013).

Ahuja, Ravi, '"Produce or Perish": the Crisis of the Late 1940s and the Place of Labour in Postcolonial India', *Modern Asian Studies* (2019), 1–72.

Anderson, Michael. 'Work Construed: Ideological Origins of Labour Law in British India to 1918', in Peter Robb (ed.) *Dalit Movements and the Meanings of Labour in India* (Delhi, Oxford University Press, 1993), pp. 87–120.

Anderson, Michael, 'India 1858–1930: the Illusion of Free Labour', in Douglas Hay and Paul Craven (eds), *Masters, Servants and Magistrates in Britain and the Empire, 1562–1955* (London, University of North Carolina Press, 2004), pp. 422–54.

Appadurai, Arjun, 'Introduction', in Arjun Appadurai (ed.), *The Social Life of Things: Commodities in Cultural Perspective* (Cambridge, Cambridge University Press, 1986), pp. 3–56.

Arasaratnam, Sinnapah, 'Weavers, Merchants and Company: the Handloom Industry in Southeastern India, 1750–1790', *The Indian Economic and Social History Review*, 17(3) (1980), 257–81.

Arasaratnam, Sinnapah, *Merchants, Companies and Commerce on the Coromandel Coast 1650–1740* (Delhi, Oxford University Press, 1986).

Archer, Mildred, *Company Paintings: Indian Paintings of the British Period* (London, Victoria and Albert Museum, Indian Art Series, 1993).

Arnold, David, 'Looting, Grain Riots and Government Policy in South India 1918', *Past and Present*, 84(1) (1979), 111–45.

Arterburn, Yvonne J., *The Loom of Interdependence: Silk Weaving Cooperatives in Kanchipuram* (Delhi, Hindustan Publishing, 1982).

Bagchi, Amiya Kumar, 'Deindustrialization in India in the Nineteenth Century: Some Theoretical Implications', *Journal of Development Studies*, 12(2) (1976), 135–64.

Baker, C. J., *An Indian Rural Economy 1880–1955: the Tamilnad Countryside* (Delhi, Oxford University Press, 1984).

Balachandran, Aparna, *Christ and the Pariah: Colonialism, Religion and Outcaste Labor in South India, 1780–1830* (PhD thesis, Columbia University, 2008).

Basile, Elisabetta and Harriss-White, Barbara, 'Introduction', *International Review of Sociology*, 20(3) (2010), 457–71.

Basu, Raj Sekhar, *Nandanar's Children: the Paraiyan's Tryst with Destiny. Tamilnadu 1850–1956* (New Delhi, Sage, 2011).

Bayly, C. A., 'The Origins of Swadeshi (Home Industry): Cloth and Indian Society, 1700–1930', in Arjun Appadurai (ed.), *The Social Life of Things: Commodities in Cultural Perspective* (Cambridge, Cambridge University Press, 1986).

Bayly, C. A. and Subrahmanyam, Sanjay, 'Portfolio Capitalists and the Political Economy of Early Modern India', *The Indian Economic and Social History Review*, 25(4) (1988), 401–24.

Berg, Maxine, *The Age of Manufactures: Industry, Innovation and Work in Britain, 1700–1820* (London, Fontana Press, 1985).

Berg, Maxine, 'Passionate Projectors: Savants and Silk on the Coromandel Coast, 1780–98', *The Journal of Colonialism and Colonial History*, 14(3) (2013).

Berg, Maxine, 'Skills, Craft and Histories of Industrialisation in Europe and Asia', *Transactions of the Royal Historical Society*, 24 (December 2014), 127–48.

Bhattacharya, Sabyasachi, 'Laissez Faire in India', *The Indian Economic and Social History Review*, 2(1) (1965), 1–22.

Bhattacharya, Sabyasachi, Guha, Sumit, Mahadevan, Raman, Padhi, Sakti, Rajasekhar, D., and Rao, G. N. (eds), *The South Indian Economy: Agrarian Change, Industrial Structure and State Policy, c.1914–1947* (Delhi, Oxford University Press, 1991).

Bhattacharya, Shahana, 'Labour in the Leather Industry in India, 1870s–1970s' (PhD thesis, University of Delhi, 2012).

Borpujari, Jitendra G., 'Indian Cottons and the Cotton Famine, 1860–65', *The Indian Economic and Social History Review*, 10(1) (1973), 37–49.

Borpujari, Jitendra G., 'The Impact of the Transit Duty System in British India', *The Indian Economic and Social History Review*, 10(3) (1973), 218–41.

Brennig, Joseph J., 'Textile Producers and Production in Late Seventeenth Century Coromandel', *The Indian Economic and Social History Review*, 23(4) (1986), 334–55.

Chandavarkar, Rajnarayan, 'Industrialisation in India before 1947: Conventional Approaches and Alternative Perspectives', *Modern Asian Studies*, 19(3) (1985), 623–68.

Chandavarkar, Rajnarayan, *The Origins of Industrial Capitalism in India: Business Strategies and the Working Classes in Bombay 1900–1940* (Cambridge, Cambridge University Press, 1994).

Chatterji, Basudev, 'The Abolition of the Cotton Excise, 1925: a Study in Imperial Priorities', *The Indian Economic and Social History Review*, 17(4) (1980), 355–79.

Chaudhuri, K. N., *The Trading World of Asia and the English East India Company 1660–1760* (Cambridge, Cambridge University Press, 1978).

Chaudhuri, K. N., 'The Structure of the Indian Textile Industry in the Seventeenth and Eighteenth Centuries', in Tirthankar Roy (ed.), *Cloth and Commerce in Colonial India* (Delhi, Sage Publications, 1996).

Chibber, Vivek, *Locked in Place: State-building and Late Industrialisation in India* (Delhi, Tulika Books, 2004).

Chung, Tan, 'The Britain–China–India Trade Triangle (1771–1840)', *The Indian Economic and Social History Review*, 11(4) (1974), 411–31.

Clingingsmith, David and Williamson, Jeffrey G., 'De-industrialization in 18th and 19th Century India: Mughal Decline, Climate Shocks and British Industrial Ascent', *Explorations in Economic History*, 45(3) (2008), 209–34.

de Neve, Geert, *The Everyday Politics of Labour: Working Lives in India's Informal Economy* (Delhi, Social Science Press, 2005).

Deliege, Robert, *The Untouchables of India* (Oxford, Berg, 1999).

Dietrich Wielenga, Karuna, 'The Emergence of the Informal Sector: Labour Legislation and Politics in South India, 1940–1960', *Modern Asian Studies* (2019), 1–36.

Dirks, Nicholas B., *Castes of Mind: Colonialism and the Making of Modern India* (Delhi, Permanent Black, 2002).

Frankel, Francine R., *India's Political Economy 1947–1977: the Gradual Revolution* (New Delhi, Oxford University Press, 1978).

Frankel, Francine R., and Rao, M. S. A. (eds), *Dominance and State Power in Modern India: Decline of a Social Order* (New Delhi, Oxford University Press, 1989).

Gallagher, John and Robinson, Ronald, 'The Imperialism of Free Trade', *Economic History Review*, 2nd series, 6(1) (1953), 1–15.

Govindu, Venu Madhav and Malghan, Deepak, *The Web of Freedom: J. C. Kumarappa and Gandhi's Struggle for Economic Justice* (Delhi, Oxford University Press, 2016).

Guha, Sumit, *The Agrarian Economy of the Bombay Deccan, 1818–1941* (Delhi, Oxford University Press, 1987).

Guha, Sumit, 'The Handloom Industry of Central India: 1825–1950', *The Indian Economic and Social History Review*, 26(3) (1989), 297–318.

Guha, Sumit, *Health and Population in South Asia: from Earliest Times to the Present* (Delhi, Permanent Black, 2001).

Hardgrave, Robert L., *The Nadars of Tamilnad: the Political Culture of a Community in Change* (Berkeley, University of California Press, 1969).

Harnetty, Peter, 'India and British Commercial Enterprise: the Case of the Manchester Cotton Company, 1860–64', *The Indian Economic and Social History Review*, 3(4) (1966), 396–421.

Harnetty, Peter, *Imperialism and Free Trade: Lancashire and India in the Mid-Nineteenth Century* (Vancouver, University of British Columbia Press, 1972).

Harnetty, Peter, 'Deindustrialization' Revisited: the Handloom Weavers of the Central Provinces of India, c. 1800–1947', *Modern Asian Studies*, 25(3) (1991), 455–510.

Harriss-White, Barbara, *India Working: Essays on Society and Economy* (Delhi, Cambridge University Press, 2004).

Haynes, Douglas E., 'Market Formation in Khandesh, c.1820–1930', *The Indian Economic and Social History Review*, 36(3) (1999), 287–8.

Haynes, Douglas E., 'Artisan Cloth-Producers and the Emergence of Powerloom Manufacture in Western India, 1920–1950', *Past and Present*, 172(1) (2001), 170–98.

Haynes, Douglas E., *Small Town Capitalism in Western India: Artisans, Merchants and the Making of the Informal Economy, 1870–1960* (Cambridge, Cambridge University Press, 2012).

Haynes, Douglas E., McGowan, Abigail, Roy, Tirthankar and Yanagisawa, Haruka (eds), *Towards a History of Consumption* (Delhi, Oxford University Press, 2010).

Haynes, Douglas E. and Prakash, Gyan (eds), *Contesting Power: Resistance and Everyday Social Relations in South Asia* (Delhi, Oxford University Press, 1991).

Haynes, Douglas E. and Roy, Tirthankar, 'Conceiving Mobility: Weavers' Migrations in Pre-colonial and Colonial India', *The Indian Economic and Social History Review*, 36(1) (1999), 35–67.

Hensman, Rohini, *Workers, Unions and Global Capitalism: Lessons from India* (Delhi, Tulika Books, 2011).

Horn, Jeff, *The Path not Taken: French Industrialisation in the Age of Revolution, 1750–1830* (Cambridge, MA, MIT Press, 2006).

Horn, Jeff, Rosenband, Leonard N. and Roe Smith, Merritt (eds), *Reconceptualizing the Industrial Revolution* (Cambridge, MA, MIT Press, 2010).

Hossain, Hameeda, *The Company Weavers of Bengal: the East India Company and the Organization of Textile Production in Bengal, 1750–1813* (Delhi, Oxford University Press, 1988).

Humphries, Jane and Schneider, Benjamin, 'Stranded Spinsters', *British Academy Review*, 34 (Autumn 2018).

Ishii, Kazuya, 'The Socioeconomic Thoughts of Mahatma Gandhi as an Origin of Alternate Development', *Review of Social Economy*, 59(3) (2001), 297–312.

Jayaraj, D. and Nagaraj, K., *Socio-economic Factors Underlying Growth of Silk-weaving in the Arni Region – a Preliminary Study*, Themes in Social Sector Research: the S. Guhan Memorial Series, Monograph 5 (Madras, Madras Institute of Development Studies, 2006).

Jha, Amalendu, 'Raw Cotton of Western India: 1750–1850', *The Indian Economic and Social History Review*, 9(1) (1972), 1–41.

Jha, P. S., *The Political Economy of Stagnation* (Delhi, Oxford University Press, 1980).

Joshi, Chitra, 'Histories of Indian Labour: Predicaments and Possibilities', *History Compass*, 6(2) (2008), 439–54.

Karuna, D. W., 'Weaving Histories: the Handloom Industry in South India: Aspects of Production, Work and Identities, c. 1800–1960' (PhD thesis, University of Delhi, 2014).

Kela, Shashank, *A Rogue and Peasant Slave: Adivasi Resistance 1800–2000* (New Delhi, Navayana, 2012).

Kela, Shashank, 'Federalism and its Discontents', *The Caravan*, 1 February (2019). https://caravanmagazine.in/literature/doctrine-state-rights-india.

Kriedte, Peter, Medick, Hans and Schlumbohm, Jürgen, *Industrialisation before Industrialisation: Rural Industry in the Genesis of Capitalism* (Cambridge, Cambridge University Press, 1981).

Kumar, Dharma, *Land and Caste in South India* (Delhi, Manohar, 1992).

Kumar, Dharma and Desai, Meghnad (eds), *Cambridge Economic History of India*, vol. 2, *c.*1757–*c.*1970 (Cambridge, Cambridge University Press, 1983).

Krishnamurty, J., 'De-industrialization in Gangetic Bihar during the Nineteenth Century: another Look at the Evidence', *The Indian Economic and Social History Review*, 22(4) (1985), 399–416.

Leacock, Seth and Mandelbaum, David G., 'A Nineteenth Century Development Project in India: the Cotton Improvement Program', *Economic Development and Cultural Change*, 3(4) (July 1955), 334–51.

Liu, Tessie P., *The Weaver's Knot: the Contradictions of Class Struggle and Family Solidarity in Western France, 1750–1914* (Ithaca, NY, Cornell University Press, 1994).

McGowan, Abigail, *Crafting the Nation in Colonial India* (New York, Palgrave Macmillan, 2009).

Machado, Pedro. 'Cloths of a New Fashion: Indian Ocean Networks of Exchange and Cloth Zones of Contact in Africa and India in the Eighteenth and Nineteenth Centuries', Giorgio Riello and Tirthankar Roy (eds), *How India Clothed the World: the World of South Asian Textiles, 1500–1850* (Leiden and Boston, MA, Brill, 2009), pp. 53–83.

Menon, Meena and Bilgrami, Uzramma, *A Frayed History: the Journey of Cotton in India* (New Delhi, Oxford University Press, 2017).

Mines, Mattison, *The Warrior Merchants: Textiles, Trade and Territory in South India* (Cambridge, Cambridge University Press, 1984).

Mohapatra, Prabhu, 'Regulated Informality: Legal Construction of Labour Relations in Colonial India, 1800–1926', in Jan Lucassen and Sabyasachi Bhattacharya (eds), *Workers in the Informal Sector: Studies in Labour History, 1800–2000* (Delhi, Macmillan, 2004), pp. 65–95.

Morris, Morris D., 'Towards a Reinterpretation of Nineteenth-Century Indian Economic History', *The Indian Economic and Social History Review*, 5(1) (1968), 1–15.

Mosse, David, 'Idioms of Subordination and Styles of Protest among Christian and Hindu Harijan Castes in Tamilnadu', *Contributions to Indian Sociology*, 28(1) (1994), 67–106.

Murphy, Veronica and Crill, Rosemary, *Tie-dyed Textiles of India: Tradition and Trade* (London, Victoria and Albert Museum in association with Mapin Publishing, 1991).

O'Brien, Patrick, 'The Geopolitics of a Global Industry: Eurasian Divergence and the Mechanization of Cotton Textile Production in England', in Giorgio Riello and Prasannan Parthasarathi (eds), *The Spinning World: a Global History of Cotton Textiles, 1200–1850* (Delhi, Primus Books, 2012), pp. 351–65.

O'Brien, Patrick and Keyder, Caglar, *Economic Growth in Britain and France, 1780–1940: Two Paths to the Twentieth Century* (London, Allen and Unwin, 1978).

Omvedt, Gail, *Dalits and the Democratic Revolution: Dr. Ambedkar and the Dalit Movement in Colonial India* (Delhi, Sage Publications, 1994).

Parthasarathi, Prasannan, 'Rethinking Wages and Competitiveness in the Eighteenth Century: Britain and South India', *Past and Present* 158(1) (1998), 79–109.

Parthasarathi, Prasannan, *The Transition to a Colonial Economy: Weavers, Merchants and Kings in South India, 1720–1800* (Cambridge, Cambridge University Press, 2001).

Parthasarathi, Prasannan, 'Historical Issues of Deindustrialisation in Nineteenth-Century South India', in Giorgio Riello and Tirthankar Roy (eds), *How India Clothed the World: the World of South Asian Textiles, 1500–1850* (Leiden, Brill, 2009), pp. 415–35.

Pascoe, C. F. *Two Hundred Years of the S.P.G.: an Historical Account of the Society for the Propagation of the Gospel in Foreign Parts, 1701-1900*, vol. 1 (London, SPG, 1901).

Perlin, Frank, 'Proto-Industrialisation and Pre-Colonial South Asia', *Past and Present*, 98 (February 1983), 30–95.

Perlin, Frank, 'Growth of Money Economy and some Questions of Transition in Late Pre-colonial India', *The Journal of Peasant Studies*, 11(3) (1984), 96–107.

Piore, Michael J. and Sabel, Charles, *The Second Industrial Divide: Possibilities for Prosperity* (New York, Basic Books, 1984).

Prasad, C. Shambu, 'Suicide Deaths and Quality of Indian Cotton: Perspectives from History of Technology and Khadi Movement', *Economic and Political Weekly*, 34(5) (1999) PE-12–PE-20.

Rai, Santosh Kumar, 'Becoming a Grihasta: Hierarchies of Work among Handloom Weavers in Early Twentieth Century United Provinces, India', in Rana Behal, Alice Mah and Babcar Fall (eds), *Rethinking Work: Global Historical and Sociological Perspectives* (New Delhi, Tulika, 2011) pp. 73–88.

Raju, Sarada, *Economic Conditions in the Madras Presidency 1800–1850* (Madras, University of Madras, 1941).

Ramagundam, Rahul, *Gandhi's Khadi: a History of Contention and Conciliation* (Delhi, Orient Longman, 2008).

Ramaswamy, Vijaya, *Textiles and Weavers in Medieval South India* (Delhi, Oxford University Press, 1985).

Ramaswamy, Vijaya, 'The Genesis and Historical Role of the Master-weavers in South Indian Textile Production', *Journal of Economic and Social History of the Orient*, 28(3) (1985), 300–13.

Rawat, Ramnarayan S., *Reconsidering Untouchability: Chamars and Dalit History in North India* (Delhi, Permanent Black, 2012).

Ray, Raka and Katzenstein, Mary, 'Introduction', in Raka Ray and Mary Katzenstein (eds), *Social Movements in India: Poverty, Power and Politics* (Lanham, MD, Rowman and Littlefield, 2005).

Raychaudhuri, Tapan, *Jan Company in Coromandel 1605–1690: a Study in the Interrelations of European Commerce and Traditional Economies* (The Hague, Martinus Nijhoff, 1962).

Remesh, Babu, P., *Organizational Structure, Labour Relations and Employment in Kancheepuram Silk Weaving* (Noida, V. V. Giri National Labour Institute, 2001).

Riello, Giorgio, *Cotton: the Fabric that Made the Modern World* (Cambridge, Cambridge University Press, 2013).

Riello, Giorgio and Parthasarathi, Prasannan (eds), *The Spinning World: a Global History of Cotton Textiles, 1200–1850* (Delhi, Primus Books, 2012).

Riello, Giorgio and Roy, Tirthankar (eds), *How India Clothed the World: the World of South Asian Textiles, 1500–1850* (Leiden, Brill, 2009).

Robb, Peter, 'Introduction', in Peter Robb (ed.) *Dalit Movements and the Meanings of Labour in India* (Delhi, Oxford University Press, 1993), pp. 44–7.

Roy, Tirthankar, 'Relations of Production in Handloom Weaving in the Mid-Thirties', Working Paper No. 223 (Trivandrum, Centre for Development Studies, 1987).

Roy, Tirthankar, 'Size and Structure of Handloom Weaving in the Mid-thirties', *The Indian Economic and Social History Review*, 25(1) (1988), 1–24.

Roy, Tirthankar, *Artisans and Industrialization: Indian Weaving in the Twentieth Century* (Delhi, Oxford University Press, 1993).

Roy, Tirthankar, 'Capitalism and Community: a Study of the Madurai Sourashtras', *The Indian Economic and Social History Review*, 34(4) (1997), 438–63.

Roy, Tirthankar, 'Growth and Recession in Small-scale Industry: a Study of Tamil Nadu Powerlooms', *Economic and Political Weekly*, 34(44) (30 October–5 November 1999), 3137–45.

Roy, Tirthankar, *Traditional Industry in the Economy of Colonial India* (Cambridge, Cambridge University Press, 1999).

Roy, Tirthankar, 'De-industrialization: an Alternative View', *Economic and Political Weekly*, 35(17) (2000), 1442–7.

Roy, Tirthankar, *The Economic History of India, 1857–1947* (New Delhi, Oxford University Press, 2000).

Roy, Tirthankar, 'Traditional Industry in Colonial India', *Economic and Political Weekly*, 35(48) (25 November 2000), 4287.

Roy, Tirthankar, 'Acceptance of Innovation in Early Twentieth Century Indian Weaving', *The Economic History Review* (New Series), 55(3) (August 2002), 507–32.

Sabel, Charles and Zeitlin, Jonathan, 'Historical Alternatives to Mass Production: Politics, Markets and Technology in Nineteenth Century Industrialization', *Past and Present*, 108 (1985), 133–76.

Sahai, Nandita Prasad, *Politics of Patronage and Protest: the State, Society, and Artisans in Early Modern Rajasthan* (New Delhi, Oxford University Press, 2006).

Sarkar, Aditya, *Trouble at the Mill: Factory Law and the Emergence of the Labour Question in Late Nineteenth-century Bombay* (New Delhi, Oxford University Press, 2018).

Schumacher, E. F. *Small is Beautiful: a Study of Economics as if People Mattered* (London, Blond and Briggs, 1973).

Simmons, Colin, '"De-industrialization", Industrialization and the Indian Economy, c. 1850–1947', *Modern Asian Studies*, 9(3) (1985), 593–622.

Specker, Konrad, *Weber in Wettbewerb: Das Schicksal des suidindischen Textilhandwerks im 19.Jahrhundert* (Wiesbaden, Steiner, 1984).

Specker, Konrad, 'Madras Handlooms in the Nineteenth Century', *The Indian Economic and Social History Review*, 26(2) (1989), 131–66.

Styles, John, 'Fibres, Yarns and the Invention of the Spinning Jenny', paper presented at the World Economic History Congress, Boston, MA, 29 July–3 August 2018.

Subrahmanyam, Sanjay, 'Rural Industry and Commercial Agriculture in Late Seventeenth-Century South-Eastern India', *Past and Present*, 126 (February 1990), 76–114.

Subrahmanyam, Sanjay, *The Political Economy of Commerce in Southern India, 1500–1650* (Cambridge, Cambridge University Press, 2004).

Swaminathan, Padmini, 'State Intervention in Industrialisation: a Case Study of the Madras Presidency', *The Indian Economic and Social History Review*, 29(4) (1992), 479–508.

Swaminathan, Padmini, 'Technical Education and Industrial Development in Madras Presidency: Illusions of a Policy in the Making', *Economic and Political Weekly*, 27(30) (1992), 1611–22.

Swarnalatha, P., 'Revolt, Testimony and Petition: Artisanal Protests in Colonial Andhra', in Lex Heerma van Voss (ed.), *Petitions in Social History*, International Review of Social History, Supplement 9 (Cambridge, Cambridge University Press, 2001).

Swarnalatha, P., *The World of the Weaver in Northern Coromandel, c. 1750–c. 1850* (New Delhi, Orient Longman, 2005).

Tarlo, Emma, *Clothing Matters: Dress and Identity in India* (Chicago, University of Chicago Press, 1996).

Thorner, Daniel, 'De-industrialization in India, 1881–1931', Daniel Thorner and Alice Thorner (eds), *Land and Labour in India* (Bombay, Asia Publishing House, 1965), pp. 70–81.

Tilly, Charles, *Regimes and Repertoires* (Chicago, University of Chicago Press, 2006).

Tomlinson, B. R., 'India and the British Empire 1880–1935', *The Indian Economic and Social History Review*, 12(4) (1975) 337–80.

Trivedi, Lisa, *Clothing Gandhi's Nation: Homespun and Modern India* (Bloomington, IN, Indiana University Press, 2007).

Tsukasa, Mizushima, *Nattar and the Socio-economic Change in South India in the 18th–19th Centuries* (Tokyo, ILCAA, 1986).

Twomey, Michael J., 'Employment in Nineteenth Century Indian Textiles', *Explorations in Economic History*, 20(1) (1983), 37–57.

Tyabji, Nasir, *The Small Industries Policy in India* (Calcutta, Oxford University Press, 1989).

Tyabji, Nasir, *Forging Capitalism in Nehru's India: Neo-colonialism and the State, c. 1940–1970* (Delhi, Oxford University Press, 2015).

van der Linden, Marcel, 'Charles Tilly's Historical Sociology', *The International Review of Social History*, 54(2) (2009), 237–74.

Vicziany, M., 'The De-industrialization of India in the Nineteenth Century: a Methodological Critique of Amiya Kumar Bagchi', *The Indian Economic and Social History Review*, 16(2) (1979), 105–46.

Warrier, Shobana, 'Class and Gender: a Study of Women Workers in Cotton Textile Mills of Madras, Madurai and Coimbatore' (PhD thesis, Delhi, Jawaharlal Nehru University, 1993).

Washbrook, David, 'Land and Labour in Late Eighteenth-century South India: the Golden Age of the Pariah?', in Peter Robb (ed.), *Dalit Movements and the Meanings of Labour in India* (Delhi, Oxford University Press, 1993).

Washbrook, David, 'India in the Early Modern World Economy: Modes of Production, Reproduction and Exchange', *The Journal of Global History*, 2(1) (2007), 87–111.

Washbrook, David, 'The Textile Industry and The Economy of South India, 1500–1800', in Giorgio Riello and Tirthankar Roy (eds), *How India Clothed the World: the World of South Asian Textiles* (Leiden, Brill, 2009), pp. 173–99.

Wendel, Jonathan F. and Grover, Corrine E., 'Taxonomy and Evolution of the Cotton Genus Gossypium', in D. D. Fang and R. G. Percy (eds), *Cotton*, 2nd edn, Agronomy Monograph, vol. 57 (Madison, WI; ASA, CSA and CSSA; 2015), pp. 25–44.

Wendt, Ian, 'The Social Fabric: Textile Industry and Community in Early Modern South India'(PhD thesis, University of Wisconsin – Madison, 2005).

Wendt, Ian, 'Four Centuries of Decline? Understanding the Changing Structure of the South Indian Textile Industry', in Giorgio Riello and Tirthankar Roy (eds), *How India Clothed the World* (Leiden, Brill, 2009), pp. 193–215.

Wilson, Jon E., '"A Thousand Countries to Go to": Peasants and Rulers in Eighteenth-century Bengal', *Past and Present*, 189(1) (2005), 81–109.

Yanagisawa, Haruka, 'The Handloom Industry and Its Market Structure: the Case of the Madras Presidency in the First Half of the Twentieth Century', *The Indian Economic and Social History Review*, 30(1) (1993), 1–27.

Websites:

https://indiankanoon.org/
http://tmoi.org.uk/
https://indiankanoon.org/

Index

Page numbers in **bold** refer to tables; page numbers in *italics* refer to illustrations and plates; 'n.' after a page number indicates the footnote number. Chronological references are placed at the beginning of the entries and follow chronological order.